International Business Management

International Business Management

(SECOND EDITION)

N. Venkateswaran
Assistant Professor
Department of Management Studies
Panimalar Engineering College
Chennai, Tamil Nadu

An Imprint of

NEW AGE INTERNATIONAL (P) LIMITED, PUBLISHERS
New Delhi • Bangalore • Chennai • Cochin • Guwahati
Hyderabad • Kolkata • Lucknow • Mumbai
Visit us at **www.newagepublishers.com**

Published by New Age International (P) Ltd., Publishers
First Edition: 2008
Second Edition: 2012

Branches:

- 37/10, 8th Cross (Near Hanuman Temple), Azad Nagar, Chamrajpet, **Bangalore**-560 018. Tel.: (080) 2675 6823, Telefax: 2675 6820, E-mail: bangalore@newagepublishers.com
- 26, Damodaran Street, T. Nagar, **Chennai**-600 017. Tel.: (044) 24353401, Telefax: 24351463, E-mail: chennai@newagepublishers.com
- CC-39/1016, Carrier Station Road, Ernakulam South, **Cochin**-682 016. Tel.: (0484) 2377004, Telefax: 4051303. E-mail:cochin@newagepublishers.com
- Hemsen Complex, Mohd. Shah Road, Paltan Bazar, Near Starline Hotel, **Guwahati**-781 008. Tel.: (0361) 2513881. Telefax: 2543669, E-mail: guwahati@newagepublishers.com
- 105, 1st Floor, Madhiray Kaveri Tower, 3-2-19, Azam Jahi Road, Nimboliadda, **Hyderabad**-500 027. Tel.: (040) 24652456, Telefax: 24652457, E-mail:hyderabad@newagepublishers.com
- RDB Chambers (Formerly Lotus Cinema)106A, 1st Floor, S.N. Banerjee Road, **Kolkata**-700 014. Tel.: (033) 22273773, Telefax: 22275247, E-mail:kolkata@newagepublishers.com
- 16-A, Jopling Road, **Lucknow**-226 001. Tel.: (0522) 2209578, 4045297, Telefax: 2204098 E-mail: lucknow@newagepublishers.com
- 142C, Victor House, Ground Floor, N.M. Joshi Marg, Lower Parel, **Mumbai**-400 013. Tel.: (022) 24927869. Telefax: 24915415, E-mail: mumbai@newagepublishers.com
- 22, Golden House, Daryaganj, **New Delhi**-110 002. Tel.: (011) 23262370, 23262368, Telefax: 43551305. E-mail: sales@newagepublishers.com

---

ISBN : 978-81-224-3236-7

₹ 295.00

C-11-07-5714

Printed in India at Parmanand Offset, Delhi.
Typeset at In-house.

PUBLISHING FOR ONE WORLD
NEW AGE INTERNATIONAL (P) LIMITED, PUBLISHERS
4835/24, Ansari Road, Daryaganj, New Delhi-110002
Visit us at **www.newagepublishers.com**

Dedicated to

My Parents, Wife, Brother

and

My Son V. Jayakanth and

Daughter V. Sangeethapriya

Preface to the Second Edition

The first print of the first edition was sold out within a few months. Encouraged by such an overwhelming response, I have endeavoured to make the book more and more useful by periodically revising it by updating the information and widening the content.

The second edition was characterized by a thorough revision and substantial modification of the text. Obsolete materials were deleted and new ones including boxes and tables added. Several chapters were reworked. Added features of this edition included chapter end summary and model questions.

There has been a tremendous increase in the number of institutes offering courses in the broad area of international business in order to cater to the growing demand for managerial personnel for this task. This book is an attempt to capture the different aspects and dimensions of international business so that the course material requirement of the students of this discipline is catered to a certain extent.

Students of international business are fortunate enough to be living in a laboratory where the principles in this book can be used on a daily basis. Virtually every management decision being made today is influenced by global events, and naive thinking about international politics, economics, cultures, exchange rates and foreign competitors can have quick and adverse effects on a firms bottom line. The objective of this introduction to international business is to provide relevant theoretical and practical insights to management students so that the real world of global business is better understood.

The text incorporates the latest theoretical advances in a manner easily comprehensible for university and college students from BA to MBA level. This second edition integrates both the practical and theoretical issues through a sustained use of the concepts of international business management. Indeed, this is the first text to have a focus in the teaching of introductory international business. This unique feature helps students choose from the extraordinarily broad menu of events in the international environment by building confidence in understanding which ones are use for international business analysis at the firm level.

The success of the first edition of International Business was based in part upon the incorporation of leading edge research into the text, the use of the up-to-date examples and statistics to illustrate global trends and enterprise strategy, and the discussion of current events within the context of the appropriate theory. Building on these strengths, my goals of the second edition have been threefold:

- Incorporate new insights from recent scholarly research wherever applicable.
- Make sure the content of the text covers all appropriate issues.
- Make sure the text is as up-to-date as possible with regard to current events, statistics and examples.
- Updated material and new frameworks to analyze the World Trade Organization, Free Trade Agreement of the Americas, APEC, SAPTA, South-South Cooperation, UNIDO and other international institutions.

As part of the revision process, changes have been made to every chapter in the book. All statistics have been updated to incorporate the most recently available data. For example Chapter 9 has been updated to discuss the new round of talks by the WTO that are aimed at reducing barriers to trade, particularly in agriculture (the Doha Round and Uruguay Round). In Chapter 17, there have been additions to the section discussing how multinationals expatriate managers can gain a competitive advantage by leveraging skills between subsidiaries. This addition reflects the substantial academic research addressing this issue that has been published in recent years.

Reflecting this rapid pace of change, in this edition of this book I have tried to ensure that all material and statistics are as up-to-date as possible. However, being absolutely up-to-date is impossible since change is always with us. What is current today may be outdated tomorrow. Readers and instructors will find this a very student friendly second edition of an already popular textbook. Throughout the book, chapter summary of topics discussed in chapters is pointed out to the students to reinforce their understanding of how the material comprises an integrated whole.

N. VENKATESWARAN

Preface to the First Edition

Going into this first edition, the premise has changed from unlimited growth to uncertainty and cautions, but importantly, the premise of opportunity in global business remain unchanged. The uncertain economy and increasing geopolitical complexity simply levels the playing field of managers around the world. How managers respond, how they manage and turn the increasing threats into opportunities becomes vital to success in today's environment.

The whole world is now connected electronically and psychologically; it is hard to imagine any business or non-business organization that is not directly affected by globalization. The challenge in the uncertain global economy is to learn and effectively practice international management. Those with the knowledge and skills to apply the contents of this text on international management will be taking a big step toward gaining a competitive advantage in today's uncertain, unprecedented environment.

The book has the following chapter distribution: Environment (Chapter 2), Regional Economic Integration (Chapter 3), Various Trade and Investment Theories (Chapter 4), Foreign Direct Investment (Chapter 5), Globalization (Chapter 6), International Strategic Planning (Chapter 7), Country Evaluation and Selection (Chapter 8), WTO Issues (Chapter 9), International Control Strategies (Chapter 10), Negotiations (Chapter 11) and Sample Case Study Discussions. Obviously, since international business management is such a dramatically changing field, all the chapter have been completely updated and improved.

At the end of all the chapters interactive cases are given. About half of the cases are new to this edition. These cases were retained or newly selected for high-interest discussion and strategic analysis.

This book has been revised from its original form offered to the students of Management Studies –Anna University Stream. It is now fit for the general reader and students particularly of most Indian Universities offering this subject in their stream. Last and finally, I hope that this edition continues the tradition and remains the best "world-class' text for the study of International Business Management. I also thank the team of New Age International Publishers who worked on various stages of this manuscript.

N. VENKATESWARAN

Acknowledgement

Authoring a book bears string similarities to sailing a boat in the ocean, and working as a team to author a book is like working as the crew of the boat. As appropriate, team members take turns charting the course, navigating the surf, and fixing the riggings. Skill, patience, luck and interpersonal skills are needed in abundance.

I would like to thank many people who provided help and support while I was on my journey. Without their help, I would still be at sea. I acknowledge the contributions of the following people from my institution.

- **Dr. Jeppiaar M.A., B.L., Ph.D.** – Founder and Chairman
- **Dr. P. Chinnadurai M.A., Ph.D.**, Secretary and Correspondent
- **Mrs. C. Vijaya Rajeswari** and **Mr. C. Sakthikumar M.E., M.Phil.,** Directors
- **Dr. K. Mani M.E., Ph.D.,** – Principal
- Dean and Faculties of my Department

These people provided me with valuable help, though I must ultimately be held accountable for the results. Now that I have returned to harbor, I owe them a vote a thanks for their help.

In writing the second edition of the book I would particularly like to thank the reviewers, and the instructors who adopted the text, for their valuable comments on the first edition. I endeavoured to incorporate their insights and criticisms to improve this edition.

I am highly indebted to the students of the Department of Management Studies, **Panimalar Engineering College** who provided me helpful comments on the learning comments and a number or other universities and institutes where I have had the opportunity to deliver guest lectures, whose doubts, questions and encouragement have immensely helped me academically. I have also benefited from discussions with a number of entrepreneurs, executives and officials of international business organizations who helped me to compile and edit this book.

I would like to thank my publisher **New Age International Publishers** for patiently bearing with me as I went through many challenges in getting permission to use the results of the previously conducted research studies that are incorporated (with proper citations) throughout this book.

I owe this book to my family members. At home my parents, wife and brother have been extremely nice and supportive. They go to any extent in accommodating my working style and idosyncracises. All my academic contributions embody essential ingredient of support which they unfailingly extends to me. Every activity has an opportunity cost. In writing this book I missed the world's most valuable thing. That is, the time I could have spent my son and daughter. They probably have the highest claim on my time, but which I spent on furthering my ends. I am indebted to them for which I have achieved at their cost and repent.

N. VENKATESWARAN

Contents

Chapter 1

International Business: An Overview

International Business is all commercial transactions–private and governmental between two or more countries. Private companies undertake such transactions for profit; governments may or may not do the same in their transactions. These transactions include sales, investments and transportation.

Why should you study international business? A simple answer is that international business comprises a large and growing portion of the world's total business. Today global events and competition affect almost all companies – large or small – because most sell output to and secure supplies from foreign countries. Many companies also compete against products and services that come from abroad.

The conditions within a company's external environment (the conditions outside a company as opposed to its internal ones) affect the way business functions such as marketing are carried out. These conditions are physical, societal and competitive. When a company operates internationally, it adds foreign conditions to its domestic ones making its external environment more diverse.

Even if you never have direct international business responsibilities, you may find it useful to understand some of its complexities. Companies international operations and governmental regulation of international business affect company profits, employment security and wages, consumer prices and national security. A better understanding of international business may help you to make more informed decisions, such as where you want to work and what governmental policies you want to support.

Today, business is acknowledged to be international and there is a general expectation that this will continue for the foreseeable future. International business may be defined simply as business transactions that take place across national borders. This broad definition includes the very small firm that exports (or imports) a small quantity to only one country, as well as the very large global firm with integrated operations and strategic alliances around the world. Within this broad array, distinctions are often made among different types of international firms, and these distinctions are helpful in understanding a firm's strategy, organization, and functional decisions (for example, its financial, administrative, marketing, human resource, or operations decisions).

One distinction that can be helpful is the distinction between multi-domestic operations, with independent subsidiaries which act essentially as domestic firms, and global operations, with integrated subsidiaries which are closely related and interconnected. These may be thought of as the two ends of a continuum, with many possibilities in between. Firms are unlikely to be at one end of the continuum, though, as they often combining aspects of multi-domestic operations with aspects of global operations.

International business grew over the last half of the twentieth century partly because of liberalization of both trade and investment, and partly because doing business internationally had become easier. In terms of liberalization, the General Agreement on Tariffs and Trade (GATT) negotiation rounds resulted in trade liberalization, and this was continued with the formation of the World Trade Organization (WTO) in 1995.

At the same time, worldwide capital movements were liberalized by most governments, particularly with the advent of electronic funds transfers. In addition, the introduction of a new European monetary unit, the euro, into circulation in January 2002 has impacted international business economically. The euro is the currency of the European Union, membership in March 2005 of 25 countries, and the euro replaced each country's previous currency. As of early 2005, the United States dollar continues to struggle against the euro and the impacts are being felt across industries worldwide.

In terms of ease of doing business internationally, two major forces are important:

- Technological developments which make global communication and transportation relatively quick and convenient; and
- The disappearance of a substantial part of the communist world, opening many of the world's economies to private business.

WHY COMPANIES ENGAGE IN INTERNATIONAL BUSINESS

When operating internationally, a company should consider its **mission** (what it will seek to do and become over the long term), its **objectives** (specific performance targets to fulfill its mission) and **strategy** (the means to fulfill its objectives). There are seven major objectives that may influence companies to engage in international business. They are:

- ❑ To expand sales
- ❑ To acquire resources

- To diversify sources of sales and supplies
- To minimize competitive risk
- Profit advantage
- Growth opportunities
- Government policies and regulations

Expand Sales: Companies sales are dependent on two factors: the consumers' interest in their products or services and the consumers' willingness and ability to buy them. The number of people and the amount of their purchasing power are higher for the world as a whole than for a single country, so companies may increase their sales by reaching international business.

Ordinarily, higher sales means higher profits, assuming each unit sold has the same markup. For example, the *Star Wars* cost millions of dollars to produce, but as more people see the films, the average production cost per viewer decreases.

So, increasing the sales will be major motive for a company's expansion into international business. Many of the world's largest companies derive over half their sales from outside their home country. You've heard of many of these companies (with their home country in parenthesis) – BASF (Germany), Electrolux (Sweden), Gillette (the United States), Michelin (France), Nestle (Switzerland), Philips (the Netherlands) and Sony (Japan). However, smaller companies also may depend on foreign sales. Many small companies also depend on sales of components to large companies, which in turn put them in finished products that they sell abroad.

Acquire Resources: Manufacturers and distributors seek out products, services and components produced in foreign countries. They also look for foreign capital, technologies, and information they can use at home. Acquiring resources may enable a company to improve its product quality and differentiate itself from competitors – in both cases, potentially increasing market share and profits. Although a company may initially use domestic resources to expand abroad, once the foreign operations are in place, the foreign earnings may the serve as resources for domestic operations.

Diversify Sources of Sales and Supplies: To minimize swings in sales and profits, companies may seek out foreign markets to take advantage of business cycle—recessions and expansions—differences among countries. Sales decrease in a country that is in a recession and increase in one that is expanding economically. By obtaining supplies of the same product or component from different countries, companies may be able to avoid the full impact of price swings or shortages in any one country.

Minimize Competitive Risk: Many companies enter into international business for defensive reasons. They want to counter advantages competitors might gain in foreign markets that, in turn, could hurt them domestically. For example Company A and Company B compete in the same domestic market. Company A may fear that Company B will generate large profits from a foreign market if left alone to serve that market. Company B may then use those profits in various ways (such as additional advertising or development of improved products) to improve its competitive position in the domestic market. Companies harboring such a fear may enter foreign markets primarily to prevent a competitor from gaining advantages.

Profit Advantage: The international business provides more profit advantage. International business is more profitable than the domestic. When we examine the average unit cost of production, we may find that the average cost of production per unit will be lowest if the plant is operated at optimum capacity. The relative rate of profit per unit will increase when the total profit from domestic business increase.

Growth Opportunities: In most of the foreign markets there is a vast growth prospects to attract foreign companies. In many countries, both the population and income are growing fast. Though the market for several goods in many domestic markets is not very substantial at present. So, many companies/countries are eager to establish a foothold in foreign market considering their future potential in mind.

Government Policies and Regulations: In developing countries like India, Government policies and regulations do encourage and motivate the exporters to go international. Most of the governments provide a number of incentives and other forms of positive support to domestic companies to export and to invest in foreign market. With the recent changes in the Government of India's economic policy, now most of the companies are entering international market.

MODES OF INTERNATIONAL BUSINESS

When pursuing international business, private enterprises and governments have to decide how to carry out their business, such as what mode of operation to use. The topic discusses how a company has a number of modes from which to choose.

MERCHANDISE EXPORTS AND IMPORTS

Companies may export or import either goods or services. More companies are involved in exporting and importing than in any other international mode. This is especially true of smaller companies, even though they are less likely than large companies to engage in exporting. **Merchandise exports** are tangible products —goods—sent out a country; **merchandise imports** are goods brought in. Because these goods can be seen leaving and entering a country, they are sometimes called *visible exports and imports.* The terms *exports* and *imports* frequently apply to merchandise, not service. For most countries, exporting and importing of goods are the major sources of international revenue and expenditures.

SERVICE EXPORTS AND IMPORTS

Service exports and imports are non-product international earnings. The company or individual receiving payment is making a **service export**. The company or individual paying is making a **service import**. Service exports and imports take many forms. In this section, we discuss the following sources of such earnings:

- Tourism and transportation
- Performance of services
- Use of assets

Tourism and Transportation: International tourism and transportation are important sources of revenue for airlines, shipping companies, travel agencies and hotels. Some countries' economies, too, depend heavily on revenue from these economic sectors. For example, in Greece and Norway, a significant amount of employment, profits, and foreign exchange comes from foreign cargo that is carried on ships owned by citizens of these countries. Earnings from foreign tourism are more important for the Bahamian economy than are earnings from the export of merchandise.

Performance of Services: Some services—banking, insurance, rentals (such as of *Star Wars* films), engineering, management services and so on – net companies earnings in the form of fees, that is, payments for the performance of those services. On an international level, for example, companies pay fees for engineering services that are often handled through **turnkey operations** – construction, performed under contract, of facilities that are transferred to the owner when they are ready to begin operating. Companies also pay fees for **management contracts** – arrangements in which one company provides personnel to perform general or specialized management functions for another company.

Use of Assets: When companies allow others to use their assets, such as trademarks, patents, copyrights, or expertise under contracts, also known as **licensing agreements**, they receive earnings called **royalties**. Royalties also come from franchise contracts. **Franchising** is a mode of business in which one party (the franchisor) allows another party (the franchisee) the use of a trademark that is an essential asset for the franchisee's business. The franchisor also assists on a continuing basis in the operation of the business, such as by providing components, management services and technology.

INVESTMENTS

Foreign investment means ownership of foreign property in exchange for financial return, such as interest and dividends. Foreign investment takes two forms: direct and portfolio.

Direct Investment: A **direct investment** is one that gives the investor a controlling interest in a foreign company. Such a direct investment is also a **foreign direct investment (FDI)**, a term common to this text. If a company holds a minority stake and the remaining ownership is widely dispersed, no other owner may be able to counter the company effectively. When two or more companies share ownership of an FDI, the operation is a **joint venture.** When a government joins a company in an FDI, the operation is called a **mixed venture**, which is a type of joint venture.

Portfolio Investment: A portfolio investment is a non-controlling interest in a company or ownership of a loan to another party. Usually a portfolio investment takes one of two forms: stock in a company or loans to a company or country in the form of bonds, bills or notes that the investor purchases.

Foreign portfolio investments are important for most companies that have extensive international operations. Companies use them primarily for short-term financial gain, that is, as a means for a company to earn more money on its money with relative safety.

EVOLUTION OF STRATEGY IN THE INTERNATIONAL PROCESS

When we think of multinational enterprises, we often think of giant companies like IBM or Nestle, which have sales and production facilities in scores of countries. But companies do not start out as giants, and few think globally at their inception. As we discuss strategies, we shall note that companies are at different levels of internationalization and that their current status affects the strategic alternatives available to them.

Although there are variations in how international operations evolve, some overall patterns do emerge. Most of these patterns are a product of risk minimization behavior – most companies view foreign operations as being riskier than domestic ones because they must operate in unfamiliar environments. Thus, they initially undertake international activities reluctantly and follow practices to minimize their risks.

PATTERNS OF EXPANSION

In order to perform internationalization process the company has to follow several steps or axis. However, a company does not necessarily move at the same speed along each axis. A slow movement along one axis may free up resources that allow faster expansion along another. A company may lack initial capacity to own facilities wholly in multiple foreign countries, so it may choose either to limit its foreign capital commitment by moving slowing from one axis to another axis. The various axis are defined below:

- Axis A – Impetus for International Business
- Axis B – Internal versus external handling for foreign operations
- Axis C – Mode of operations
- Axis D – Number of foreign countries in which a firm does business
- Axis E – Degree of similarity between foreign and domestic countries

Passive to Active Expansion: The impetus of strategic focus is defined in Axis A. Most new companies are established in response to domestic needs, and they frequently think only of domestic opportunities until a foreign opportunity presents itself to them. Often these companies have no idea of how their products became known abroad, but at this juncture, they must make a decision to export or not. Even large companies may move from passive to active expansion with aspects of their business.

External to Internal Handling of Operations: A company commonly uses intermediaries to handle foreign operations during early stages of international expansion because it minimizes risk. It commits fewer of its resources to international endeavors and relies on intermediaries that already know how to operate in the foreign market. But if the business grows successfully, the company will usually want to handle the operations with its own staff. This is because it has learned more about foreign operations, considers them less risky than at the onset, and realizes that the volume of business may justify the development of internal capabilities such as hiring trained personnel to maintain a department for foreign sales or purchases. This evolution is defined in Axis B.

Deepening Mode of Commitment: Axis C defined the importing and exporting is usually the first mode a company undertakes in becoming international. At an early stage of international involvement, importing and exporting require the least commitment and least risk to the company's resources, such as capital, personnel, equipment and production facilities.

A company often moves into some type of foreign production after successfully building an export market. Initially this foreign production is apt to minimize the use of its resources by licensing to handle production abroad, sharing ownership in the foreign facility, or limiting the amount of manufacture, such as assembling output abroad.

A company typically does not abandon its early modes of operating abroad, such as importing and exporting, when it adopts other means of operating internationally. Rather, it usually either continues them by expanding its trade to new markets or complements them with new types of business activities.

Geographic Diversification: When companies first move internationally, they are most apt to do business in only one or very few foreign locations. Axis D shows that over time, the number of countries in which they operate increases. The initial narrow geographic expansion parallels the low early commitment of resources abroad. The choice of countries in this geographic expansion also tends to follow certain patterns as Axis E indicates. Initially, companies tend to go to those locations that are geographically close and similar.

The patterns most companies have followed in their international expansion are not necessarily optimal for their long-range performance. The initial movement into a nearby country, such as a U.S. company moving into Canada, may delay entry into faster growing markets. There is, however, evidence that many new companies are starting out with a global focus because of the international experience and education of their founders. Further, because of technological advancements, especially in communications and the World Wide Web, these start-up companies have a better idea of where their markets are globally and how they may gain resources from different countries.

COUNTERVAILING FORCES

In addition to the effect of external and competitive environmental factors, countervailing forces complicate decision making in international business. The strength of one force compared to that of another influences those choices available to companies that compete internationally. Some opposing choices that companies contend with are whether to institute global or national company practices, whether to focus on country or company competitiveness.

GLOBALLY STANDARDIZED VERSUS NATIONALLY RESPONSIVE PRACTICES

Any company operating internationally must decide between the advantages of globally standardized practices and those practices that respond to different national preferences. These advantages may vary by product, function, and country of operation.

The trends that have influenced the recent worldwide growth in international business –

- Rapid expansion of technology
- Liberalization of governmental trade policies
- Development of the institutions and services needed to support and facilitate international trade
- Increased global competition
- Reduce costs

However, when a company goes abroad, it faces conditions very different from those it encounters at home. The company may need to engage in national responsiveness, meaning it makes operating adjustments where it does business to reach a satisfactory level of performance. In such cases, a multi-domestic approach often works better than a global one because the company managers abroad are best able to assess and deal with the environments of the foreign countries in which the company operates.

COUNTRY VERSUS COMPANY COMPETITIVENESS

Companies at least those that are not government owned, may compete by seeking maximum production efficiency on a global scale. To accomplish this goal, the company's production would use the best inputs for the price, even if the production location moved abroad. The company would then sell the output wherever it would fetch the best price. Such practices should lead to maximum performance for the company.

But countries also compete with each other. They do so in terms of fulfilling economic, political and social objectives. Countries are concerned not only with the absolute achievement of these objectives but also with how well they do compared to other countries. Keep in mind that competition among countries is the means to an end – the end being the well-being of a country's citizens. However, there is no consensus on how to measure well-being and accepted indicators of current prosperity actually may foretell longer-term problems.

SOVEREIGN VERSUS CROSS-NATIONAL RELATIONSHIPS

Countries compete. They also cooperate. Countries sometimes cede sovereignty (freedom from external control) reluctantly because of coercion and international conflicts. However, they willingly cede sovereignty through treaties and agreements with other countries for the following reasons:

- To gain reciprocal advantages
- To attack problems that one country acting alone cannot solve
- To deal with areas of concern that lie outside the territory of all countries

Countries want to ensure that companies headquartered within their borders are not disadvantaged by foreign-country policies, so they enter into treaties and agreements with other countries on a variety of commercial activities, such as transportation and trade.

INSTRUMENTS OF INTERNATIONAL TRADE CONTROL

A country's trade policy will have repercussions abroad, retaliation from foreign governments looms as a potential obstacle to achieving the desired objectives. The chose of instruments for achieving is therefore important, because each may elicit different responses from domestic and foreign groups. One way to understand the types of instruments is to distinguish between those that affect the amount traded indirectly by directly influencing the prices of exports or imports and those that directly limit the amount that can be traded.

TARIFFS

Another common distinction is between tariff barriers and non-tariff barriers. Tariff barriers affect prices; non-tariff may affect either price or quantity directly. A **tariff**, or **duty**, which is the most common type of trade control, is a tax government's levy on a good shipped internationally. If collected by the exported country, it is known as an **export tariff**; if collected by a country through which the goods have passed, it is a **transit tariff**; if collected by the importing country, it is an **import tariff**;

A government may assess a tariff on a per unit basis, in which case it is a **specific duty**. It may assess a tariff as a percentage of the value of the item, in which case it is an **ad valorem duty**. If it assesses both a specific duty and an ad valorem duty on the same product, the combination is a **compound duty**. A specific duty is easy for customs officials who collect duties to assess because they do not need to determine a good's value on which to calculate a percentage tax.

NONTARIFF BARRIERS: DIRECT PRICE INFLUENCES

We have shown how tariff raise prices and limit trade. We will now explain other instruments governments use to limit trade by altering prices.

Subsidies: Countries sometimes make direct payments to domestic companies to compensate them for losses incurred from selling abroad, such as U.S. subsidies to cotton exporters. However, they most commonly provide other types of assistance to make it cheaper or more profitable for them to sell overseas. From an economic or market efficiency standpoint, service subsidies frequently are more justifiable than tariffs because they usually seek to overcome, rather than create, market imperfections, such as export and import promotion offices to help companies in emerging economies find foreign markets for the products.

Aid and Loans: Governments also give aid and loans to other countries. If the recipient is required to spend the funds in the donor country, which is known as tied aid or tied loans, some products can compete abroad that might otherwise be non-competitive. Most industrial countries also provide repayment insurance for their exporters, thus reducing the risk of non-payment for overseas sales.

Customs Valuation: Most countries have agreed on a procedure for assessing values when their customs agents levy tariffs. First, customs officials must use the invoice price. If there is none, of if its authenticity is doubtful, they must assess on the basis of similar goods coming in at about the same time. If this basis cannot be used, officials may compute a value based on final sales value or on reasonable cost.

Other Direct Price Influences: Countries frequently use other means to affect prices, including special fees requirements that customs deposits be placed in advance of shipment, and minimum price levels at which goods can be sold after they have customs clearance.

NONTARIFF BARRIERS: QUANTITY CONTROLS

We have described the instruments governments use to alter prices so that their domestic products are more competitive internationally. But governments also limit import and export quantities directly.

Quotas: The most common type of import or export restriction based on quantity is the quota. From the standpoint of imports, a quota most frequently limits the quantity of a product allowed to be imported in a given year. The amount frequently reflects a guarantee that domestic producers will have access to a certain percentage of the domestic market in that year. This sort of restriction of supply usually will increase the consumer price because there is little incentive to use price as a means of increasing sales.

A specific type of quota that prohibits all trade is an **embargo.** Like quotas, countries–or groups of countries–may place embargos on either imports or exports, on whole categories of products regardless of destination, on specific products to specific countries or on all products to given countries.

Standards: Countries commonly have set classification, labeling and testing standards in a manner that allows the sale of domestic products but inhibits that of foreign made ones. The requirement that companies indicate on a product where it is made provides information to consumers who prefer buying products from certain locales. But this adds to a firm's production costs, particularly if the components, design, and labour increasingly come from a variety of countries, so most products today are of mixed origin.

"Buy Local" Legislation: Another form of quantitative trade control is "buy local" legislation. If government purchases are a large part of total expenditure within a country, they comprise an important part of the market. Most governments favour domestic producers in their purchases of goods. Sometimes they favour domestic producers through price mechanisms. There is abundant legislation worldwide that simply prescribes a minimum percentage of domestic content that a given product must have for it to be sold legally within the country.

Specific Permission Requirements: Some countries require that potential importers or exporters secure permission from governmental authorities before conducting trade transactions, a requirement known as an **import license.**

To gain a license, a company may have send samples abroad, which can restrict import or exports directly by denying permission or indirectly because of the cost, time, and uncertainty involved in the process. Similar to an import license is a **foreign-exchange control,** which requires an importer of a given product to apply to a governmental agency to secure the foreign currency to pay for the product.

Administrative Delays: Closely akin to specific permission requirements are international administrative delays, which create uncertainty and raise the cost of carrying inventory. But correcting delays may be difficult. For example, exporters to Japan have complained that stevedore practices at Japanese ports excessively delay and add costs to their shipments.

Reciprocal Requirements: Governments sometimes require that exporters take merchandize in lieu of money or that they promise to buy merchandize or services in the country to which they export. This requirement is common in the aerospace and defense industries-sometimes because the importer is short of foreign currency to purchase what it wants. More frequently, however, reciprocal requirements are made between countries with ample access to foreign currency that wants to secure jobs to technology as part of the transaction. These barter transactions are called **counter trade**, or **offsets**. They often require exporters to find markets for goods outside their lines of expertise or to engage in complicated organizational arrangements over which they lose desired control. Many companies avoid counter trade. However, some have developed competencies in these types of arrangements.

MAJOR DIFFERENCES BETWEEN INTERNATIONAL AND DOMESTIC BUSINESS

Conducting and managing international business operations is more complex than undertaking domestic business. Differences in the nationality of parties involved, relatively less mobility of factors of production, customer heterogeneity across markets, variations in business practices and political systems, varied business regulations and policies, use of different currencies are the key aspects that differentiate international businesses from domestic business. These, moreover, are the factors that make international business much more complex and a difficult activity.

Scope: Scope of international business is quite wide. It includes not only merchandise exports, but also trade in services, licensing and franchising as well as foreign investments. Domestic business pertains to a limited territory all the trading activities are inside a single boundary.

Benefits: International business benefits both the nations and firms.

- Nations gain by way of earning foreign exchange, more efficient use of domestic resources, greater prospects of growth and creation of employment opportunities.

- The advantages to the business firms include prospects for higher profits, greater utilization of production capacities, way out to intense competition in domestic market and improved business vision.

Market Fluctuations: Firms have to face this situation which results in low profits and in some cases losses too. International trade provides for stabilizing seasonal market fluctuations which in consequence provides them to withstand the huge losses as their operations are wide spread which is not available for those operating locally.

Modes of Entry: A firm desirous of entering into international business has several options available to it. These range from exporting/importing to contract manufacturing abroad, licensing and franchising, joint ventures and setting up wholly owned subsidiaries abroad. Each entry mode has its own advantages and disadvantages which the firm needs to take into account while deciding as to which mode of entry it should prefer.

Purvey: Providing goods and services as a business within a territory is much easier than doing the same globally. Restrictions such as custom procedures do not bother domestic entities but whereas globally operating firms need to follow complicated customs procedures and trade barriers like tariff etc.

Sharing of Technology: International business provides for sharing of the latest technology that is innovated in various firms across the globe which in consequence will improve the mode and quality of their production.

Political Relations: International business obviously improve the political relations among the nations which gives rise to cross-national cooperation and agreements. Nations cooperate more on transactional issues.

An international business is a business whose activities are carried out across national borders. This differs from a domestic business because a domestic business is a business whose activities are carried out within the borders of its geographical location.

A domestic company is one that confines its activities to the local market, be it city, state, or the country it is in. It deals, generally, with one currency, local customs and cultures, business laws of commerce, taxes and products and services of a local nature.

The international company, on the other hand deals with businesses and governments in one or more foreign countries and is subject to treaties, tariffs, currency rates of exchange, politics, cultural differences, taxes, fees, and penalties of each country it is doing business in. It may also be conducting business in it's home country, but the emphasis is on trading in the international marketplace.

WHAT CAN YOU DO WITH A MAJOR IN INTERNATIONAL BUSINESS

With globalization and international business becoming the mantra of today, there is a great demand for professionals with a major in international business, and this demand is expected to increase as global economy continues to expand.

As a specialist with a major in international business, you are equipped to understand the diversity present in international business and you can end up being a valuable participant in any global business venture.

So, what can you do with a major in international business? Well, having a major in international business means that you are prepared to compete in the global market. Any American company involved in international business and trade can only survive if it has the ability to expand into new markets and to do so, they have be open to change and to new learning needs of their international customers and clients. This itself poses a big challenge and your skills and knowledge will help the business immensely. Most American businesses tend to be insular and companies do not take into account the broader perspective of trade regulations of the various governing bodies.

International business is one area where a comprehensive high level education is very important. This is also true for anyone joining at entry level positions. Your college degree clubbed with your personality and business sense will go a long way in opening door for your career and advancing it. However, you should ensure that you are well versed in cultural differences of the various countries and it would be well worth your time and time to learn multi-cultural business etiquette so that you prove to be an invaluable asset to your organization.

CHALLENGES OF INTERNATIONAL TRADING SYSTEM

The international trading system was developed after World War II as way of protecting major economies. Concerned with the emergence of protectionist trends, the United States and other countries joined hands to move toward liberalization of trade to help develop world and domestic economies.

However, in recent years, there are major challenges in the international trading system. The international trading system has been characterized by wider range of players involved in free trade negotiations; instances where an important role has been played by regional cohesion and integration like the liberalization efforts by NAFTA.

Protectionism has recently been seen with the form of tariff hikes by countries. However, the international trading system is important not just at domestic level but also on the global scale. There is no doubt that rules have to developed for areas like intellectual properties, competition policy, anti-dumping, electronic commerce and international harmonization and the World Trade

Organization should be used as a forum where many countries can participate simultaneously and thus allowing efficient rule formulation.

While the world trading system has seen substantial enhancement of the international trading system, it is also characterized by worldwide surge in groupings in the form of regional cohesion and integration. However, regional integration has shown positive impact for countries, especially the Asian countries which are focusing on cross-border corporate activities and intra-regional trade.

If the challenges of international trading system are resolved to a certain extent, many countries will see increased merits, especially those that have similar economic and social circumstances.

Several businesses today are global businesses too and with the increase of technology and real time experiences on the internet conducting global business has become simpler than ever. All the aspects of global business like interacting with people, business planning, holding conferences and communication happens on the internet and not at the actual location.

Every business has its difficulties and presents is own challenges in when it comes to operating it successfully. For example, the nature of business may not be accepted openly in the targeted country because of cultural differences. Also, international businesses face several restrictions like acceptance, usability, application of the product locally and customer service issues. Even though English is a very popular language it is in the end spoken only in a few countries as a primary language. Some of the people in other countries have never uttered a single word in English their entire lives. So the company which is starting a business in such a place should have a contingency plan where they can provide service in their language for example.

If a company can cross over the language and cultural barriers, then most of their blocks have been cleared. Also the business ethics matter and the any international organization cannot have standard ethics that apply globally. They have to be changed and altered.

IMPACT OF GLOBALIZATION ON INTERNATIONAL BUSINESS

Globalization is not a new concept. It has been around throughout history with mankind exchanging goods and services, shared social traditions and blended cultures. The difference today is the development of new technologies, primarily tools of communication like the internet, which have played a major role in accelerating exchanges.

Globalization is a process which cannot be stopped or slowed. What we can do is to ensure that globalization is shaped by common and deliberate efforts so that all involved, people and countries, are benefited by it.

Economists have proven that those countries experiencing the most accelerated growth have also been those with greatest increase in exports. For countries with small population, export-led growth is the principal source of jobs and government revenue. However, increasing exports is just part of the development challenge that both governments and private sector face. They have to prepare people to take advantage of globalization and one of the best ways to promote globalization is to promote well-paying, high-skilled jobs through investment in education which is essential for the development of any business.

International business community should play a role in helping to reduce the downsides of globalization while availing the benefits. Reducing the disadvantages in the long run help to create wealth in a country and thus playing an important role in reducing global poverty through economic development.

Most international businesses try to gain a foothold in a foreign country by formulating sustainable development so that repay the community they work in. International business community sees globalization as a way of reaching out to the masses and this has definitely altered the way global business is conducted, the way existing technologies are utilized and the way products are produced and consumed.

ADVANTAGES OF INTERNATIONAL BUSINESS

- **Faster Growth:** Firms that have operate internationally tend to develop at a much quicker pace than those operating locally.
- **Access to Cheaper Inputs:** Operating internationally may enable the firm to source raw materials or labor at lower prices.
- **Increased Quality and Efficiency:** Exposure to foreign competition will encourage increased efficiency. Doing business in the international market allows firms to improve the quality of their product in order to gain a competitive advantage.
- **New Market Opportunities:** International business presents firms with new market opportunities. These new markets provide more opportunities for expansion, growth and income. A bigger market means more customers, increased revenue, a larger profit margin and allows the business to realize economies of scale.
- **Diversification:** As the firm diversifies its market, it becomes less vulnerable to changes in local demand. This reduces wild swings in a company's sales and profits.

After launching a business related to product or service and being successful, the requirements of the business change and needs also differ. By tending to the same market the product or service can become extremely redundant. However, venturing into global markets gives a new prospect and also it is like restarting a business with new challenges. It is like going to a different vacation spot every year instead of returning to the same holiday home in a broad perspective.

A new market not only presents new opportunities but also creates an option of recognition once more. Now the product has expanded credibility and more presence. Global recognition goes a long way and the country can consider setting up business in several countries. There is no end for recognition in global markets. General Electric is a good example of that.

Another perspective is risk sharing. If the business is not doing well in the native country due to poor economic conditions, or saturated market or increased competition, the new location could actually be more productive and profit earning for the business. So, the loss in one location can be compensated with the profits from the other location. These are some of the major advantages of international business.

DISADVANTAGES OF INTERNATIONAL BUSINESS

- **Increased Costs:** There are increased operating expenses including the establishment of facilities abroad, the hiring of additional staff, traveling of personnel, specialized transport networks, information and communication technology.
- **Foreign Regulations and Standards:** The firm may need to conform to new standards. This may require changes such as in the production process, inputs and packaging, incurring additional costs.
- **Delays in Payments:** International trade may cause delays in payments, adversely affecting the firm's cash flow.
- **Complex Organizational Structure:** International business usually requires changes to the firms operating structure. Training/retraining of management may be necessary to facilitate restructuring.

BARRIERS TO INTERNATIONAL BUSINESS

When we talk about international business we mean the exchange of goods and/or services. This exchange usually takes place between two parties from different countries or between two countries located anywhere on the globe.

There are basically three barriers to international business that are used by countries, and they are as follows:

- **Non-tariff Barrier:** Usually this type of barrier is imposed by a country on imports so that the quantity of imported items is restricted. Due to this, the availability of the imported item or items is restricted in the domestic market and the price too is very high.
- **Tariff Barrier:** This is barrier is in the form of duties, taxes, quotas etc. Because of this barrier, imports decrease and price of imported

products increase which results in the fall in the demand giving boost to domestic products.

- **Voluntary Constraint:** This is a type of international trade barrier wherein a country voluntarily restricts or stops imports from coming in. This is usually used to limit the competition that domestic industries will face with the coming in of imported goods.

Whenever a country starts international business with another country, these three barriers to international trade are always taken into account. It has been seen that lower developed countries and developing countries tend to favor these three barriers to international trade as the countries can earn foreign exchange by introducing tariff and non-tariff barrier, the local industries are protected from competition by foreign companies and industries and as less imported goods are available in the country, consumers tend to buy local products giving the local industries a boost.

The benefits of these barriers are as follows:

- Country receives foreign exchange by placing Tariff and non-Tariff barriers.
- The local industry of the nation is safeguarded by the overseas competitive industries.
- Less of products are imported into the country as a result of which customer also buys local items.
- The currency remains in the country as a result of which government expands profits in the form of revenue.

RISKS IN INTERNATIONAL BUSINESS

Having an international business is great and it opens a lot of more options globally for the company. However, there are several risks involved in locating a company in a different country. The company has to face difficulties in multiple levels in the local business community. There are other factors that are out of anyone's control like terrorism and anti social attitudes.

A firm should have plenty of freedom for making strategic decisions and in an international place and a new business environment this becomes a restrictive factor.

- An **operational risk** is faced by company when it comes to their assets and financial capital required to carry out their day to day business. There can be several hindrances faced by the company with breakdown of machinery, infrastructural problems and local conditions.
- **Politics** play a very important role in a country's business and in several countries where it is not a Presidential government it is ever problematic for international businesses to prosper. As the political party changes

the policies relate to international companies are susceptible for change as per the party's beliefs. Politics can make a business volatile. One of the biggest examples in this category is Coca cola in India. They had to pull out of the country for a brief while.

- **Economic risk** is another big restricting factor and if the overall economy of the country is and the company may suffer in several ways. They may not get essential tools for running the business locally and this may even apply to essential commodities like petrol and gas.

Companies doing business across international borders face many of the same risks as would normally be evident in strictly domestic transactions. For example,

- Buyer insolvency (purchaser cannot pay);
- Non-acceptance (buyer rejects goods as different from the agreed upon specifications);
- Credit risk (allowing the buyer to take possession of goods prior to payment);
- Regulatory risk (e.g., a change in rules that prevents the transaction);
- Intervention (governmental action to prevent a transaction being completed);
- Political risk (change in leadership interfering with transactions or prices); and
- War and other uncontrollable events.

In addition, international business also faces the risk of unfavorable exchange rate movements (and, the potential benefit of favorable movements).

REASONS WHY GOVERNMENT INTERVENE IN INTERNATIONAL BUSINESS

The reasons why governments intervene in international business are usually to correct market failures or distortions, redistribution of income and non-economic objectives.

Market Failures

- Economies usually follow the principles of optimization which state that the marginal benefit should always exceed marginal cost for any discreet change that is made in a policy; and the marginal benefit should be equal to marginal cost for a choice to be optimal.
- With properly defined costs and benefits, the principles of optimization have been used to explain behavior throughout the economy. Many firms apply these principles in deciding how to produce in order to be profitable. Consumers apply these principles in deciding how much to

consume in order to be satisfied and government apply these principles to decide when and how to intervene in the economy and international business.

- Governments intervene in international business so that government policies can redirect the economy of a country towards the preferred outcome. That is why it is quite common for governments to levy a tax or introduce a subsidy and this alters the marginal costs or benefits for a business involved in international business.

Distribution of Income

- In a competitive market, income will accrue to whoever owns the economy's productive assets in proportion to their productivity. Therefore, the government has a legitimate reason to intervene so that distribution of income and wealth. Sometimes, depending on who controls the government, it can end up enriching the members of the governments themselves rather than the people who deserve it. Government policies are usually designed to shift wealth from some people to others without changing the total resources available.

Changes in policy occur in real time and are usually anticipated by those who they affect. This results in people changing their behavior to avoid adverse consequences of the change.

Non-economic Objectives

- One of the major reasons why governments intervene in international business is national security. In order survive, all countries have to arrange their defense from military attack and this cannot be left to the private sector because national security is a public good. Therefore, it is quite possible that a government might subsidize defense, wherein the defense establishment is usually operated by the government itself.

ROLE OF COMMERCIAL BANKS IN INTERNATIONAL BUSINESS

Commercial banks are vital to the success of international trade and they form a major link between the buyer and the seller. In an international market every business needs a strong link between the seller and the buyer for easy financial transactions.

The advantage with commercial banks is that they will have a global presence and tie ups with many other international banks. This will help the business further to have transactions worldwide and also enable to transfer funds quickly to their destination.

Commercial banks are easy to operate because they usually are more flexible with international businesses as they need the funds and also they can make a lot of things happen in a short period of time for the new businesses. The same amount of flexibility may not be available with the local banks. Local banks that are run by the state or the federal governments have more rigid rules and they do not offer as many facilities as the commercial banks. However, the only advantage that a government run bank would offer is immense security and people do not have to be scared that they will disappear one day. However there are several commercial banks that are present in many countries like Standard Chartered, HSBC, and American Express that can also offer the same amount of security.

Commercial banks understand the work ethos of international business firms and also have several ready-made solutions that suit business needs. These business solutions are offered are designed keeping in mind the international business.

LAWS AFFECTING INTERNATIONAL BUSINESS TRANSACTION

An international business which is conducting their business in a different country would need to abide by the laws and regulations of that particular country always. The court that is located in the specific country would make the judicial decisions pertaining to the business. There will be several laws affecting the business and its day to day transactions. They will have several obligations to fulfill before carrying out any transaction that involves finances or product transfers.

If the international business is shipping products to another country, then their products or services should comply with all the legalities of the country. For example, if it is food products that are being exported, then they should meet the legal quality standards set forth by the country.

Several countries observe laws related to culture and religion and the company has to make sure that they do not cross the set limitations or else they will land themselves in legal trouble. All the material that comes into direct contact with the people living in the country should comply with their cultural, ethical and religious values. For example, it is okay if a swim suit model in a bikini exhibits her body on a soft drink bottle. However, if the same tradition is carried out in Afghanistan, the company can set off a major issue with religious leaders and it can backfire. Advertising material and campaigns have to be handled very carefully keeping in mind the country's cultural and religious values. These are some of the laws relating to International businesses.

REASONS FOR DOING CULTURAL ANALYSIS BEFORE STARTING AN INTERNATIONAL BUSINESS

Every business that is planning to start its operation in an international location should first study the location thoroughly. They should completely understand the local market and also do a through cultural analysis of the place.

Cultural analysis helps the business in setting several parameters for decision making, adapting to new needs, implementation and also monitoring the effectiveness of the business. Executing a business in a cross cultural environment is very difficult. Every country has its own unique cultural requirements and you can notice this on a wider perspective. People in China are different from people in Russia. Eating, living, clothing and language and other habits are different form place to place.

The nation's culture will also determine if the product of the international business set up has any scope at all. One cannot launch an alcohol brand in an extremely conservative and orthodox society. They will basically find no market and it will be the most foolish thing for them to do to venture in such markets without checking the cultural background. A business that is extremely successful in India cannot expect the same result in Saudi Arabia for example and the reason is cultural differences.

The satisfaction of the end user matters in the end and this also has a cultural bearing. For example in some communities people do not eat meat at all. Take Tibet as a country where most monks do not eat commercially cooked food. Launching fast food businesses in this country may still be successful because of the number of tourists who visit here. However, they have to also study the environmental needs before staring out.

COUNTERTRADE

Sometimes countries have so much difficulty generating enough foreign exchange to pay for imports that they need to devise creative ways to get the products they want. Both companies and governments often must find creative ways of settling payment such as trading goods for goods as part of the transaction. **Countertrade** is any one of several different arrangements by which goods and services are traded for each other. Countertrade can be divided into two basic types:

- Barter, based on clearing arrangements used to avoid money-based exchange
- Buybacks
- Offsets
- Counterpurchase

BARTER

Barter, the oldest form of countertrade, is a transaction in which goods of equal value without any flow of cash trade goods. There are barter firms that act as an intermediary between the exporter and importer, often taking title to the goods received by the exporter for a price or selling the goods for a fee and a percentage of the sales value.

Buybacks are products the exporter receives as payment that are related to or originate from the original export. An example would be where a company exports capital equipment for a country's mining operation and receives as payment minerals to sell on world markets.

OFFSET TRADE

Another type of countertrade, called offset trade, is becoming increasingly important. Offset trade is when an exporter sells products for cash and then helps the importer find opportunities to earn hard currency. Offsets are most often used for big-ticket items, such a military sales. Offset arrangements are usually one of two types:

- *Direct offsets* include any business that relates directly to the export. Generally the exporters seek contractors in the importer's country to joint venture or co-produce certain parts if applicable.
- *Indirect offsets* include all business unrelated to the export. Generally the exporter is asked by the importers government to buy a country's goods or invest in an unrelated business. Examples of indirect offsets might include assisting in the export of unrelated products from the host country or generating tourist revenues for the host country.

Counterpurchase: Under the counterpurchase agreement the seller receives the full payment in cash but agrees to spend an equivalent amount of money in that country within a specified period.

Why Counter Trade?

- Expand or maintain foreign markets
- Increase sales
- Sidestep liquidity problems
- Repatriate blocked funds
- Clean up bad debt situations
- Build customer relationships
- Keep from losing markets to competitors
- Gain foreign contracts for future sales
- Find lower-cost purchasing sources

Four Main Reasons Why Counter Trade is Used

- **Money:** some people cannot pay in the currency you want "to enable trade to take place in markets which are unable to pay for imports. This can occur as a result of a non-convertible currency, a lack of commercial credit or a shortage of foreign exchange".
- **The Political Environment:** local jobs and industry "to protect or stimulate the output of domestic industries (including agriculture and mineral extraction) and to help find new export markets".
- **The Political Environment:** rules and regulations to protect the host country "as a reflection of political and economic policies which seek to plan and balance overseas trade".
- "To gain a competitive advantage over competing suppliers."

Reasons for the Growth of Countertrade

1. Countertrade was very common between the communist countries. It also became popular in respect of trade between the Communist Block and many developing countries because many developing countries were eagerly looking towards this block for increasing their exports among other things and this naturally led to the acceptance of the trade practice preferred by these centrally planned economies.
2. Some countries have also made the countertrade a means to increase sales through disguised undercutting of the cartel prices.
3. When the foreign exchange problem became more severe for the developing countries following the oil price hikes, they began to actively pursue countertrade in a frantic bid to increase their exports by all means.
4. Having realized the potential of increasing the business by engaging in countertrade, many international trading corporations became active in the countertrade. Their trading with many countries enabled them even to take up such complex transactions as the case of Daimler Benz cited earlier.

Pros of Counter Trade

- The world debt crisis has made ordinary trade financing very risky.
- The use of counter trade permits the covert reduction of prices and therefore allows the circumvention of price and exchange controls.
- "You scratch my back and I'll scratch yours" – Bilateralism.
- Excellent mechanism to gain entry into new markets.
- Counter trade can be a good way to attract new buyers.
- Counter trade also can provide stability for long-term sales.

DEVELOPING A CORPORATE COUNTERTRADE STRATEGY

An exporter confronted with a countertrade demand can react in four possible ways:

- The first is to refuse to consider the proposal; although this will certainly lose the sale, it will save the company trouble.
- The second is to push the demand aside and delay any action as long as possible.
- The third is to respond positively to the demand, having prepared beforehand to engage in countertrade.
- The fourth is for the company to have a commitment to a pro-active countertrade marketing strategy and accept countertrade as a way to give the company a competitive edge and to develop a long-term relationship with the customer.

IMPACT OF GLOBALIZATION ON INDIAN ECONOMY – AN OVERVIEW

Today, the word has acquired a much wider connotation and significance. The International Monetary Fund has defined globalization as "the growing interdependence of countries worldwide through the increasing volume and variety of cross-border transactions in goods and services, and of international capital flows, and also, through the more rapid and widespread diffusion of technology."

To understand the structure and grammar of globalization, at least in respect of its impact on economic governance, it is essential to examine the critical driving forces and key building blocks behind the process. The growing interdependence has taken place only because of the increasing acceptance and enthronement of economic liberalism as the preferred method of managing the market forces.

In fact, this, in the context of a liberal approach, is a paradox and self-contradiction. Liberal economics demands little politics. The role of the political rulers must be confined to the provision of an enabling environment and a conducive climate, in which trade and commerce will feel free, and find their own way to the fulfillment of their target.

The market in India will witness more and more alliances, joint ventures, and networks, thanks to the **LPG** syndrome — an acronym popular with the financial analysts to describe the process of **liberalization, privatization, and globalization** — which has been predominant since 1991.

We are into the millennium: Already the third year is nearly coming to an end. Change is the name of the game in this new epoch. "You cannot step into the same river twice," wrote Heraclitus. In this whirlwind of change, only such organizations will thrive and survive — which stick their necks out, and which are proactive and not reactive.

It is possible and probable that such changes may usher in a new world order, and spell a different dimension to the global economic environment. Already Europe has a new currency (the euro), and a closely collaborating comity of nations. China and the US, which were till sometime back, poles apart politically and economically, are now hand-in-glove in respect of trade pacts and partnerships. The WTO, which has emerged as a worthy successor to the GATT, has brought sunshine into the field of economic cooperation between countries. All these are harbingers of a cataclysm in commerce, and a revolution in international trade, which are already on the cards.

The spectrum of a shift to a global level of governance, on a number of erstwhile local and domestic issues, has further reinforced the trend and thinking towards obliterating national boundaries, and countenancing in cross-border transactions. The world seems to be progressing clearly on the path of a multi-level system of national management, in which regional and global interests will operate in tandem and transcend all other parochial parameters.

The establishment of a totally integrated global economy, however, has a long way to go. It is a protracted process, and in the current scenario of a clear emphasis on regional cooperation and concepts such as the European Union, SAARC, ASEAN, and so on, globalization appears to be a pipe-dream.

While the regional organizations may want to exclude third-party nations from their conglomerate, it is also possible that they may serve as a stepping stone to eventual globalization on a full-fledged scale. The range and spectrum may extend from the locus of a country to a region, and then from a region to the globe; this way, the growth will be gradual and logical. Unity in diversity may be the idiom and grammar of globalization.

The growth of trade and investment in sequel to globalization warrants parallel movements of capital and finance. Traditional and orthodox public finance, however, has always been highly regimented and regulated; and hence, a localized and fragmented phenomenon. Therefore, the advocates of integrated financial markets claim and clamour that creating a global resource base is *sine qua non* for fostering international trade and commerce.

Globalization adds an incremental dimension to the cultural issues inside a company. All organizations cultivate over a period of time, their own institutional behavior, norms, culture, code of conduct ethics and values. This psyche becomes more pronounced, when the corporate extends its presence to other countries.

The tendency to preserve, protect, and persevere with one's own value system is accentuated, when it is in competition with an alien ethos. The confluence of corporate and country culture brings about a social synergy par excellence. In fact, such a synthesis is a condition precedent for globalization. It is a virtuous circle.

Nevertheless, the depth and roots of the philosophy of diverse cultures across the world are intensive and extensive; they are almost immune to any external influence. On the other hand, if at all any cultural convergence is possible, it can transpire only when there shall be no clash with such profoundly professed and practiced indigenous beliefs and faiths such as religion, ethnic tradition etc.

Liberalization, Privatization and Globalization (LPG) of the economies and companies has fuelled the competitiveness among corporate. A number of factors have lead to the increasing globalization of the world economy and as a result the competitive environment faced by the corporate has changed dramatically since the last decade. The drivers of globalization include: decreasing tariffs, improved transportation, communications and information technology, global manufacturing of products and availability of services across markets.

These changes have enabled the global competitors to make the products and services available to customers worldwide, and the results have been a proliferation of choices for consumers and a need for the companies to offer greater products and service quality at lower costs in order to remain competitive. These pressures have led to an increased emphasis on reengineering internal business processes and working more collaboratively with the customers and suppliers to better integrate planning and operations throughout the supply chain as a means to reduce costs and improve services.

Changes in technology and globalization of products and services have also resulted in increasingly dynamic markets and greater uncertainty in customer demand. Consumers have greater access to more goods and services, and the introduction of new products is occurring at a faster pace. Thus a company's competitive position depends upon its ability to understand changes in customer demands and respond appropriately with goods and services that will meet those demands.

LIBERALISATION AND GLOBALISATION: MEANING AND PROCESSES

LIBERALISATION contains two components:

- Allow the private sector to run those activities which were restricted earlier only to public sector.
- Relaxation of rules and regulations which were restricted to the growth of private sector.

PROCESSES:

- Private sector has been allowed to produce all the goods except alcohol, cigarettes, hazardous chemicals, industrial explosives, electronic aerospace and drugs and pharmaceuticals.
- Industries reserved for public sector has been reduced from 17 to 3.
- Private sector can also enter in to core industries like iron and steel, electricity, air transport, shipbuilding, heavy machinery and some defense goods.

  The private sector has been freed from many regulations such as (a) licensing (b) permission to import raw materials (c) regulation on price and distribution and (d) restriction on investment by large business companies.

GLOBALISATION: Integrating the Indian economy with the world economy.

- Many producers from outside the country can sell their goods and services in India.
- India can also sell its goods and services to other countries.
- Globalization facilitates those who have capital to establish enterprises in India, produce goods for sale within the country or export them.
- Entrepreneurs from India also can go and invest in other countries.
- Not only the movement of capital but also the movement of people takes place.
- Exchange of capital, technology and experience take place between the various countries of the world.
- Government has removed restrictions on import of goods, reduced taxes on imported goods and encouraged investors from abroad to invest in India.

The Important Reform Measures (Step towards Liberalization, Privatization and Globalization)

Indian economy was in deep crisis in July 1991, when foreign currency reserves had plummeted to almost $1 billion; Inflation had roared to an annual rate of 17 per cent; fiscal deficit was very high and had become unsustainable; foreign investors and NRIs had lost confidence in Indian Economy. Capital was flying out of the country and we were close to defaulting on loans. Along with these bottlenecks at home, many unforeseeable changes swept the economies of nations in Western and Eastern Europe, South East Asia, Latin America and elsewhere, around the same time. These were the economic compulsions at home and abroad that called for a complete overhauling of our economic policies and programs. Major measures initiated as a part of the liberalization and globalization strategy in the early nineties included the following:

- **Devaluation:** The first step towards globalization was taken with the announcement of the devaluation of Indian currency by 18-19 per cent against major currencies in the international foreign exchange market. In fact, this measure was taken in order to resolve the BOP crisis.
- **Disinvestment:** In order to make the process of globalization smooth, privatization and liberalization policies are moving along as well. **Under the privatization scheme, most of the public sector undertakings have been/are being sold to private sector.**
- **Dismantling of the Industrial Licensing Regime:** At present, only six industries are under compulsory licensing mainly on accounting of environmental safety and strategic considerations. A significantly amended locational policy in tune with the liberalized licensing policy is in place. No industrial approval is required from the government for locations not falling within 25 kms of the periphery of cities having a population of more than one million.
- **Allowing Foreign Direct Investment** (FDI) across a wide spectrum of industries and encouraging non-debt flows. The department has put in place a liberal and transparent foreign investment regime where most activities are opened to foreign investment on automatic route without any limit on the extent of foreign ownership. Some of the recent initiatives taken to further **liberalize the FDI regime,** inter alias, include opening up of sectors such as Insurance (upto 26%); development of integrated townships (upto 100%); defense industry (upto 26%); tea plantation (upto 100% subject to divestment of 26% within five years to FDI); enhancement of FDI limits in private sector banking, allowing FDI up to 100% under the automatic route for most manufacturing activities in SEZs; opening up B2B e-commerce; Internet Service Providers (ISPs) without Gateways; electronic mail and voice mail to 100% foreign investment subject to 26% divestment condition; etc. The Department has also strengthened investment facilitation measures through Foreign Investment Implementation Authority (FIIA).
- **Non Resident Indian Scheme** the general policy and facilities for foreign direct investment as available to foreign investors/companies are fully applicable to NRIs as well. In addition, government has extended some concessions especially for NRIs and overseas corporate bodies having more than 60% stake by NRIs.
- **Throwing Open Industries Reserved for the Public Sector to Private Participation:** Now there are only three industries reserved for the public sector.
- **Abolition of the (MRTP) Act,** which necessitated prior approval for capacity expansion.
- **The Removal of Quantitative Restrictions on Imports.**

- **The Reduction of the Peak Customs Tariff** from over 300 per cent prior to the 30 per cent rate that applies now.
- **Wide-ranging Financial Sector Reforms** in the banking, capital markets, and insurance sectors, including the deregulation of interest rates, strong regulation and supervisory systems, and the introduction of foreign/private sector competition.

INDIA'S DEVELOPMENT STRATEGY PRIOR TO 1991–AN EVALUATION

Prior to 1991, India followed mixed economy and the control of critical industries such as coal mining; steel, power and roads were under the control of the govt. The private sectors were allowed to establish certain industries again under the rules and regulations of the govt. In case of the public sector, the Government invested a large amount and the purpose behind this strategy was to remove poverty, reduce inequalities in the distribution of income and wealth and to achieve economic growth and social justice.

Positive Aspects

This strategy has created:

- A large industrial base and increase in industrial production.
- The proportion of population living below poverty line has declined.
- India has become self sufficient in food grains.
- A base for export-oriented industries has been created.
- India has mobilized savings and created their own resources.
- Educational institutions have produced large number of scientists and technically skilled working people.
- This has helped in industrial and technological growth and self-reliance.

Negative Aspects

- Industrialization did not take place as per the expectation.
- The growth rate of industrial production declined from 8% to 4%.
- The laws that were framed to regulate the private sector were responsible for slow growth of industrial sector.
- These laws have also failed to reduce the concentration of economic power in the private sector.
- Corruption, lack of efficiency in work and ineffective management became the common features of the public sector.
- Many public sector companies were making losses.
- Official machinery became a major hindrance to the development.

Impact of Globalization on Indian Economy

The novel Tale of Two Cities of Charles Dickens begins with a piquant description of the contradictions of the times: It was the best of times, it was the worst of times; it was the age of wisdom, it was the age of foolishness; it was the epoch of belief, it was the epoch of incredulity; we had everything before us, we had nothing before us.

At the present, we can also say about the tale of two India's: We have the best of times; we have the worst of times. There is sparkling prosperity, there is stinking poverty. We have dazzling five star hotels side by side with darkened ill-starred hovels. **We have everything by globalization, we have nothing by globalization.**

Though some economic reforms were introduced by the Rajiv Gandhi government (1985–89), it was the Narasimha Rao Government that gave a definite shape and start to the new economic reforms of globalization in India. Presenting the 1991–92 Budget, Finance Minister Manmohan Singh said: After four decades of planning for industrialization, we have now reached a stage where we should welcome, rather fear, foreign investment. Direct foreign investment would provide access to capital, technology and market.

In the Memorandum of Economic Policies dated August 27, 1991 to the IMF, the Finance Minister submitted in the concluding paragraph: The Government of India believes that the policies set forth in the Memorandum are adequate to achieve the objectives of the program, but will take any additional measures appropriate for this purpose. In addition, the Government will consult with the Fund on the adoption of any measures that may be appropriate in accordance with the policies of the Fund on such consultations.

The Government of India affirmed to implement the economic reforms in consultation with the international bank and in accordance of its policies. Successive coalition governments from 1996 to 2004, led by the Janata Dal and BJP, adopted faithfully the economic policy of liberalization. With Manmohan Singh returned to power as the Prime Minister in 2004, the economic policy initiated by him has become the lodestar of the fiscal outlook of the government.

The Bright Side of Globalization

The rate of growth of the **Gross Domestic Product** of India has been on the increase from 5.6 per cent during 1980-90 to seven per cent in the 1993–2001 period. In the last four years, the annual growth rate of the GDP was impressive at 7.5 per cent (2003–04), 8.5 per cent (2004–05), 9 per cent (2005-06) and 9.2 per cent (2006–07). Prime Minister Manmohan Singh is confident of having a 10 per cent growth in the GDP in the Eleventh Five Year Plan period.

The foreign exchange reserves (as at the end of the financial year) were $39 billion (2000–01), $107 billion (2003–04), $145 billion (2005–06) and $180 billion (in February 2007). It is expected that India will cross the $200 billion mark soon.

The cumulative FDI inflows from 1991 to September 2006 were ₹1, 81,566 crores (US $43.29 billion). The sectors attracting highest FDI inflows are electrical equipments including computer software and electronics (18 per cent), service sector (13 per cent), telecommunications (10 per cent), transportation industry (nine per cent), etc. In the inflow of FDI, India has surpassed South Korea to become the fourth largest recipient. India controls at the present 45 per cent of the global outsourcing market with an estimated income of $50 billion.

In respect of market capitalization (which takes into account the market value of a quoted company by multiplying its current share price by the number of shares in issue), India is in the fourth position with $894 billion after the US ($17,000 billion), Japan ($4800 billion) and China ($1000). India is expected to soon cross the trillion dollar mark.

As per the Forbes list for 2007, the number of billionaires of India has risen to 40 (from 36 last year) more than those of Japan (24), China (17), France (14) and Italy (14) this year. A press report was jubilant: This is the richest year for India. The combined wealth of the Indian billionaires marked an increase of 60 per cent from $106 billion in 2006 to $170 billion in 2007. The 40 Indian billionaires have assets worth about ₹7.50 lakh crores whereas the cumulative investment in the 91 Public Sector Undertakings by the Central Government of India is ₹3.93 lakh crores only.

The Dark Side of Globalization

On the other side of the medal, there is a long list of the worst of the times, the foremost casualty being the agriculture sector. Agriculture has been and still remains the backbone of the Indian economy. It plays a vital role not only in providing food and nutrition to the people, but also in the supply of raw material to industries and to export trade. In 1951, agriculture provided employment to 72 per cent of the population and contributed 59 per cent of the gross domestic product. However, by 2001 the population depending upon agriculture came to 58 per cent whereas the share of agriculture in the GDP went down drastically to 24 per cent and further to 22 per cent in 2006-07. This has resulted in a lowering the per capita income of the farmers and increasing the rural indebtedness.

The agricultural growth of 3.2 per cent observed from 1980 to 1997 decelerated to two per cent subsequently. The Approach to the Eleventh Five Year Plan released in December 2006 stated that the growth rate of agricultural GDP including forestry and fishing is likely to be below two per cent in the Tenth Plan period.

The reasons for the deceleration of the growth of agriculture are given in the Economic Survey 2006–07: Low investment, imbalance in fertilizer use, low seeds replacement rate, a distorted incentive system and low post-harvest value addition continued to be a drag on the sectors performance. With more than half the population directly depending on this sector, low agricultural growth has serious implications for the inclusiveness of growth.

ETHICAL ISSUES IN INTERNATIONAL BUSINESS

Business ethics is an important part of the education of any manager, but managers with responsibility for foreign operations are confronted with many ethical issues that do not arise in domestic business. The distinctive ethical problems of international business are due to many factors, including:

- Different ethical traditions and political and legal systems; diverse forms of economic organization and
- Different levels of economic development;
- Inadequate or ineffectual regulation, especially in less-developed countries; conflicts between national and regional economic and political interests;
- A lack of background institutions and guidelines for international business; the scope and power of multinational corporations and their ability to evade regulation; and pervasive corruption in some parts of the world.

Importance of ethics in the business world is superlative and global. New trends and issues arise on a daily basis which may create an important burden to organizations and end-consumers. Nowadays, the need for proper ethical behavior within organizations has become crucial to avoid possible lawsuits. The public scandals of corporate malfeasance and misleading practices, have affected the public perception of many organizations. It is widely known that advertising does not promote the advancement of human moral sensibility.

The recent expansion of global business and fall of trade barriers worldwide have further underlined the interest in the topics of ethical behavior and social responsibility. In addition, as many scholars believe, human rights and environmental conservation are gaining increasing more recognition in both academic and commercial settings.

International business ethics is becoming very important in view of the globalization of business activity. Companies all over the world have been forced to come to grips with the costs and consequences of unethical behavior that result from cultural differences. There is no true global consensus on what is morally correct.

As multinational companies expand globally and enter foreign markets, ethical conduct of the officers and employees assume added importance since the very cultural diversity associated with such expansion may undermine the much shared cultural and ethical values observable in the mores homogeneous organizations. Although understanding of other cultures and recognition of differences among them will enhance the cross-cultural communication, it may not be sufficient to provide viable guidelines of proper ethical behavior in organizations.

Thus, concerns about unethical behavior of corporations in other countries, are manifested in legislations such as the Foreign Corrupt Practices Act of 1977, and the Sarbane-Oxley Act of 2002. In the academic arena, on the other hand, the culture-based consequentiality model is developed to explain, among other things, how cultural differences alter the ethical perception and actions of individuals engaged in making decisions with ethical overtones.

"Ethics is the moral principle that individuals inject into their decision making process and that helps temper the last outcome to conform to the norms of their society." Moreover, ethical principles have the very profound function of making behavior predictable. The truly global companies must come to grips with the legal and moral atmosphere in which they operate. But above all, they need to establish an environment that fosters ethical behavior, because in the final analysis to do otherwise cuts into their profitability.

Ethical investment is a useful aspect for considering ethical business, since large scale investment is ultimately subject to market forces, which largely reflect public opinion. As such ethical investment criteria and examples tend to be a good guide towards ethical attitudes of large sections of people and society, rather than the 'expert' views of leaders and gurus.

Ethical investment has been a growing aspect of business investment since the 1970s, although arguably the first types of ethical businesses can be traced back to the Quaker and Methodist movements of the 1800s.

Then as now ethical business and investments regard **socially responsible** activities and aims with far greater priority and emphasis than the traditional profit and free market business approach.

Traditional profit-based business models, which arose and came to dominate global commerce from the beginnings of industrialisation, inherently do not require a socially responsible element, other than compliance with the law, and a reflection of public reaction for pragmatic marketing (and ultimately profit) purposes.

Ethical business or investment is concerned with **how profit is made and how much profit is made**, whereas traditional profit-centred free-market based business is essentially only concerned with **how much profit is made**.

While business ethics emerged as a field in the 1970s, international business ethics did not emerge until the late 1990s, looking back on the international developments of that decade. Many new practical issues arose out of the international context of business. Theoretical issues such as cultural relativity of ethical values receive more emphasis in this field. Other, older issues can be grouped here as well.

Issues and Subfields Include:

- The search for universal values as a basis for international commercial behavior.
- Comparison of business ethical traditions in different countries. Also on the basis of their respective GDP and [Corruption rankings].
- Comparison of business ethical traditions from various religious perspectives.
- Ethical issues arising out of international business transactions; e.g. Bioprospecting and biopiracy in the pharmaceutical industry; the fair trade movement; transfer pricing.
- Issues such as globalization and cultural imperalism.
- Varying global standards - e.g. the use of child labor.
- The way in which multinationals take advantage of international differences, such as outsourcing production (e.g. clothes) and services (e.g. call centres) to low-wage countries.
- The permissibility of international commerce with pariah states.

Foreign countries often use dumping as a competitive threat, selling products at prices lower than their normal value. This can lead to problems in domestic markets. It becomes difficult for these markets to compete with the pricing set by foreign markets. In 2009, the International Trade Commission has been researching anti-dumping laws. Dumping is often seen as an ethical issue, as larger companies are taking advantage of other less economically advanced companies.

Global interdependence is a compelling dimension of the global business environment, creating demands on international managers to take a positive stance on issues of ethical behavior, social responsibility, economic development in host countries, and environmental protection around the world. However, there were still several large multinational companies indulging in ethically questionable practices. If MNEs behave unethically, it soon comes to the notice of the public and the company's image is tainted. Multinationals are often worse off for having behaved unethically in the interest of short term gains, as the bad publicity generated by unethical practices leads to far greater losses in the long run.

In order to deal effectively with the ethical challenges of international business, **managers** need to:

- Understand the increasingly complex global environment of business and the specific ethical problems that it raises.
- Develop a sensitivity to different ethical perspectives and a tolerance for the conflicts and ambiguity of international business.
- Develop guidelines for personal decision making and for formulating and implementing ethical corporate policies under the conditions of international business.
- Learn how to work toward more effective background institutions and forms of international business regulation.

ETHICAL PROBLEMS IN INTERNATIONAL BUSINESS

Getz analyzed international codes of conduct in **four** entities:

- The **Organization for Economic Cooperation and Development** (OECD), which is the primary policy-maker for industrialized nations,
- The **International Chamber of Commerce (ICC)**, which is concerned with fair treatment among multinational corporations,
- The **International Labor Organization (ILO)**, which is concerned with direct investment in developing countries, and
- The **Center for Transnational Corporations (CTC)**, whose objective is to maximize the contributions of transnational corporations to economic development and growth and to minimize the negative effects of the activities of these corporations.

These various codes were developed in order to establish order among multinational corporations; although, some organizations refuse to abide by these codes, mainly because national governments have not sanctioned them completely. Without uniform and full enforcement, multinational organizations could have rampant choice in international ethical issues. Underlying this lack of consensus is the issue of national as well as corporate culture. Every nation is different and every multinational organization is in one way or another distinct in the way they do business, especially in other countries.

In addition to these codes, the moral corporation should address human rights and whistle blowing and the international ethics code under which it operates. These issues are not very new. In a survey of 300 multinational corporations, 80 per cent agreed with seven items being ethical issues for business:

- employee conflict of interest,
- inappropriate gifts to corporate personnel,

- sexual harassment,
- unauthorized payments,
- affirmative action,
- employee privacy, and
- environmental issues

ETHICAL CLIMATE AND ETHICAL PROBLEMS

Strategies, such as these codes of ethics, are only one means of achieving the ultimate goal of having ethical international responsibility in the engagement of business worldwide. As stated above, there are many ethical responsibilities faced by multinational organizations. Theorists generally agree that situational variables such as organizational climate can affect ethical behavior of individuals. However, there have been no attempts to study the relationship of ethical climate of an organization and ethical behavior of its members.

Ethical climate, it must be emphasized, is not the same as culture is commonly perceived, but rather a broader concept of culture. Culture is believed to be more associated with deeper beliefs, values and assumptions. Therefore, just as one can value an individual's culture by his or her actions and personal activities, ethical climate can be observed on a larger scale; in this case, the organization. Ethical climate is, in essence, the employee's perception of the norms of an organization.

It is imperative for managers to consider developing strong ethical climates if they aim to provide organizational members the ability to handle ethical dilemmas and to avoid any inherent liabilities. Managers must create and maintain a clear and strong set of norms to promote good ethical behavior.

Global corporations must recognize the need for a uniform code of business ethics since without such a code, behavior of actors in this arena remains unpredictable. Furthermore, national governments must realize that probably the most effective means of protecting their citizens, their national interests, and the global environment against the ravages of the over-reaching global business rest in the development, adoption and enforcement of such a code. Until then, it is not realistic to hope for any such international agreement to be adopted.

However, a growing momentum for such a movement is observable. As stated in previous pages, international organizations, especially those involved in international business, finance, labor, economics and environment are developing rules and policies that can be regarded as the building blocks of a universal code of business ethics. Until such a uniform body of rules is drawn, signed and enforced, global corporations and organizations will be doing well to develop their own codes of conduct, applicable to all of their officers regardless of location.

EXAMPLES OF UNETHICAL BEHAVIORS, ACTIVITIES, POLICIES, ETC.

Instead of trying to arrive at a standard or all-encompassing rule of what is ethical, it is helpful to illustrate the depth and variety of ethics through suitable examples. This is an extension of the ethical business investment items listed above, and goes into far greater detail of different behaviors which might often be regarded as unethical.

The first category might seem obvious and clear-cut, and actually it's a reasonable starting point for the vast majority of ethical decisions, but this one point cannot be applied exclusively in assessing whether something is ethical or not:

- anything unlawful in the territory or area covered by such law—is probably unethical. Not always.

Conversely, and more importantly, very many legal activities and behaviors can be extremely unethical. For example, behaviors that are not necessarily unlawful but which are generally considered to be unethical to Western society would now typically include:

- dishonesty, withholding information, distortion of facts
- misleading or confusing communications or positioning or advertising
- manipulation of people's feelings
- deception, trickery, kidology, rule-bending, fooling people
- exploitation of weakness and vulnerability
- excessive profit
- greed
- anything liable to harm or endanger people
- breach of psychological contract (breaking trust, changing agreed or implied expectations-modern theory within **Transactional Analysis** offers a useful approach for contracting-agreeing expectations-in this sense)
- avoidance of blame or penalty or payment of compensation for wrong-doing
- inertia-based 'approvals' and 'agreements' (in which action proceeds unless objected to)
- failing to consult and notify people affected by change

- secrecy and lack of transparency and resistance to reasonable investigation
- coercion or inducement
- harming the environment or planet
- unnecessary waste or consumption
- invasion of privacy or anything causing privacy to be compromised
- recklessness or irresponsible use of authority, power, reputation
- nepotism (the appointment or preference of family members)
- favoritism or decision-making based on ulterior motives (e.g., secret affiliations, deals, memberships, etc.)
- alienation or marginalization of people or groups
- conflict of interests (having a foot in two or more competing camps)
- neglect of duty of care
- betrayal of trust
- breaking confidentiality
- causing suffering of animals
- 'bystanding'-failing to intervene or report wrong-doing within area of responsibility (this does not give licence to interfere anywhere and everywhere, which is itself unethical for various reasons)
- unfairness
- unkindness
- lack of compassion and humanity

ETHICAL DECISION MAKING

Individuals are the instruments who enact the ethical guidelines set before them. It may be possible to provide an environment that supports ethical decisions by accommodating factors that influence the individual. Early childhood ethical understanding appears to be influenced by the examples of parents, teachers, organization leaders, and spiritual leaders. Adult relationships influencing ethical decisions including organizational superiors, friends, spouses, government officials, parents and spiritual leaders also play a formative role. Consistent behavior, honesty, openness, and willingness to listen appear to be appreciably related to perception of another's ethicality and influence. Codes of conduct influence ethical decision making if those codes were observed in the daily actions of others.

Businesses seek to influence the ethical decision-making process by establishing codes of conduct and publishing ethical guidelines. Attempts are made to train employees how to make ethical decisions. Governments seek to establish legal guidelines for business that protect stakeholders by requiring business practices designed to provide mechanisms that prevent the abuse of power or misuse of funds.

Ethical behavior deals with the philosophy behind that morality which determines the individual's perception of right and wrong. The distinction was important because rather than attempting to define participant actions as morally right or wrong, an attempt has been made to understand how individuals make ethical decisions. Factors influencing decisions individuals judged to be ethical, whether morally correct or not, were explored.

It is hoped that with additional knowledge from this study, ethical courses of action may be defined objectively in order to build an ethical environment and culture for others. Knowledge of influencing factors may lead to introspective, proactive, purposeful, and personal evaluation as situations demanding ethical judgment arise in the future. Understanding how significant factors influence ethical decisions may be useful to those seeking to improve the ethicality of self and others. Knowing these factors may also help those in managerial or leadership roles guide others to strengthen ethical decision making.

Popular opinion alone is an unreliable measurement of what is ethical for **several reasons:**

- A poorly informed majority of people or anyone poorly informed is not able to make an informed decision about the ethics of a particular decision. The extent to which people are helped to understand longer-term consequences of a situation is also a limiting factor in the value of majority opinion.
- Democratic decision-making is vulnerable to whim and 'herding' instincts-especially if the national press and other mainstream media have anything to do with it.
- Leadership—as a function within civilizations features in the organization of human systems and societies because people generally accept that many sorts of complex and large scale decision-making are best made by full-time experts working in the areas concerned, rather than such decisions being left to the vagaries of popular inexpert view. This is not to say that people have no right to consultation or a vote on crucial issues (in fact generally people need more involvement in decisions which affect them)—it is more to illustrate that majority view, especially when colored with apathy or misinformation or prejudice for whatever reason, is not the only basis for deciding what's ethical or not.

Popular opinion is a significant factor in the consideration of what is ethical, but it is not the only factor, and the significance of popular opinion in determining ethical decisions will vary according to the situation.

So what is the basis of ethical decision-making?

My best suggestion is:

Objectivity and fairness are the basis of ethical decision-making.

In simple terms this means you must be able to see the other people's points of view. This might seem a simple statement of the bleeding obvious, and it might be, but it is not often practiced. True objectivity is quite difficult to achieve, especially for leaders under pressure. Similarly, fairness is difficult to define, let alone apply.

Detachment is a huge part of the process. Objectivity is impossible without personal detachment. Fairness cannot begin to be achieved without detachment, since it's about other people, not the leader, nor the leader's supporters and environment.

Being ethical is being fair. Being fair means understanding implications from other people's perspectives not your own. The more widely and well you appreciate other people's issues and implications, then the easier you will find it to be ethical.

Cybernetics is a really useful way to look at objectivity. Objectivity entails understanding how systems work and inter-relate. But systems here mean merely the general sense of people and the way life is organized. Systems do not refer to complex mathematics or scientific formulae. Again, it requires you to step back - to detach yourself, resist personal bias and emotion step back, be objective, adult, mature-fair.

- Objectivity is a wonderfully potent and extremely flexible ability to pursue. Especially if you can combine it with the ability to facilitate rather than influence.
- Objectivity is flexible because it can be approached and achieved in so many different ways - intuitively, logically, systematically, creatively- anyone can do it. In the same way that the truth—purity, probity is available to anyone who cares to look for it.

Ethical considerations comprise several variables in one combination or another, if you are striving for real objectivity:

- The society and/or situation.
- Short-term and long-term effects.
- 'The greater good'—the flip-side of the issue; i.e., what are the other options and their consequences—the costs or implications of the choices?
- Cultural issues.
- Issues of personal conscience of those affected—beware of relying on your own ideas of 'faith' or 'belief' or 'what is right', because this will not be the view held by many people affected by your decision. You are not a god, nor an agent of a god.

- Religious influence and personal beliefs of those affected, rather than the decision-makers, really, I cannot emphasise this enough. Religion is a subjective belief system. Your own religion is therefore not a basis for objective ethical decision-making.
- Informed enlightened educated and truly objective views.
- Majority views.
- Significant minority views.
- Unrepresented very small minority views.

SOME PRINCIPLES OF ETHICAL DECISION MAKING

- Step back from every decision before you make it and look at it objectively. Use the above list of examples of unethicals as a check-list to see if you might possibly be falling into one of these traps. It's easily done: to get swept along by excitement and urgency; or by apparently demanding expectations, whether self-imposed or otherwise. Aim for objectivity and fairness—not for personal power, 'winning', strategic plotting, high drama, etc.
- Strive for **fairness** rather than polarised 'winner takes all' outcomes. Try to facilitate solutions rather than actually deciding and imposing decisions, unless all parties are happy for you to do so.
- Learn from history and previous situations. Reviewing how previous situations were handled reduces the risks of making daft mistakes: not many things are fundamentally new in this world, despite how unique you believe your situation to be. Also history is a superb store of already invented wheels, which can often save you the time and agonies of trying unsuccessfully to invent a new one.
- Get the facts from all possible perspectives. Often a challenging issue offers three main options: (a) your instinctive or personal view; (b) a main alternative option; and (c) the commonly under-estimated ever-available third main option of **doing nothing**. Doing nothing in times of real emergency can be disastrous, but for a very large number of situations doing nothing is the only truly wise way. Doing nothing is not weakness or procrastination if it done in the right way for the right reasons.
- Understand the long-term consequences. Model or brainstorm the 'what if' scenarios. Again look at previous examples and history.
- Check the law. In whatever territories are affected by the decision. But do not base your decision wholly on the law.

- Consult widely—especially with critical people, and especially **beyond** your close circle of (normally) biased and friendly advisors, colleagues, friends, etc. You have not properly consulted if you merely seek and obtain confirmation from a tame advisor. After the event such 'consultation' can very easily be interpreted as a conspiracy, in which your 'advisor' is deemed not to have been an advisor but a co-conspirator. Consult especially the people affected by the situation and potential actions, and if using a survey of any sort then ensure the positioning and questions used are balanced and objective, because to be otherwise is unethical in itself. You should even consult about how to frame the survey and wording of the questions if the issue is anything but a minor one.
- Consider cause and effect in the deepest possible sense. Life and all that surrounds it is one huge interconnected system. If you are making big decisions or even apparently little fleeting decisions within a potentially big and sensitive environment, these decisions will affect many people and aspects of life, now and especially into the future.
- Resist the delusion and arrogance that power and authority tends to foster. This is especially important to guard against if you live and work in a protected, insulated or isolated situation, as many large scale leaders and decision-makers tend to do. Being a leader for a long time, or for any duration in a culture of arrogance, privilege and advantage, provides great nourishment for personal delusion. Many unethical decisions are borne of arrogance and delusion. Guard against becoming so dangerous.
- Beware of justifying decisions according to religious faith. There is nothing wrong with having a religious faith, but there are various risks in leaning too heavily on a god or faith when making serious decisions.
- Aim for solutions and harmony, objectivity and detachment. Facilitate rather than influence. Help, don't sell. Diffuse situations—find common ground—don't polarise or inflame. Whenever you see a big swell of expectation looming (among your immediate team, not those affected by your decision) which is borderline ethical/unethical, remember the ever-available third option to decide clearly and firmly to do nothing, in the right way for the right reason. The best ethical decisions are usually decided by people who are most affected by them, rather than by leaders who don't trust the people.

SUMMARY

- **International Business** is all commercial transactions–private and governmental between two or more countries. Private companies undertake such transactions for profit; governments may or may not do the same in their transactions.
- When a company operates internationally, it adds foreign conditions to its domestic ones making its external environment more diverse.
- When operating internationally, a company should consider its **mission, objectives and strategy.**

The objectives that may influence companies to engage in international business. They are:

1. To expand sales
2. To acquire resources
3. To diversify sources of sales and supplies
4. To minimize competitive risk
5. Profit advantage
6. Growth opportunities
7. Government policies and regulations

Merchandise exports are tangible products–goods–sent out a country; **merchandise imports** are goods brought in. The company or individual receiving payment is making a **service export**. The company or individual paying is making a **service import**.

Turnkey operations–construction, performed under contract, of facilities that are transferred to the owner when they are ready to begin operating. **Management contracts**–arrangements in which one company provides personnel to perform general or specialized management functions for another company.

- When companies allow others to use their assets, such as trademarks, patents, copyrights, or expertise under contracts, also known as **licensing agreements**, they receive earnings called **royalties**. **Franchising** is a mode of business in which one party (the franchisor) allows another party (the franchisee) the use of a trademark that is an essential asset for the franchisee's business.
- Foreign investment means ownership of foreign property in exchange for financial return, such as interest and dividends. Foreign investment takes two forms: Direct and Portfolio. When two or more companies share ownership of an FDI, the operation is a **joint venture.** When a government joins a company in an FDI, the operation is called a **mixed venture.** A **portfolio investment** is a non-controlling interest in a company or ownership of a loan to another party.

The various patterns of expansion axis are:

1. Axis A – Impetus for International Business

2. Axis B – Internal versus external handling for foreign operations
3. Axis C – Mode of operations
4. Axis D – Number of foreign countries in which a firm does business
5. Axis E – Degree of similarity between foreign and domestic countries.

- Any company operating internationally must decide between the advantages of globally standardized practices and those practices that respond to different national preferences. These advantages may vary by product, function, and country of operation.
- Companies at least those that are not government owned, may compete by seeking maximum production efficiency on a global scale. To accomplish this goal, the company's production would use the best inputs for the price, even if the production location moved abroad. Countries sometimes cede sovereignty (freedom from external control) reluctantly because of coercion and international conflicts.
- A **tariff**, or **duty**, which is the most common type of trade control, is a tax government's levy on a good shipped internationally. If collected by the exported country, it is known as an **export tariff**; if collected by a country through which the goods have passed, it is a **transit tariff**; if collected by the importing country, it is an **import tariff**.
- A government may assess a tariff on a per unit basis, in which case it is a **specific duty**. It may assess a tariff as a percentage of the value of the item, in which case it is an **ad-valorem duty**. If it assesses both a specific duty and an ad valorem duty on the same product, the combination is a **compound duty.**
- The various non-tariff barriers are: Subsidies, Aids and Loans, Customs Valuation.
- The most common type of import or export restriction based on quantity is the quota. A specific type of quota that prohibits all trade is an **embargo.** Another form of quantitative trade control is "buy local" legislation. If government purchases are a large part of total expenditure within a country, they comprise an important part of the market.
- There are basically three barriers to international business that are used by countries they are tarrif barrier, non-tarrif barrier, voluntary constraint.
- **Counter trade** is any one of several different arrangements by which goods and services are traded for each other. **Barter**, the oldest form of counter trade, is a transaction in which goods of equal value without any flow of cash trade goods. **Buybacks** are products the exporter receives as payment that are related to or originate from the original export. **Offset trade** is when an exporter sells products for cash and then helps the importer find opportunities to earn hard currency. **Counterpurchase** agreement the seller receives the full payment in cash but agrees to spend an equivalent amount of money in that country within a specified period.
- Examination of the recent development in the international trade and the far-reaching expansion of global entities lead to the inevitable conclusion that

ethical issues and concerns facing business entities are no longer related to the limited frameworks of national or even regional arenas. These issues have assumed global dimensions and as such require global solutions.

- To that end, it is postulated that probably an international organization is the best vehicle through which a code of ethics covering all aspects of business can be developed. Once, on the basis of such a code, an international treaty is drafted, signed and ratified; it may be prudent to leave the implementation of the treaty to the member nations subject to regular audit by an independent international body. WTO may eventually take on this role.
- Meanwhile, global organizations need to develop and enforce their own codes of ethics specifically directed at the issues related to a multicultural, multinational business environment.
- The market in India will witness more and more alliances, joint ventures, and networks, thanks to the **LPG** syndrome—an acronym popular with the financial analysts to describe the process of **liberalization, privatization, and globalization**—which has been predominant since 1991.
- Liberalization allow the private sector to run those activities which were restricted earlier only to public sector.

Chapter 2

International Environments

CULTURAL ENVIRONMENTS

The major problems of cultural collision in international business are when:

- A company implements practices that work less well than intended, and
- A company's employees encounter distress because of an inability to accept or adjust to foreign behaviors.

Business employs, sells to, buys from, is regulated by, and is owned by people. Because international business includes people from different cultures, every business function—managing a workforce, marketing output, and purchasing supplies, dealing with regulators, securing funds– is subject to potential cultural problems. An international company must be sensitive to these cultural differences to predict and control its relationships and operations. When doing business abroad, a company first should determine what business practices in a foreign country differ from those it's used to. Management then must decide what, if any, adjustments are necessary to operate efficiently in the foreign country.

CULTURAL AWARENESS

Building cultural awareness is not an easy task, and no foolproof method exists for doing so. Culture consists of specific learned norms based on attitudes, values and beliefs all of which exist in every nation. Visitors remark on cultural differences, experts write about them, and international businesspeople find that they affect operations. Yet, controversy surrounds these differences because people disagree on what they are, whether they are widespread or exceptional differences, and whether the differences are deep-seated or superficial.

Some people seem to have an innate ability to do and say the right thing at the right time and others offend unintentionally or misrepresent what they want to convey. Nevertheless, there is general agreement that businesspeople can improve their awareness and sensitivity and that training about other cultures will enhance the likelihood of succeeding in those cultures.

There are so many cultural variations that businesspeople cannot expect to memorize all of them for every country. Wide variations exist even in addressing people. Making a mistake may be construed by foreign businesspeople as ignorance or rudeness, which may jeopardize a business arrangement. Fortunately, there are guidebooks for particular geographical areas, based on the experiences of many successful international managers. A manager also may consult with knowledgeable people at home and abroad, from governmental offices or in the private sector.

When a company engages in few foreign functions – for example, just exporting its home country production – it must be aware of only those cultural factors that may influence its marketing program. Consider advertising, which may be affected by the target market's perception of different words and images. A company undertaking a purely resource-seeking foreign activity by manufacturing abroad can ignore the effects of cultural variables on advertising but must consider factors that may influence management of a foreign workforce, such as management styles and operational practices most likely to motivate its workforce.

For multifunctional activities, such as producing and selling a product in a foreign country, a company must be concerned with a wide array of cultural relationships. The more countries in which a company does business, the more cultural nuances it must consider.

A company may handle foreign operations on its own or contract with another company to handle them. The risk of making operating mistakes because of cultural misunderstandings goes down if it turns foreign operations over to another company at home or abroad that is experienced in the foreign country. If the operations are contracted to a company abroad, then each company needs some cultural awareness to anticipate and understand the other company's reactions.

BEHAVIORAL PRACTICES AFFECTING BUSINESS

Attitudes and values affect business behavior, from what products to sell to how to organize, finance, manage and control operations. Researchers define cultural variables differently, attaching different names to slightly different and sometimes overlapping attitudes and values. Similarly, businesspeople define business functions differently. The following discussion merely highlights those that international managers and academic researchers have most noted to influence business practices differently from one country to another.

Social Stratification Systems

Every culture values some people more highly than others and this dictates a persons' class or status within that culture. In business, this might mean valuing members of managerial groups more highly than members of production groups. A persons' making is partly determined by individual factors and partly by the persons' affiliation or membership in given groups.

Affiliations determined by birth – known as **ascribed group memberships** – include those based on gender, family, age, caste and ethnic, racial or national origin. Affiliations not determined by birth are called **acquired group memberships** and include those based on religion, political affiliation, and professional and other associations. Social stratification affects such business functions as marketing. For example, companies choose to use people in their advertisements that their target market admires or associates.

Gender-Based Groups: There are strong country-specific differences in attitudes toward males and females. In China and India there is an extreme degree of male preference. Because of their governmental and economic restrictions on family size and the desire to have a son to carry on the family name, the practices of aborting female fetuses and killing female babies are widespread despite governmental opposition. However, many Chinese and Indian females have been successful in business and government positions.

In Saudi Arabia, schools and most of social life separate the sexes, and women cannot drive cars. Few women work outside the home, and most of their work in professions entails little or no contact with males, such as teaching or providing medical treatment to other women. When women do work in integrated organizations, Saudis commonly place partitions between them and male employees.

Even among countries in which women constitute a large portion of the working population, vast differences exist in the types of jobs regarded as "male" or "female". For example, in the United States, women fill 40 per cent of administrative and managerial positions while in Japan, that figure is less than 10 per cent.

Barriers to employment based on gender are easing substantially in many parts of the world. Statistical and attitudinal studies from even a few years ago may be considered unreliable. One change has been the growing numbers of women and men in the United States employed in occupations previously dominated by the other gender. Even in Saudi Arabia women now work at hotel reception desks.

Age-Based Groups: Many cultures assume that age and wisdom are correlated. These cultures usually have a seniority-based system of advancement. But in the United States, retirement at age 60 or 65 was mandatory in most companies until the 1980s, revealing that youth has the professional advantage. For example, US television scriptwriters complain of an inability of finding jobs after age 30. Clearly, companies need to examine reference groups when considering whom they may hire and how best to promote their products.

Family-Based Groups: In some societies, the family is the most important group membership. An individual's acceptance in society largely depends on the family's social status or respectability rather than on the individual's achievement. Because family ties are so strong, there also may be a compulsion to cooperate closely within the family unit while distrusting relationships with others. But the difficulty of sustaining family-run companies retards these countries' economic development because large-scale operations are often necessary for many products.

Occupation: In every society, people perceive certain occupations as having greater economic and social prestige than others. This perception usually determines the numbers and qualifications of people who will seek employment in a given occupation. The importance of business as a profession also is predictive of how difficult it may be for an international company to hire qualified managers. If say, jobs in business are not as desirable as jobs in government, a company may have to spend more to attract and train local managers, or it may have to rely more on managers transferred from abroad.

Jobs with low prestige usually go to people whose skills are in low demand. In the United States occupations such as baby-sitting, delivering newspapers, and carrying groceries traditionally go to teenagers, who leave these jobs as they age and gain additional training. In most poor countries, these are not transient occupations but are filled by adults who have very little opportunity to move on to more rewarding positions.

Motivation

Employees who are motivated to work long and hard are normally more productive than those who are not. On an aggregate basis, this influences economic development positively. International companies are concerned about economic development because markets for their products grow as economies grow. They are also interested in motivation because higher productivity normally reduces production costs.

Materialism and Leisure

Some societies take less leisure time than others, which means they work longer hours, take fewer days for holidays and vacation, and spend less time and money on leisure. In the most economically developed countries, most people work to satisfy materialistic needs. Good international managers know that the motives for working vary in different countries. Employees' work attitudes may change as they achieve economic gains. Leisure time is a sign of upward mobility. In parts of some poor countries, such as in rural India, living a simple life with minimum material achievements is a desirable end in itself. When there are productivity gains, people are prone to work less rather than earn and buy more.

Need Hierarchy

The hierarchy of needs is a well-known motivation theory. According to this theory, people try to fulfill lower-order needs sufficiently before moving on to higher ones. People will work to satisfy a need, but once it is fulfilled, it is no longer a motivator. Because lower-order needs are more important than higher-order ones, they must be nearly fulfilled before any higher-order need becomes an effective motivator.

The hierarchy of needs theory is helpful for differentiating the reward preferences of employees in different countries. In very poor countries, a company can motivate workers simply by providing enough compensation for food and shelter. Elsewhere, other needs will motivate workers. Researchers have noted that people from different countries attach different degree of importance to needs and even rank some of the higher order needs differently.

RELATIONSHIP PREFERENCES

We have discussed two categories of behavioral practices affecting business – social stratification systems and motivation. Within social stratification systems, not everyone within a reference group is necessarily an equal. Further, they may be strong or weak pressures for conformity within one's group. In both cases, there are national differences in norms that influence management styles and marketing behavior. The following section discusses the values underlying these differences.

Power Distance: Employee preferences in how to interact with their bosses, subordinates and peers vary substantially internationally. There is considerable anecdotal evidence that they perform better when their interactions fit their preferences. Therefore, companies may need to align their management styles to those preferences.

Power distance is a term describing the relationship between superiors and subordinates-usually wanting and having an autocratic or paternalistic management style in their organizations. Interestingly, those employees preferring an autocratic style of superior-subordinate relationship are also willing to accept decision making by a majority of subordinates. Clearly it may be easier for organizations to initiate certain types of worker-participation methods in some countries than in others.

Individualism versus Collectivism: The degree of individualism and collectivism also influences how employees interact with their colleagues. Japan has a much more collectivist culture than the United States does, especially concerning the work group, and this causes contrasts at work. Levi's introduced team-based production for US plants because its management had observed high productivity from that system in Asian plants. US employees – especially the faster, more skilled ones – detected the system, productivity decreased, and Levi's abandoned the team-based production system.

Although China and Mexico are also characterized as collectivist cultures, they differ from Japan in that the collectivism is based on kinship that does not carry over to the workplace. The concept of China and Mexico includes not only a nuclear family (a husband, wife and minor children) and also a vertically extended family (several generations) and perhaps a horizontally extended one (aunts, uncles and cousins). This difference affects business in several ways.

First, material rewards from an individual's work may be less motivating because these rewards are divided among more people. Second, geographical mobility is reduced because relocation means other members of a family also have to find new jobs. Third, purchasing decisions may be more complicated because of the interrelated roles of family members. Fourth, security and social needs may be met more extensively at home than in the workplace. Where collectivism is high, companies find their best marketing successes when emphasizing advertising themes that express group values.

STRATEGIES FOR DEALING WITH CULTURAL DIFFERENCES

After a company identifies cultural differences in the foreign country where it intends to do business, must it alter its customary practices to succeed there? How can it avoid misrepresenting its intents? Can individuals overcome adjustment problems when working abroad? What strategies can companies follow to get host cultures to accept the innovations they would like to introduce?

Some countries are relatively similar to one another, usually because they share many attributes that help mold their cultures, such as language, religion, geographical location, ethnicity and level of economic development. A company should expect fewer differences when moving within a cluster than when moving from one cluster to another. However, there still may be significant differences within similar countries that could affect business dealings. Managers may expect that seemingly similar countries are more alike than they really are; a company may be lulled into a complacency that overlooks important subtleties.

Cost Benefit Change: Some adjustments to foreign cultures are costly to undertake, while others are inexpensive. Some adjustments result in greatly improved performance such as higher productivity or sales. Other changes may improve performance only marginally. A company must consider the expected cost-benefit relationship of any adjustments it makes abroad.

Resistance to too much Change: When German company Gruner + Jahr bought the US magazine McCall's it quickly began to overhaul the format. Gruner + Jahr changed its editor, eliminated long stories and advice columns, increased coverage on celebrities made the layouts more dense, started using sidebars and boxes in articles and refused discounts for big advertisers. But employee turnover began to increase because of low morale. Gruner + Jahr made fewer demands at one time and phased in other policies more slowly.

Participation: One way to avoid problems that could result from change is to discuss a proposed change with stakeholders in advance. By doing so, the company may learn how strong resistance to the change will be, stimulate in the stakeholders recognition of the need for improvement, and ease their fears of adverse consequences resulting from the change. Managers sometimes think that stakeholder participation is unique to countries where people have educational backgrounds that enable them to make substantial contributions.

Reward Sharing: Sometimes a proposed change may have no foreseeable benefit for the people who must support it. A company's solution may be to develop a bonus system for productivity and quality based on using the new approach.

Timing: Many good business changes fall flat because they are ill timed. However, less employee fear and resistance will occur if management introduces the laborsaving method when there is a labor shortage. A culture's attitudes and needs may change slowly or rapidly, so keeping abreast of these changes helps in determining timing. In some cases, poor company profits have stimulated a rapid change from "a family running the business" to a "family only on the board". But in other cases, family members continue to exert substantial influence on company's practices even after they have no official responsibilities.

Learning Abroad: As companies operate abroad, they affect the host society and are affected by it. The company may learn things that will be useful in its home country or in other operations. This last point is the essence for undertaking transnational practices in which the company seeks to capitalize on diverse capabilities among the countries in which it operates. Basically, companies believe natural intelligence exists in about the same proportion throughout the world and that innovations and good ideas may come from anywhere.

POLITICAL AND LEGAL ENVIRONMENTS

INTRODUCTION

Multinational Enterprises (MNEs) must operate in countries with different political and legal conditions. For the company to succeed, its management must carefully analyze whether its corporate policies will fit a desirable political and legal environment. This chapter discusses the political and legal systems that managers encounter and the factors they need to consider when operating in different countries.

THE POLITICAL ENVIRONMENT

A political system integrates the parts of a society into a viable, functioning unit. A major challenge of the political system is to bring together people of different ethnic or other backgrounds and allow them to work together to govern themselves. A country's political system influences how business is conducted domestically and internationally.

Political policies are established by aggregating, or bringing together, different points of view that are articulated by key constraints, such as *politicians, individuals, businesses or other special-interest groups.* In the case of Hong Kong, business has always been the key constituency in establishing government policies. However, that is beginning to change; other interest groups are emerging to balance off the needs of business. Given the interests of different constituencies, governments identify policy alternatives and then decide on a specific policy to pursue.

The policy is then implemented, and it may be altered depending on the reactions from political parties, government bureaucracies, legislatures, courts and other constituencies. Normally, the chief executive officer (CEO) of an MNE watches policies as they develop and makes sure that the company voices its concerns in the interest articulation stage.

BASIC POLITICAL IDEOLOGIES

A **political ideology** is the body of constructs (complex ideas), theories, and aims that constitute a sociopolitical program. The liberal ideology of the Democratic Party and the conservative ideology of the Republican Party in the United States are examples of political ideology. Most modern societies are **pluralistic** politically, meaning different ideologies coexist because there is no one ideology that everyone accepts. Pluralism arises because groups within countries often differ significantly from each other in language ethnic background or religion. These and other cultural dimensions strongly influence the political system.

The ultimate test of any political system is its ability to hold a society together despite pressures from different ideologies tending to split it apart. The more different and strongly held the ideas are, the more difficult it is for a government to formulate policies that everyone can accept. The resulting political instability has made it difficult for them to attract foreign investment and for managers to feel comfortable operating in and committing resources to them.

A POLITICAL SPECTRUM

MNEs may be able to operate equally effectively in democratic and totalitarian regimes, but they prefer democracies because democracies usually have economic freedom and legal rules that safeguard individual rights. Let's now learn about the world's major political ideologies.

DEMOCRACY

Winston Churchill once called democracy the worst form of government – except for all the others. The ideology of pure democracy derives from the ancient Greeks, who believed all citizens should be equal politically and legally, should enjoy widespread freedoms, and should actively participate in the political process. In reality, society's complexity increases as the population increases, and so full participation by citizens in the decision-making process has become impossible in these modern times.

Contemporary democratic political systems share the following:

- Freedom of opinion, expression, press and freedom to organize
- Elections in which voters decide who is to represent them
- Limited terms for elected officials
- An independent and fair court system with high regard for individual rights and property.
- A nonpolitical bureaucracy and defense infrastructure
- Accessibility to the decision-making process.

Political Rights and Civil Liberties: A key element of democracy is freedom in the areas of political rights and civil liberties. The major indicators for political rights are:

- The degree to which fair and competitive elections occur.
- The ability of voters to endow their elected representatives with real power.
- The ability of people to organize into political parties or other competitive political groupings of their choice.
- The existence of safeguards on the rights of minorities.

The major indicators for civil liberties are:

- The existence of freedom of the press.
- Equality under the law for all individuals.
- The extent of personal social freedoms.
- The degree of freedom from extreme governmental indifference or corruption.

Stability in Democracies: In surveys on democracy in the United States, it is clear that confidence in politicians and government have continued to decline over the past quarter-century. People are concerned about whether or not politicians are trustworthy and care about voters. The loss of faith in political institutions and the feeling that professional pressure groups and lobbying organizations are increasingly more influential than individuals are causes of concern in democracy.

TOTALITARIANISM

Totalitarianism takes several form, including fascism, authoritarianism, and communism.

Mussolini (Italy's dictator, 1924–1943) defined fascism as follows: "The Fascist conception of the state of all-embracing; outside of it no human or spiritual value may exist, much less have any value. Thus understood Fascism is totalitarian and the Fascist State, as a synthesis and a unit, which includes all values, interprets, develops and lends additional power to the whole life of a people.

Communism is a form of secular totalitarianism in which political and economic systems are virtually inseparable. Communists believe in the equal distribution of wealth, which entails total government ownership and control of resources. As communism moves toward democracy, the link between economics and politics in communist countries has been weakened, making countries such as Estonia, Latvia with strong centralized authoritarian control over the political process.

POLITICAL RISK

As managers evaluate countries as a potential place to do business and as they struggle to succeed once they have committed resources, they need to be aware of **political risk.** Political risk is when international companies fear that the political climate in a foreign country will change in such a way that their operating position will deteriorate.

Types and Causes of Political Risk

Political actions that may affect company operations adversely are governmental takeovers of property, either with or without compensation; operational restrictions that impede the company's ability to take certain actions; and agitation that disrupts sales or causes damage to property or personnel. Political risk may occur for the following reasons:

- Opinion of political leadership
- Civil disorder
- External relations

Micro and Macro Political Risks: If political actions are aimed only at specific foreign investments, they are known as **micro political risks**. Companies most likely to be affected by micro political risk are those that may have a considerable and visible impact on a given country because of their size, monopoly position, importance to their home country's national defense, and dependence of other industries on them.

If political actions affect a broad spectrum of foreign investors, they are **macro political risks**. For example, after the communist revolution in Cuba, the takeover of property was aimed at all foreign investors regardless of industry, nationality or whether or not the investors past behavior had been socially responsive. Today most countries realize that they need the stability of foreign direct investment in order to grow.

FORMULATING AND IMPLEMENTING POLITICAL STRATEGIES

Formulating political strategies often is more complicated for managers than formulating competitive marketplace strategies. When dealing in the political arena, manager's needs to know how decisions are made that could influence their ability to operate. Then they need to know what the rules are for trying to influence political decisions.

There are certain steps that a company must follow if it wants to establish an appropriate political strategy in its countries of operation:

1. Identify the issue.
2. Define the political aspect of the issue.
3. Assess the potential political action of other companies and special-interest groups.
4. Identify important institutions and key individuals-legislatures, regulatory agencies, courts, important personalities.
5. Formulate strategies.
6. Determine the impact of implementation
7. Select the most appropriate strategy and implement.

Implementing a strategy means marshaling whatever resources are necessary to accomplish the company's political objectives. In a representative democracy, lobbyists represent constituencies and perform the important role of aggregating ideas and communicating them to decision makers. A company also can attempt to influence governmental action from consumers on up by using a grassroots campaign or by building coalitions of different groups that share the company's interests.

Part of the problem with establishing a global political strategy is that democracies deal with companies differently than do totalitarian regimes. In general, foreign companies can influence democracies through lobbying.

However, companies sometimes abuse their power by engaging in bribery and other illicit activities. Sometimes, a totalitarian regime might seem more stable because it doesn't have to deal with the pressure of democracy.

THE LEGAL ENVIRONMENT

Managers must be aware of the legal systems in the countries in which they operate, the nature of legal profession, both domestic and international and the legal relationships that exist between countries. Legal systems differ in terms of the nature of the system – common law, civil law and theocratic law – and the degree of independence of the judiciary from the political process. Also, some of the totalitarian countries that are going through a transition to democracy and to a free-market economy don't have a legal system in place that deals with business transactions in global market context.

Kinds of Legal Systems

Legal systems usually fall into one of three categories: common law, civil law and theocratic law.

Common Law: Common Law is based on tradition, precedent and custom and usage. The courts fulfill an important role in interpreting the law according to those characteristics. Because the United Kingdom originated common law in the modern setting, its former and current colonies, such as Hong Kong, also have common law systems.

Civil Law: The civil law system, also called a codified legal system, is based on a detailed set of laws that make up a code. Rules for conducting business transactions are a part of the code. Over 70 countries, including Germany, France and Japan operate on a civil law basis.

The two legal systems differ primarily in that common law is based on the courts' interpretations of events, while civil law is based on how the law is applied to the facts. In a common law country, contracts tend to be detailed, with all contingencies spelled out. In a civil law country, contracts tend to be shorter and less specific because many of the issues that a common law contract should cover already are included in the civil code.

Theocratic Law: The third type of legal system is the **theocratic law system**, which is based on religious precepts. The best example of this system is Islamic law, which is found in Muslim countries, Islamic law is based on the following sources:

- The Koran, the sacred text.
- The Sunnah, or decision and sayings of the Prophet Muhammad.
- The writings of Islamic scholars, who derive rules by analogy from the principles established in the Koran and the Sunnah.
- The consensus of Muslim countries legal communities.

An example of how Islamic law influences international business can be found in banking. According to Islamic law, banks cannot charge interest or benefit from interest. Instead, banks have to structure fees into their loans to allow them to make a profit. For example, assume that a company needs to borrow money to purchase merchandise. It can approach a bank, which would buy the goods and sell them to the company, which will pay the bank at a future date at an agreed upon markup. Also, banks can structure loans so that they share in the profits of a venture rather than receive interest.

LEGAL ISSUES IN INTERNATIONAL BUSINESS

National laws affect business within the country or business among countries. Some national laws on local business activity influence both domestic and foreign companies, especially in the areas of health and safety standards, employment practices, antitrust prohibitions, contractual relationships, environmental practices and patents and trademarks.

Laws also exist that govern cross border activities, such as the investment of capital, the payment of dividends to foreign investors, and customs duties on imports. International laws, such as treaties governing the cross border transfer of hazardous waste, can also determine how a firm operates in transporting shipments across borders.

THE ECONOMIC ENVIRONMENT

INTRODUCTION

Understanding the economic environments of foreign countries and markets can help managers predict how trends and events in those environments might effect their company's future performance there.

There are economic forces, which play an important part of the physical and societal factors that help comprise the external influences on company strategy. Economic forces include such issues as the general economic framework of a country, economic stability, the existence and influence of capital markets, factor endowments, the size of the market, and the availability of a good economic infrastructure such as transportation and communication. Managers need to understand the nature of the world's economies if they are going to make wise investment decisions.

COUNTRIES CLASSIFIED BY INCOME

We can classify countries along any of the dimensions mentioned above; the key dimension we use to distinguish one country from another is the size of demand, or **Gross National Product (GNP).** In particular, we classify countries according to per capital GNP, or the size of GNP of a nation divided by its total population. Those with low per capita GNP and low populations are least desirable, and the other countries fit somewhere in between.

What is GNP? It is the broadest measure of economic activity. It is the market value of final goods and services newly produced by domestically owned factors of production. An alternative to GNP is **Gross Domestic Product** (GDP), the value of production that takes place within a nation's borders, without regard to whether the production is done by domestic or foreign factors of production.

The **World Bank** a multilateral lending agency uses per capita GNP as a basis for its lending policies. The World Bank Group was founded in 1944 by the United Nations. It consists of five closely associated institutions: the International Bank for Reconstruction and Development (IBRD), the International Development Association (IDA), the International Finance Corporation (IFC), the Multilateral Guarantee Agency (MIGA) and the International Center for Settlement of Investment Disputes (ICSID). It uses per capita income to identify those countries that need help the most. In particular, its programs include:

- Investing in people, particularly through basic health and education
- Protecting the environment
- Supporting and encouraging private business development
- Strengthening the ability of the governments to deliver quality services, efficiently and transparently.
- Focusing on social development, inclusion, governance, and institution building as key elements of poverty reduction.

COUNTRIES CLASSIFIED BY REGION

Much of the World Bank data is provided by geographic region, and this will be especially important as we discuss economic growth in a future section of this chapter. However, the following groups listed include only the developing countries in their region. It is obvious from the map that Japan, Australia and New Zealand are included in East Asia and Pacific geographically although they are also high-income countries and therefore colored differently on the map. The major regions are:

- East Asia and Pacific
- Europe (East and Central Europe) and Central Asia
- Middle East and North Africa
- South Asia
- Sub-Saharan Africa

These designations are important to MNEs, which tend to organize their operations along geographic lines. For example, IBM organizes its firm along the following lines: Africa, Americas, Asia Pacific, Europe and Middle East.

Managers can use the data compiled and disclosed by the World Bank to spot trends in key markets. Investors can use the data to analyze where potential growth and risks exist in the regions where their companies operate.

COUNTRIES CLASSIFIED BY ECONOMIC SYSTEM

A final way of classifying countries is by their economic system. Every government struggles with the right mix of *ownership* and *control* of the economy. Ownership means those who own the resources engaged in economic activity – the public sector, the private sector or both. Public sector ownership of economic activity refers to the existence of state-owned enterprises.

Market Economy: A market economy is one in which resources are primarily owned and controlled by the private sector, not the public sector. The key factors that make the market economy work are consumer sovereignty–that is, the right of consumers to decide what to buy–and freedom for companies to operate in the market. Prices are determined by supply and demand. In a market economy, for example, the prices of gasoline rise during holidays because of the excess of demand over supply.

Command Economy: In a command economy, also known as **centrally planned economy**, all dimensions of economic activity, including pricing and production decisions are determined by a central government plan. The government owns and controls all resources. The government sets goals for every business enterprise in the country–how much they produce and for whom. In this type of economy, the government considers itself a better judge of resource allocation than its businesses or citizens.

Mixed Economy: In actuality, no economy is purely market or completely commands. Most market economies have some degree of government ownership and control, while most command economies are moving toward a market economy and away from command concepts. Another example of a mixed economy is market socialism, where the state owns significant resources, but allocation of the resources comes from the market price mechanism. Although the market determines prices, a lot of economic activity is controlled by government fiscal policies.

TRANSITION TO A MARKET ECONOMY

So far we've been learning about economic systems with the assumption that countries are in one economic system or another and that they were not in transition from one classification to another. Many countries are undergoing transition from command economies to market economies because of the failure of central planning to generate economic growth. The process of transition has made the world of international business very interesting indeed.

What does transition mean? In general, transition implies

- Liberalizing economic activity, prices, and market operations, along with reallocating resources to their most efficient use.
- Developing indirect, market-oriented instruments for macroeconomic stabilization.
- Achieving effective enterprise management and economic efficiency, usually through privatization.
- Imposing hard budget constraints, which provides incentives to improve efficiency.
- Establishing an institutional and legal framework to secure property rights, the rule of law, and transparent market-entry regulations.

A study of the countries in transition have shown that a few key things must be done for successful transition:

- Sustained macroeconomic stabilization (inflation control) is essential.
- No, pain, no gain. Delayed reforms may defer the pain, but they defer sustained recovery and increase the risk that growth will be reversed.
- There is no royal road to reform. There is no one key to growth; countries have to implement all the different components of reform.
- Developing an appropriate legal structure is indispensable.

SUMMARY

- Culture includes norms of behavior based on learned attitudes, values, and beliefs. Businesspeople agree that there are cross-country differences but disagree as to what they are.
- International companies must evaluate their business practices to ensure they take into account national norms in behavioral characteristics.
- A given country may encompass very distinct societies. People also may have more in common with similar groups in foreign countries than with groups in their own country.
- Companies can build awareness about other cultures. The amount of effort needed to do this depends on the similarity between countries and the type of business operation undertaken.
- People fall into social stratification systems according to their ascribed and acquired group memberships. These memberships determine a person's degree of access to economic resources, prestige, social relations, and power. An individual's affiliations may determine his or her qualifications and availability for given jobs.
- The political process involves inputs from various interest groups, articulation of issues that affect policy formulation, aggregation of those issues into key alternatives, development of policies, and implementation and adjudication of the policies.

(Contd...)

- Most complex societies are pluralistic, which means they encompass a variety of ideologies.
- The ultimate test of any political system is its ability to hold a society together despite pressures from different ideologies.
- Political risk occurs because of changing opinions of political leadership, civil disorder, or external relations between the host country and foreign investor's home country.
- Micro political risks occur when actions are taken against specific foreign investments; macro political risks occur when actions are taken against a broad spectrum of foreign investors.
- Managers of MNEs must learn to cope with varying degrees of governmental intervention in economic decisions, depending on the countries in which a company is doing business.
- In formulating political strategies, managers must consider the possible political actions that could affect the company, the different constituencies that might influence those political actions, the political strategies that would be in the best interests of the company, and the costs of implementing those strategies.
- Common law systems are based on tradition, precedent and custom and usage. Civil law systems are based on a detailed set of laws organized into a code. Theocratic legal systems are based on religious precepts, as exemplified by Islamic law.
- Understanding the economic environments of foreign companies and markets can help managers predict how trends and events in those environments might effect their company's future performance there.
- Gross national product is a broad measure of national income that is the market value of final goods and services produced by domestically owned factors of production. Per capita GNP is used to rank countries in terms of their individual wealth.
- The transition to a market economy is where former command economies liberalize their economic policies and move from ownership and control of the economy by government to reliance on market forces to control economic activity.
- The process of transition differs from country to country-no one formula applies to all. Countries differ greatly in their commitment and progress to transformation to a market economy.
- In addition to general economic issues, countries in transition need to deal with environmental damage and the development of human capital.

Chapter 3

Regional Economic Integration (Trade Blocks)

INTRODUCTION

Regional trading groups are an important influence on MNEs' strategies. They can define the size of the regional market and the rules under which companies must operate. Companies in the initial stages of foreign expansion must be aware of the regional economic groups that encompass countries with good manufacturing locations or market opportunities. As companies expand internationally, they must change their organizational structure and operating strategies to take advantage of regional trading groups.

Economic integration schemes–also referred to as trade blocks, Regional Integration Agreement (RIAs), Regional Trade Agreements (RTAs)–is an important international business environment. As economic integration scheme is conceived as a building block of economic development of the member countries. It may sometimes become a stumbling block for companies located outside the block. Besides the integration schemes, there have been other efforts to foster economic cooperation between countries.

There has been a significant growth of regional economic integration schemes designed to achieve various economic, social and political purposes. Most countries in the world are members of–or discussing participation in–one or more trade block known as regional integration agreement/arrangement (RIA). Such agreement have been concluded among high-income countries, among low-income countries, and, more recently, starting with the North American Free Trade Area (NAFTA)–between high-income and developing countries.

Regional integration schemes tend to increase intra-regional trade. There has, in fact, been a fast growth of the intra-regional trade. Some people view world trade as consisting broadly of intra-regional trade. There is also talk of rationalization versus globalization of world trade.

Rationale/Objectives

The motivation to form trading blocks may vary from region to region and from country to country. Nevertheless, as Shiells suggests, the following motivations seem to play a key role in the formation of trading blocks.

- To obtain economic benefits from achieving a more efficient production structure by exploiting economies of scale through spreading fixed costs over larger regional markets increased economic growth from foreign direct investment, learning from experience etc.
- To pursue non-economic objectives such as strengthening political ties and managing migration flows.
- To ensure increased security of market access for smaller countries by forming regional trading blocks with larger countries.
- To improve members bargaining strength in multilateral trade negotiations or to protect against the slow pace of trade negotiations.
- Finally, to prevent further damage to their trading strength due to further trade diversion from third countries.
- To promote regional infant industries, which cannot be viable cannot a protected regional market.

There are four basic types of regional economic integration:

1. **Free Trade Agreement (FTA):** The goal of an FTA is to abolish all tariffs between member countries. FTA usually begins modestly by eliminating tariffs on goods that already have low tariffs, and there is usually an implementation period over which all tariffs are eliminated on all products. In addition, each member country maintains its own external tariff against non-FTA countries.
2. **Customs Union:** In addition to eliminating internal tariffs, member countries levy a common external tariff on goods being imported from non-members. It not only eliminates all restrictions on trade among members but also adopts a uniform commercial policy against the non-members.
3. **Common Market:** The common market is step ahead of the customs union. A common market allows free movement of labor and capital within the common market, besides having the two characteristics of the customs union, namely, free trade among members and uniform tariff policy towards outsiders.

4. **Complete Economic Integration:** Countries create even greater economic harmonization through the adoption of common economic policies. This level of cooperation creates a degree of political integration among member countries, which means they lose a bit of their sovereignty.

THE EFFECTS OF INTEGRATION

Regional economic integration can affect member countries in social, cultural, political and economic ways. It reduces or eliminates barriers for member countries. It produces both **static effects** and **dynamic effects**.

Static effects are the shifting of resources from inefficient to efficient companies as trade barriers fall. *Dynamic effects* are the overall growth in the market and the impact on a company of expanding production and achieving greater economies of scale. *Static effects* may develop when either of two conditions occurs.

- **Trade Creation:** production shifts to more efficient producers for reasons of comparative advantage, allowing consumers access to more goods at a lower price than would have been possible without integration. The strategic implication is that companies that might not have been able to export to another country, even though they might be more efficient that producers in that country, are now able to export when the barriers come down.
- **Trade Diversion:** trade shifts to countries in the group at the expense of trade with countries not in the group, even though the non-member company might be more efficient in the absence of trade barriers.

EUROPEAN UNION

The European Economic Community (EEC), also known as European Common Market (ECM), European Community (EC) and European Union (EU), is by far the most successful of the regional economic integration schemes.

The EEC, which originally comprised six nations namely Belgium, France, Federal Republic of Germany, Italy, Luxembourg and Netherlands, was brought into being on 1st January 1958, by the Treaty of Rome, 1957.

Initially the objectives of the EEC were the

- Elimination of customs duties between member states
- Establishment of an external common customs tariff
- Introduction of a common policy for agriculture and transport
- Creation of a European Social Fund

- Establishment of a European Investment Bank
- Development of closer relations between member states

The EEC was expanded in 1973 with the inclusion of the United Kingdom, Denmark and Ireland. Greece joined the Community in 1981. Spain and Portugal became members on January 1, 1986, raising the number of members to twelve. With Austria, Finland and Sweden joining the union in the early 1990s, the number rose to 15. It increased to 25 in 2003.

Many more countries will be joining the union in due course.

EU EXPANSION

One of the EU's major challenges is that of expansion. The EU's first step in expansion was the creation of the European Economic Area (EEA) in 1991, which expanded the custom union privileges of the EU to European Free Trade Association (EFTA) member countries. EFTA was established in 1960 as an alternative to the EEC, and it was simply a free trade agreement. With the loss of Austria, Finland and Sweden to the EU as full members in 1995, EFTA was reduced to only four countries: Norway, Iceland, Switzerland and Liechtenstein. The EEA agreement with the EU allows the freedom of people, goods, services, and capital to Norway, Iceland and Liechtenstein.

Prior to the end of the Soviet empire, the countries of the USSR and Central and Eastern Europe were linked together in a trading relationship known as the **Council for Mutual Economic Assistance (CMEA** or also known as **COMECON**). However, the breakup of the Soviet Union and its allied countries in Eastern Europe dissolved the CMEA in June 1991. On July 1, 1992, the **Central European Free Trade Association (CEFTA)** went into effect, with the Czech Republic, Slovakia, Hungary and Poland as members.

WHERE NEXT FOR THE EU?

The Economist identified five fundamental shifts that have occurred in the EU that will dramatically affect its future:

- The inversion of the Franco-German balance. France had always had political control of the EU and could take the high road as a result of World War II. However, Germany's confidence has returned with its reunification between East and West, and Germany is now the largest and richest country in Europe. Germany may be the only country that can lead Europe in the future.
- A sense that the EU should possess a capacity for collective military action separate or separable from NATO. This was confirmed in the

Kosovo conflict where the United States took control of a European conflict.

- The introduction of the euro, discussed later in more detail.
- The weakening of the European Commission and the ascendancy of national governments in controlling the destiny of the EU.
- The planned enlargement of the EU to include at least 12 and possibly as many as 20 new members, most of them former communist countries in Central and Eastern Europe.

These shifts in Europe are impacting and being affected by top priorities identified by Europeans themselves:

- Job creation
- Promoting peace
- Protecting the environment
- Reining in EU spending
- Protecting the food supply.

EC 1992

By July 1968, a Customs Union has been established among the original six members of the EEC as they abolished tariffs on trade among themselves and imposed a common tariff schedule on imports from other countries. The community members had also taken some noteworthy steps towards approximating their economic policies including adoption of Common Agricultural Policy (CAP) in 1962 and establishment of the European Monetary System in 1979. A detailed program for attaining a single integrated market was set forth by the EC commission in June 1985 in a White Paper entitled "Completing the Internal Market".

The White Paper listed 300 specific areas and made for action by 1992. The barriers targeted for removal pertained to the following eight categories:

- Border control
- Limitations on the movement of people and their right of establishment
- Differing internal taxation regimes
- Lack of common legal framework for business
- Heavy and differing regulation of services
- Divergent product regulations and standards
- Protectionist public procurement policies.

Some observers refer to the EC 1992 as the European Fortress/Fortress–92 implying that henceforth exports from non-member countries to the EC will have to encounter a mounting barrier, EC officials, however, say that the Fortress Europe story is senseless and groundless and that they will not be tempted by protectionism. They argue that the single European market will boost world trade and growth.

Indo-EU Trade

The EC, taken as a single unit, is India's largest partner. India's exports to EC grew from ₹282 crores in 1970–71 to ₹1447 crores in 1980–81 and ₹8951 crores in 1990–91. The corresponding figures of India's exports from the EC were ₹320 crores, ₹320 crores, ₹2639 crores and ₹12860 crores. In 2001–02, India's exports and imports with the EU were ₹45,524 crores and ₹46,771 crores respectively. In 2000–01 India, however, had a trade surplus with the EU.

India's main exports to EC include textiles, jute, leather and leather manufacturers, polished diamonds, engineering goods, chemicals, marine products etc. Imports include edible oils, fertilizers, dairy products, steel, capital goods, optical instruments, synthetic rubber and photo and cinematographic goods. India also receives technology, investment and development aid from EC countries.

India's export performance has been regulated as poor. Several factors such as lack of price competitiveness, poor quality, poor quality image, bad reputation in respect of delivery schedules, poor export marketing skills, and protectionist policy pursued by the EEC countries etc. have contributed to this.

The EC is very potential market and India should pay sufficient attention to taking advantage of this enlarging market. Many countries, including Japan and South-East Asian countries, have been taking measures to overcome the Fortress by setting up manufacturing/assembling units in the Community. India's achievements in this direction have, however, been not very significant.

The Euro

Euro, the common currency of European Union, was launched by 11 of the 15 members of the Union, on January 1, 1999. The exchange rates per euro determined at the time of the Euro launch were about US $1.7; British pound 0.70; Yen 133; and German mark 1.96. One Euro was equivalent to ₹49.

Euro currency and coins will not come into circulation until 2002, although banking and trading transactions in Euro have commenced since January 1, 1999. The national currencies of the 11 Euro nations will continue in circulation until 2002. The deadline for the withdrawal of national currencies and coins was July 1, 2002. Beyond this date they will not be legal tender.

The monetary policy decisions for the Euro area are made by the European Central Bank (ECB), which along with the National Central Banks (NCB) of all EU members comprise the European System of Central Banks (ESCB). The single currency will bring a single interest rate, eliminate currency risk and give equity and bond markets the necessary scope and liquidity to attract big investors. Europe will rank alongside the US as the deepest and most liquid market in the world.

Consumers will benefit in several ways. The single currency will impart price transparency throughout the Euroland–when there were many currencies price comparisons were not so easy. Prices now will tend to be equal throughout the Euro area.

The euro (sign: €; code: EUR) is the official currency of the European Union (EU), and is currently in use in 16 of the 27 Member States. The states, known collectively as the eurozone, are Austria, Belgium, Cyprus, Finland, France, Germany, Greece, Ireland, Italy, Luxembourg, Malta, the Netherlands, Portugal, Slovakia, Slovenia and Spain. Estonia is due to join the eurozone on the 1st January 2011. The currency is also used in a further five European countries, with and without formal agreements, and is consequently used daily by some 327 million Europeans. Over 175 million people worldwide use currencies which are pegged to the euro, including more than 150 million people in Africa.

The euro is the second largest reserve currency (a status it inherited from the German mark) as well as the second most traded currency in the world after the US dollar. As of October 2009, with more than € 790 billion in circulation, the euro is the currency with the highest combined value of banknotes and coins in circulation in the world, having surpassed the US dollar. Based on IMF estimates of 2008 GDP and purchasing power parity among the various currencies, the eurozone is the second largest economy in the world.

The name *euro* was officially adopted on 16 December 1995. The euro was introduced to world financial markets as an accounting currency on 1 January 1999, replacing the former European Currency Unit (ECU) at a ratio of 1:1. Euro coins and banknotes entered circulation on 1 January 2002.

Evidence on the Effect of the Introduction of the Euro

In conformity with the economic predictions, empirical studies have found that the introduction of the euro has had a positive impact on the movement of goods, financial assets, and people within the eurozone. In addition, countries which previously had weak currencies have benefited from lower interest rates and their firms now have easier access to capital.

Trade

The consensus from the studies of the effect of the introduction of the euro is that it has increased trade within the eurozone by 5% to 10%. On the lower bound, one study suggested an increase of 3%. A recent study estimates this effect to be between 9 and 14%.

Investment

Studies have found a positive effect of the introduction of the euro on investment. Physical investment seems to have increased by 5% in the eurozone due to the introduction. Regarding foreign direct investment, a study found that the intra-eurozone FDI stocks have increased by about 20% during the first four years of the EMU. Concerning the effect on corporate investment, there is evidence that the introduction of the euro has resulted in an increase in investment rates and that it has made it easier for firms to access financing in Europe. The euro has most specifically stimulated investment in companies that come from countries that previously had weak currencies. A study found that the introduction of the euro accounts for 22% of the investment rate after 1998 in countries that previously had a weak currency. The effect is however less clear for firms coming from the strong currency countries; the introduction has not been beneficial for most of them.

Exchange Rate Risk

One of the advantages of the adoption of a common currency is the reduction of the risk associated with changes in currency exchange rates. It has been found that the introduction of the euro created "significant reductions in market risk exposures for non-financial firms both in and outside of Europe". These reductions in market risk "were concentrated in firms domiciled in the eurozone and in non-Euro firms with a high fraction of foreign sales or assets in Europe". These changes were however "statistically and economically small".

Effect on Interest Rates

The introduction of the euro has decreased the interest rates of most members countries, in particular those with a weak currency. As a consequence the market value of firms from countries which previously had a weak currency has very significantly increased. The countries whose interest rates fell most as a result of the euro are Greece, Ireland, Portugal, Spain and Italy.

Price Convergence

The evidence on the convergence of prices in the eurozone with the introduction of the euro is mixed. Several studies failed to find any evidence of convergence following the introduction of the euro after a phase of convergence in the early 1990s. Other studies have found evidence of price convergence, in particular for cars. A possible reason for the divergence between the different studies is that the processes of convergence may not have been linear, slowing down substantially between 2000 and 2003, and resurfacing after 2003 as suggested by a recent study (2009).

NORTH AMERICAN FREE TRADE AGREEMENT (NAFTA)

NAFTA, which includes Canada, the United States, and Mexico, went into effect in 1994, but it originated with the Canada–US Free Trade Agreement. The United States and Canada historically have had various forms of mutual economic cooperation. One is the Automotive Products Trade Agreement, effective in 1965, which provides for qualified duty free trade in specified automotive products. In the early 1980, the two countries discussing developing free trade in specific industries such as steel and textiles. The discussion led to broader discussion of free trade, and by 1987 negotiations were underway to open up trade even more.

In February 1991, Mexico approached United States to establish a free trade agreement. The formal negotiations that began in June 1991 included Canada. The resulting NAFTA became effective on January 1, 1994.

NAFTA covers the following areas:

- Market access: tariff and non-tariff barriers, rules of origin, governmental procurement.
- Trade rules: safeguards, subsidies, countervailing and antidumping duties, health and safety standards.
- Services: provides for the same safeguards for trade in services (consulting, engineering, software etc.) that exist for trade in goods.
- Investment: establishes investment rules governing minority interests, portfolio investment, real property and majority-owned or controlled investment from the NAFTA countries.
- Intellectual property: all three countries pledge to provide adequate and effective protection and enforcement of intellectual property rights, while ensuring that enforcement measures do not themselves become barriers to legitimate trade.

- Dispute settlement: provides a dispute settlement process what will be followed instead of countries taking unilateral action against an offending party.

NAFTA has achieved substantial trade liberalization. The trade between the US and Canada and the US and Mexico is substantial and has been rising fast. The two-way trading relationship between the US and Canada is the largest in the world. Mexico replaced Japan as the second-largest market for US exports while remaining as the third most important supplier to the US market after Canada and Japan.

Foreign investment in Mexico has risen substantially since the Agreement. Companies from outside NAFTA have been making large investment in Mexico to gain a free entry to the huge NAFTA market. NAFTA has been resulting in a lost of trade diversion.

In addition, NAFTA is a good example of trade diversion. Many US and Canadian companies have established manufacturing facilities in Asia to take advantage of cheap labor. Now US and Canadian companies can establish manufacturing facilities in Mexico rather than in Asian countries to take advantage of relatively cheap labor.

An important component of NAFTA is the concept of rules of origin and regional value content. Because NAFTA is a free trade agreement and not a customs union, each country sets its own tariffs to the rest of the world. Rules of origin ensure that only goods that have been the subject of substantial economic activity within the free trade area are eligible for the more liberal tariff conditions created by the NAFTA.

From the **labor standpoint** the NAFTA side agreement set forth the following general objectives:

- Improving working conditions and living standards
- Promoting compliance with and effective enforcement of labor laws
- Promoting the Agreement's principles through cooperation and coordination
- Promoting publication and exchange of information to enhance mutual understanding of Parties laws, institutions and legal systems.

From the **environmental standpoint**, the NAFTA side agreement include:

- Promotion of sustainable development
- Cooperation on the conversation
- Protection and enhancement of the environment
- Effective enforcement of and compliance with domestic environmental laws.

However, Mexican environmental standards are getting tougher and enforcement of those standards is improving. There is no evidence to support the idea that environmental standards and enforcement would lag behind as the economy grows. One could argue that NAFTA actually could force Mexico to strengthen its standards and enforcement.

Economic Integration of Developing Countries

The United Nations Conference on Trade and Development (UNCTAD) has felt that "Regional economic groupings, integration or other forms of economic cooperation should be promoted among developing countries as a means of expanding".

For many developing countries in Latin America and Sub-Saharan Africa, regional trade agreements have been a key element in their policy agendas over the past three decades.

Similarly, Latin American countries have been involved in regional integration schemes since the late 1950s.

Regional trade agreements among developing countries include the Latin American Free Trade Association (LAFTA), the Central American Common Market (CACM), the Andean Pact, and the Carribean Common Market (CARICOM) in Latin America; the Economic Community of West African States (ECOWAS), the Preferential Trade Area (PTA), and the Southern African Development Coordination Conference (SADCC) in Sub-Saharan Africa.

The Southern Cone Common Market (Mercado Comun del Sur–MERCOSUR) consisting of Argentina, Brazil, Paraguay and Uruguay was formed in 1991. The Mercosur, the world's third largest customs union, announced in May 2000, the decision to transform the block into a common market.

Association of South East Asian Nations (ASEAN): Formed by the Bangkok Declaration, 1967, by five countries, viz., Indonesia, Malaysia, the Philippines, Singapore and Thailand with a view to accelerate economic progress.

The ASEAN now constitutes a larger market for Japan than does the United States. For two of the members–Indonesia and Malaysia–Japan is now the leading trade partner for exports as well as imports.

The economic growth rate of the ASEAN that is richly endowed with natural resources has been very high. This region accounts for the lion's share of the world's natural rubber, palm oil and tin. It is also an important producer of sugar, coffee, timber, petroleum, nickel, bauxite, tungsten and coal.

A comprehensive economic partnership between ASEAN and Japan would provide greater market opportunities to their economies, through the creation of larger and new markets and enabling the industries to enjoy bigger economies of scale.

A strong ASEAN free trade area (AFTA) and the new ASEAN-China deal would give companies an expanded consumer base with a combined gross domestic product of more than $1.5 trillion. Under AFTA, which came into force in 2002, six of ASEAN's established members have cut tariffs on most goods traded within the region to between 0 to 5 per cent. The new members Cambodia, Laos, Myanmar and Vietnam have until 2005 to comply.

Economic cooperation in ASEAN does not entail only trade liberalisation measures but also trade facilitation, non-border measures and investment promotion activities. New areas of cooperation, such as in services and intellectual property rights are being implemented. Bold decisions have also been made to elevate and strengthen ASEAN industrial cooperation through a new scheme which will take into account present industrial needs and economic situation in ASEAN. Cooperation in private sector development, small and medium size enterprises, infrastructural development and regional investment promotion measures have also made considerable progress.

The thrusts of **ASEAN** economic cooperation in the 1990s include the following:

- to fully implement the ASEAN Free Trade Area (AFTA);
- to develop the region into a global base for the manufacture of value added and technologically sophisticated products geared towards servicing the region and world markets;
- to enhance the industrial efficiency of the region through exploiting complementary location advantages based on the principles of market sharing and resource pooling;
- to enhance the attractiveness of the region for investment and as a tourist destination;
- to cooperate in enhancing greater infrastructural development which will contribute towards more efficient business environment; and
- to ensure that the rich resources (minerals, energy, forestry and others) of the region are exploited effectively and efficiently.

Guiding Principles

The success of ASEAN Economic Cooperation, seen as a possible model for regional cooperation among developing countries, is very much the result of the wisdom, foresight and bold decisions of the Bangkok Declaration of 1967 and the past four Summits' guidance. ASEAN Economic Cooperation was first stressed in the Bangkok Declaration of 1967 which laid the foundation for economic cooperation. The Declaration emphasized among other things, the following aims and purposes:

- to accelerate economic growth, social progress and cultural development in the region;
- to promote active collaboration and mutual assistance of matters of common interest in the economic, social, cultural, technical, scientific and administrative fields;
- to collaborate more effectively for the greater utilization of the region's agriculture and industries, the expansion of trade, including the study of the problems of international commodity trade, the improvement of its transportation and communications facilities and the raising of the living standards of its peoples.

INDIA-ASEAN

Since its start about a decade ago, the partnership between India and the Association of South East Asian Nations (ASEAN) comprising Brunei, Cambodia, Indonesia, Laos, Malaysia, Myanmar, the Philippines, Singapore, Thailand and Vietnam has been developing at quite a fast pace.

India became a sectoral dialogue partner of ASEAN in 1992. Mutual interest led ASEAN to invite India to become its full dialogue partner during the fifth ASEAN summit in Bangkok in 1995. India also became a member of the ASEAN Regional Forum (ARF) in 1996. India and ASEAN have been holding summit-level meetings on an annual basis since 2002.

In October 2009, India signed a Free Trade Agreement (FTA) with the ASEAN members in Thailand. Under the ASEAN-India FTA, ASEAN member countries and India will lift import tariffs on more than 80 per cent of traded products between 2013 and 2016.

Also, tariffs on sensitive goods will be reduced to 5 per cent in 2016, while tariffs will be maintained on up to 489 very sensitive items. India and ASEAN are currently negotiating agreements on trade in services and investment. The services negotiations are taking place on a request-offer basis, wherein both sides make requests for the openings they seek and offers are made by the receiving country based on the requests. There are four meetings scheduled between January and July and the deal is expected to be finalised by August 2010.

India has made requests in a number of areas including teaching, nursing, architecture, chartered accountancy and medicine as it has a large number of

English speaking professionals in these areas who can gain from job opportunities in the ASEAN region. India is also keen on expanding its telecom, IT, tourism and banking network in ASEAN countries.

Trade

The deepening of ties between India and ASEAN is reflected in the continued buoyancy in trade figures. The ASEAN is India's fourth-largest trading partner after the EU, US and China. In 2008–09 India's exports to ASEAN totalled US$ 19.14 billion, an increase of 16.62 per cent. During April-June 2009, India exported goods worth US$ 4.41 billion to ASEAN.

India imported goods worth US$ 26.20 billion in 2008–09 from ASEAN. During the period April-June 2009, India's imports totaled US$ 6.24 billion.

Singapore

The growing bilateral economic relationship is reflected in the rapidly rising bilateral trade between Singapore and India. Singapore continues to be the single largest investor in India amongst the ASEAN countries with FDI inflows into India and the second largest amongst all countries, rising to US$ 3.45 billion in 2008–09. FDI inflows from Singapore between April-December 2009 stood at US$ 1.70 billion, taking the cumulative inflows in the April 2000-December 2009 period to US$ 9.51 billion.

The total bilateral trade during 2008–09 was US$ 16.1 billion, an increase of 3.86 per cent over US$ 15.5 billion in 2007–08.

ICICI Bank is all set to become the second Indian financial institution to get a full-fledged banking licence in Singapore, which will allow it to set up branches, ATMs, take deposits and disburse loans like a local bank. State Bank of India is already a fully-recognised bank in Singapore.

Malaysia

The bilateral economic relationship between India and Malaysia has been steadily moving ahead. Malaysia has been a huge source of FDI for India. In fact, Malaysia is the twenty-fourth largest overall investor and second largest investor among ASEAN countries with a total inflow of US$ 244.45 million during the April 2000-December 2009 period.

Bilateral trade among the two countries amounted to US$ 10.5 billion during 2008–09. During the same period, US$3 8.7 million worth of Malaysian investments in India were primarily in sectors like construction, real estate and business services.

SAARC

The South Asian Association for Regional Cooperation (SAARC) involving seven countries, namely, India, Bangladesh, Pakistan, Nepal, Bhutan, Sri Lanka and Maldives was formally launched in December 1995. These neighbors had come together in an act of faith.

The fundamental goal of SAARC is to accelerate economic and social development through optimum utilization of their human and material resources. The objectives of the Association are as follows:

- To promote the welfare of the people of South Asia and to improve their quality of life.
- To promote and strengthen collective self-reliance among the countries of South Asia.
- To strengthen cooperation with other developing countries.
- To strengthen cooperation among them in international forums on matter of common interests.
- To cooperate with international and regional organizations with similar aims and purposes.
- To promote active collaboration and mutual assistance in the economic, social, cultural, technical and scientific fields.

A major share of the world's poor lives in these countries. All these are low-income economies. India holds about two-thirds of the total population of the Association. On the other extreme is the tiny country of Maldives with a land area of 298 sq.kms, inhabited by about 2 lakh people. Bhutan is a comparatively small country, with a total population much less than that of population of Bangalore, where the second SAARC summit was held.

In general, there has also been a decline in the intra-regional trade of each country during the last decade or so, reflecting a more rapid expansion of trade with extra-regional countries—developed and developing.

Some of the member countries are major exporters of certain commodities and therefore major competitors in the international market. For example, jute exports of India and Bangladesh and tea exports by Sri Lanka and India. Let us hope that the SAARC will become a forum to help avoid unhealthy competition in such areas and to help formulate joint strategies to get a better deal, particularly for the primary commodities in the international market.

The member countries of SAARC have many common features and problems which are characteristic of the developing countries. There are number of areas which offer scope for development through mutual help and cooperation.

The second summit of the SAARC held in Bangalore in November 1986 decided to expand and strengthen the cooperative programs of the Association and wanted the following actions to be taken:

- South-Asian broadcasting program covering both radio and television.
- Concrete steps to develop tourism in the region, including facilities for limited convertibility of national currencies for tourists from SAARC countries.
- Cooperation in educational, scientific, technical and research and development fields.

SAARC SUMMIT HELD SINCE 1985

	Date	Place Held
1st SAARC Summit	07–08 December 1985	Dhaka
2nd SAARC Summit	16–17 November 1986	Bangalore
3rd SAARC Summit	02–04 November 1987	Kathmandu
4th SAARC Summit	29–31 December 1988	Islamabad
5th SAARC Summit	21–23 November 1990	Maldives
6th SAARC Summit	21 December 1991	Colombo
7th SAARC Summit	10–11 April 1993	Dhaka
8th SAARC Summit	02–04 May 1995	New Delhi
9th SAARC Summit	12–14 May 1997	Maldives
10th SAARC Summit	29–31 July 1998	Colombo
11th SAARC Summit	04–06 January 2002	Kathmandu
12th SAARC Summit	02–06 January 2004	Islamabad
13th SAARC Summit	12–13 November 2005	Bangladesh
14th SAARC Summit	3–4 April 2007	New Delhi
15th SAARC Summit	1–3 August 2008	Colombo
16th SAARC Summit	28–29 April 2010	Bhutan
17th SAARC Summit	April 2011 (Tentative)	Maldives

SAPTA

The Agreement on SAARC Preferential Trading Arrangement (SAPTA) was signed on 11 April 1993 and entered into force on 7 December 1995, with the desire of the Member States of SAARC (India, Pakistan, Nepal, Sri Lanka, Bangladesh, Bhutan and the Maldives) to promote and sustain mutual trade and economic cooperation within the SAARC region through the exchange of concessions.

The establishment of an Inter-Governmental Group (IGG) to formulate an agreement to establish a SAPTA by 1997 was approved in the ***Sixth Summit*** *of SAARC* held in Colombo in December 1991.

The basic principles underlying SAPTA are:

1. *overall reciprocity* and *mutuality of advantages* so as to benefit equitably all Contracting States, taking into account their respective level of economic and industrial development, the pattern of their external trade, and trade and tariff policies and systems;
2. negotiation of *tariff reform* step by step, improved and extended in successive stages through periodic reviews;
3. recognition of the special needs of the Least Developed Contracting States and agreement on *concrete preferential measures* in their favour;
4. inclusion of all products, manufactures and commodities in their raw, semi-processed and processed forms.

So far, four rounds of trade negotiations have been concluded under SAPTA covering over 5000 commodities.

The declared **objectives** of the SAPTA are:

- To promote and sustain mutual trade, and
- To develop economic cooperation among developing countries (members of Group of 77).

Rules of Origin

1. The objective of these rules is to determine the origin of products eligible for preferential concessions under SAPTA. Products, which have achieved the status 'originating in India', are eligible for preferential tariff treatment upon imports into participant countries.

2. Following products are considered as originating in India, if they are consigned directly to a participant country.

   (a) Products that are wholly obtained in India, as defined at 4 below

   (b) Products obtained in India in the manufacture of which, in addition to the materials referred to at 4 below and materials originating in participant countries, materials imported from non-participant countries and/or materials of undetermined origin are also used, provided the value of materials imported from non-participant countries and/or materials of undetermined origin does not exceed

50% of the f.o.b. value of the product, subject to condition detailed at 5 below.

3. For the purpose of 2 (b), value of non-originating materials means the c.i.f. value at the time of importation of such materials or, if this is not known and cannot be ascertained and proved, the first ascertainable price paid for the materials in India.

4. Within the meaning of 2 (a) above, the following are considered as wholly obtained in India:

   (a) raw or mineral products extracted from its soil, its water or its seabed;

   (b) agricultural products harvested there;

   (c) animals born and raised there;

   (d) products obtained from animals referred to in clause (c) above;

   (e) products obtained by hunting or fishing conducted there;

   (f) products of sea fishing and other marine products taken from the high seas by its vessels;

   (g) products processed and/or made on board its factory ships exclusively from products referred to in clause

   (h) above;

   (i) used articles collected there, fit only for the recovery of raw materials;

   (j) waste and scrap resulting from manufacturing operations conducted there;

   (k) goods produced there exclusively from the products referred to in clauses (a) to (i) above.

5. Products which comply with origin requirements provided for at 2 and which are used by a participant as input for a finished product eligible for preferential treatment by another participant are considered as a product originating in the territory of the participant where working or processing of the finished product has taken place provided that the aggregate content originating in the territory of the participant is not less than 60 per cent of its f.o.b. value.

6. The following are considered to be directly consigned from India to the importing country:

   (a) If the products are transported without passing through the territory of any non-participant country.

(b) The products whose transport involves transit through one or more non-participant countries with or without transhipment or temporary storage in such countries; provided that

1. the transit entry is justified for geographical reason or by considerations related exclusively to transport requirements;
2. the products have not entered into trade or consumption there; and
3. the products have not undergone any operation there other than unloading and reloading or any operation required to keep them in good condition.

7. When determining the origin of the products, packing forms a whole with the product it contains.

SAFTA

The Agreement on the South Asian Free Trade Area is an agreement reached at the **12th SAARC summit** at Islamabad, capital of Pakistan on 6 January 2004. It creates a framework for the creation of a free trade area covering 1.4 billion people in India, Pakistan, Nepal, Sri Lanka, Bangladesh, Bhutan and the Maldives.

The seven foreign ministers of the region signed a framework agreement on SAFTA with zero customs duty on the trade of practically all products in the region by end 2016. The new agreement i.e. SAFTA, came into being on 1 January 2006 and will be operational following the ratification of the agreement by the seven governments.

SAFTA requires the developing countries in South Asia that is, India, Pakistan and Sri Lanka, to bring their duties down to 20 percent in the first phase of the two year period ending in 2007. In the final five year phase ending 2012, the 20 per cent duty will be reduced to zero in a series of annual cuts.

The least developed nations in South Asia consisting of Nepal, Bhutan, Bangladesh and Maldives have an additional three years to reduce tariffs to zero. India and Pakistan have signed but not ratified the treaty.

What is SAFTA Ultimate Goal?

It will replace the earlier South Asia Preferential Trade Agreement (SAPTA), which was limited in its scope. The ultimate aim of SAFTA will be to put in place a full-fledged South Asia Economic Union on the lines of the EU. SAFTA is scheduled for launch in January 2006 and will lead to reduction of tariffs for intra-regional trade among SAARC countries.

What are the Objectives Guiding SAFTA?

Among its aims are: promoting and enhancing mutual trade and economic cooperation by eliminating barriers in trade, promoting conditions of fair competition in the free trade area, ensuring equitable benefits to all and establishing a framework for further regional cooperation to expand the mutual benefits of the agreement.

What other Benefits can SAFTA bring to Member-countries?

It could lead to enhancement of foreign investment among SAARC nations. The visible spurt in foreign investment within ASEAN countries and the increase in investments by India in Sri Lanka and *vice versa* following the India-Sri Lanka FTA bear testimony to the potential of such agreements in boosting investments.

The agreement can be structured to ensure that such investments don't harm the domestic industries of member-nations. RTAs, like the proposed SAFTA, can also catalyze beneficial industrial restructuring in member-countries through cross-border corporate marriages and acquisitions.

SOUTH-SOUTH COOPERATION

Historically, South-South cooperation was promoted only by the governments as a model to exhibit "South-solidarity" for collectively influencing the international political and economic order.

The **rich diversity of the South** provides an excellent opportunity for forging mutually beneficial partnerships to work towards the common goal of economic growth, industrial development and poverty reduction. The trends in South-South Cooperation have been quite encouraging. **Developing countries are now increasingly investing in each others' economies**, with FDI rising from US$ 14 billion in 1995 to US$ 47 billion in 2003.

These investments accounted for 37% of the total FDI in all of the developing countries in 2003. Trade within the South has also risen significantly from US$222 billion in 1995 to US$ 562 billion in 2004; or representing 26% of their global trade. Talking of Asia; South and East Asian countries in 2005 accounted for 70 per cent of the total manufacturing value-added in developing countries in 2005, an increase from around 50 per cent in 1990. During the period 2002–2004, average annual intra-Asian investment flows amounted to US$ 48 billion, i.e. more than four-fifth of all intra-South FDI in the period.

South-South cooperation promotes **economic and technical cooperation among developing countries** and is an important **complement to North-South cooperation**. The role of technical cooperation among developing countries for industrial development is widely recognized. The growing importance of developing countries in world trade is associated with a sharp rise in manufactured exports and an increasing role of South-South trade in commodities and manufactures. If the rise of some countries in the South is to be harnessed for the **mutual benefit** of all, it calls for a qualitative enhancement of South-South cooperation.

To tackle the new challenges in **trade and investment promotion** and industrial development, new institutions and systems are needed and UNIDO responded with a project to launch South-South Cooperation Centers in some of the more advanced developing countries like India and China.

The UNIDO South-South Cooperation Program

The **essence** of South-South cooperation is that the **wealth of knowledge and capacity in the South**, when systematically mobilized and shared, can facilitate the effective participation of the developing countries in the global economy. UNIDO's South-South Cooperation Program aims to create and strengthen **technical and business capacities** of developing countries in order to increase their competitive strengths and to base their cooperation on shared interests and on their economic and social needs.

The South-South cooperation program will **focus** on:

- Technology transfer, management and upgrading of skills
- Investment promotion in industries
- Information technology applications for industrial development and knowledge networking
- Business linkages for Small and Medium Size Enterprises (SMEs) and cluster development
- Micro enterprise and rural industry development
- Building trade capacities and market linkages
- Grassroots innovations and renewable energy sources
- Commercialization of research findings and skill development
- Value-chain participation

South Assisting South

To **enhance greater interaction** between developing countries, the UNIDO Centre for South-South Industrial Cooperation will:

- Exchange expertise and experience
- Network institutions and enterprises

- Replicate best practices to reduce poverty
- Strengthen national and local innovation systems

Specifically, the centre aims to:

- Design **practical and innovative projects** to exploit new areas of technical competence and economic opportunity. The emphasis will be on launching projects in established fields as well as in new ones with social and economic development potential for LDCs;
- **Provide a platform** to encourage closer cooperation in policy formulation among developing countries. The aim is to ensure that the less developed countries can benefit from the experience of successful strategies in the more developed ones. Benchmarking will be encouraged between the more developed economies of the South-India, China, South Africa and Brazil–so that through increased productivity their pace of development could be maintained and strengthened, enabling them to become engines of growth in their respective regions. For this, the Centre will network with the UNIDO International Technology Promotion Centres, the Investment and Technology Promotion Offices (ITPOs) and the Africa Investment Promotion Agency Network (AFRIPA-NET). The Centre will also coordinate its activities with UNIDO's field offices all over the world;
- **Act as a catalyst** to leverage various on-going projects of governments, as well as of UNIDO, where relevant, and channelize them into coherent initiatives, to enhance their effectiveness, and leverage their benefits to sharpen their South-South cooperation component.

South-South Initiative on Cotton

The initiative focuses on **11 selected cotton-producing countries:**

1. Benin, Burkina Faso, Cameroon, Chad, Côte d'Ivoire, Mali, Nigeria, Senegal, Uganda, United Republic of Tanzania and Zambia.

Issues Addressed by the Initiative

Cotton plays a **significant role** in African countries. The cotton-producing countries in Africa export most their cotton fibre directly without adding value. Despite competitive labour costs, African cotton and textile companies cannot meet the challenges of international **competition on a quota-free cotton market**.

- Trade distorting subsidies in developed countries
- Products do not meet international standards

- Low productivity
- Lack of modern production facilities
- Lack of knowledge and experience on how to run a business in a competitive market
- Inefficient use of domestic resources
- Lack of foreign direct investments (FDI)
- Lack of regional and national strategies for developing cotton-textile-garment value chains

The Key Stakeholders of the Initiative

- Government authorities
- Representatives of the private sector
- Cotton farmer representatives
- Private and public cotton textile and garment operators
- Regional and national support institutions

Technical Cooperation Counterpart Organization

- African Cotton Association (ACA)
- International Cotton Advisory Committee (ICAC)
- South India Cotton Association (SICA)
- China Cotton Association (CCA)

Purpose of the Initiative: The **goal** of the program is to ensure sustained competitiveness of the Cotton-Textile-Garment sector in African countries. The program focuses on product innovation and investment promotion. The South-South Initiative contributes to poverty reduction through employment generation and value chain improvement.

Immediate Goal and Expected Outcomes and Outputs: The immediate goal of the program is to assist African cotton-producing countries to **improve productive capacity-building in cotton processing** through south-south cooperation with India and China. The cotton and textile industry is more advanced in China and India than in Africa. African countries could benefit from the transfer of equipment, technology and niche product ranges from China and India. Comprehensive supply chain and infrastructure development shall attract foreign direct investment from China and India.

Expected End-of-program Situation

- Creation of new jobs
- Stimulation of business creation

- Training for 250 experts and technicians
- Productivity enhancement of selected textile companies
- Increase of export revenues of selected textile companies
- Boosting the cotton processing industry
- Promotion of investment opportunities
- Stronger worldwide partnerships
- Replication of the program in other cotton producing countries

APEC

The **Asia Pacific Economic Cooperation** was formed in November 1989 to promote multilateral economic cooperation in trade and investment in the Pacific Rim. It is comprised of 21 countries that border the Pacific Rim – both in Asia as well as the Americas. The members of APEC can be Australia, Brunei, Darussalam, Canada, Indonesia, Japan, Malaysia, New Zealand, Philippines, the Republic of Korea, Singapore, Thailand and United States.

By 1991 China, Hong Kong (China), Taiwan (China); 1993: Mexico Papua New Guinea; 1994: Chile; 1998: Peru, Russia, Vietnam.

APEC major objectives are to:

- Resist protectionist pressures and maintain the momentum of trade liberalization.
- Counter inward-looking regionalism elsewhere, such as in the EU and NAFTA
- Provide ways to deal with economic conflicts in the region

To accomplish the objectives APEC leaders committed to achieve free and open trade in the region by 2010 for the industrial nations (which generate 85 per cent of the regional trade) and by 2020 for the rest of the members. Heads of the state have met annually since their first meeting in the United States in 1993.

APEC has the potential to become a significant economic block, especially because it generates such as large percentage of the world's output and merchandise trade. APEC is trying to establish "open regionalism," whereby individual member countries can determine whether to apply trade liberalization to non-APEC countries on an unconditional most favored nation basis on a reciprocal, free trade agreement basis.

Objectives and Aims of APEC: The main purpose of APEC's inception was to decrease the number of obstacles in trade and also to reduce tariffs across Asia Pacific nations. This in turn created domestic economies, which were efficient. It also gave a boost to export activities in all the APEC countries. The APEC has set its eye on achieving the "Bogor Goals" by the year 2010 for economies, which are industrialized. It has set its target for fulfilling the "**Bogor Goals**" by the year 2020 in case of developing economies.

These goals are related to open and free trade across all member economies of APEC. The name "**Bogor Goals**" was adopted because these goals were framed in the 1994 meeting, by different leaders in Bogor, a place in Indonesia.

A Brief Overview of the "Bogor Goals": Investment, trade, which is free and open, facilitates economic growth. It also creates employment opportunities and new vistas open in the field of international trade. On the contrary, industrial inefficiencies as well as rise in prices are consequences of excessive protectionism. By carrying out free and open trade, production cost is greatly reduced and this in turn reduces the cost of services and goods. APEC also looks into the efficient as well as safe movement of services and goods. This is achieved by means of technical cooperation, economic cooperation and policy alignment.

APEC's Mode of Operation: APEC is successful because it believes in respecting the views expressed by the member nations. It operates by encouraging dialogs between member economies. In order to achieve its goals pertaining to free trade, investments and open trade, it takes decisions depending on consensus.

Funding of APEC: Funding by the different member economies, keeps APEC functioning and aids in carrying out the various activities of APEC.

Achievements of APEC: From the time, APEC was established in the year 1989, the APEC member economies have been the most active nations as far as economic dynamism is concerned. Within few years of its inception, the different APEC economies together accounted for 70% of the growth in the economy worldwide. All the APEC member nations surpassed the other economies of the world. This was true, even during the period, when Asia was going through financial crisis. APEC has managed to streamline economies of the member nations.

INDO-LANKA FREE TRADE AGREEMENT

The main objective of this Free Trade Agreement, according to its preamble, is the following:

1. To promote through the expansion of trade the harmonious development of the economic relations between India and Sri Lanka.
2. To provide fair conditions of competition for trade between India and Sri Lanka.

3. In the implementation of this agreement both the countries would pay due regard to the principle of reciprocity.
4. To contribute, in this way, by the removal of barriers to trade to the harmonious development and expansion of world trade.

According to the Bilateral Free Trade Agreement signed by India and Sri Lanka on 28 December 1998, a large number of items will be eligible for duty free trade. India has offered to permit as much as 1000 items on zero duty from Sri Lanka and Sri Lanka will allow duty free exports of 900 items from India.

It is feared that the India-Sri Lanka Free Trade Agreement would very adversely affect the farmers of India, as several cash crops would enter India duty free from Sri Lanka depressing their domestic prices.

As India is a very large market, the Free Trade Agreement is likely to benefit Sri Lanka a lot and the benefits to India may not be much as Sri Lanka is a small market.

UNCTAD

The **United Nations Conference on Trade and Development** (UNCTAD) was established in 1964 as a permanent intergovernmental body. It is the principal organ of the United Nations General Assembly dealing with trade, investment, and development issues.

Established in 1964, UNCTAD promotes the development-friendly integration of developing countries into the world economy. UNCTAD has progressively evolved into an authoritative knowledge-based institution whose work aims to help shape current policy debates and thinking on development, with a particular focus on ensuring that domestic policies and international action are mutually supportive in bringing about sustainable development.

The organization works to fulfill this mandate by carrying out **three key functions:**

- It functions as a **forum for intergovernmental deliberations**, supported by discussions with experts and exchanges of experience, aimed at **consensus building**.
- It undertakes **research, policy analysis and data collection** for the debates of government representatives and experts.
- It provides **technical assistance** tailored to the specific requirements of developing countries, with special attention to the needs of the least developed countries and of economies in transition. When appropriate, UNCTAD cooperates with other organizations and donor countries in the delivery of technical assistance.

The organization's goals are to "maximize the trade, investment and development opportunities of developing countries and assist them in their efforts to integrate into the world economy on an equitable basis." (from official website). The creation of the conference was based on concerns of developing countries over the international market, multinational corporations, and great disparity between developed nations and developing nations.

In the 1970s and 1980s, UNCTAD was closely associated with the idea of a New International Economic Order (NIEO).

The United Nations Conference on Trade and Development was established in 1964 in order to provide a forum where the developing countries could discuss the problems relating to their economic development. UNCTAD grew from the view that existing institutions like GATT and IMF were not properly organized to handle the particular problems of developing countries. UNCTAD has **193** members.

The primary objective of the UNCTAD is to formulate policies relating to all aspects of development including trade, aid, transport, finance and technology.

One of the principal achievements of UNCTAD has been to conceive and implement the **Generalised System of Preferences (GSP)**. It was argued in UNCTAD, that in order to promote exports of manufactured goods from developing countries, it would be necessary to offer special tariff concessions to such exports. Accepting this argument, the developed countries formulated the GSP Scheme under which manufacturers' exports and some agricultural goods from the developing countries enter duty-free or at reduced rates in the developed countries. Since imports of such items from other developed countries are subject to the normal rates of duties, imports of the same items from developing countries would enjoy a competitive advantage.

The conference ordinarily meets once in **four** years.

- UNCTAD I was held in Geneva in 1964,
- UNCTAD II was held in New Delhi in 1968,
- UNCTAD III was held in Santiago in 1972,
- UNCTAD IV was held in Nairobi in 1976,
- UNCTAD V was held in Manila in 1979,
- UNCTAD VI was held in Belgrade in 1983,
- UNCTAD VII was held in Geneva in 1987,
- UNCTAD VIII was held in Cartagena (Colombia) in 1992
- UNCTAD IX was held in Johannesburg (South Africa) in 1996
- UNCTAD X was held in Bangkok, Thailand in 12-19 February 2000

- UNCTAD XI was held in São Paulo, Brazil in 13-18 June 2004
- UNCTAD XII was held in Accra, Ghana in 21-25 April 2008
- UNCTAD XIII will be held in Doha, Qatar in 2012

MAIN ACTIVITIES OF UNCTAD

Trade and Commodities

- **Commodity Diversification and Development:** Promotes the diversification of production and trade structures. Helps Governments to formulate and implement diversification policies and encourages enterprises to adapt their business strategies and become more competitive in the world market.
- **Competition and Consumer Policies:** Provides analysis and capacity building in competition and consumer protection laws and policies in developing countries. Publishes regular updates of a Model Law on Competition.
- **Trade Negotiations and Commercial Diplomacy:** Assists developing countries in all aspects of their trade negotiations.
- **Trade Analysis and Information System (TRAINS):** Comprehensive computer-based information system on trade control measures that uses UNCTAD's database. The CD-ROM version includes 119 countries.
- **Trade and Environment:** Assesses the trade and development impact of environmental requirements and relevant multilateral agreements and provides capacity-building activities to help developing countries participate in and derive benefits from international negotiations on these matters.

Investment and Enterprise Development

- **International Investment and Technology Arrangements:** Helps developing countries to participate more actively in international investment rule making at the bilateral, regional and multilateral levels. These arrangements include the organization of capacity-building seminars and regional symposia and the preparation of a series of issues papers.
- **Investment Policy Reviews:** Intended to familiarize Governments and the private sector with the investment environment and policies of a given country. Reviews have been carried out in a number of countries, including Ecuador, Egypt, Ethiopia, Mauritius, Peru, Uganda and Uzbekistan.

- **Investment Guides and Capacity Building for the LDCs:** Some of the countries involved are Bangladesh, Ethiopia, Mali, Mozambique and Uganda.
- **Empretec:** Promotes entrepreneurship and the development of small and medium-sized enterprises. Empretec programmes have been initiated in 27 countries, assisting more than 70,000 entrepreneurs through local market-driven business support centres.

Macroeconomic Policies, Debt and Development Financing

- **Policy Analysis and Research** on issues concerning global economic interdependence, the international monetary and financial system, and macroeconomic and development policy challenges.
- **Technical and Advisory Support** to the G24 group of developing countries (the Intergovernmental Group of 24) in the World Bank and the International Monetary Fund; advisory services to developing countries for debt rescheduling negotiations under the Paris Club.
- **DMFAS Programme:** Computer-based debt management and financial analysis system specially designed to help countries manage their external debt. Started in 1982, and now installed in 62 countries.

Technology and Logistics

- **ASYCUDA Program:** Integrated customs system that speeds up customs clearance procedures and helps Governments to reform and modernize their customs procedures and management. Installed in over 80 countries, ASYCUDA has become the internationally accepted standard for customs automation.
- **ACIS Program:** Computerized cargo tracking system installed in 20 developing countries of Africa and Asia.
- **E-Tourism Initiative:** Linking sustainable tourism and Information and communication technologies (ICTs) for development, UNCTAD has developed this Initiative to help developing countries' destinations to become more autonomous by taking charge of their own tourism promotion by using ICT tools.
- **Technology:** Services the UN Commission on Science and Technology for Development and administers the Science and Technology for Development Network; carries out case studies on best practices in transfer of technology; undertakes Science, Technology and Innovation Policy Reviews for interested countries, as well as capacity-building activities.

- **Train for Trade Program:** Builds training networks and organizes training in all areas of international trade to enable developing countries to increase their competitiveness. Currently developing distance learning programs focusing on the LDCs.

Africa, least developed countries, landlocked developing countries and small island developing States:

- **Africa:** Provides analytical work aimed at increasing the understanding of problems faced by African countries in their development efforts, and facilitating a better integration of Africa into the world economy. Particular emphasis is placed on supporting the New Partnership for Africa's Development (NEPAD).
- **Least Developed Countries (LDCs):** Provides analytical work and technical assistance aimed at enabling relevant States to make the best possible use of LDC status in the framework of the Program of Action for the Least Developed Countries for the Decade 2001–2010, and to better understand the policy-related issues that are specially relevant to LDCs, notably with a view to developing productive capacities and reducing poverty in these countries.
- **Landlocked Developing Countries (LLDCs):** Provides analytical work and technical assistance to LLDCs in support of the implementation of the 2003 Almaty Program of Action, which deals with the special needs of LLDCs within a new global framework for transit transport cooperation for landlocked and transit developing countries.
- **Small Island Developing States (SIDS):** Provides analytical work and technical assistance to SIDS in support of the implementation of the 2005 Mauritius Strategy for the Further Implementation of the Program of Action for the Sustainable Development of Small Island Developing States, with particular emphasis on issues of economic vulnerability and specialization.

OECD

The Organization for Economic Co-opertaion and Development (OECD) was formed in 1961 as an expansion of the Organization for European Economic Co-operation (OEEC). The OEEC developed strategies for restructuring Europe after World War II. Conversely, the OECD expanded its reach and included not only European countries, but also Canada, Mexico, Australia, New Zealand, Japan, Korea and the United States.

The OECD's goals are to promote economic stability and democracy in its member countries and in developing countries. One of the main methods that the OECD uses to analyze countries is collecting and publishing statistics on social and economic issues. These statistics are reviewed by governments and during OECD meetings to address how best to foster OECD goals.

Aim

The OECD defines itself as a forum of countries committed to democracy and the market economy, providing a setting to compare policy experiences, seek answers to common problems, identify good practices, and co-ordinate domestic and international policies. Its mandate covers economic, environmental and social issues. It acts by peer pressure to improve policy and implement "soft law"—non-binding instruments that can occasionally lead to binding treaties. In this work, the OECD cooperates with businesses, trade unions and other representatives of civil society. Collaboration at the OECD regarding taxation, for example, has fostered the growth of a global web of bilateral tax treaties.

The OECD promotes policies designed:

- to achieve the highest sustainable economic growth and employment and a rising standard of living in Member countries, while maintaining financial stability, and thus to contribute to the development of the world economy;
- to contribute to sound economic expansion in Member as well as non-member countries in the process of economic development; and
- to contribute to the expansion of world trade on a multilateral, non-discriminatory basis in accordance with international obligations.

OECD counsels are comprised of representatives from member countries. These representatives draft recommendations or international agreements on various issues. For example, in 2006, the OECD made strong recommendations to countries to adopt anti-spam policies, encouraging nations to educate both the public and industries to reduce internet spam.

At the same meeting in 2006, the OECD debated and discussed the economic future and potential of China, not a member country, and recommended that China allow more foreign investment, which is frequently held up by Chinese laws. The OECD analysis of this issue suggests that more foreign investors would increase the economic growth of China, while fostering good relationships between China and other countries. Member countries of the OECD take these recommendations back to their governments, and often these recommendations influence foreign policy.

The OECD also has influence over the issue of sustainable development. The OECD looks for solutions that allow for current economic growth without negatively impacting the economic growth and survival of future generations.

Through statistical analysis and discussion, the OECD can draft agreements, or at least strongly encourage corporate responsibility or high environmental standards and policies. It can also examine developing countries to see if they progress along sustainable lines. Education and recommendations can be offered to these countries, which if agreed upon, will further the aims of the OECD.

Not all counsel from the OECD is accepted, and some counsel is harshly criticized. Recommendations and agreements are not binding to either member or non-member countries. The OECD fails to find approval by governments opposing democracy and capitalism. Frequently, however, the OECD continues to recommend and exert pressure on governments they deem irresponsible in their policies. This can be an effective method for ultimately achieving the OECD's aims.

G-7

The G7 (also known as the G-7) is the meeting of the finance ministers from a group of seven industrialized nations. It was formed in 1976, when Canada joined the Group of Six: France, Germany, Italy, Japan, United Kingdom and United States.

An economic and political group of the seven largest industrialized nations, the powerful group of nations does not include any developing nations. The finance ministers of these countries meet several times a year to discuss economic policies. Their work is supported by regular, functional meetings of officials, including the G7 Finance Deputies.

It is not to be confused with the **G8**, which is the annual meeting of the heads of government of the aforementioned nations, plus Russia.

The G7 held a meeting on April 11, 2008, in Washington D.C., met again on October 10, 2008, in Washington D.C., and then met again on February 14, 2009, in Rome, to discuss the global financial crisis of 2007–2010. The group of finance ministers has pledged to take "all necessary steps" to help stem the crisis.

"G8" can refer to the member states or to the annual summit meeting of the G8 heads of government. The former term, G6, is now frequently applied to the six most populous countries within the European Union. G8 ministers also meet throughout the year, such as the G7/8 finance ministers (who meet four times a year), G8 foreign ministers, or G8 environment ministers.

The G8 summit is an international event which is observed and reported by news media, but the G8's relevance is unclear. The member country holding the G8 presidency is responsible for organizing and hosting the year's summit, held for three days in mid-year; and for this reason, Tony Blair and the United

Kingdom accumulated the lion's share of the credit for what went right (and wrong) at Gleneagles in 2005.

Each of the 35 G8 summit meetings could have been called a success if the events had been re-framed as venues to generate additional momentum for solving problems at the other multilateral conferences that meet throughout the year. The G8 annual summit sets the stage for what needs to be done and establishes an idea of how to do it, even if that idea is, at best, rough and patchy.

G-20 MAJOR ECONOMIES

The Group of Twenty Finance Ministers and Central Bank Governors (known as the G-20 and also the G20 or Group of Twenty) is a group of finance ministers and central bank governors from 20 economies: 19 countries plus the European Union. Recently summits meeting at level of Heads of government have been introduced. The 2010 chair country of the G-20 is South Korea.

Collectively, the G-20 economies comprise 85% of global gross national product, 80% of world trade (including EU intra-trade) and two-thirds of the world population. The G-20 is a forum for cooperation and consultation on matters pertaining to the international financial system. It studies, reviews, and promotes discussion (among key industrial and emerging market countries) of policy issues pertaining to the promotion of international financial stability, and seeks to address issues that go beyond the responsibilities of any one organization.

With the G-20 growing in stature since the 2008 Washington summit, its leaders announced on September 25, 2009, that the group will replace the G8 as the main economic council of wealthy nations.

The G-20 operates without a permanent secretariat or staff. The chair rotates annually among the members and is selected from a different regional grouping of countries. The chair is part of a revolving three-member management group of past, present and future chairs referred to as the Troika. The incumbent chair establishes a temporary secretariat for the duration of its term, which coordinates the group's work and organizes its meetings. The role of the Troika is to ensure continuity in the G-20's work and management across host years.

In 2010, there are 20 members of the G-20. These include **South Africa, Argentina, Brazil, Mexico, Canada, United States, China, Japan, South Korea, India, Indonesia, Saudi Arabia, European Union, France, Germany, Italy, Russia, Turkey, United Kingdom, Australia** etc.

G-20 Summits

The G-20 summit was created as a response both to the financial crisis of 2007–2010 and to a growing recognition that key emerging countries were not adequately included in the core of global economic discussion and governance. The G-20 summits of heads of state or government were held in addition to the G-20 Meetings of Finance Ministers and Central Bank Governors who continued to meet to prepare the Heads Summits and implement their decisions.

	Date	Host Country	Host City
I Summit	November 2008	United States	Washington, D.C.
II Summit	April 2009	United Kingdom	London
III Summit	September 2009	United States	Pittsburgh
IV Summit	June 2010	Canada	Toronto
V Summit	November 2010	South Korea	Seoul
VI Summit	2011	France	-

In addition to these 20 members, the following forums and institutions, as represented by their respective chief executive officers, participate in meetings of the G-20:

- the Managing Director of the International Monetary Fund
- the Chairman of the International Monetary Fund
- the President of the World Bank
- International Monetary and Financial Committee
- the Chairman of the Development Committee

GROUP OF 77

The Group of 77 at the United Nations is a loose coalition of developing nations, designed to promote its members' collective economic interests and create an enhanced joint negotiating capacity in the United Nations. There were 77 founding members of the organization, but the organization has since expanded to 130 member countries. The Republic of Yemen holds the Chairmanship in New York for 2010.

The group was founded on June 15, 1964 by the "Joint Declaration of the Seventy-Seven Countries" issued at the United Nations Conference on Trade and Development (UNCTAD). The first major meeting was in Algiers in 1967, where the *Charter of Algiers* was adopted and the basis for permanent institutional structures was begun. There are *Chapters of the Group of 77* in Rome (FAO), Vienna (UNIDO), Paris (UNESCO), Nairobi (UNEP) and the Group of 24 in Washington, D.C. (IMF and World Bank).

Aims of G77: The Group of 77 is the largest intergovernmental organization of developing states in the United Nations, which provides the means for the countries of the South to articulate and promote their collective economic interests and enhance their joint negotiating capacity on all major international economic issues within the United Nations system, and promote South-South cooperation for development.

Structure of G77: The operation and modalities of work of the G-77 in the various Chapters have certain minimal features in common such as a similarity in membership, decision-making and certain operating methods. A Chairman, who acts as its spokesman, coordinates the Group's action in each Chapter. The Chairmanship, which is the highest political body within the organizational structure of the Group of 77, rotates on a regional basis (between Africa, Asia and Latin America and the Caribbean) and is held for one year in all the Chapters. Currently the Republic of the Ymen holds the Chairmanship of the Group of 77 in New York for the year 2010. Ambassador Abdullah M. Alsaidi is the Permanent Representative of the Republic of Yemen to the United Nations and Chairman of the Group of 77 in New York.

The South Summit is the supreme decision-making body of the Group of 77. It is convened once in every five years. The First and the Second South Summits were held in Havana, Cuba, on 10–14 April 2000 and in Doha, Qatar, on 12–16 June 2005, respectively. In accordance with the principle of geographical rotation, the Third South Summit is due to be held in Africa in 2010.

The Annual Meeting of the Ministers for Foreign Affairs of the Group of 77 is convened at the beginning of the regular session of the General Assembly of the United Nations in New York. Periodically, Sectoral Ministerial Meetings in preparation for UNCTAD sessions and the General Conferences of **UNIDO** and **UNESCO** are convened. Special Ministerial Meetings are also called as needed such as on the occasion of the Group's 25th anniversary (Caracas, June 1989), 30th anniversary (New York, June 1994), and 40th anniversary (Sao Paulo, Brazil, June 2004). Other Sectoral Ministerial Meetings in various fields of cooperation of interest to the Group are convened, in order to pursue South-South cooperation.

Starting in 1995, the Group convened a series of sectoral meetings in the **following fields:**

- Sectoral Review Meeting of the Group of 77 on Energy, Jakarta, Indonesia, 5–7 September 1995;
- Sectoral Meeting of the Group of 77 on Food and Agriculture, Georgetown, Guyana, 15–19 January, 1996;
- South-South Conference on Trade, Investment and Finance, San Jose, 13–15 January 1997;

- High-level Conference on Subregional and Regional Economic Cooperation among Developing Countries, Bali, Indonesia, 2–5 December 1998;
- South-South High-level Conference on Science and Technology of the Group of 77, Dubai, United Arab Emirates, 27–30 October 2002;
- High-level Conference on South-South Cooperation, Marrakech, Morocco, 16–19 December 2003;
- High-level Forum on Trade and Investment, Doha, Qatar, 5–6 December 2004;
- Open-ended Intergovernmental Study Group Workshop on the Trade and Development Bank, New York, 2–3 May 2005;
- Group of Experts Meeting on Development Platform for the South, Kingston, Jamaica, 29–30 August 2005;
- Meeting of the Ministers of Science and Technology of the Member States of the Group of 77, Angra dos Reis, Rio de Janeiro, Brazil, 3 September 2006.

In addition to the Sectoral Meetings, the Intergovernmental Follow-up and Coordination Committee on Economic Cooperation among Developing Countries (IFCC), which is a plenary body consisting of senior officials, meets once every two years to review the state of implementation of the Caracas Program of Action (CPA) adopted by the Group of 77 in 1981 and the progress made in the implementation of the outcomes of the South Summits in the field of South-South cooperation.

UNESCO

UNESCO **(United Nations Educational, Scientific and Cultural Organization)** works to create the conditions for dialogue among civilizations, cultures and peoples, based upon respect for commonly shared values. It is through this dialogue that the world can achieve global visions of sustainable development encompassing observance of human rights, mutual respect and the alleviation of poverty, all of which are at the heart of UNESCO's mission and activities.

The broad goals and concrete objectives of the international community – as set out in the internationally agreed development goals, including the Millennium Development Goals (MDGs) – underpin all UNESCO's strategies and activities. Thus UNESCO's unique competencies in education, the sciences, culture and communication and information contribute towards the realization of those goals.

And on a number of overarching **objectives**:

- Attaining quality education for all and lifelong learning
- Mobilizing science knowledge and policy for sustainable development
- Addressing emerging social and ethical challenges
- Fostering cultural diversity, inter-cultural dialog and a culture of peace
- Building inclusive knowledge societies through information and communication

Activities of UNESCO

UNESCO implements its activities through the five programme areas of Education, Natural Sciences, Social and Human Sciences, Culture, and Communication and Information.

Education: UNESCO is providing international leadership in creating learning societies with educational opportunities for all; it supports research in Comparative education; and provides expertise and fosters partnerships to strengthen national educational leadership and the capacity of countries to offer quality education for all. This includes:

- Eight specialized Institutes in different topics of the sector
- UNESCO Chairs, an international network of 644 UNESCO Chairs, involving over 770 institutions in 126 countries.
- Environmental Conservation Organization
- Organization of the International Conference on Adult Education (CONFINTEA) in an interval of 12 years
- UNESCO ASPNet, an international network of 8,000 schools in 170 countries
- UNESCO also issues public 'statements' to educate the public:
- Seville Statement on Violence: A statement adopted by UNESCO in 1989 to refute the notion that humans are biologically predisposed to organized violence.

UNIDO

The United Nations Industrial Development Organization (UNIDO) is a specialized agency of the United Nations. Its mandate is to promote and accelerate sustainable industrial development in developing countries and economies in transition, and work towards improving living conditions in the world's poorest countries by drawing on its combined global resources and expertise.

The United Nations Industrial Development Organization (UNIDO), French/Spanish acronym **ONUDI**, is a specialized agency in the United Nations system, headquartered in Vienna, Austria. The Organization's primary objective is the promotion and acceleration of industrial development in developing countries and countries with economies in transition and the promotion of international industrial cooperation.

In recent years, UNIDO has assumed an enhanced role in the global development agenda by focusing its activities on poverty reduction, inclusive globalization and environmental sustainability. Our services are based on two core functions: as a global forum, we generate and disseminate industry-related knowledge; as a technical cooperation agency, we provide technical support and implement projects.

Today, the Organization is recognized as a highly relevant, specialized and efficient provider of key services in support of the interlinked challenges of reducing poverty through productive activities, promoting the integration of developing countries in global trade through trade capacity building, fostering environmental sustainability in industry, and improving access to energy.

UNIDO believes that competitive and environmentally sustainable industry has a crucial role to play in accelerating economic growth, reducing poverty and achieving the **Millennium Development Goals**. The Organization therefore works towards improving the quality of life of the world's poor by drawing on its combined global resources and expertise in the following three interrelated thematic areas:

- Poverty reduction through productive activities;
- Trade capacity-building; and
- Energy and environment.

Activities in these fields are strictly aligned with the priorities of the current United Nations Development Decade and related multilateral declarations, and reflected in the long-term vision statement, business plan and mid-term programme frameworks of UNIDO.

In order to fulfill these objectives, UNIDO

- assists developing countries in the formulation of development, institutional, scientific and technological policies and programs in the field of industrial development;
- analyzes trends, disseminates information and coordinates activities in their industrial development;
- acts as a forum for consultations and negotiations directed towards the industrialization of developing countries; and

- provides technical cooperation to developing countries for implementing their development plans for sustainable industrialization in their public, cooperative and private sectors.

UNIDO Functions and Services

UNIDO Delivers Value via Two Core Functions

- **Global Forum Facilitator:** We produce and disseminate knowledge relating to industrial development. In addition, we act as a forum for various actors in the public and private sectors, civil society organizations and the policy-making community to establish dialog and develop partnerships. Technology Cooperation Agency–We design and implement programs to support, in cooperation with our partners, sustainable industrial development efforts.
- These functions are both complementary and mutually supportive: on one hand, the experience gained in technical cooperation activities can be shared with policy-makers; on the other hand, the Organization's analytical work provides for the necessary empiric evidence to optimally unfold our technical cooperation activities.

More specifically, UNIDO delivers on its thematic priorities through the following services:

- Industrial Governance and Statistics
- Investment and Technology Promotion
- Industrial Competitiveness and Trade
- Private Sector Development
- Agro-Industries
- Sustainable Energy and Climate Change
- Montreal Protocol
- Environmental Management

In addition, UNIDO's activities are divided by:

- Geography—Focusing on least developed countries and Africa
- Sectors—Focusing on agro-based industries
- Target areas—Focusing on small and medium enterprises (SMEs)

INTERNATIONAL MONETARY FUND (IMF)

The International Monetary Fund (IMF) is the international organization that oversees the global financial system by following the macroeconomic policies of its member countries, in particular those with an impact on exchange rate and the balance of payments.

It is an organization formed with a stated objective of stabilizing international exchange rates and facilitating development through the enforcement of liberalizing economic policies on other countries as a condition for loans, restructuring or aid. It also offers highly leveraged loans, mainly to poorer countries. Its headquarters are in Washington, D.C., United States.

Key IMF Activities

The IMF supports its membership by providing:

- policy advice to governments and central banks based on analysis of economic trends and cross-country experiences;
- research, statistics, forecasts, and analysis based on tracking of global, regional, and individual economies and markets;
- loans to help countries overcome economic difficulties;
- concessional loans to help fight poverty in developing countries; and
- technical assistance and training to help countries improve the management of their economies.

More Specifically, the IMF Continues to

- provide a forum for cooperation on international monetary problems;
- facilitate the growth of international trade, thus promoting job creation, economic growth, and poverty reduction;
- promote exchange rate stability and an open system of international payments; and
- lend countries foreign exchange when needed, on a temporary basis and under adequate safeguards, to help them address balance of payments problems.

PURPOSE

The International Monetary Fund was created in July 1944, originally with 45 members, with a goal to stabilize exchange rates and assist the reconstruction of the world's international payment system. Countries contributed to a pool which could be borrowed from, on a temporary basis, by countries with payment imbalances. The IMF was important when it was first created because it helped the world stabilize the economic system. The IMF is still important because it works to improve the economies of its member countries (Inaccurate citation, does not justify assertion of importance).

The IMF provides policy advice and financing to members in economic difficulties and also works with developing nations to help them achieve macroeconomic stability and reduce poverty.

Marked by massive movements of capital and abrupt shifts in comparative advantage, globalization affects countries' policy choices in many areas, including labor, trade, and tax policies. The global economic crisis has highlighted just how interconnected countries have become in today's world economy.

The IMF describes itself as "an organization of 186 countries (as of June 29, 2009), working to foster global monetary cooperation, secure financial stability, facilitate international trade, promote high employment and sustainable economic growth, and reduce poverty".

The IMF's influence in the global economy steadily increased as it accumulated more members. The number of IMF member countries has more than quadrupled from the 44 states involved in its establishment, reflecting in particular the attainment of political independence by many developing countries and more recently the collapse of the Soviet bloc. The expansion of the IMF's membership together with the changes in the world economy has required the IMF to adapt in a variety of ways to continue serving its purposes effectively.

In 2008, faced with a shortfall in revenue, the International Monetary Fund's executive board agreed to sell part of the IMF's gold reserves. On April 27, 2008, IMF welcomed the board's decision of April 7, 2008 to propose a new framework for the fund, designed to close a projected $400 million budget deficit over the next few years. The budget proposal includes sharp spending cuts of $100 million until 2011 that will include up to 380 staff dismissals.

At the 2009 G-20 London summit, it was decided that the IMF would require additional financial resources to meet prospective needs of its member countries during the ongoing global financial crisis. As part of that decision, the G-20 leaders pledged to increase the IMF's supplemental cash tenfold to $500 billion, and to allocate to member countries another $250 billion via Special Drawing Rights.

As of May 2010 Hungary ($11.6 billion), Romania ($12.5 billion) and Ukraine (the IMF granted a $16.4-billion loan to Ukraine in 2008, of which the government has so far received $10.6 billion) are the largest borrowers of the fund.

Working with the World Bank

The IMF and the World Bank are different, but complement each other's work. Whereas the IMF's focus is chiefly on macroeconomic and financial sector issues, the World Bank is concerned mainly with longer-term development and poverty reduction. Its loans finance infrastructure projects, the reform of particular sectors of the economy, and broader structural reforms. Countries must join the IMF to be eligible for World Bank membership.

Given the World Bank's focus on antipoverty issues, the IMF collaborates closely with the Bank in the area of poverty reduction and helping countries draw up poverty reduction strategies. Other areas of collaboration include assessments of member countries' financial sectors, development of standards and codes, and improvement of the quality, availability, and coverage of data on external debt.

Cooperating with Other International Organizations

The IMF is a member of the Switzerland-based Financial Stability Board, which brings together government officials responsible for financial stability in the major international financial centers, international regulatory and supervisory bodies, committees of central bank experts, and international financial institutions. It also works with standard-setting bodies such as the Basel Committee on Banking Supervision and the International Association of Insurance Supervisors.

The IMF collaborates with the World Trade Organization (WTO) both formally and informally. The IMF has observer status at WTO meetings and IMF staff contribute to the work of the WTO Working Group on Trade, Debt, and Finance. And the IMF is involved in the WTO-led Integrated Framework for Trade-Related Technical Assistance to Least Developed Countries, whose other members are the International Trade Commission, UNCTAD, UNDP, and the World Bank.

The IMF has a Special Representative to the United Nations, located at the UN Headquarters in New York. The Special Representative facilitates the liaison between the IMF and the UN system. The general arrangements for collaboration and consultations between the IMF and the UN include areas of mutual interest, such as cooperation between the statistical services of the two organizations, and reciprocal attendance and participation at events.

DATA DISSEMINATION SYSTEMS

In 1995, the International Monetary Fund began work on data dissemination standards with the view of guiding IMF member countries to disseminate their economic and financial data to the public. The International Monetary and

Financial Committee (IMFC) endorsed the guidelines for the dissemination standards and they were split into two tiers: The General Data Dissemination System (**GDDS**) and the Special Data Dissemination Standard (**SDDS**).

The International Monetary Fund executive board approved the SDDS and GDDS in 1996 and 1997 respectively and subsequent amendments were published in a revised "Guide to the General Data Dissemination System". The system is aimed primarily at statisticians and aims to improve many aspects of statistical systems in a country. It is also part of the World Bank Millennium Development Goals and Poverty Reduction Strategic Papers.

The IMF established a system and standard to guide members in the dissemination to the public of their economic and financial data. Currently there are two such systems: General Data Dissemination System (GDDS) and its superset Special Data Dissemination System (SDDS), for those member countries having or seeking access to international capital markets.

The primary objective of the GDDS is to encourage IMF member countries to build a framework to improve data quality and increase statistical capacity building. This will involve the preparation of metadata describing current statistical collection practices and setting improvement plans. Upon building a framework, a country can evaluate statistical needs, set priorities in improving the timeliness, transparency, reliability and accessibility of financial and economic data.

INTERNATIONAL COMMODITY AGREEMENTS

International Commodity Agreements are inter-governmental arrangements concerning the production of, and trade in, certain primary products with a view to stabilizing their prices.

Commodity Agreements have been tried in different cases for quite sometime now. These commodity agreements could be used as a way of raising (or halting a fall in) the world prices of commodities, and in this way of transferring income from consuming to producing countries.

Commodity Agreements may take any of the four forms namely, quota, buffer stock, bilateral contract and multilateral contract.

Quota Agreements

Under this agreement, export quotas are determined and allocated to participating countries according to some mutually agree formula, and they undertake to restrict the export or production by a certain percentage of the basic quota decided by the central committee or council.

Quota agreements have already been tried in case of coffee and sugar, and commodities like tea and bananas have been suggested as prospective candidates for new agreement.

Quotas have the advantage, however, of being manageable. They avoid accumulation of stocks, require no financing and do not call for continuous operating decisions. In practice, quotas would probably have to be combined with buffer pools in order to provide the necessary short-run flexibility of supply.

Buffer Stock Agreements

International buffer stock agreements seek to stabilize commodity prices by maintaining the demand-supply balance.

Buffer stock agreements stabilize the price by increasing the market supply by the sale of the commodity when the price tends to rise and by absorbing the excess supply to prevent a fall in the price. The buffer stock plan requires an international agency to set a range of prices and to buy the commodity at the minimum and sell at the maximum.

The buffer stock arrangements, however, suffer from certain limitations. It can be affected only for those products, which can be stored at a relatively low cost without the danger of deterioration. Finally, the present division of the world into different currency areas would hamper the functioning of buffer pools.

Setting up and administering a buffer stock program is beset with practical difficulties:

- It is difficult to arrive at a target price range that reflects correctly the long term market trend and is agreeable to all members. Fixing a too low or high target price range will prove disastrous.
- The long run price level may change over time, requiring updating of the target price range.
- Even if the target price range is appropriately defined, the international agency may lack resources to keep the price within the range.
- The cost of holding the stocks, which includes transportation, insurance and labor expenses, tends to be very high. Sharing of such costs among the members equitably poses a problem of consensus.
- Distribution of respective gains to producers and consumers may prove to be tricky.

Bilateral / Multilateral Contracts

Bilateral contract to purchase and sell certain quantities of a commodity at agreed prices may be entered into between a major importer and exporter of the commodity. In such an agreement, an upper price and a lower price are specified. If the market price, throughout the period of the agreement, remains within these specified limits, the agreement becomes inoperative. But if the market price rises above the upper limit specified, the exporting country is obliged to sell to the importing country a certain specified quantity of the commodity at the upper price fixed by the agreement. On the other hand, if the market price falls below the lower limit specified, the importer is obliged to purchase the contracted quantity at the specified lower price.

Bilateral/multilateral agreements are usually concluded between the major suppliers and the major importers of the commodities.

Some difficulties are encountered in the implementation of multilateral contracts:

- To be effective, multilateral contract should cover a large proportion of the total trade of the members.
- The spread of minimum and maximum price should not be wide.
- If the target price does not reflect the long term equilibrium price, discrepancies will arise between supply and demand.
- The agreement provides only limited market stability, with provision for relatively easy withdrawal and entry by participating countries.

CARTELS

Existence of international cartels hampers free trade in the concerned products. International cartels are agreements between producers located in different countries or between governments of different countries to restrict competition.

Cartels are common in the market structure known as oligopoly, which is characterized, by a relatively small number of firms. As Wilson observers, "it is characteristic of this type of market that firms tacitly collude to keep out potential competitors and to reduce the degree of competition between themselves.

Cartels should be distinguished from International Commodity Agreements. The Cartel is basically a unilateral decision by producers to co-operate while a commodity agreement, in principle, includes consumers in the negotiations, although in practice consumers have little direct say in their operation.

Cartels are defined as international business agreements to regulate price, division of markets or other aspects of enterprises. An international Cartel is formed by a group of producers in the same industry based in different countries with a view to limit selling competition and to regulate the production and sales in order to earn high profits.

The major objective of a cartel is to raise price and restrict competition, it may have other goals as well.

A Cartel will be successful only if the following conditions are fulfilled:

- There are few suppliers of the commodity in the world market
- The members of the cartel have large share in the world production and supply
- There are no close substitutes for the commodity
- The price elasticity for the commodity is low
- The members strictly follow the quota and price restriction
- There is no wide variance among members on costs

Generalized System of Preferences (GSP)

The Generalized System of Preferences (GSP) is a scheme designed by the UNCTAD to encourage exports of developing countries to developed countries. Under this scheme, developed countries grant duty concession on imports of specified manufacturers and semi-manufacturers from developing countries.

The GSP facility is available only to developing countries; it is subject to certain stringent limitations. Each scheme has a safeguard clause or an escape clause to protect the sensitive sectors in its economy.

A particular item is qualified for GSP benefits only if the following conditions are satisfied:

1. The product must be included in the GSP list.
2. The country exporting the item should be declared under the GSP as a beneficiary country.
3. The value added requirements / process criteria must be compiled with.
4. The product must be imported into the GSP donor country from a GSP beneficiary country.
5. The exporter must send to his buyer/importer a certificate of origin in the prescribed form duly filled in and duly signed by him, and then certified by a designated Government authority.

Global System of Trade Preferences (GSTP)

Expansion of trade among the developing countries is viewed as an important aspect of economic cooperation among developing countries (ECDC). It is felt that trade preferences can help achieve expansion of South-South trade.

The Group of 77 ministerial conference held in New Delhi in July 1985, resolved to complete the first round of negotiations on GSTP by May 1, 1987. The agreement reached at the conference included across the board tariff preference margin of 10 per cent, the removal of reduction of non-tariff barriers, selection of specific sectors and products where trade preferences could be extended and trade creating production sharing and marketing arrangements.

The agreement of GSTP adopted at the Ministerial meeting of the developing countries of the Group of 77 held in Belgrade in April 1988 annexed a list of tariff concessions exchange amongst 48 participating countries of G77 in the first round of negotiations. India exchanged tariff concessions with 14 countries.

SUMMARY

- Economic integration schemes – also referred to as trade blocks, Regional Integration Agreement (RIAs), Regional Trade Agreements (RTAs)–is an important international business environment.
- Some people view world trade as consisting broadly of intra-regional trade. There is also talk of rationalization versus globalization of world trade.
- There are different degrees or levels of economic integration viz., free trade area, customs union, common market, economic union and full economic integration.
- The EEC, which originally comprised six nations namely Belgium, France, Federal Republic of Germany, Italy, Luxembourg and Netherlands, was brought into being on 1st January 1958, by the Treaty of Rome, 1957.
- *Static effects* are the shifting of resources from inefficient to efficient companies as trade barriers fall. *Dynamic effects* are the overall growth in the market and the impact on a company of expanding production and achieving greater economies of scale.

The EC 1992 barriers targeted for removal pertained to the following eight categories:

1. Border Control
2. Limitations on the movement of people and their right of establishment
3. Differing internal taxation regimes
4. Lack of common legal framework for business
5. Heavy and differing regulation of services
6. Divergent product regulations and standards
7. Protectionist public procurement policies

- India's main exports to EC include textiles, jute, leather and leather manufacturers, polished diamonds, engineering goods, chemicals, marine products etc. Imports include edible oils, fertilizers, dairy products, steel, capital goods, optical instruments, synthetic rubber and photo and cinematographic goods. India also receives technology, investment and development aid from EC countries.

- Euro, the common currency of European Union, was launched by 11 of the 15 members of the Union, on January 1, 1999. The exchange rates per euro determined at the time of the Euro launch were about US $1.7; British pound 0.70; Yen 133; and German mark 1.96. One Euro was equivalent to ₹49.
- NAFTA, which includes Canada, the United States, and Mexico, went into effect in 1994. NAFTA covers the following areas such Market Access, Trade rules, Services, Investment, Intellectual property, Dispute Settlement.
- Regional trade agreements among developing countries include the Latin American Free Trade Association (LAFTA), the Central American Common Market (CACM), the Andean Pact, and the Carribean Common Market (CARICOM) in Latin America; the Economic Community of West African States (ECOWAS), the Preferential Trade Area (PTA), the Economic Community of West African State (CEEAC).
- ASEAN formed by the Bangkok Declaration, 1967, by five countries, viz., Indonesia, Malaysia, The Philippines, Singapore and Thailand with a view to accelerate economic progress. The main objectives are to achieve free and open trade in the region by 2010 for the industrial nations (which generate 85 per cent of the regional trade) and by 2020 for the rest of the members.
- The Bilateral Free Trade Agreement signed by India and Sri Lanka on 28 December 1998, a large number of items will be eligible for duty free trade. India has offered to permit as much as 1000 items on zero duty from Sri Lanka and Sri Lanka will allow duty free exports of 900 items from India.
- Commodity Agreements may take any of the four forms namely, quota, buffer stock, bilateral contract and multilateral contract.
- The cartel is basically a unilateral decision by producers to cooperate while a commodity agreement, in principle, includes consumers in the negotiations, although in practice consumers have little direct say in their operation.
- The Generalized System of Preferences (GSP) is a scheme designed by the UNCTAD to encourage exports of developing countries to developed countries. The GSP facility is available only to developing countries; it is subject to certain stringent limitations.
- The Group of 77 ministerial conferences held in New Delhi in July 1985, resolved to complete the first round of negotiations on GSTP by May 1, 1987. The agreement of GSTP adopted at the Ministerial meeting of the developing countries of the Group of 77 held in Belgrade in April 1988.
- The International Monetary Fund (IMF) is the international organization that oversees the global financial system by following the macroeconomic

policies of its member countries; in particular those with an impact on exchange rate and the balance of payments.

- UNCTAD functions as a **forum for intergovernmental deliberations**, supported by discussions with experts and exchanges of experience, aimed at **consensus building**.
- The United Nations Industrial Development Organization (UNIDO) is a specialized agency of the United Nations. Its mandate is to promote and accelerate sustainable industrial development in developing countries and economies in transition, and work towards improving living conditions in the world's poorest countries by drawing on its combined global resources and expertise.
- UNESCO implements its activities through the five program areas of Education, Natural Sciences, Social and Human Sciences, Culture, and Communication and Information.
- The ultimate aim of SAFTA will be to put in place a full-fledged South Asia Economic Union on the lines of the EU. SAFTA is scheduled for launch in January 2006 and will lead to reduction of tariffs for intra-regional trade among SAARC countries.
- The basic principle of SAPTA is *overall reciprocity* and *mutuality of advantages* so as to benefit equitably all Contracting States, taking into account their respective level of economic and industrial development, the pattern of their external trade, and trade and tariff policies and systems;
- South-South cooperation was promoted only by the governments as a model to exhibit "South-solidarity" for collectively influencing the international political and economic order.
- The ultimate aim of SAFTA will be to put in place a full-fledged South Asia Economic Union on the lines of the EU.
- The G7 (also known as the G-7) is the meeting of the finance ministers from a group of seven industrialized nations. It was formed in 1976, when Canada joined the Group of Six: France, Germany, Italy, Japan, United Kingdom and United States.
- The OECD's goals are to promote economic stability and democracy in its member countries and in developing countries. One of the main methods that the OECD uses to analyze countries is collecting and publishing statistics on social and economic issues.
- The main purpose of APEC 's inception was to decrease the number of obstacles in trade and also to reduce tariffs across Asia Pacific nations. This in turn created domestic economies, which were efficient. It also gave a boost to export activities in all the APEC countries.

- IMF facilitate the growth of international trade, thus promoting job creation, economic growth, and poverty reduction; provides only limited market stability, with provision for relatively easy withdrawal and entry by participating countries.
- IMF provides policy advice and financing to members in economic difficulties and also works with developing nations to help them achieve macroeconomic stability and reduce poverty.

Chapter 4

Trade and Investment Theories

INTRODUCTION

Why study trade theory? It shows that trade in goods and services are one of the means by which countries are linked economically. Authorities in all countries wrestle with the questions of what, how much, and with whom their country should import and export. Once they make decisions, officials enact policies to achieve the desired results. These policies have an impact on business because they affect which countries can produce given products more efficiently and whether countries will permit imports to compete against their domestically produced goods and services.

Two general types of theories about trade pertain to international business:

- Descriptive Theory
- Prescriptive Theory

Descriptive Theory deals with the natural order of trade. They examine and explain trade patterns under laissez-faire conditions. Theories of this type pose questions of which products, how much, and with whom a country will trade in the absence of restrictions.

Prescriptive Theory prescribes whether governments should interfere with the free movement of goods and services among countries to alter the amount, composition and direction of trade.

Both the above theories influence international business. They provide insights favorable market locales for exports as well as potentially successful export products. They also help companies determine where to locate their production facilities because, in the absence of governmental trade restrictions, exports of given products will move from lower-cost to higher-cost production locations.

MERCANTILISM

Mercantilism, the trade theory that formed the foundation of economic thought from about 1500 to 1800. According to this theory, countries should export more than they import and, if successful, receive gold from countries that run deficits.

To export more than they imported, government imposed restrictions on most imports, and subsidized production of many products that could otherwise not compete in domestic or export markets. Some countries used their colonial possessions, such as Sri Lanka under British rule, to support their trade objective. Mercantilist theory was intended to benefit the colonial powers. The imposition of regulations based on this theory caused much discontent in the British colonies and was one cause of the American Revolution.

Enhancement of state power was, indeed, inherent in the mercantilist philosophy. A strong army, strong navy and merchant marine, control over navigation, shipping and trade routes, colonization of nations to ensure low-cost source of raw materials and agricultural products and export market for manufactures were all part of the statistic policy under mercantilism.

NON-MERCANTILISM

Non-mercantilism has emerged to describe the approach of countries that try to run favorable balances of trade in an attempt to achieve some social or political objectives. A country may attempt to maintain political influence in an area by sending more merchandise to the area that it receives from it, such as a government granting aid or loans to a foreign government to use for the purchase of the granting country's excess production.

ABSOLUTE COST THEORY

Adam Smith, developed the theory of *absolute advantage*, which holds that different countries produce some goods more efficiently than other countries; thus, global efficiency can increase through free trade. Based on this theory, he questioned why the citizens of any country should have to buy domestically produced goods when they could buy those goods more cheaply from abroad.

According to this theory, trade between two countries would be mutually beneficial if one country could produce one commodity at an absolute advantage and the other country could, in turn, produce another commodity at an absolute advantage over the first.

Table 3.1: Absolute Cost Differences

	Sri Lanka	USA
No. of units of Tea per unit of labor	15	4
No. of units of Wheat per unit of labor	5	10

In the above example, Sri Lanka has an absolute advantage in the production of Tea over USA and USA has an absolute advantage in the production of wheat over Sri Lanka. According to the above theory, Sri Lanka should specialize in the production of Tea and meet its requirement of wheat through import from USA. On the other hand, USA should specialize in the production of Wheat and meet its requirement of Tea through import from Sri Lanka.

Through specialization, countries could increase their efficiency because of three reasons:

- Labor could become more skilled by repeating the same tasks
- Labor would not lose time in switching from the production of one kind of product to another
- Long production runs would provide incentives for the development of more effective working methods.

COMPARATIVE COST THEORY

David Ricardo expanded on Adam Smith's theory of absolute advantage to develop the theory of Comparative advantage. Ricardo reasoned that there might still be global efficiency gains from trade if a country specializes in those products that it can produce more efficiently than other products – regardless of whether other countries can produce those same products even more efficiently.

The Ricardian theory is based on the following assumptions:

1. Labor is the only element of cost of production.
2. Production is subject to the law of constant returns.
3. There is no transport cost.
4. There is full employment.
5. There is perfect competition.
6. There are only two countries and two commodities.

In this example, assume that the United States is more efficient in producing both tea and wheat than Sri Lanka is. The United States has an absolute advantage in the production of both products. As in the earlier example of absolute advantage, again assume that there are only two countries and each country has a total of 100 units of resources available.

Although the United States has an absolute advantage in the production of both tea and wheat, it has a comparative advantage only in the production of wheat. This is because its advantage in wheat production is comparatively greater that its advantage in tea production.

Using two-country-two-commodity model, trade between nations can be profitable even if one of the two nations can produce both the commodities more efficiently than the other nation provided that it can produce one of these commodities with comparatively greater efficiency than the other commodity.

According to this theory, free and unrestricted trade among nations encourages specialization on a larger scale. It, thereby, tends to bring about:

- The most efficient allocation of world resources as well as maximization of world production.
- A redistribution of relative product demands, resulting in greater equality of product prices among trade nations, and
- A redistribution of relative demands to correspond with relative product demands, resulting in relatively greater equality of resource prices among trading nations.

THEORY OF COUNTRY SIZE

The theories of absolute and comparative advantage do not deal with country-by-country differences in how much and what products will be traded through specialization. However, research based on country size helps explain these differences.

VARIETY OF RESOURCES

The theory of country size says that countries with large land areas are apt to have varied climates and an assortment of natural resources, making them more self-sufficient than smaller countries. Most large countries, such as Brazil, China, India, the United States and Russia, import much less of their consumption and export much less of their production than do small countries, such as Uruguay, the Netherlands and Iceland.

TRANSPORT COSTS

Although the theory of absolute advantage ignores transport costs in trade, these costs affect large and small countries differently. Normally, the farther the distance, the higher the transport costs. The average distance between production location and markets is higher for the international trade of large countries. Most U.S. production locations and markets are more than 100 miles from the Canadian or Mexican border. In the Netherlands, however, almost all foreign production locations and markets are within 100 miles of its borders. Transport costs make it more likely that small countries will trade internationally because their costs of getting products over their borders are worth the effort.

SIZE OF ECONOMY AND PRODUCTION SCALES

Countries with large economies and high per capita incomes are more likely to produce goods that use technologies requiring long production runs. This is because these countries develop industries to serve their large domestic markets, which in turn tend to be competitive in export markets. In industries where long production runs are important for gaining competitive advantages, companies tend to locate their production in few countries, using these locations as sources of exports to other countries. Where long production runs are unimportant, companies are more apt to minimize exporting. Therefore, the technologically intensive company from a small nation may have a more compelling need to sell abroad than would a company with a large domestic market.

FACTOR-PROPORTIONS THEORY

Smith and Ricardo theories did not help to identify the types of products that would most likely give a country an advantage. Those theories assumed that the workings of the free market would lead producers to the goods they could produce more efficiently and away from those they could not produce efficiently.

Eli Heckscher and Bertil Ohlin developed the **factor-proportion theory** based on countries production factors – land, labor and capital (funds for investment in plant and equipment). This theory said that differences in countries endowments of labor compared to their endowments of land or capital explained differences in the cost of production factors. These economists proposed that if labor were abundant in comparison to land and capital, labor costs would be low relative to land and capital costs.

LAND-LABOR RELATIONSHIP

In countries in which there are many people relative to the amount of land– for example, Hong Kong and the Netherlands – land price is very high because it is in demand. Regardless of climate and soil conditions, neither Hong Kong nor the Netherlands excels in the production of goods requiring large amounts of land, such as wool or wheat. Businesses in countries such as Australia and Canada produce these goods because land is abundant compared to the number of people.

In Hong Kong the most successful industries are those in which technology permits the use of a minimum amount of land relative to the number of people employed. Clothing production occurs in multistory factories where workers share minimal space.Hong Kong does not compete in the production of automobiles, however, which requires much more space per worker.

LABOR-CAPITAL RELATIONSHIP

In countries where there is little capital available for investment and where the amount of investment per worker is low, managers might expect cheap labor rates and export competitiveness in products requiring large amounts of labor relative to capital. They can anticipate the opposite when labor is scarce.

However, the factor proportions theory assumes production factors to be homogeneous. Labor skills, in fact, vary within and among countries because people have different training and education. Training and education require capital expenditures that do not show up in traditional capital measurements, which include only plant and equipment values. When the factor proportions theory accounts for different labor groups and the capital invested to train these groups, it seems to hold.

Exports of emerging economies, though, show a high intensity of less skilled labor. This variation in labor skills among countries has led to more international specialization by task to produce a given product.

TECHNOLOGICAL COMPLEXITIES

The factor proportions analysis becomes more complicated when the same product can be produced by different methods, such as with labor or capital. Canada produces wheat in a capital-intensive way because of its abundance of low-cost capital relative to labor. In contrast, India produces wheat by using a much smaller number of machines in comparison to its abundant and cheap labor. In the final analysis managers must compare the cost in each locale based on the type of production that will minimize costs there.

THE PRODUCT LIFE CYCLE THEORY OF TRADE

Raymond Vernon's international product life cycle (PLC) theory of trade states that certain kinds of products go through a continuum, or cycle, that consists of four stages – introduction, growth, maturity and decline. The location of production to serve world markets will shift internationally depending on the stage of the cycle.

STAGE 1: INTRODUCTION

Most new products are produced in and exported from the high-income industrial countries because of their combined demand conditions and labor skills. This combination is explained in the following sections:

Innovation, Production and Sales in Same Country: Companies develop new products because there is a nearby observed need and market for them. This means that a US company is most apt to develop a new product for the US market, a French company for the French market and so on. Once a company has created a new product, theoretically it can manufacture that product anywhere in the world.

Location and Importance of Technology: Companies use technology to create new ways to produce old products, both of which can give them competitive advantages. Their abilities to harvest technology differ substantially by country, so they locate production to take advantage of technological capabilities in order to serve world markets. Almost all-new technology that results in new products and production methods originates in industrial countries.

Export and Labor: At this stage, companies may sell a small part of their production to customers in foreign markets who have heard about the new product and actively seek it. These foreign customers are mostly found in other industrial countries because they have incomes to spend on newer products. The early production is most apt to occur in industrial countries, which have high labor rates. This implies high labor input as opposed to automated production, which is more capital intensive. When production becomes highly automated, this labor becomes less competitive because unskilled labor may be quickly trained to perform highly repetitive tasks efficiently.

STAGE 2: GROWTH

As sales of the new product grow, competitors enter the market. At the same time, demand is likely to grow substantially in foreign markets, particularly in other industrial countries. In fact, demand may be sufficient to justify producing in some foreign markets to reduce or eliminate transport charges, but the output at this stage is likely to stay almost entirely in the foreign country with the additional manufacturing unit.

However, product technology may not yet be well developed because of the number of product variations introduced by competitors also trying to gain market share. So, the production process may still be labor intensive during this stage, although it is becoming less so.

STAGE 3: MATURITY

In this stage, demand begins to level off, although it may be growing in some countries and declining in others. There often is a shakeout of products such that product models become highly standardized, making cost an important competitive weapon. Because markets and technologies are widespread, the innovating country no longer has a production advantage. There are incentives to begin moving plants to emerging markets where unskilled, inexpensive labor is efficient for standardized processes. Exports decrease from the innovating country as foreign production displaces it.

STAGE 4: DECLINE

As a product moves to this stage, those factors occurring during the mature stage continue to evolve. The markets in industrial countries decline more rapidly than those in emerging markets, as affluent customers demand ever-newer products. By this time, market and cost factors have dictated that almost all production is in emerging markets, which export to the declining or small-niche markets in industrial countries.

LIMITATIONS OF PLC THEORY

1. Products that, because of very rapid innovation, have extremely short life cycles, which make it impossible to achieve cost reductions by moving production from one country to another.
2. Luxury products for which cost is of little concern to the consumer.
3. Products for which a company can use a differentiation strategy, perhaps through advertising, to maintain consumer demand without competing on the basis of price.
4. Products that require specialized technical labor to evolve into their next generation. This seems to explain the long-term US dominance of medical equipment production and German dominance in rotary printing presses.

COUNTRY SIMILARITY THEORY

The above-mentioned theories, explaining why trade takes place have focused on the differences among countries. These theories tend to explain most of the trade among dissimilar countries, such as trade between an industrial country and an emerging economy or trade between a temperate country and a tropical one.

For example, great differences in climatic conditions will lead to highly differentiated agricultural products. Countries that differ in labor or capital intensities will differ in the types of products they can produce efficiently.

Economic Similarity of Industrial Countries

This theory explains that once a company has developed a new product in response to observed market conditions in the home market, it will turn to markets it sees as most similar to those at home. In addition, markets in industrial countries can support products and their variations. Thus companies from different countries produce different product models, and each may gain some markets abroad.

Although the markets within the industrial countries might have similar demands, countries also specialize to gain acquired advantages, such as by apportioning their research efforts more strongly to some sectors than to others. The importance of industrial countries in world trade is due, in addition to specialization, to these countries economic size. In other words, these countries produce so much, there is more to sell – both domestically and internationally. Instead they mainly export primary products and labor-intensive mature products to industrial countries in exchange for new and technologically advanced products.

Similarity of Location

Although the theories regarding country differences and similarities help to explain broad world trade patterns, such as between industrial countries and emerging economies, they do little to explain specific pairs of trading relationships. For example, Finland is a major exporter to Russia because transport costs are cheap and fast compared to transport to other countries. Acer, a Taiwanese computer maker, built a plant in Finland to serve Russia because of savings compared with shipments from Asia and because Finland provided more secure storage and ease of operations that if the plant were in Russia.

But transport cost is not only factor in trade partner choice. For example, New Zealand competes with Chile, Argentina, and South Africa for out-of-season sales of apples to the Northern Hemisphere, but with a disadvantage in freight costs. It has countered this disadvantage by increasing yields, developing new premium varieties, bypassing intermediaries to sell directly to supermarkets abroad, and consolidating efforts through a national marketing board. However, such methods to overcome distance disadvantages are difficult to maintain.

Cultural Similarity

Cultural similarity, as expressed through language and religion, also helps explain much of the direction of trade. Importers and exporters find it easier to do business in a country they perceive as being similar. Likewise, historic colonial relationships explain much of the trade between specific industrial countries and emerging economies.

Similarity of Political and Economic Interests

Political relationships and economic agreements among countries may discourage or encourage trade between them or their companies. Military conflicts disrupt traditional international business trade patterns as participants divert their transportation systems and much of their productive capacity to the war effort. In addition, political animosity and transport difficulties may interfere with trading channels. The composition of trade changes from consumer goods to industrial goods, which the warring countries use to meet military objectives.

OPPORTUNITY COST THEORY

One of the main drawbacks of the Ricardian comparative cost theory was that it was based on the labor theory of value, which stated that the value or price of a commodity was equal to the amount of labor time going into the production of the commodity. Gottfried Haberler gave new life to comparative cost theory by restating the theory in terms of opportunity costs in 1933.

The opportunity cost of anything is the value of the alternatives or other opportunities, which have to be foregone in order to obtain that particular thing. For example, assume that a given amount of productive resources can produce either 10 units of cloth or 20 units of wine. Then the opportunity cost of 1 unit of cloth is 2 units of wine. Thus, the opportunity cost approach defines cost in terms of the value of the alternatives of other opportunities, which have to be foregone in order to achieve a particular thing.

To sum up, the opportunity cost theory demonstrates that trade is beneficial as long as opportunity costs differ. As far as the basis of international specialization and trade are concerned, the logic behind the comparative cost approach and the opportunity cost approach are the same.

FACTOR ENDOWMENT THEORY

This theory was developed by Swedish economist Eli Heckscher and his student Bertil Ohlin. Paul Samuelson and Wolfgang Stolper have also made significant contributions to this theory.

This theory consists of two important theorems, namely the *Heckscher-Ohlin Theorem* and the *Factor Price Equalization Theorem.*

The former theorem examines the reasons for comparative cost differences of that commodity which uses more intensively the country's more abundant factor. Whereas the later theorem examines the effect of international trade on factor prices and states that free international trade equalizes factor prices between countries, relatively and absolutely and thus serves for international factor mobility.

INVESTMENT THEORIES

A number of attempts have been made to formulate a theory to explain the international investment. A brief outline of the important attempts in this direction is given below.

MARKET IMPERFECTIONS THEORY

One of the important market imperfections approach to the explanation of the foreign investments if the *Monopolistic Advantage Theory* pro-founded by Stephen in 1960. FDI is motivated by market imperfections, which permit the multinational to exploit its monopolistic advantages in foreign markets. Hymer (1960) observers that foreign firms must possess advantages over local firms to make such investment viable and, usually the market for the sale of the product or service are imperfect.

This view is elaborated further by Kindleberger (1969) who suggests that market imperfections offer multinationals compensating advantages of magnitude that exceeds the disadvantages due to their lack of origins within a host environment, and it is the financial effects of this underpin FDI. Again, FDI is a direct outcome of imperfect markets.

Multinational firms are typically oligopolists. Virtually all multinationals enjoy considerable market power. The market in which they operate is usually one of international oligopoly with shades of monopolistic competition. In a British study, Dunning (1985) identified oligopoly as a distinguishing feature of markets in which multinationals operate, confirming many other investigators findings.

Market imperfections may be created in a number of ways:

- Internal or external economies of scale often exist, possibly due to privileged access to raw materials or to final markets, possibly from the exploitation of firm-specific knowledge assets, possibly from increases in physical production. The oligopolies, which may result, do not react, as would firms in perfectly competitive markets.
- Effective differentiation – not only to products and processes but also to marketing and organizational skills – may create substantial imperfections.
- Government policies have an impact on fiscal and monetary matters, on trade barriers and so on. Due to their stronger credit ratings, multinationals may often borrow funds in international markets at favorable rates when host government policies make domestic capital expensive or unavailable for indigenous firms.

INTERNALIZATION THEORY

Internalization theory suggests that a firm internalizes a transaction whenever the cost of using markets or contractual agreements is higher than that of organizing it internally. Applied to multinationals, the suggestion is that international markets may be difficult to organize, monitor and control. Multinationals will tend to develop and use their own internal organizational hierarchy whenever intra-firm transactions are less costly than market transactions.

The incentive to internalize depends upon the four key groups of factors:

- Industry-specific factors, for example, economies of scale, external market structure, and so on.
- Region-specific factors, for example, geographical distance and cultural differences.
- Nation-specific factors, for example, political and fiscal conditions.
- Firm-specific factors, for example, management expertise and technical know-how.

The multinational may realize valuable cost savings via the process of internalization. According to Giddy (1978), such economies may arise through bypassing any of the following:

- Concentrated markets for raw materials and arm's length supply which may be both expensive and risky.
- Imperfect markets for the firm's resources, for example as created by brand names.
- Imperfect markets for product resources, due perhaps to government imposed barriers to entry, such as tariffs.
- Imperfect markets for outputs due to monopolistic control over distribution channels–a significant factor in many small countries.

Of course, internalizing markets through FDI also imposes further costs, for example:

- Additional communication costs which will vary with geographical and cultural distance.
- The cost of operating in an unfamiliar environment.
- The cost of overcoming political and social preferences for domestically owned firms.
- The administrative cost of managing an internal market.

From the internalization point of view, multinationals are merely searchers after efficiency, ready to substitute hierarchies for markets as the balance of transaction costs changes. The internalization argument does not assume a precise, risk-adjusted analysis of markets against hierarchies – in practice such an analysis would be difficult and complex, if not impossible.

LOCATION-SPECIFIC ADVANTAGES

Hood and Young (1979) advance four factors that are relevant to the location-specific theory of FDI, which involves the multinational in seeking locations such that the differences between benefits and costs are maximized. Their four key factors are follows:

- *Labor Costs:* Real wage costs vary, not only between developing and industrialized countries, but also within these groupings. Thus low-technology international industries may logically locate in low-wage economies.
- *Marketing Factors:* FDI decisions may be affected by host country characteristics like market size, market growth, stage of development, and the presence of local competition.
- *Trade Barriers:* Such impositions are used by many host countries trying to encourage inward investment. Often multinationals set up local production facilities to protect an already developed export market when trade barriers are erected or mooted.
- *Government Policy:* This may have a significant effect on the investment climate in a particular host country, either directly through fiscal invectives, monetary policies or the regulatory regimes, or indirectly through the prevailing social environment.

ECLECTIC THEORY

The ideas summarized above about firm-specific advantages, location-specific advantages and internalization have been melded by Dunning in his eclectic theory of international production. For him, these sources of profit are competitive advantages to the multinational and are defined in the following terms:

- *Firm-specific Advantages:* The multinational possesses ownership advantages, which may be held temporarily or permanently and are held exclusively. They promise superior returns over competitors in foreign markets. Firm-specific advantages include intangible assets like expertise or patents.
- *Location-specific Advantages*: These include factors specific to a particular place and have to be used in that place. They would embrace trade barriers, which restrict import, labor advantages, natural resources, proximity to final markets, conditions of transportation and communication, favorable government intervention and cultural factors.
- *Internalization Advantages*: These include factors for which a company gains by using its ownership internally instead of buying or selling on the market from or to third parties, respectively.

Dunning formulated his main hypothesis in the following way. Given the possession of net ownership advantages over local firms, the most profitable development for the multinational is to internalize them by extending its own activities. It must then be beneficial for the multinational to combine these internalized advantages with some factor inputs in some foreign countries –

otherwise foreign markets would be served entirely by exports and home markets by home production.

Even when a firm internalizes its exclusive resources it may be able to serve a foreign market without foreign investment. Therefore, for the production to take place in the foreign country there should be some location specific advantages. One important deficiency of the Eclectic Theory is that it does not explain the foreign investment for acquisitions, which have become a very important route to internationalization.

SUMMARY

Two general types of theories about trade pertain to international business:

- Descriptive Theory
- Prescriptive Theory
- *Descriptive Theory* deals with the natural order of trade. They examine and explain trade patterns under laissez-faire conditions. Theories of this type pose questions of which products, how much, and with whom a country will trade in the absence of restrictions.
- *Prescriptive Theory* prescribes whether governments should interfere with the free movement of goods and services among countries to alter the amount, composition and direction of trade.
- **Mercantilism** theory, countries should export more than they import and, if successful, receive gold from countries that run deficits. To export more than they imported, government imposed restrictions on most imports, and subsidized production of many products that could otherwise not compete in domestic or export markets.
- **Non-mercantilism** has emerged to describe the approach of countries that try to run favorable balances of trade in an attempt to achieve some social or political objectives.
- **Absolute cost theory** defines when trade between two countries would be mutually beneficial if one country could produce one commodity at an absolute advantage and the other country could, in turn, produce another commodity at an absolute advantage over the first.
- **Comparative cost theory** defines that there is global efficiency gains from trade if a country specializes in those products that it can produce more efficiently than other products – regardless of whether other countries can produce those same products even more efficiently.
- **Theory of country size** explains the difference between variety of resources, Transport costs, size of economy and Production Scales.

- **Factor-proportion theory** based on countries production factors – land, labor and capital (funds for investment in plant and equipment). This theory said that differences in countries endowments of labor compared to their endowments of land or capital explained differences in the cost of production factors.
- **International product life cycle** (PLC) theory of trade states that certain kinds of products go through a continuum, or cycle, that consists of four stages – introduction, growth, maturity and decline.
- **Country similarity theory** describes the differences in climatic conditions will lead to highly differentiated agricultural products. Countries that differ in labor or capital intensities will differ in the types of products they can produce efficiently.
- Gottfried Haberler gave new life to comparative cost theory by restating the theory in terms of opportunity costs in 1933. The opportunity cost of anything is the value of the alternatives or other opportunities, which have to be foregone in order to obtain that particular thing.
- **Factor endowment theory** consists of two important theorems, namely the *Heckscher-Ohlin Theorem* and the *Factor Price Equalization Theorem.*
- **Market imperfections** approach to the explanation of the foreign investments if the *Monopolistic Advantage Theory* pro-founded by Stephen in 1960. FDI is motivated by market imperfections, which permit the multinational to exploit its monopolistic advantages in foreign markets.
- **Internalization theory** suggests that a firm internalizes a transaction whenever the cost of using markets or contractual agreements is higher than that of organizing it internally. Internalization depends upon the four key groups of factors: (1) industry-specific factors (2) region-specific factors (3) nation-specific factors (4) firm-specific factors.
- **Location-specific advantages** theorem four key factors are follows: (1) Labor costs (2) Marketing factors (3) Trade barriers (4) Government Policy.
- **Eclectic theory** defined in the following terms: (1) Firm-specific advantages (2) Location-specific advantages (3) Internalization advantages.

Chapter 5

International Investment Decisions

INTRODUCTION

When making an investment decision, individuals often face the problem of asymmetric information on the domestic level and, even more so, on the international level. Risk assessment firms, international organizations, and governmental agencies try to provide information in order to evaluate investments more objectively, or to make an investment in a particular country appear profitable or attractive. This provides the individual investor with additional information; however, the problem of informational asymmetries is not alleviated. Often, it remains unclear which bias is inherent in the source. Yet, the quality or objectiveness of the information is crucial to investment choices.

Compared to the average investor, diaspora members have potential access to alternative channels of information gathering. Depending on personal, political and social variables – e.g. connection to the homeland, closeness to the diaspora community in the host-country or time of migration from the homeland—their sources can be significantly different from publicly accessible information sources in a particular country.

Foreign investment decisions are typically taken using mainly economic evaluation criteria. Nowadays many companies are becoming aware that there are additional risks associated with foreign investment that arise as a direct consequence of choosing to operate in a different environment. Country risk assessment as an emerging function in international business reflects a growing recognition of the need to include an evaluation of these additional risks in any comprehensive foreign investment proposal.

A decision to undertake foreign investment in a particular country is the outcome of a decision process where projected revenues and costs are evaluated. Increased knowledge of a foreign country reduces the cost and the uncertainty of operating in a foreign market and should increase the probability of an investment made in that country. Experience creates increased market knowledge and uncertainty reduction, and experience is therefore considered an owner-specific advantage in the so-called eclectic theory of international production.

FIVE DIFFERENT WAYS COMPANIES MADE FOREIGN INVESTMENT

The **first** type of investment is taken to gain access to specific factors of production, e.g. resources, technical knowledge, material know-how, patent or brand names, owned by a company in the host country. If such factors of production are not available in the home economy of the foreign company, and are not easy to transfer, then the foreign firm must invest locally in order to secure access.

The **second** type of foreign investment is developed by **Raymond Vernon** in his product cycle hypothesis. According to this model the company shall invest in order to gain access to cheaper factors of production, e.g. low-cost labor. The government of the host country may encourage this type of FDI if it is pursuing an export-oriented development strategy. Since it may provide some form of investment incentive to the foreign company, in form of subsidies, grants and tax concessions. If the government is using an import-substitution policy instead, foreign companies may only be allowed to participate in the host economy if they possess technical or managerial know-how that is not available to domestic industry. Such know-how may be transferred through licensing. It can also result in a joint venture with a local partner.

The **third** type of investment involves international competitors undertaking mutual investment in one another, e.g. through cross-shareholdings or through establishment of joint venture, in order to gain access to each other's product ranges. As a result of increased competition among similar products and R&D-induced specialization this type of investment emerged. Both companies often find it difficult to compete in each other's home market or in third-country markets for each other's products. If none of the products gain the dominant advantage, the two companies can invest in each other's area of knowledge and promote sub-product specialization in production.

The **fourth** type of investment concerns the access to customers in the host country market. In this type of investment there are not observed any underlying shift in comparative advantage either to or from the host country. Export from the companies' home base may be impossible, e.g. certain services, or the capability to request immediate design modifications. The limited tradability of many services has been an important factor explaining the growth of investment in these sectors.

The **fifth** type of investment relates to the trade diversionary aspect of regional integration. This type occurs when there are location advantages for foreign companies in their home country but the existence of tariffs or other barriers of trade prevent the companies from exporting to the host country. The foreign companies therefore jump the barriers by establishing a local presence within the host economy in order to gain access to the local market. The local manufacturing presence need only be sufficient to circumvent the trade barriers, since the foreign company wants to maintain as much of the value-added in its home economy.

Understanding Foreign Direct Investment

Foreign direct investment (FDI) plays an extraordinary and growing role in global business. It can provide a firm with new markets and marketing channels, cheaper production facilities, access to new technology, products, skills and financing. For a host country or the foreign firm which receives the investment, it can provide a source of new technologies, capital, processes, products, organizational technologies and management skills, and as such can provide a strong impetus to economic development.

Foreign direct investment, in its classic definition, is defined as a company from one country making a physical investment into building a factory in another country. The direct investment in buildings, machinery and equipment is in contrast with making a portfolio investment, which is considered an indirect investment. In recent years, given rapid growth and change in global investment patterns, the definition has been broadened to include the acquisition of a lasting management interest in a company or enterprise outside the investing firm's home country.

In the past decade, FDI has come to play a major role in the internationalization of business. Reacting to changes in technology, growing liberalization of the national regulatory framework governing investment in enterprises, and changes in capital markets profound changes have occurred in the size, scope and methods of FDI. New information technology systems, decline in global communication costs have made management of foreign investments far easier than in the past. The sea change in trade and investment policies and the regulatory environment globally in the past decade, including trade policy and tariff liberalization, easing of restrictions on foreign investment and acquisition in many nations, and the deregulation and privatization of many industries, has probably been the most significant catalyst for FDI's expanded role.

Proponents of foreign investment point out that the exchange of investment flows benefits both the home country (the country from which the investment originates) and the host country (the destination of the investment). Opponents of FDI note that multinational conglomerates are able to wield great power over smaller and weaker economies and can drive out much local competition. The truth lies somewhere in the middle.

For small and medium sized companies, FDI represents an opportunity to become more actively involved in international business activities. In the past 15 years, the classic definition of FDI as noted above has changed considerably. This notion of a change in the classic definition, however, must be kept in the proper context. Very clearly, over 2/3 of direct foreign investment is still made in the form of fixtures, machinery, equipment and buildings. Moreover, larger multinational corporations and conglomerates still make the overwhelming percentage of FDI. But, with the advent of the Internet, the increasing role of technology, loosening of direct investment restrictions in many markets and decreasing communication costs means that newer, non-traditional forms of investment will play an important role in the future.

Within the past decade, however, there has been a dramatic increase in the number of technology startups and this, together with the rise in prominence of Internet usage, has fostered increasing changes in foreign investment patterns. Many of these high tech startups are very small companies that have grown out of research and development projects often affiliated with major universities and with some government sponsorship. Unlike traditional manufacturers, many of these companies do not require huge manufacturing plants and immense warehouses to store inventory. Another factor to consider is the number of companies whose primary product is an intellectual property right such as a software program or a software-based technology or process. Companies such as these can be housed almost anywhere and therefore making a capital investment in them does not require huge outlays for fixtures, machinery and plants.

In many cases, large companies still play a dominant role in investment activities in small, high tech oriented companies. However, unlike in the past, these larger companies are not necessarily acquiring smaller companies outright. There are several reasons for this, but the most important one is most likely the risk associated with such high tech ventures. In the case of mature industries, the products are well defined. The manufacturer usually wants to get closer to its foreign market or wants to circumvent some trade barrier by making a direct foreign investment. The major risk here is that you do not sell enough of the product that you manufactured. However, you have added additional capacity and in the case of multinational corporations this capacity can be used in a variety of ways.

High tech ventures tend to have longer incubation periods. That is, the product tends to require significant development time. In the case of software and other intellectual property type products, the product is constantly changing even before it hits the marketplace. This makes the investment decision more complicated. When you invest in fixtures and machinery, you know what the real and book value of your investment will be. When you invest in a high tech venture, there is always an element of uncertainty. Unfortunately, the recent spate of dot.com failures is quite illustrative of this point.

Therefore, the expanded role of technology and intellectual property has changed the foreign direct investment playing field. Companies are still motivated to make foreign investments, but because of the vagaries of technology investments, they are now finding new vehicles to accomplish their goals. Consider the following:

- **Licensing and Technology Transfer:** Licensing and tech transfer have been essential in promoting collaboration between the academic and business communities. Ever since legal hurdles were removed that allowed universities to hold title to research and development done in their labs, licensing agreements have helped turned raw technology into finished products that are viable in competitive marketplaces. With some help from a variety of government agencies in the form of grants for R&D as well as other financial assistance for such things as incubator programs, once timid college researchers are now stepping out and becoming cutting edge entrepreneurs. These strategic alliances have had a serious impact in several high tech industries, including but not limited to: medical and agricultural biotechnology, computer software engineering, telecommunications, advanced materials processing, ceramics, thin materials processing, photonics, digital multimedia production and publishing, optics and imaging and robotics and automation. Industry clusters are now growing up around the university labs where their derivative technologies were first discovered and nurtured. Licensing agreements allow companies to take full advantage of new and exciting technologies while limiting their overall risk to royalty payments until a particular technology is fully developed and thus ready to put new products into the manufacturing pipeline.

- **Reciprocal Distribution Agreements:** Actually, this type of strategic alliance is more trade-based, but in a very real sense it does in fact represent a type of direct investment. Basically, two companies, usually within the same or affiliated industries, agree to act as a national distributor for each other's products. The classical example is to be found in the furniture industry. A U.S.-based manufacturer of tables signs a reciprocal distribution agreement with a Spanish-based manufacturer of chairs. Both companies gain direct access to the other's distribution network without having to pay distributor support payments and other related expenses found within the distribution channel and neither company can hurt the other's market for its products. Without such an agreement in place, the Spanish manufacturer might very well have to invest in a national sales office to coordinate its distributor network, manage warehousing, inventory and shipping as well as to handle administrative tasks such as accounting, public relations and advertising.

- **Joint Venture and other Hybrid Strategic Alliances:** The more traditional joint venture is bi-lateral, that is it involves two parties who are within the same industry who are partnering for some strategic advantage. Typical reasons might include a need for access to proprietary technology that might tip the competitive edge in another competitor's favor, desire to gain access to intellectual capital in the form of ultra-expensive human resources, access to heretofore closed channels of distribution in key regions of the world. One very good reason why many joint ventures only involve two parties is the difficulty in integrating different corporate cultures. With two domestic companies from the same country, it would still be very difficult. However, with two companies from different cultures, it is almost impossible at times. This is probably why pure joint ventures have a fairly high failure rate only five years after inception. Joint ventures involving three or more parties are usually called syndicates and are most often formed for specific projects such as large construction or public works projects that might involve a wide variety of expertise and resources for successful completion. In some cases, syndicates are actually easier to manage because the project itself sets certain limits on each party and close cooperation is not always a prerequisite for ultimate success of the endeavor.

- **Portfolio Investment:** Yes, we know that you're paying attention and no we're not trying to trip you up here. Remember our definition of foreign direct investment as it pertains to controlling interest. For most of the latter part of the 20th century when FDI became an issue, a company's portfolio investments were not considered a direct investment if the amount of stock and/or capital was not enough to garner a significant voting interest amongst shareholders or owners. However, two or three companies with "soft" investments in another company could find some mutual interests and use their shareholder power effectively for management control. This is another form of strategic alliance, sometimes called "shadow alliances". So, while most company portfolio investments do not strictly qualify as a direct foreign investment, there are instances within a certain context that they are in fact a real direct investment.

Why is FDI Important for any Consideration of Going Global?

The simple answer is that making a direct foreign investment allows companies to accomplish several tasks:

- Avoiding foreign government pressure for local production.
- Circumventing trade barriers, hidden and otherwise.
- Making the move from domestic export sales to a locally-based national sales office.
- Capability to increase total production capacity.
- Opportunities for co-production, joint ventures with local partners, joint marketing arrangements, licensing, etc.

A more complete response might address the issue of global business partnering in very general terms. While it is nice that many business writers like the expression, "think globally, act locally", this often used cliché does not really mean very much to the average business executive in a small and medium sized company. The phrase does have significant connotations for multinational corporations. But for executives in SME's, it is still just another buzzword.

The simple explanation for this is the difference in perspective between executives of multinational corporations and small and medium sized companies. Multinational corporations are almost always concerned with worldwide manufacturing capacity and proximity to major markets. Small and medium sized companies tend to be more concerned with selling their products in overseas markets. The advent of the Internet has ushered in a new and very different mindset that tends to focus more on access issues. SME's in particular are now focusing on access to markets, access to expertise and most of all access to technology.

What would be Some of the Basic Requirements for Companies Considering a Foreign Investment?

Depending on the industry sector and type of business, a foreign direct investment may be an attractive and viable option. With rapid globalization of many industries and vertical integration rapidly taking place on a global level, at a minimum a firm needs to keep abreast of global trends in their industry. From a competitive standpoint, it is important to be aware of whether a company's competitors are expanding into a foreign market and how they are doing that. At the same time, it also becomes important to monitor how globalization is affecting domestic clients. New market access is also another major reason to invest in a foreign country. At some stage, export of product or service reaches a critical mass of amount and cost where foreign production or location begins to be more cost effective. Any decision on investing is thus a combination of a number of key factors including:

- assessment of internal resources,
- competitiveness,
- market analysis
- market expectations

IMPACT OF POLITICAL RISK ON FOREIGN INVESTMENT DECISIONS

Political risk may alter operating cash flows via discriminatory regulations as well as the investment via expropriation. Political risk refers to the risk that,

- political events and processes within the host country,
- changing relationships between the host and the home country, as well as between the host country and third countries, will influence the economic well-being of the parent firm.

Political risk is defined as unexpected changes in future cash flows due to political events in the host country. Political risk may thus lead to unexpected increases or decreases in future cash flows. Political risk exists because there is no legal recourse if the foreign government chooses to expropriate an asset or otherwise increase the cost for foreign firms.

The necessity and importance of foreign investment for strengthening economic stability and quickly evolving towards a developing economy in developing countries has determined interest in foreign investment decisions of multinational corporations.

Many multinational corporations consider the political risk of the host country as one of the most important determinants in investment decision making. This concern is due to the belief that unpredictability and volatility in the political environment of the host market increases the perceived risk and uncertainty experienced by the firm. In turn, this disinclines firms from entering with heavy resource commitments (e.g. wholly owned subsidiary, majority equity participation in joint venture).

Political risk is also relevant for government project decision-making, whereby government initiatives (be they diplomatic or military or other) may be complicated as a result of political risk. Whereas political risk for business may involve understanding the host government and how its actions and attitudes can impact a business initiative, government political risk analysis requires a keen understanding of politics and policy that includes both the client government as well as the host government of the activity.

TYPES OF POLITICAL RISK

Political risk can be classified as **macro** political risk and **micro** political risk.

Macro political risk is country-specific political risk and will influence all foreign firms in the host country alike. Macro risks include expropriations of all foreign firms in a country, non-discriminatory measures such as changes in tax laws, price controls, environmental regulations, and constraints which affect foreign firms only, such as limitations on the repatriation of capital, restrictions on expatriate employment and foreign ownership, and local content regulations.

Macro-level political risk looks at non-project specific risks. Macro political risks affect all participants in a given country. A common misconception is that macro-level political risk only looks at country-level political risk; however, the coupling of local, national, and regional political events often means that events at the local level may have follow-on effects for stakeholders on a macro-level. Other types of risk include government currency actions, regulatory changes, sovereign credit defaults, endemic corruption, war declarations and government composition changes. These events pose both portfolio investment and foreign direct investment risks that can change the overall suitability of a destination for investment. Moreover, these events pose risks that can alter the way a foreign government must conduct its affairs as well.

Micro political risk is specific to a certain industry, firm, or project. Political risk may affect the ownership of the assets, via full or partial forced divestitures, or the operations of the firm. Macro risk is more visible, micro risk is of more importance to firms.

A micro-level political risk report might include a full analysis of the **CFIUS (Committee on Foreign Investment in US)** regulatory climate as it directly relates to project components and structuring, as well as analysis of congressional climate and public opinion in the US toward such a deal. This type of analysis can prove crucial in the decision-making process of a company assessing whether to pursue such a deal.

The alternatives for host governments to alter the cash flows from foreign operations range from reducing cash flow due to higher taxes to completely eliminating any cash flows in case of full expropriation. Foreign governments will likely choose to do so only if the expected benefits of the expropriation or other cost to the multinational firm exceed the expected costs to the foreign government of these actions. The focus in most of the studies examining the motivation of host countries to impose political costs has been on the effects of expropriation.

The benefits of expropriation to the host country are the ownership of new productive assets. Any cash flow generated from these assets will benefit residents of the host country. The costs to the host country include foregone future investments by foreign firm's loss of skilled labor supplied by the foreign investor and loss of export markets.

POLITICAL RISK AND INSTABILITY

We have to note that there is no single universally accepted definition of political risk. It is most commonly conceived in terms of (usually host) government interference with business operation. The term 'political risk' refers to the possibility that political decisions and/or events in a country will affect the business climate in such a manner that investors will lose money or not make as much money as they expected when the investment was made.

The existing definitions of political risk focus on the concept of political risk from two different perspectives. One view political risk in terms of governmental or sovereign interference actions. This concept, which is related to all undesired outcomes of political activities of the host government with private businesses, is represented by confiscation, currency repatriation, limits to business transactions and so on. The second perspective identifies political risk as occurrences of any political events imposed upon the firm. The examples are violence, terrorism and guerilla groups.

In the process of defining political risk it is useful to distinguish it from political instability. Instability is a feature of the general environment, whereas risk is something narrower in focus which directly affects the multinational corporations. For example, political instability by an unexpected change in government leadership may not involve political risk for international business. Political stability in itself is not a sufficient guarantee to any economic activity, especially in the absence of favorable economic conditions.

Political risk may be defined more precisely, as "the application of host government policies that constrain the business operations of a given foreign investment". It may be subdivided into three main categories: transfer risk – concerning risk to capital payments, operational risk – with threats over local source or content, and ownership control risk – highlighting possibilities of expropriation or confiscation. Moreover, political risk can be defined as the risk of a strategic, financial or personnel loss of a firm because of non-market factors as macroeconomics and social policies (fiscal, monetary, trade, investment, industrial, income, labor and development) or events related to political instability (terrorism, riots, civil war, insurrection). These two-types of non-market factors can be called legal – governmental and extra legal political risk. Legal-governmental risks are caused by events that are considered illegitimate by the existing political system.

The difficulty in finding a proper and commonly accepted definition of political risk has presumably prevented many researchers from contributing to this issue and it is also troublesome for building a solid model easily applicable.

POLITICAL RISK AND FOREIGN INVESTMENT

The growing amount of resource commitment assigned to foreign investment by the increasing number of multinational corporations has generated particular interest I assessing the relationship between the foreign investment and factors influencing the investment decision. Among these factors, political conditions have demonstrated to be one of the leading factors in assessing a company's foreign direct investment in a foreign company.

Interviews and surveys of executives of multinational corporations have found political events to be one of the most important factors in foreign investment decision. In particular, executives cite the stability of the host government and the attitude of the host government toward to foreign investment as most important considerations in the investment decision.

There is a negative relationship between political instability and foreign direct investment. After controlling for the effect of economic variables on the flow of foreign investment, the statistical result supported the association between political stability and foreign direct investment is more likely to be conspicuous when there is an economically rooted conflict and the government has sufficient administrative capability to indirectly respond to it.

There are a number of political events which can cause a loss or harm to a business operating in a foreign environment. Nationalization and expropriation became the greatest fears for foreign companies in the developing world during this era. The impact of politics on business operations has almost always been seen in the negative. Unexpected political activity by guerilla or other political groups is another means of political risk. Discriminatory taxation, absence of patent protections, and limits on foreign national employment have also crucial impact on international business in foreign country.

POLITICAL RISK ASSESSMENT

A rational approach to foreign investment decision process requires a careful examination by the firm of numerous factors which relate to both the general environment of a proposed investment and the specific operating functions of the firm in that environment. The main element of the environmental analysis is the question of political risk. Most studies of dealing with political risk focus on determining the variables composing that specific risk, or aim to find an association between political events and foreign investment. The significance of political risk is generally acknowledged, but the studies that analyze it are too often vague and difficult to examine and apply in practice.

Analysts providing political risk assessments to multinational corporations have attempted to overcome the problems of accurately predicting future scenarios which incorporate the dualistic, and often incompatible, components of academic theory and business clarity. Various political risk analysis approaches are used either by in-house or outside specialists. These range from qualitative, subjective, and discursive briefings by respected "experts" at one end of the spectrum, to quantitative computer-based assessments drawn from a numerical ranking of various societal variables. The more sophisticated quantitative approaches are not significantly different from econometric forecasting used by economists; political risk analysis instead tracks political trends with multivariate data analysis techniques. Objective and subjective methodologies can be integrated in order to allow for the best features of management science to be combined with insights and intuition of regional experts.

Traditional studies assessing political risk and its relation with foreign investment have taken into consideration a variety of data from different countries and industries. This generic perspective has led to a failure in determining reliable assessments of the dimension of political risk and its relationship with investments from outside the host country. Political risk assessment must address both the peculiar characteristics of the host country and attribute of the investment project. The project plays a critical role in determining potential risks because different projects can be differently affected by the political events of a host country.

Some industry types may be more vulnerable than others to specific problems in a country's political economy, especially if political stability is the major concern. The multinational corporations belonging to different industries do not perceive the same degree of risk when facing the same political turmoil in a given country.

MANAGERS' PERCEPTION ON POLITICAL RISK

The assessment of political risk and more importantly, investment decision, depend upon prevailing attitudes, first impressions, and generalization on single events occurring in the host country. Most managers' understanding of the concept of political risk, their assessment and evaluation of politics, and the manner in which they integrate political information into decision making are all rather general, subjective and superficial. Many empirical studies supported that the evaluation of political risk is based on generalization and impressionistic knowledge of a developing nation. Experience indicated the executive responsible for international operations of multinational companies rely very little on systematic environmental scanning methods. Executives' attitudes play a major role in their evaluation of risk and profitability of the investment opportunities.

Political risk assessments are not necessarily based on structured decision-making processes. Often times, managers are not provided with, or are unable to interpret, the information required to make the optimal choice.

POLITICAL RISK MITIGATION

Companies may have a **Chief Risk Officer** who is charged with managing political risk or, in many cases, this job falls to the **Chief Financial Officer.**

At the macro-level, political risk mitigation largely involves understanding political uncertainties of the operating environment and the risks faced by all business operations in individual countries. Such information can come in the form of customized analysis or in-depth subject matter reporting; information that can enable an investor or firm to calibrate their risk appetite. Mitigation tactics involve both macro and micro level strategies. A recent article on the subject suggested that political risk mitigation should not simply revolve around the decision to enter or avoid a given country's marketplace, but should rather center on the pragmatic usage of contingency planning, intellectual property safeguards, risk diversification, and sound exit planning to guard against uncertainty.

At the micro-level, political risk insurance and hedges play a larger role. **MIGA (Multilateral Investment Guarantee Agency)** and **OPIC (Overseas Private Investment Corporation)**, both public sector insurers, provide project-specific political risk insurance while private market insurers can provide cover for projects as well as a portfolio of investments. This type of insurance usually outlines specific triggers, such as expropriation or breach of contract by a local party, which entitle the insured entity to a pay-out after relinquishing control of the insured project to the insurer.

Political risk insurance, however, often involves premiums which must factor in considerable uncertainty and the threat that arbitrary decisions will affect the value of insured property. Policies therefore can be expensive and are manuscripted after extensive negotiations. An experienced and specialist broker can assess the availability of appropriate cover from private and public insurers and then, based on their experience and expertise, negotiate appropriate policies. Businesses can also purchase hedges, which could be derivative instruments, which allow them to reduce risk by selecting a level of return based on a given set of outcomes.

Political risk mitigation takes place before, during, and after an investment. Prior to investment, businesses can perform due diligence related to local partners and carefully word and structure their contracts. While a project is on-going, the investor may benefit from building local political leverage through community activities. After a risk has been realized, its effects may be mitigated through post-hoc litigation and retaliation, as well as the implementation of a previously developed contingency plan, or exit from the market.

SOURCES OF FUNDS

Sourcing money may be done for a variety of reasons. Traditional areas of need may be for capital asset acquirement - new machinery or the construction of a new building or depot. The development of new products can be enormously costly and here again capital may be required. Normally, such developments are financed internally, whereas capital for the acquisition of machinery may come from external sources. In this day and age of tight liquidity, many organizations have to look for short term capital in the way of overdraft or loans in order to provide a cash flow cushion. Interest rates can vary from organization to organization and also according to purpose.

Funds are typically defined as Working Capital or cash. Sources of working capital include: (1) working capital provided from operations (net income plus non-working capital expenses less non-working capital revenue); (2) decrease in Non-current Assets; (3) increase in non-current liabilities; and (4) increase in stockholders' equity. If funds are defined as cash rather than working capital, the following two additional sources of funds are used: (1) decrease in current assets other than cash; and (2) increase in current liabilities.

A company might raise new funds from the following sources:

- The capital markets
- Loan stock
- Retained earnings
- Bank borrowing
- Government sources
- Business expansion scheme funds
- Venture capital
- Franchising

Ordinary (Equity) Shares

Ordinary shares are issued to the owners of a company. They have a nominal or 'face' value, typically of $1 or 50 cents. The market value of a quoted company's shares bears no relationship to their nominal value, except that when ordinary shares are issued for cash, the issue price must be equal to or be more than the nominal value of the shares.

Deferred Ordinary Shares

Deferred ordinary shares are a form of ordinary shares, which are entitled to a dividend only after a certain date or if profits rise above a certain amount. Voting rights might also differ from those attached to other ordinary shares.

Ordinary shareholders put funds into their company:

(a) by paying for a new issue of shares

(b) through retained profits.

Simply retaining profits, instead of paying them out in the form of dividends, offers an important, simple low-cost source of finance, although this method may not provide enough funds, for example, if the firm is seeking to grow.

A new issue of shares might be made in a variety of different circumstances:

(a) The company might want to raise more cash. If it issues ordinary shares for cash, should the shares be issued pro-rata to existing shareholders, so that control or ownership of the company is not affected? If, for example, a company with 200,000 ordinary shares in issue decides to issue 50,000 new shares to raise cash, should it offer the new shares to existing shareholders, or should it sell them to new shareholders instead?

   (i) If a company sells the new shares to existing shareholders in proportion to their existing shareholding in the company, we have a *rights issue.* In the example above, the 50,000 shares would be issued as a one-in-four rights issue, by offering shareholders one new share for every four shares they currently hold.

   (ii) If the number of new shares being issued is small compared to the number of shares already in issue, it might be decided instead to sell them to new shareholders, since ownership of the company would only be minimally affected.

(b) The company might want to issue shares partly to raise cash, but more importantly to float' its shares on a stick exchange.

(c) The company might issue new shares to the shareholders of another company, in order to take it over.

New Shares Issues

A company seeking to obtain additional equity funds may be:

(a) an unquoted company wishing to obtain a Stock Exchange quotation.

(b) an unquoted company wishing to issue new shares, but without obtaining a Stock Exchange quotation.

(c) a company which is already listed on the Stock Exchange wishing to issue additional new shares.

The methods by which an unquoted company can obtain a quotation on the stock market are:

(a) an offer for sale

(b) a prospectus issue

(c) a placing

(d) an introduction.

Offers for Sale

An offer for sale is a means of selling the shares of a company to the public.

(a) An unquoted company may issue shares, and then sell them on the Stock Exchange, to raise cash for the company. All the shares in the company, not just the new ones, would then become marketable.

(b) Shareholders in an unquoted company may sell some of their existing shares to the general public. When this occurs, the company is not raising any new funds, but just providing a wider market for its existing shares (all of which would become marketable), and giving existing shareholders the chance to cash in some or all of their investment in their company.

When companies 'go public' for the first time, a 'large' issue will probably take the form of an offer for sale. A smaller issue is more likely to be a placing, since the amount to be raised can be obtained more cheaply if the issuing house or other sponsoring firm approaches selected institutional investors privately.

Rights Issues

A rights issue provides a way of raising new share capital by means of an offer to existing shareholders, inviting them to subscribe cash for new shares in proportion to their existing holdings.

For example, a rights issue on a one-for-four basis at 280c per share would mean that a company is inviting its existing shareholders to subscribe for one new share for every four shares they hold, at a price of 280c per new share.

A company making a rights issue must set a price which is low enough to secure the acceptance of shareholders, who are being asked to provide extra funds, but not too low, so as to avoid excessive dilution of the earnings per share.

Preference Shares

Preference shares have a fixed percentage dividend before any dividend is paid to the ordinary shareholders. As with ordinary shares a preference dividend can only be paid if sufficient distributable profits are available, although with 'cumulative' preference shares the right to an unpaid dividend is carried forward to later years. The arrears of dividend on cumulative preference shares must be paid before any dividend is paid to the ordinary shareholders.

From the company's point of view, **preference shares** are advantageous in that:

- Dividends do not have to be paid in a year in which profits are poor, while this is not the case with interest payments on long term debt (loans or debentures).
- Since they do not carry voting rights, preference shares avoid diluting the control of existing shareholders while an issue of equity shares would not.
- Unless they are redeemable, issuing preference shares will lower the company's gearing. Redeemable preference shares are normally treated as debt when gearing is calculated.
- The issue of preference shares does not restrict the company's borrowing power, at least in the sense that preference share capital is not secured against assets in the business.
- The non-payment of dividend does not give the preference shareholders the right to appoint a receiver, a right which is normally given to debenture holders.

However, dividend payments on preference shares are not tax deductible in the way that interest payments on debt are. Furthermore, for preference shares to be attractive to investors, the level of payment needs to be higher than for interest on debt to compensate for the additional risks.

For the investor, preference shares are less attractive than loan stock because:

- they cannot be secured on the company's assets.
- the dividend yield traditionally offered on preference dividends has been much too low to provide an attractive investment compared with the interest yields on loan stock in view of the additional risk involved.

Loan Stock

Loan stock is long-term debt capital raised by a company for which interest is paid, usually half yearly and at a fixed rate. Holders of loan stock are therefore long-term creditors of the company.

Loan stock has a nominal value, which is the debt owed by the company, and interest is paid at a stated "coupon yield" on this amount. For example, if a company issues 10% loan stocky the coupon yield will be 10% of the nominal value of the stock, so that $100 of stock will receive $10 interest each year. The rate quoted is the gross rate, before tax.

Debentures are a form of loan stock, legally defined as the written acknowledgment of a debt incurred by a company, normally containing provisions about the payment of interest and the eventual repayment of capital.

Debentures with a Floating Rate of Interest

These are debentures for which the coupon rate of interest can be changed by the issuer, in accordance with changes in market rates of interest. They may be attractive to both lenders and borrowers when interest rates are volatile.

Security

Loan stock and debentures will often be *secured.* Security may take the form of either a *fixed charge* or a *floating charge.*

(a) **Fixed Charge;** Security would be related to a specific asset or group of assets, typically land and buildings. The company would be unable to dispose of the asset without providing a substitute asset for security, or without the lender's consent.

(b) **Floating Charge;** With a floating charge on certain assets of the company (for example, stocks and debtors), the lender's security in the event of a default payment is whatever assets of the appropriate class the company then owns (provided that another lender does not have a prior charge on the assets). The company would be able, however, to dispose of its assets as it chose until a default took place. In the event of a default, the lender would probably appoint a receiver to run the company rather than lay claim to a particular asset.

The Redemption of Loan Stock

Loan stock and debentures are usually redeemable. They are issued for a term of ten years or more, and perhaps 25 to 30 years. At the end of this period, they will "mature" and become redeemable (at par or possibly at a value above par).

Most redeemable stocks have an earliest and latest redemption date. For example, 18% Debenture Stock 2007/09 is redeemable, at any time between the earliest specified date (in 2007) and the latest date (in 2009). The issuing company can choose the date. The decision by a company when to redeem a debt will depend on:

- how much cash is available to the company to repay the debt.
- the nominal rate of interest on the debt. If the debentures pay 18% nominal interest and the current rate of interest is lower, say 10%, the company may try to raise a new loan at 10% to redeem the debt which costs 18%. On the other hand, if current interest rates are 20%, the company is unlikely to redeem the debt until the latest date possible, because the debentures would be a cheap source of funds.

There is no guarantee that a company will be able to raise a new loan to pay off a maturing debt, and one item to look for in a company's balance sheet is the redemption date of current loans, to establish how much new finance is likely to be needed by the company, and when.

Mortgages are a specific type of secured loan. Companies place the title deeds of freehold or long leasehold property as security with an insurance company or mortgage broker and receive cash on loan, usually repayable over a specified period. Most organizations owning property which is unencumbered by any charge should be able to obtain a mortgage up to two thirds of the value of the property.

As far as companies are concerned, debt capital is a potentially attractive source of finance because interest charges reduce the profits chargeable to corporation tax.

Retained Earnings

For any company, the amount of earnings retained within the business has a direct impact on the amount of dividends. Profit re-invested as retained earnings is profit that could have been paid as a dividend. The major reasons for using retained earnings to finance new investments, rather than to pay higher dividends and then raise new equity for the new investments, are as follows:

(a) The management of many companies believes that retained earnings are funds which do not cost anything, although this is not true. However, it is true that the use of retained earnings as a source of funds does not lead to a payment of cash.

(b) The dividend policy of the company is in practice determined by the directors. From their standpoint, retained earnings are an attractive source of finance because investment projects can be undertaken without involving either the shareholders or any outsiders.

(c) The use of retained earnings as opposed to new shares or debentures avoids issue costs.

(d) The use of retained earnings avoids the possibility of a change in control resulting from an issue of new shares.

Another factor that may be of importance is the financial and taxation position of the company's shareholders. If, for example, because of taxation considerations, they would rather make a capital profit (which will only be taxed when shares are sold) than receive current income, then finance through retained earnings would be preferred to other methods.

A company must restrict its self-financing through retained profits because shareholders should be paid a reasonable dividend, in line with realistic expectations, even if the directors would rather keep the funds for re-investing. At the same time, a company that is looking for extra funds will not be expected by investors (such as banks) to pay generous dividends, nor over-generous salaries to owner-directors.

Bank Lending

Borrowings from banks are an important source of finance to companies. Bank lending is still mainly short term, although medium-term lending is quite common these days.

Short term lending may be in the form of:

(a) an overdraft, which a company should keep within a limit set by the bank. Interest is charged (at a variable rate) on the amount by which the company is overdrawn from day to day;

(b) a short-term loan, for up to three years.

Medium-term loans are loans for a period of from three to ten years. The rate of interest charged on medium-term bank lending to large companies will be a set margin, with the size of the margin depending on the credit standing and riskiness of the borrower. A loan may have a fixed rate of interest or a variable interest rate, so that the rate of interest charged will be adjusted every three, six, nine or twelve months in line with recent movements in the Base Lending Rate.

Lending to smaller companies will be at a margin above the bank's base rate and at either a variable or fixed rate of interest. Lending on overdraft is always at a variable rate. A loan at a variable rate of interest is sometimes referred to as a *floating rate loan.* Longer-term bank loans will sometimes be available, usually for the purchase of property, where the loan takes the form of a mortgage. When a banker is asked by a business customer for a loan or overdraft facility, he will consider several factors, known commonly by the mnemonic PARTS.

- **Purpose:** The purpose of the loan. A loan request will be refused if the purpose of the loan is not acceptable to the bank.
- **Amount:** The amount of the loan. The customer must state exactly how much he wants to borrow. The banker must verify, as far as he is able to do so, that the amount required to make the proposed investment has been estimated correctly.
- **Repayment:** How will the loan be repaid? Will the customer be able to obtain sufficient income to make the necessary repayments?
- **Term:** What would be the duration of the loan? Traditionally, banks have offered short-term loans and overdrafts, although medium-term loans are now quite common.
- **Security:** Does the loan require security? If so, is the proposed security adequate?

Leasing

A lease is an agreement between two parties, the "lessor" and the "lessee". The lessor owns a capital asset, but allows the lessee to use it. The lessee makes payments under the terms of the lease to the lessor, for a specified period of time.

Leasing is, therefore, a form of rental. Leased assets have usually been plant and machinery, cars and commercial vehicles, but might also be computers and office equipment. There are two basic forms of lease: "operating leases" and "finance leases".

Operating Leases

Operating leases are rental agreements between the lessor and the lessee whereby:

(a) the lessor supplies the equipment to the lessee.

(b) the lessor is responsible for servicing and maintaining the leased equipment.

(c) the period of the lease is fairly short, less than the economic life of the asset, so that at the end of the lease agreement, the lessor can either

  (i) lease the equipment to someone else, and obtain a good rent for it, or

  (ii) sell the equipment secondhand.

Finance Leases

Finance leases are lease agreements between the user of the leased asset (the lessee) and a provider of finance (the lessor) for most, or all, of the asset's expected useful life.

Suppose that a company decides to obtain a company car and finance the acquisition by means of a finance lease. A car dealer will supply the car. A finance house will agree to act as lessor in a finance leasing arrangement, and so will purchase the car from the dealer and lease it to the company. The company will take possession of the car from the car dealer, and make regular payments (monthly, quarterly, six monthly or annually) to the finance house under the terms of the lease.

Other important characteristics of a finance lease:

(a) The lessee is responsible for the upkeep, servicing and maintenance of the asset. The lessor is not involved in this at all.

(b) The lease has a primary period, which covers all or most of the economic life of the asset. At the end of the lease, the lessor would not be able to lease the asset to someone else, as the asset would be worn out. The lessor must, therefore, ensure that the lease payments during the primary period pay for the full cost of the asset as well as providing the lessor with a suitable return on his investment.

(c) It is usual at the end of the primary lease period to allow the lessee to continue to lease the asset for an indefinite secondary period, in return for a very low nominal rent. Alternatively, the lessee might be allowed to sell the asset on the lessor's behalf (since the lessor is the owner) and to keep most of the sale proceeds, paying only a small percentage (perhaps 10%) to the lessor.

Hire Purchase

Hire purchase is a form of instalment credit. Hire purchase is similar to leasing, with the exception that ownership of the goods passes to the hire purchase customer on payment of the final credit instalment, whereas a lessee never becomes the owner of the goods.

Hire purchase agreements usually involve a finance house.

(i) The supplier sells the goods to the finance house.

(ii) The supplier delivers the goods to the customer who will eventually purchase them.

(iii) The hire purchase arrangement exists between the finance house and the customer.

The finance house will always insist that the hirer should pay a deposit towards the purchase price. The size of the deposit will depend on the finance company's policy and its assessment of the hirer. This is in contrast to a finance lease, where the lessee might not be required to make any large initial payment.

An industrial or commercial business can use hire purchase as a source of finance. With industrial hire purchase, a business customer obtains hire purchase finance from a finance house in order to purchase the fixed asset. Goods bought by businesses on hire purchase include company vehicles, plant and machinery, office equipment and farming machinery.

Government Assistance

The government provides finance to companies in cash grants and other forms of direct assistance, as part of its policy of helping to develop the national economy, especially in high technology industries and in areas of high unemployment. For example, the Indigenous Business Development Corporation of Zimbabwe (IBDC) was set up by the government to assist small indigenous businesses in that country.

Venture Capital

Venture capital is money put into an enterprise which may all be lost if the enterprise fails. A businessman starting up a new business will invest venture capital of his own, but he will probably need extra funding from a source other than his own pocket. However, the term 'venture capital' is more specifically associated with putting money, usually in return for an equity stake, into a new business, a management buy-out or a major expansion scheme.

The institution that puts in the money recognizes the gamble inherent in the funding. There is a serious risk of losing the entire investment, and it might take a long time before any profits and returns materialize. But there is also the prospect of very high profits and a substantial return on the investment. A venture capitalist will require a high expected rate of return on investments, to compensate for the high risk.

A venture capital organization will not want to retain its investment in a business indefinitely, and when it considers putting money into a business venture, it will also consider its "exit", that is, how it will be able to pull out of the business eventually (after five to seven years, say) and realize its profits. Examples of venture capital organizations are: Merchant Bank of Central Africa Ltd. and Anglo American Corporation Services Ltd.

Franchising

Franchising is a method of expanding business on less capital than would otherwise be needed. For suitable businesses, it is an alternative to raising extra capital for growth. Franchisors include Budget Rent-a-Car, Wimpy, Nando's Chicken and Chicken Inn.

Under a franchising arrangement, a franchisee pays a franchisor for the right to operate a local business, under the franchisor's trade name. The franchisor must bear certain costs (possibly for architect's work, establishment costs, legal costs, marketing costs and the cost of other support services) and will charge the franchisee an initial franchise fee to cover set-up costs, relying on the subsequent regular payments by the franchisee for an operating profit. These regular payments will usually be a percentage of the franchisee's turnover.

Although the franchisor will probably pay a large part of the initial investment cost of a franchisee's outlet, the franchisee will be expected to contribute a share of the investment himself. The franchisor may well help the franchisee to obtain loan capital to provide his-share of the investment cost.

The advantages of franchises to the firm franchisor are as follows:

- The capital outlay needed to expand the business is reduced substantially.
- The image of the business is improved because the franchisees will be motivated to achieve good results and will have the authority to take whatever action they think fit to improve the results firm.

The advantage of a franchise to a franchisee is that he obtains ownership of a business for an agreed number of years (including stock and premises, although premises might be leased from the franchisor) together with the backing of a large organisation's marketing effort and experience. The franchisee is able to avoid some of the mistakes of many small businesses, because the franchisor has already learned from its own past mistakes and developed a scheme that works.

EXCHANGE RATE RISK AND MANAGEMENT

DEFINITION

The risk that a business' operations or an investment's value will be affected by changes in exchange rates. For example, if money must be converted into a different currency to make a certain investment, changes in the value of the currency relative to the American dollar will affect the total loss or gain on the investment when the money is converted back. This risk usually affects businesses, but it can also affect individual investors who make international investments also called currency risk.

Exchange rate risk management is an integral part of every firm's decisions about foreign currency exposure. Currency risk hedging strategies entail eliminating or reducing this risk, and require understanding of both the ways that the exchange rate risk could affect the operations of economic agents and techniques to deal with the consequent risk implications. Selecting the appropriate hedging strategy is often a daunting task due to the complexities involved in measuring accurately current risk exposure and deciding on the appropriate degree of risk exposure that ought to be covered. The need for currency risk management started to arise after the breakdown of the Bretton Woods system and the end of the US dollar peg to gold in 1973.

The issue of currency risk management for non-financial firms is independent from their core business and is usually dealt with by their corporate treasuries. Most multinational firms also have risk committees to oversee the treasury's strategy in managing the exchange rate (and interest rate) risk. This shows the importance that firms attach to risk management issues and techniques. Conversely, international investors usually manage their exchange rate risk independently from the underlying assets and/or liabilities. Since their currency exposure is related to translation risks on assets and liabilities denominated in foreign currencies, they tend to consider currencies as a separate asset class requiring a currency overlay mandate.

A common definition of exchange rate risk relates to the effect of unexpected exchange rate changes on the value of the firm. In particular, it is defined as the possible direct loss (as a result of an unhedged exposure) or indirect loss in the firm's cash flows, assets and liabilities, net profit and, in turn, its stock market value from an exchange rate move. To manage the exchange rate risk inherent in every multinational firm's operations, a firm needs to determine the specific type of current risk exposure, the hedging strategy and the available instruments to deal with these currency risks.

Multinational firms are participants in currency markets by virtue of their inter-national transactions. To measure the impact of exchange rate movements on a firm that is involved in foreign-currency denominated operations, i.e., the implied Value-at-Risk (VaR) from exchange rate moves, we need to identify the type of risks that the firm is exposed to and the amount of risk encountered.

TYPES OF EXCHANGE RATE RISK

- **Transaction risk**, which is basically cash flow risk and deals with the effect of ex-change rate moves on transactional account exposure related to receivables (export contracts), payables (import contracts) or repatriation of dividends. An exchange rate change in the currency of denomination of any such contract will result in a direct transaction exchange rate risk to the firm;

- **Translation risk,** which is basically balance sheet exchange rate risk and relates exchange rate moves to the valuation of a foreign subsidiary and, in turn, to the consolidation of a foreign subsidiary to the parent company's balance sheet. Translation risk for a foreign subsidiary is usually measured by the exposure of net assets (assets less liabilities) to potential exchange rate moves. In consolidating financial statements, the translation could be done either at the end-of-the-period exchange rate or at the average exchange rate of the period, depending on the accounting regulations affecting the parent company. Thus, while income statements are usually translated at the average exchange rate over the period, balance sheet exposures of foreign subsidiaries are often translated at the prevailing current exchange rate at the time of consolidation; and
- **Economic risk,** which reflects basically the risk to the firm's present value of future operating cash flows from exchange rate movements. In essence, economic risk concerns the effect of exchange rate changes on revenues (domestic sales and exports) and operating expenses (cost of domestic inputs and imports). Economic risk is usually applied to the present value of future cash flow operations of a firm's parent company and foreign subsidiaries. Identification of the various types of currency risk, along with their measurement, is essential to develop a strategy for managing currency risk.

Measurement of Exchange Rate Risk

After defining the types of exchange rate risk that a firm is exposed to, a crucial aspect of a firm's exchange rate risk management decisions is the measurement of these risks. Measuring currency risk may prove difficult, at least with regards to translation and economic risk. At present, a widely-used method is the value-at-risk (VaR) model. Broadly, value at risk is defined as the maximum loss for a given exposure over a given time horizon with z% confidence.

The VaR methodology can be used to measure a variety of types of risk, helping firms in their risk management. However, the VaR does not define what happens to the exposure for the (100 – z) % point of confidence, i.e., the worst case scenario. Since the VaR model does not define the maximum loss with 100% confidence, firms often set operational limits, such as nominal amounts or stop loss orders, in addition to VaR limits, to reach the highest possible coverage.

Value-At-Risk Calculation

The VaR measure of exchange rate risk is used by firms to estimate the riskiness of a foreign exchange position resulting from a firm's activities, including the foreign exchange position of its treasury, over a certain time period under normal conditions.

The VaR calculation depends on three parameters:

- The holding period, i.e., the length of time over which the foreign exchange position is planned to be held. The typical holding period is 1 day.
- The confidence level at which the estimate is planned to be made. The usual confidence levels are 99% and 95%.
- The unit of currency to be used for the denomination of the VaR.

Assuming a holding period of x days and a confidence level of y%, the VaR measures what will be the maximum loss (i.e., the decrease in the market value of a foreign exchange position) over x days, if the x-days period is not one of the (100-y)% x-days periods that are the worst under normal conditions. Thus, if the foreign exchange position has a 1-day VaR of $10 million at the 99% confidence level, the firm should expect that, with a probability of 99%, the value of this position will decrease by no more than $10 million during 1 day, provided that usual conditions will prevail over that 1 day. In other words, the firm should expect that the value of its foreign exchange rate position will decrease by no more than $10 million on 99 out of 100 usual trading days, or by more than $10 million on 1 out of every 100 usual trading days.

To calculate the VaR, there exists a variety of models. Among them, the more widely-used are: (1) the **historical simulation**, which assumes that currency returns on a firm's foreign exchange position will have the same distribution as they had in the past; (2) **the variance-covariance model**, which assumes that currency returns on a firm's total foreign exchange position are always (jointly) normally distributed and that the change in the value of the foreign exchange position is linearly dependent on all currency returns; and (3) **Monte Carlo simulation**, which assumes that future currency returns will be randomly distributed.

Historical Simulation Model

The historical simulation is the simplest method of calculation. This involves running the firm's current foreign exchange position across a set of historical exchange rate changes to yield a distribution of losses in the value of the foreign exchange position, say 1,000, and then computing a percentile (the VaR). Thus, assuming a 99% confidence level and a 1-day holding period, the VaR could be computed by sorting in ascending order the 1,000 daily losses and taking the 11th largest loss out of the 1,000 (since the confidence level implies that 1 per cent of losses–10 losses –should exceed the VaR). The main benefit of this method is that it does not assume a normal distribution of currency returns, as it is well documented that these returns are not normal but rather leptokurtic. Its shortcomings, however, are that this calculation requires a large database and is computationally intensive.

Variance-Covariance Model

The variance-covariance model assumes that (1) the change in the value of a firm's total foreign exchange position is a linear combination of all the changes in the values of individual foreign exchange positions, so that also the total currency return is linearly dependent on all individual currency returns; and (2) the currency returns are jointly normally distributed. Thus, for a 99% confidence level, the VaR can be calculated as:

$$VaR = -Vp\ (Mp + 2.33\ Sp)$$

where Vp is the initial value (in currency units) of the foreign exchange position

- Mp is the mean of the currency return on the firm's total foreign exchange position, which is a weighted average of individual foreign exchange positions.
- Sp is the standard deviation of the currency return on the firm's total foreign exchange position, which is the standard deviation of the weighted transformation of the variance-covariance matrix of individual foreign exchange positions (note that the latter includes the correlations of individual foreign exchange positions).

While the variance-covariance model allows for a quick calculation, its drawbacks include the restrictive assumptions of a normal distribution of currency returns and a linear combination of the total foreign exchange position. Note, however, that the normality assumption could be relaxed. When a non-normal distribution is used instead, the computational cost would be higher due to the additional estimation of the confidence interval for the loss exceeding the VaR.

Monte-Carlo Simulation

Monte-Carlo simulation usually involves principal components analysis of the variance-covariance model, followed by random simulation of the components. While its main advantages include its ability to handle any underlying distribution and to more accurately assess the VaR when non-linear currency factors are present in the foreign exchange position (e.g., options), its serious drawback is the computationally intensive process.

Management of Exchange Rate Risk

After identifying the types of exchange rate risk and measuring the associated risk exposure, a firm needs to decide whether or not to hedge these risks. In international finance, the issue of the appropriate strategy to manage (hedge) the different types of exchange rate risk has yet to be settled. In practice, however, corporate treasurers have used various currency risk management strategies depending, *ceteris paribus*, on the prevalence of a certain type of risk and the size of the firm.

Hedging Strategies

Indicatively, transaction risk is often hedged tactically (selectively) or strategically to preserve cash flows and earnings, depending on the firm's treasury view on the future movements of the currencies involved. Tactical hedging is used by most firms to hedge their transaction currency risk relating to short-term receivable and payable transactions, while strategic hedging is used for longer-period transactions. However, some firms decide to use passive hedging, which involves the maintenance of the same hedging structure and execution over regular hedging periods, irrespective of currency expectations–that is, it does not require that a firm takes a currency view.

Translation, or balance sheet, risk is hedged very infrequently and non-systematically, often to avoid the impact of possible abrupt currency shocks on net assets. This risk involves mainly long-term foreign exposures, such as the firm's valuation of subsidiaries, its debt structure and international investments. However, the long-term nature of these items and the fact that currency translation affects the balance sheet rather than the income statement of a firm, make hedging of the translation risk less of a priority for management. For the translation of currency risk of a subsidiary's value, it is standard practice to hedge the net balance sheet exposures, i.e., the net assets (gross assets less liabilities) of the subsidiary that might be affected by an adverse exchange rate move.

Economic risk is often hedged as a residual risk. Economic risk is difficult to quantify, as it reflects the potential impact of exchange rate moves on the present value of future cash flows. This may require measuring the potential impact of an exchange rate deviation from the benchmark rate used to forecast a firm's revenue and cost streams over a given period. In this case, the impact on each flow may be netted out over product lines and across markets, with the net economic risk becoming small for firms that invest in many foreign markets because of offsetting effects. Also, if exchange rate changes follow inflation differentials (through PPP) and a firm has a subsidiary that faces cost inflation above the general inflation rate, the firm could find its competitiveness eroding and its original value deteriorating as a result of exchange rate adjustments that are not in line with **PPP** (Purchase Power Parity). Under these circumstances, the firm could best hedge its economic exposure by creating payables (e.g., financing operations) in the currency in which the firm's subsidiary experiences the higher cost inflation (i.e., in the currency in which the firm's value is vulnerable).

Hedging Benchmarks and Performance

Hedging performance can be measured as a distance to a given benchmark rate. The risk embedded in the hedge is usually expressed as a VaR number that will be consistent with the performance measure. Hedging optimization models, as methods for optimizing hedging strategies for currency-denominated cash flows, help find the most efficient hedge for individual currency exposures, while most of them do not provide a hedging process for multiple currency hedging. Thus, both performance and VaR are measured as effective hedge rates, calculated for each hedging instrument used and the risk in terms of a confidence level.

As part of the currency risk management policy, firms use a variety of hedging benchmarks to manage their hedging strategies effectively. Such benchmarks could be the hedging level (i.e., a certain percentage), the reporting period, especially for firms that use forward hedging to limit the volatility of their net equity, (e.g., quarterly or 12-month benchmarks), and budget exchange rates, depending on the prevailing accounting rules. Moreover, benchmarks enable the performance of individual hedges to be measured against that of the firm.

Hedging and Budget Rates

Budget exchange rates provide firms with a reference exchange rate level. Setting budget exchange rates is often linked to the firm's sensitivities and benchmarking priorities. After deciding on the budget rate, the corporate treasury will have to secure an appropriate hedge rate and ensure that there is minimal deviation from that hedge rate. This process will determine the frequency and instruments to be used in hedging. It should be further pointed out that persistent moves relative to the numeraire (functional) currency should be reflected in the budget rates, or strategic positioning and hedging should be considered.

Alternatively, a firm may decide to set its budget exchange rate at the daily average exchange rate over the previous fiscal year. In such cases, the firm would need to use one hedge through, perhaps, an average-based instrument like an option or a synthetic forward. This hedging operation will usually be executed on the last day of the previous fiscal year, with starting day the first day of the new fiscal year. Furthermore, a firm may also use passive currency hedging, such as hedging the average value of a foreign currency cash flow over a specified time period, relative to a previous period, through option structures available in the market. This type of hedging strategy is fairly simple and easier to monitor.

Best Practices for Exchange Rate Risk Management

For their currency risk management decisions, firms with significant exchange rate exposure often need to establish an operational framework of best practices. These practices or principles may include:

- Identification of the types of exchange rate risk that a firm is exposed to and measurement of the associated risk exposure. As mentioned before, this involves determination of the transaction, translation and economic risks, along with specific reference to the currencies that are related to each type of currency risk. In addition, measuring these currency risks - using various models (e.g. VaR) - is another critical element in identifying hedging positions.
- Development of an exchange rate risk management strategy. After identifying the types of currency risk and measuring the firm's risk exposure, a currency strategy needs to be established for dealing with these risks. In particular, this strategy should specify the firm's currency hedging objectives – whether and why the firm should fully or partially hedge its currency exposures. Furthermore, a detailed currency hedging approach should be established. It is imperative that a firm details the overall currency risk management strategy on the operational level, including the execution process of currency hedging, the hedging instruments to be used, and the monitoring procedures of currency hedges.
- Creation of a centralized entity in the firm's treasury to deal with the practical aspects of the execution of exchange rate hedging. This entity will be responsible for exchange rate forecasting, the hedging approach mechanisms, the accounting procedures regarding currency risk, costs of currency hedging, and the establishment of benchmarks for measuring the performance of currency hedging. (These operations may be undertaken by a specialized team headed by the treasurer or, for large multinational firms, by a chief dealer.)
- Development of a set of controls to monitor a firm's exchange rate risk and ensure appropriate position taking. This includes setting position limits for each hedging instrument, position monitoring through mark-to-market valuations of all currency positions on a daily basis (or intraday), and the establishment of currency hedging benchmarks for periodic monitoring of hedging performance (usually monthly).
- Establishment of a risk oversight committee. This committee would in particular approve limits on position taking, examine the appropriateness of hedging instruments and associated VaR positions, and review the risk management policy on a regular basis.

Managing exchange rate risk exposure has gained prominence in the last decade, as a result of the unusual occurrence of a large number of currency crises. From the corporate managers' perspective, currency risk management is increasingly viewed as a prudent approach to reducing a firm's vulnerabilities from major exchange rate movements. This attitude has also been reinforced by recent international attention to both accounting and balance sheet risks.

INTERNATIONAL MONETARY SYSTEM

International Monetary System encompasses the institutions, instruments, laws, rules and procedures for handling international payments, in particular those in final settlement of inter-country debts. Money has sometimes been defined as whatever is used in final settlement of debt. Internationally, central banks have come to be the institutions, which make final settlements and hence the assets they use may be termed 'international money'. Central banks hold reserves of international money. These have also been termed 'reserve assets'.

Prior to the Second World War there was no international central bank. Usually central banks of individual countries made final settlements through transfers of gold or sterling or US dollars. A transfer of gold, sterling or US dollars from one country (other than the UK or the USA) to another (again leaving aside the UK and the USA) reduced the formers reserve assets and increased the latter's. A transfer of sterling from the UK to another country could be made by creating sterling deposit liabilities owed to the other country. The same was true for the USA. Thus reserve currency countries, as the UK and the USA came to be termed, had a different status from that of other countries.

The Gold Standard

The international monetary system that operated immediately prior to the 1914–18 wars was termed the 'gold standard'. Then, countries accepted two major assets–gold and sterling–in settlement of international debt. So the term 'gold / sterling standard' might be more appropriate.

Most major countries operated the gold standard system. A unit of a country's currency was defined as a certain weight–a part of an ounce–of gold. It also provided that gold could be obtained from the treasuries of these countries in exchange for money and coin of the country concerned.

The adoption of the gold standard began in Britain early in the nineteenth century. An attempt was made in the 1860s by a number of European countries to establish the Latin Monetary Union, involving bimetallism of gold and silver. The intention was that both gold and silver should be used for international debt settlement. But the establishment of the gold standard in Germany in 1871, together with less demand for silver in other areas, led to a diminished use of silver as international money. The United States was forced to abandon redemption of paper money in metal during the Civil War, but the redemption of paper money for gold began in 1879.

The First World War had a serious effect on the international monetary system. Britain was forced to abandon the gold standard because of the wartime deficit on its balance of payments, and its reluctance at that time to provide gold to settle international differences. This was, perhaps, the beginning of a reduction in confidence in sterling as an international reserve asset.

Many other countries abandoned the gold standard temporarily, but none had the same significance as the action of Britain because sterling had finance 90 per cent of world payments. The British government, recognizing the importance of sterling and of British institutions in international business, wished to return to the gold standard as soon as possible.

The Bretton Woods System

The framework for a new international monetary system was created in July 1944 in the USA at Bretton Woods, New Hampshire. The prime movers were John Maynard Keynes and Harry Dexter White, the respective British and US representatives. The key innovations of the Bretton Woods agreement were as follows:

- A new permanent institution, the International Monetary Fund (IMF) was to be establish to promote consultation and collaboration on international monetary problems and to lend to member countries in need due to recurring balance of payments deficits.
- Each fund member would establish, with the approval of the IMF, a par value for its currency and would undertake to maintain exchange rates for its currency within 1 per cent of the declared par value. Countries that freely bought and sold gold in settlement of international transactions were deemed to be adhering to the requirement that they maintain exchange rates within 1 per cent margins.
- Members would change their par values only after having secured IMF approval. This approval would be granted only if there were evidence that the country was suffering from a fundamental disequilibrium in its balance of payments. It was generally agreed that a long and continuing large loss of reserve assets in support of an exchange rate would be evidence of this fundamental disequilibrium.
- Each IMF member country would pay into the IMF pool a quota, one-quarter being in gold with the remainder in its own currency. The size of the quota was a function of each member's size in the world economy.
- The IMF would be in a position, from the subscription to quotas, to lend to countries in ongoing deficit.

SUMMARY

- Political factors are not only determinants which decide whole investment decision. Political, as well as economic stability are necessary conditions to attract direct investment from abroad.
- To determine and get rid of the major political barriers and risks to foreign investment development is the first step which developing countries should exercise in order to attract more inward foreign investment.
- Measuring and managing currency risk exposure are important functions in reducing a firm's vulnerabilities from major exchange rate movements. These vulnerabilities mainly arise from a firm's involvement in international operations and investments, where exchange rate changes could affect profit margins, through their effect on sources for inputs, markets for outputs and debt, and the value of assets.
- Prudent management of currency risk has been increasingly mandated by corporate boards, especially after the currency-crisis episodes of the last decade and the consequent heightened international attention to accounting and balance sheet risks.
- In managing currency risk, multinational firms utilize different hedging strategies depending on the specific type of currency risk.
- These strategies have become increasingly complicated as they try to address simultaneously transaction, translation and economic risks.
- As these risks could be detrimental to the profitability and the market valuation of a firm, corporate treasurers, even of smaller-size firms, have become increasingly proactive in controlling these risks.
- Rationalized production means producing different components or products in different countries to take advantage of factor costs.
- The least-cost production location may shift over time, especially during a product's life cycle. It also may change because of governmental incentives that subsidies production.
- Monopolistic advantages help explain why companies are willing to take what they perceive as higher risks of operating abroad. Certain countries and currencies have had such advantages, which helps explain the dominance of companies from certain countries at certain times.
- Exposure arises because currency movements may alter home currency values.
- Transaction exposure arises because a payable or receivable is denominated in a foreign currency.

- Translation exposure arises on the consolidation of foreign-currency-denominated assets, liabilities and profits in the process of preparing accounts.
- Economic exposure arises because the present value of a stream of expected future operating cash flows denominated in the home currency or in a foreign currency may vary due to changed exchange rates.
- The magnitude of a translation exposure varies according to the accounting convention used for translation of foreign-denominated items. There are four basic translation methods. These are the current / non-current method, the all-current (sometimes called closing rate) method, the monetary / non-monetary method, and the temporal method.
- Immediately prior to 1914 most major countries operated to gold standard system – two major assets, gold and sterling, were accepted in settlement of international debt.
- In 1914 Britain, in common with many other countries, left the gold standard.
- Britain abandoned the gold standard in 1931. Until the Second World War, most countries moved to a system of fluctuating exchange rates while others adopted strict exchange controls.
- The Bretton Woods agreement created the International Monetary Fund (IMF) a world central bank. It established a fixed exchange rate system with countries maintaining their exchange rates within 1 per cent of a declared par value against the US dollar. All IMF members' countries would pay a quota into the IMF pool and this would be available for loan to countries in need of the wherewithal to intervene in FX markets to keep rates at their par value.

Chapter 6

Globalization

INTRODUCTION

The world economy has been emerging as a global or transnational economy. A global or transnational economy is one, which transcends the national borders unhindered by artificial restriction like Government restriction of trade and factor movements. Globalization is a process of development of the world into a single integrated economic unit.

The transnational economy is different from the international economy. The international economy is characterized by the existence of different national economies the economic relation between them being regulated by the national Governments. The transnational economy is borderless world economy characterized by free flow of trade and factors of production across national borders.

In general, globalization represents the increasing integration of the world economy, based on five interrelated drivers of change:

- International trade (lower trade barriers and more competition)
- Financial flows (foreign direct investment, technology transfers/ licensing, portfolio investment and debt)
- Communications (traditional media and the Internet)
- Technological advances in transportation, electronics, bioengineering and related fields.
- Population mobility, especially of labor

GLOBALIZATION OF BUSINESS

Globalization is an attitude of mind – it is a mind-set, which views the entire world as a single market so that the corporate strategy is based on the dynamics of the global business environment. International marketing or international investment does not amount to globalization unless it is the result of such a global orientation.

Globalization of course is not a new phenomenon. The new phase of globalization which started around the mid 20th century became very widespread, more pronounced and overcharging since the late 1980s by gathering more momentum from the political and economic changes that swept across the communist countries, the economic reforms in other countries, the latest multilateral trade agreement which seeks to substantially liberalize international trade and investment and the technological and communication revolutions.

The following are the new features of the current phase of globalization.

New Markets

- Growing global markets in services – banking, insurance, transport
- New financial markets – deregulated, globally linked, working around the clock, with action at a distance in real time, with new instruments such as derivatives.
- Deregulation of antitrust laws and proliferation of mergers and acquisitions
- Global consumer markets with global brands.

New Actors

- Multinational corporations integrating their production and marketing, dominating food production.
- The World Trade Organization – the first multilateral organization with authority to enforce national governments' compliance with rules.
- An international criminal court system in the making.
- A booming international network of NGOs.
- More policy coordination groups – G-7, G-40, G-22, G-77, OECD.

New (Faster and Cheaper) Tools of Communication

- Internet and electronic communications linking many people simultaneously.
- Cellular phones.
- Fax machines.
- Faster and cheaper transport by air, rail and road.
- Computer-aided design.

STAGES OF GLOBALIZATION

Normally, a firm passes through different stages of development before it becomes a truly global corporation. Typically, a domestic firm starts its international business by exporting. Later it may establish joint ventures or subsidiaries abroad. From an international firm it may then develop into a multinational firm and finally into a global one.

In **stage one**, the arm's length service activity of essentially domestic company, which moves into new markets overseas by linking up with local dealers and distributors.

In **stage two**, the company takes over these activities on its own.

In **stage three**, the domestic based company begins to carry out its own manufacturing, marketing and sales in the key foreign markets.

In **stage four**, the company moves to a full insider position in these markets, supported by a complete business system including R & D and engineering. This stage calls on the managers to replicate in a new environment the hardware; systems and operational approaches that have worked so sell at home. It forces them to extend the reach of domestic headquarters, which now has to provide support functions such as personnel and finance, to all overseas activities.

In the **fifth stage**, the company moves toward a genuinely global mode of operation. The company is able to serve local customers in markets around the globe in ways that are truly responsive to their needs as well as to the global character of its industry depends on its ability to strike a new organizational balance.

After completing all the above five stages, a company must denationalize their operations and create a system of values shared by corporate managers around the globe to replace the glue a nation based orientation once provided.

ESSENTIAL CONDITIONS FOR GLOBALIZATION

There are, however, some essential conditions to be satisfied on the part of the domestic economy as well as the firm for successful globalization of the business. They are:

- **Business Freedom:** There should not be unnecessary Government restrictions, which come in the way of globalization, like import restriction, restrictions on sourcing finance or other factors from abroad, foreign investments etc. That is why the economic liberalization is regarded as first step towards facilitating globalization.

- **Facilities:** The extent to which an enterprise can develop globally from home country base depends on the facilities available like the infrastructure facilities.
- **Government Support:** Although unnecessary government interference is a hindrance to globalization, government support can encourage globalization. Government support may take the form of policy and procedural reforms, development of common facilities like infrastructure facilities, R&D support, financial market reforms and so on.
- **Resources:** Resources is one of the important factors, which often decide the ability of a firm to globalize. Resourceful companies may find it easier to thrust ahead in the global market. Resources include finance, technology, R&D capabilities, managerial expertise, company and brand image, human resource etc.
- **Competitiveness:** The competitive advantage of the company is a very important determinant of success in global business. A firm may derive competitive advantage from any one or more of the factors such as low costs and price, product quality, product differentiation, technological superiority, after sales service, marketing strength etc.
- **Orientation:** A global orientation on the part of the business firms and suitable globalization strategies are essential for globalization.

FOREIGN MARKET ENTRY STRATEGIES

One of the most important strategic decisions in international business is the mode of entering the foreign market. On the one extreme, a company may do the complete manufacturing of the product domestically and export it to the foreign market. On the other extreme, a company may do, by itself, the complete manufacturing of the product to be marketed in the foreign market there itself.

Important foreign market entry strategies are the following:

1. Exporting
2. Licensing / Franchising
3. Contract manufacturing
4. Management control
5. Assembly operations
6. Fully owned manufacturing facilities
7. Joint venturing
8. Contertrade
9. Mergers and acquisitions

10. Strategic alliance
11. Third country location

Exporting

Exporting, the most traditional mode of entering the foreign market is quite a common one even now. International trade has been growing much faster than the world output resulting in greater world economic integration.

It is the appropriate strategy when one of more of the following conditions prevails:

1. There are political or other risks of investment in the foreign country.
2. The company has no permanent interest in the foreign market concerned or that there is no guarantee of the market available for a long period.
3. The foreign country concerned does not favor foreign investment.
4. Licensing or contract manufacturing is not a better alternative.

Exporting is attractive that other modes particularly when underutilized capacity exists. Even when there is no excess capacity, expansion of the existing facility may sometimes be easier and less costly than setting up production facilities abroad.

Although exporting may turn out to be the best alternative under a given set of conditions or environmental factors, there are several sets of conditions, which make exporting less attractive than one or more of other alternatives.

Besides, in a number of a cases cost considerations make foreign production or assembly preferable to other entry strategies. Further, exporting marks the first stage in the evolution of international business of many companies. As the international business grows or as the environment changes or to expand the business it may become necessary to change the strategies.

Licensing and Franchising

Licensing and franchising, which involve minimal commitment of resources and effort on the part of the international marketer, are easy ways of entering the foreign markets.

Under international licensing, a firm in one country (the licensor) permits a firm in another country (the licensee) to use its intellectual property (such as patents, trade marks, copyrights, technology, technical know-how, marketing skill). The monetary benefit of the licensor is the royalty or fees which licensee pays.

Under franchising, a form of licensing in which a parent company (the franchiser) grants another independent entity (the franchisee) the right to do business in a prescribed manner. This right can take the form of selling the franchisor's products, using its name, production and marketing techniques, or general business approach.

International licensing/franchising have grown very substantially. As an entry strategy, it requires neither capital investment nor knowledge and marketing strength in foreign markets. Licensing will help to avoid host country regulations that are more prevalent in equity ventures. Licensing may also serve as a stage in the internationalization of the firm by providing a means by which foreign markets can be tested without major involvement or capital or management time.

When the market is closed by the host country regulations either to imports or to foreign investment, licensing may provide a viable opportunity to enter such a market. From the point of view of the licensee, licensing provides the greater advantage of entering the market with a proven product/technology or marketing intangible without having to run the risk of R & D failures.

Contract Manufacturing

Under contract manufacturing, a company doing international marketing contracts with firms in foreign countries to manufacture or assemble the products while retaining the responsibility of marketing the product.

Contract manufacturing has the following advantages:

1. The company does not have to commit resource for setting up production facilities.
2. It frees the company from the risks of investing in foreign countries.
3. It also has the advantage that it is less risky way to start with. If the business does not pick up sufficiently, dropping it is easy; but if the company had established its own production facilities, the exit would be difficult.

Contract manufacturing, has the following disadvantages:

1. In some cases, there will be the loss of potential profits from manufacturing.
2. Less control over the manufacturing process.
3. Contract manufacturing also has the risk of developing potential competitors.

4. It would not be suitable in cases of high-tech products and cases, which involve technical secrets etc.

Management Contracting

Under this contract, the firm providing the management know-how may not have any equity stake in the enterprise being managed. It could sometimes bring in additional benefits for the managing company. It may obtain the business of exporting or selling otherwise of the products of the managed company or supplying the inputs required by the managed company.

Management contract could, sometimes, bring in additional benefits for the managing company. It may obtain the business of exporting or selling otherwise of the products of the managed company or supplying the inputs required by the managed company.

Management contracts, obviously, have clear benefits for the clients. They can provide organizational skills not available locally, expertise that is immediately available rather than built up and management assistance in the form of support services that would be difficult and costly to replicate locally.

Some Indian companies–Tata Tea, Harrisons Malayalam and AVT–have contracts to manage a number of plantations in Sri Lanka. Tata Tea also has a joint venture in Sri Lanka namely, Estate Management Services Pvt. Limited.

Turnkey Contracts

Turnkey contracts are common in international business in the supply, erection and commissioning of plants, as in the case of oil refineries, steel mills, cement and fertilizer plants etc. construction projects and franchising agreements.

A turnkey operation is an agreement by the seller to supply a buyer with the facility fully equipped and ready to be operated by the buyer's personnel, who will be trained by the seller. The term is sometimes used in fast food franchising when a franchiser agrees to select a store site, build the store, equip it, train the franchisee and employees and sometimes arrange for the financing.

Wholly Owned Manufacturing Facilities

Companies with long-term and substantial interest in the foreign market normally establish fully owned manufacturing facilities there. A number of factors like trade barriers, differences in the production and other costs, government policies etc. encourage the establishment of production facilities in the foreign markets.

It provides the firm with complete control over production and quality. It does not have the risk of developing potential competitors as in the case of licensing and contract manufacturing. Fully owned enterprises may not be allowed or favored in some countries, particularly in low priority areas.

Joint Ventures

Joint venture is a very common strategy of entering the foreign market. In the widest sense, any form of association, which implies collaboration for more than a transitory period, is a joint venture. Such a broad definition encompasses many diverse types of joint overseas operations viz.,

1. Sharing of ownership and management in an enterprise
2. Licensing/franchising agreements
3. Contract manufacturing
4. Management contracts.

The essential feature of a joint ownership venture is that the ownership and management are shared between a foreign firm and a local firm. In some cases there are more than two parties involved. A foreign investor buying an interest in a local company, a local firm acquiring an interest in an existing foreign firm or by both the foreign and local entrepreneurs jointly forming a new enterprise.

One important advantage of joint venturing is that it permits a firm with limited resources to enter more foreign markets that might be possible under a policy of forming wholly owned subsidiaries.

Partnership with local firms has certain specific advantages. The local partner would be in a better position to deal with the government and the publics. Further, there would not be much public hostility when there is a local partner; it would be much less when there is equity holding by the government sector and the public.

Third Country Location

Third country location is sometimes used as an entry strategy. When there is no commercial transaction between two nations because of political reasons or when direct transactions between two nations are difficult due to political reasons or the like, a firm in one of these nations which wants to enter the other market will have to operate from a third country base.

Third country location may also be helpful to take advantage of the friendly trade relations between the third country and the foreign market concerned. Some times commercial reasons encourage third country location. It may be resorted to reduce cost of production and thereby to increase price competitiveness to facilitate market entry or for improving maintaining the market position. The incentives offered by governments, particularly of the developing countries for investment and exports encourage such third country location.

Mergers and Acquisitions

M & A have been a very important market entry strategy and expansion strategy. A number of Indian companies have also used this entry strategy. M & A have certain specific advantages.

It provides instant access to markets and distribution network. As one of the most difficult are in international marketing is the distribution, this is often a very important consideration for M & A. Another important objective of M & A is to obtain access to new technology or a patent right.

M & A may also give rise to some problems, which arise mostly because of the deficiencies of the evaluation of the case for acquisition. Sometimes the cost of acquisition may be unrealistically high. The success of the enterprise will naturally depend on the success in solving the problems.

Strategic Alliance

Strategic alliance has been becoming more and more popular in international business. It is also sometimes used as a market entry strategy. For example, a firm may enter a foreign market by forming an alliance with a firm in the foreign market for marketing or distributing the former's products.

There are different types of alliances according to purpose or structure. Based on the description of the generic forms of coalitions by Michael Porter and Mark Fuller, classifies alliances according to purpose as follows:

- Technology development alliances like research consortia, simultaneous engineering agreements, licensing or joint development agreements.
- Marketing, sales and service alliances in which a company makes use of the marketing infrastructure etc. of another company, in the foreign market, for its products. This may help easy penetration of the foreign market and pre-emption of potential competitors.
- Multiple activity alliance, which involves the combining of two or more types of alliances. While marketing alliances are often single country alliances, as international firms take on different allies in each country, technology development and operations alliances are usually multi-country since these kinds of activities can be employed over several countries.

PROS AND CONS OF GLOBALIZATION

While globalization has several benefits, it has a number of problems.

While developing countries, which in the past, were against globalization, have wide opened their doors for globalization, many people in developed countries like USA are angry against globalization. The important pros and cons of globalization according to the above survey are the following. Productivity grows more quickly when countries produce goods and services in which they have comparative advantage. Living standards can go up faster.

- Global competition and imports keep a lid on prices, so inflation is less likely to derail economic growth.
- An open economy spurs innovation with fresh ideas from abroad.
- Export jobs often pay more than other jobs.
- Unfettered capital flows give the US access to foreign investment and keep interest rates low.

True, globalization can benefit the developing countries in several ways. It is, however, apprehended that unregulated globalization will cause serious problems for developing countries. A number of countries allow high foreign stake even in industries where that is not really required. This could affect domestic enterprise of developing countries.

Replacement of traditional and indigenous products by modern products, resulting in the ruin of traditional crafts and industries and the livelihood of people in these sectors has also been happening in several countries.

In a competitive environment, a firm can survive only if it is efficient. Companies all around world, including many large multinationals, have been cutting down the size of their human resources as one of the means of achieving cost efficiency. The problem of over-manning is very severe in the developing countries.

The developing countries, in general, have been disadvantaged by the international trading system. The adverse terms of trade led to economic loss for the developing countries, in general. It should, however, be noted that a number of developing countries have improved their export performance substantially and several of them figure in the list of top 20 exporters.

Another criticism is that the liberalization increases the economic inequality. Even in China, the liberalization has created many island of affluence. If inequality increases because of the worsening of the living conditions of the poor, it certainly is unjustifiable. But, if the increase in inequality is the result of improving the economic conditions of a section, while there is no economic deterioration of any section, or because of the disproportionate benefits, the question is whether the economic progress of some sections should be curbed so that there will not be a widening of the inequality.

OBSTACLES TO GLOBALIZATION

The Indian business suffers from a number of disadvantages in respect of globalization of business. The important problems are the following:

- **Government Policy and Procedures:** Government policy and procedures in India are among the most complex, confusing and cumbersome in the world. Even after the much-publicized liberalization, they do not present a very conducive situation. Government policy and the bureaucratic culture in India in this respect are not that encouraging.
- **High Cost:** High cost of many vital inputs and other factors like raw materials and intermediates, power, finance, infrastructure facilities like port etc. tend to reduce the international competitiveness of the Indian business.
- **Poor Infrastructure:** Infrastructure in India is generally inadequate and inefficient and therefore very costly. This is a serious problem affecting the growth as well as competitiveness.
- **Obsolescence:** The technology employed, mode and style of operations etc. are, in general, obsolete and these seriously affect the competitiveness.
- **Resistance to Change:** There are several socio-political factors, which resist change and this comes in the way of modernization, rationalization and efficiency improvement. Technological modernization is resisted due to fear of unemployment. The extent of excess labor employed by the Indian industry is alarming.
- **Poor Quality Image:** Due to various reasons, the quality of many Indian products is poor. Even when the quality is good, the poor quality image, India has become a handicap.
- **Supply Problems:** Due to various reasons, like low production capacity, shortages of raw materials and infrastructure like power and port facilities, Indian companies in many instances are not able to accept large orders or to keep up delivery schedules.
- **Lack of Experience:** The general lack of experience in managing international business is another important problem.

FACTORS FAVORING GLOBALIZATION

Although India has several handicaps, there are also a number of favorable factors for globalization of Indian business.

- **Human Resources:** Apart from the low cost of labor, there are several other aspects of human resources to India's favor. India has one of the largest pools of scientific and technical manpower. The number of management graduates is also surging. It is widely recognized that given the right environment, Indian scientists and technical personnel can do excellently. Similarly, although the labor productivity in India is generally low, given the right environment it will be good.

- **Wide Base:** India has a very broad resource and industrial base, which can support a variety of businesses.
- **Growing Entrepreneurship:** Many of the established industries are planning to go international in a big way. Added to this is the considerable growth of new and dynamic entrepreneurs who could make a significant contribution to the globalization of Indian business.
- **Growing Domestic Market:** The growing domestic market enables the Indian companies to consolidate their position and the gain more strength to make foray into the foreign market or to expand their foreign business.
- **Niche Market:** There are many marketing opportunities abroad present in the form of market niche. Such niches are particularly attractive for small companies. Several Indian companies have become very successful by niche marking.
- **Expanding Markets:** The growing population and disposable income and the resultant expanding internal market provides enormous business opportunities.
- **Economic Liberalization:** The economic liberalization in India is an encouraging factor of globalization. The delicencing of industries, of restrictions of growth, opening up of industries earlier reserved for the public sector, import liberalizations, liberalization of policy towards foreign capital and technology etc. could encourage globalization of India business.
- **Competition:** The growing competition, both from within the country and abroad, provokes many Indian companies to look to foreign markets seriously to improve their competitive position and to increase the business.

GLOBALIZATION OF MARKETS

The globalization of markets means that the expansion and access of businesses to all over the world to reach the needs of the customers internationally. Now due to the advancement of technology and IT revolution there is less problems of boundaries. The main reason is due to the advent of the Internet that has facilitated to the customers and companies to interact at a common place by just sitting it home and it decreases the cost of product and other costs as well which is the benefit for the both parties. Now the companies are able to sell its product and services internationally.

It is commonly believed that the taste of the consumers living in the different parts of the worlds are now emerging now MTV has become local channel, ordinary people wear Levis Jeans and the access to the McDonald pizza is very easy.

Now not only big multinationals but also small companies who were lack of resources can now reach the customers internationally. This all happened due to the globalization of markets. Many big markets have emerged into one single market due to the customer's needs and demands. So this gives benefits to the consumers and the producers as well.

Globalization and localization should function together as companies develop globally. Localization should not be seen as an afterthought every time that a business makes the decision to move into a new market. It should be part of the globalization strategy from the beginning as it can make or break a global business strategy.

The globalization of markets can benefit—and has benefited—rich and poor alike. But the integration of the global economy is outpacing the development of a healthy global polity. To realize the values and rules critical to a secure and just world—and to make the full benefits of a global market available to all—will require a better global politics.

Economic globalization can be measures in different ways. These center around the four main economic flows that characterize globalization:

- Goods and services, e.g., exports plus imports as a proportion of national income or per capita of population.
- Labor/people, e.g., net human migration|migration rates; inward or outward migration flows, weighted by population.
- Capital (economics)|Capital, e.g., inward or outward direct investment as a proportion of national income or per head of population.
- Technology, e.g., international research and development flows; proportion of populations (and rates of change thereof) using particular inventions (especially 'factor-neutral' technological advances such as the telephone, motorcar, broadband).

Globalization of Production: It can be observed that companies are increasingly dispersing parts of their production process to different locations around the globe to take advantage of national differences in the cost and quality of production factors (land, labor, capital, legislation).

Globalization of Markets: It has been argued that the world is moving away from an economic system in which national markets are distinct entities, isolated from each other by trade barriers and barriers of distance, time, and culture, toward a system in which national markets are merging together into one huge global marketplace.

Causes of Global Shift: Two factors underlie the trend toward the increasing globalization of markets and of production. The first is the declining of barriers to enable the free flow of goods, services, and capital. The second factor are the dramatic changes in communication, information, and transportation technologies.

Consequences of Global Shift: Companies need to recognize that industry boundaries do not stop at national borders and that they have to face this change to remain competitive. Also nations or regions have to take steps to stay competitive in this global environment.

Enablers

- Global organizations like WTO, OECD, IMF, World Bank (link to driving force Power of the United Nations and Influence of the World Trade Organization (WTO)).
- Participation of China, India and other emerging markets in the global markets (link to driving force Economic Growth in China and The Rise of BRIC Economies).
- Number and importance of multinational companies.
- Technological development especially information technology (link to driving force Increasing potential to grow based on new available technology).
- Transport efficiency (link to driving force Logistics/Distribution).
- Specialization and outsourcing.
- Harmonization and reeognition of international Intellectual Property laws (link to driving force IP rights).
- Internationalization of education.
- Access to international media (link to driving force Media Globalization).
- The positive trend of world export and imports of the past years.
- The 1,2% increase expected of the industrial production of advanced economies.

Paradigms

- Market globalization decreases national governments control on unemployment, GDP fluctuations, etc. Laws and regulations should therefore be made on a global basis.

- Possible decreasing power of governments and increasing power of companies, which set a totally different political and economic arena. The rules to adhere to in this situation have yet to be created.
- The globalization of markets can benefit—and has benefited—rich and poor alike. But the integration of the global economy is outpacing the development of a healthy global policy. To realize the values and rules critical to a secure and just world—and to make the full benefits of a global market available to all—will require better global politics.
- If the globalization of the market leads to continents or countries which cannot compete anymore, trade barriers (de-globalization) might be a counter reaction.

In the past two decades, the picture has changed a bit. Some developing countries, including China and more recently India, have grown faster than the already rich countries. Incomes in China and India will not soon equal those in rich countries—it would take them almost a century of faster growth even to reach current U.S. levels. Still, some developing countries have done some dramatic catching up. And the rapid growth in India and China has caused world poverty to decline.

Global Marketing Strategy

Gone are the days when a company was confined to doing business only in their own country; with more and more companies achieving a global presence there has been a need for the corresponding development global marketing strategy. Some of the rules which apply when only focusing on the domestic market can no longer be applied once the company starts expanding overseas.

Global marketing strategy used mainly by multinational companies to sell goods or services internationally. Global marketing requires that there be harmonization between the marketing policies for different countries and that the marketing mix for the different countries can be adapted to the local market conditions. Global marketing is sometimes used to refer to overseas expansion efforts through licensing, franchises, and joint ventures.

In turbulent markets that are affected by increased political and economic unrest in the global marketplace, continuing to follow the same paths for marketing and business strategy is extremely risky. Both the pace of change and the level of complexity call for a new marketing paradigm, one that may well require companies to scrap their current models and methods and build a new approach to marketing.

Most companies tend to underestimate the market strength of their competitors and especially of new competitors from outside the traditional boundaries of the industry. In addition, many companies do a poor job developing a strong understanding of the unique cultures that exist within each country within which they do business. Many companies tend to stampede into new cultures without taking the time to learn about those cultures, the differences and similarities between the new markets and countries and the company's home country, and other countries in which it operates. The more a company truly understands the unique needs and desires of the new market, the more responsive it will be able to be to that market.

The case for change-truly radical change-is powerful if companies are to avoid the threats and capitalize on the opportunities of the changing global information age. In a time of dynamic movements in all aspects of the global marketplace, not being market driven and not acting boldly and rapidly, along the lines suggested by the new marketing strategy paradigm, is the riskiest decision of all. Rethinking, reorganizing, and reinventing the future and global marketing strategies are crucial.

Global Marketing Strategy provides a coherent and stimulating analysis of the issues related to strategic marketing in an increasingly global economy. It takes the reader from an awareness of global developments to a more informed understanding of how they apply to business now and in the near future.

To discuss the differences between global marketing strategy and domestic marketing strategy, the factors which have led to global expansion must first be analyzed.

- The first key factor is that the saturation of domestic markets has pushed companies to look for business elsewhere. For example, an electronics company in Japan would face a high level of competition due to the number of players in the market. They would be better off expanding internationally, where they not only would face less competition but may have an added advantage due to the reputation of Japanese technology.
- Secondly, the increased consumer access to foreign brands means that there is a broader market space to conquer. With many international brands like Nike cutting manufacturing costs by outsourcing overseas and using economies of scale, it is more difficult for their competitors to get the same profit margin for price parity.
- Thirdly, the current dominance of the Internet makes conducting international business and forming international collaborations much more accessible. Many small businesses are fielding business from across the globe through their websites. For them, using the Internet to

communicate is cheap and instantaneous. However, it is increasingly becoming an expectation that businesses will have a website and trade internationally in order to remain competitive.

The need to expand internationally means that companies need to consider the sensitivities of new market conditions, giving rise to the evolution of global strategics from domestic strategy. There may be different opportunities or limitations for the company in the form of economic conditions or the political/legal framework. Company communications need to be culturally sensitive; for example, showing bare soles of feet in Thailand would be considered offensive. There may also be different sets of needs that the company's product/service appeals to which require the adaptation of the market offering as well as promotions.

In the late 1980s, five stages of the evolution of global marketing were proposed. The **first stage** is **domestic marketing**, where the company's production and marketing are focused on only one market. Product development, communications and competition analysis are ethnocentric, with operations centralized in national headquarters.

In the **exporting stage**, companies start to look at selling their products overseas whilst maintaining their headquarters and operations in their home market. The majority of the time, product development will be based on the home market. Expansion in this manner is low-risk but may not allow the company to fully consider the needs of other markets.

However, when companies become international marketers, they start to look at the needs of other markets and tailoring their products and marketing mix to each country. This polycentric approach means that they are addressing the demands of each market, but with a large number of markets international marketing strategy can decentralize decisions and reduce brand consistency. Arguably, McDonalds is an international marketing company with country-specific products and separate advertising campaigns, dealing with brand consistency through global regulations.

The fourth stage is multinational marketing, where companies start to standardize product development and marketing decisions across a region in order to take advantage of economies of scale.

By the time global marketing strategies evolved they were very different to domestic strategies. Companies take a geocentric, as opposed to ethnocentric, approach. Products are global with only slight variations for each country. While marketing decisions are once again centralized, a global strategy demands that there is some flexibility to tailor the marketing mix to each market.

Global marketing strategy allows companies to expand their reach, and tap market share from other countries that they would not be able to access otherwise. They can also utilize greater economies of scale.

Global expansion also allows companies to diversify the risk of poor market conditions. A solely domestic company is subject to the economic and regulatory conditions of their country of operation. However, global companies can harvest profits from one market to support another market which is experiencing difficulties, or to push operations in another market to success. Companies have also used their global operations to minimize their taxes payable or consolidate their power structures.

However, to obtain the full benefit of global marketing strategy standardization is required. This limits the degree to which companies cater to each market's individual needs. Coca-cola was implementing a global marketing strategy until 2000, when it was realized that creating an aspirational brand required vastly different promotional techniques in different markets. There were also opportunities to produce other drinks which could not be pursued with a global marketing strategy.

Global marketing strategy has developed out of the need and opportunities for companies to occupy a greater market space. For some companies, the benefits in economies of scale, standardization of marketing and establishing of global networks has allowed them to rise to the top of their industries. However, others have found that global strategy limits their level of customization and have changed to a more flexible strategy.

Developing Global Marketing Strategies

Two opposite viewpoints for developing global marketing strategy are commonly expounded. According to one school of thought, marketing is an inherently local problem. Due to cultural and other differences among countries, marketing programs should be tailor-made for each country. The opposing view treats marketing as know-how that can be transferred from country to country. It has been argued that the worldwide marketplace has become so homogenized that multinational corporations can market standardized products and services all over the world with identical strategies, thus lowering their costs and earning higher margins.

Localized Strategy: The proponents of localized marketing strategies support their viewpoint based on four differences across countries:

- buyer behavior characteristics
- socioeconomic condition
- marketing infrastructure, and
- competitive environment

Here are the examples that show how companies often experience difficulties in foreign markets because they did not fully understand differences in buyer behavior.

- For example, Campbell's canned soups mostly vegetable and beef combinations packed in extra large cans did not catch on in soup-loving Brazil.
- Most Brazilian housewives felt they were not fulfilling their roles if they served soup that they could not call their own. Brazilian housewives had no problems using dehydrated competitive products, such as Knorr and Maggi, which they could use as soup starters and still add their own ingredients and flair.
- Also, Johnson & Johnson's baby powder did not sell well in Japan until its original package was changed to a flat box with a powder puff. Japanese mothers feared that powder would fly around their small homes and enter their spotlessly clean kitchens when sprinkled from a plastic bottle. Powder puffs allowed them to apply powder sparingly.
- For example, purple is a death color in Brazil, white is for funerals in Hong Kong, and yellow signifies jealousy in Thailand. In Egypt the use of green, which is the national color, is frowned upon for packaging.

Socioeconomic differences (i.e., per capita income, level of education, level of unemployment) among countries also call for a localized approach toward international marketing.

Differences in the character of local marketing infrastructure across countries may suggest pursuing country-specific marketing strategies. The marketing infrastructure consists of the institutions and functions necessary to create, develop, and service demand, including retailers, wholesalers, sales agents, warehousing, transportation, credit, media, and more.

Finally, differences in the competitive environment among countries may require following localized marketing strategies. Nestlé, for example, achieved more than a 60 percent market share in the instant coffee market in Japan but less than 30 percent in the United States.

Nestlé had to contend with two strong domestic competitors in the United States, namely General Foods, which markets Maxwell House and other brands, and more recently Procter & Gamble, which markets Folgers and High Point. Nestlé faced relatively weak domestic competitors in Japan. IBM, which is the leading computer company in the world, slipped to third place in the Japanese market behind Fujitsu Ltd. and NEC Corporation in terms of total revenue. Nestlé and IBM must reflect differences in their competitive environments in such marketing choices as pricing, sales force behavior, and advertising.

Standardized Strategy: In contrast to the view that marketing strategies must be localized, many scholars and practitioners argue that significant benefits can be achieved through standardization of marketing strategies on a global basis. As a matter of fact, some people recommend an extreme strategy: offering identical products at identical prices through identical distribution channels and supporting these identical products by identical sales and promotional programs throughout the world.

Among consumer durable goods, Mercedes-Benz sells its cars by following a universal marketing program. Among nondurable goods, Coca-Cola is ubiquitous. Among industrial goods, Boeing jets are sold worldwide based on common marketing perspectives.

Companies usually opt for standardization. A recent survey on the subject lends support to the high propensity to standardize all or parts of marketing strategy in foreign markets. For example, an extremely high degree of standardization appears to exist in brand names, physical characteristics of products, and packaging.

Also, standardization makes it feasible to achieve consistency in dealing with customers and in product design. Consistency in product style features, design, brand name, packaging should establish a common image of the product worldwide and help increase overall sales. For example, a person accustomed to a particular brand is likely to buy the same brand overseas if it is available. The global exposure that brands receive these days as a result of extensive world travel and mass media requires the consistency that is feasible through standardization. Finally, standardization may be urged on the grounds that a product that has proved to be successful in one country should do equally well in other countries that present more or less similar markets and similar competitive conditions.

A multinational corporation that intends to launch a new product into a foreign market should consider the nature of its products, its organizational capabilities, and the level of adaptation required to accommodate cultural differences between the home and the host country. A multinational corporation should also analyze such factors as market structures, competitors' strategic orientations, and host government demands. The international marketplace is far more competitive today than in the 1980s and most likely will remain so as we enter the next century. Thus, to enhance competitive advantage some sort of adaptation might provide a better match between a product and local marketing conditions.

Global New Product Development

Simply put, Global Product Development means maximizing the financial and operational productivity of the product development process by spreading product development activities across multiple regions of the world in order to better match value-add to cost. In this context, the definition of "product development" ranges from marketing activities that identify and document customer needs; to engineering activities that conceptualize, design, analyze and refine new product ideas; to activities that plan and document manufacturing, operation, and maintenance processes; to sustaining activities that make ongoing product changes and refinements. Regions with high costs include industrialized countries like the United States, United Kingdom, Germany, France, Italy, and Japan. The list of lower cost regions is long but includes India, China, Russia, and various other Eastern European and Asian countries.

Companies who manage to develop higher levels of productivity in product development compared to their peers enjoy a well-documented competitive advantage in the marketplace. Because productivity is ultimately defined as the amount of output per unit of input, companies who can find a means to develop great products while containing product development costs enjoy a distinct advantage in terms of market share and profitability. Within their product development process, few companies effectively balance their inputs and outputs today. By concentrating both higher value-add and lower value-add resources in a single high-cost region, most companies simply overpay for their respective level of output. Other companies may spend less across the board by mandate, but in so doing they compromise on value-add and therefore achieve correspondingly lower returns as well.

Fortunately, for most companies, there is not just an opportunity but actually an entitlement to improved productivity. Just as levels of value-add vary significantly across activities, so too do costs vary dramatically from region to region. By simply rearranging product development activities and personnel in a globally distributed fashion that better aligns cost structures with levels of value-add, companies can immediately increase product development productivity by 10%, enjoying a cost savings equal to 0.5% of total company revenues.

The Basics of Global New Product Development

Implementing Global Product Development requires reconfiguring product development activities across multiple regions of the world. This must be done, of course, with an eye toward maximizing productivity while mitigating risk. With a Global Product Development approach, process decomposition is used to identify and segregate high value activities and resources from lower value-add activities and resources. Those activities that add higher levels of value become candidates to remain in higher cost regions because their critical value-add justifies their higher cost, while many of the lower value-add activities may become candidates for subsequent transfer to lower-cost regions. The ability to characterize value-add is somewhat subjective and naturally varies from industry to industry and even company to company.

Further, given the need to mitigate risk within the mission-critical product development process, the move to Global Product Development should be viewed as evolutionary, not revolutionary. Most companies simply cannot switch to a highly globalized model overnight, but can migrate toward increasing levels of globalization over a period of years.

Off-shoring Versus Outsourcing

Ultimately, the value of Global Product Development is unlocked when a balanced alignment of cost and value-add is achieved. "Off-shoring" and "outsourcing" are fundamental tools to be appropriately used to achieve the desired balance. Off-shoring, however, is the core strategy.

As a rule of thumb, companies typically look at keeping in-house (i.e., in-sourcing) that which is "core" to their business, and distributing to others (i.e., outsourcing) that which is "context", or less critical.

Historically, manufacturing companies have done a high degree of outsourcing of components of their products to companies that specialize in their design and manufacture. Much of the outsourced work remained onshore, though some went offshore. Another form of outsourcing is the large onshore industry of "engineering services" companies within high cost regions that offer contract engineering talent. While traditional outsourcing of manufacturing and engineering will remain a viable method to improve products while managing fixed costs, many companies have little additional room to drive incremental productivity with this technique.

A Global Development Maturity Model

To help mitigate the risk of disruptions to their product develop process, most companies evolve toward a Global Product Development model over a period of time. Even within a single company, different business units or product lines may very well be at different points in their evolution toward global distribution and balance of cost and value-add.

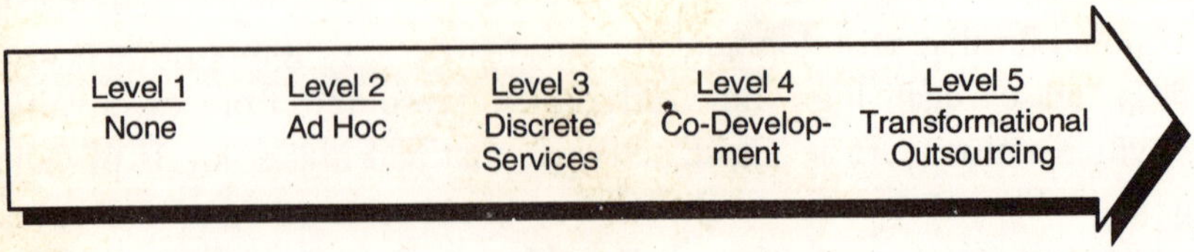

Level 1 None
Level 2 Ad Hoc
Level 3 Discrete Services
Level 4 Co-Development
Level 5 Transformational Outsourcing

Fig. 6.1: Global New Product Development Maturity Model

- Level 1 – None
- Level 2 – Ad Hoc
- Level 3 – Discrete Services
- Level 4 – Co-Development
- Level 5 – Transformational Outsourcing

The Maturity Model presented helps to characterize common states of evolution in the Global Product Development practices of various manufacturers. The states may be described as follows:

- Many Western companies are currently at **Level 1–None,** with no meaningful degree of global distribution of product development activities.
- Numerous companies at **Level 2 – Ad Hoc** find themselves with some degree of offshore product development capability, but lack a meaningful strategy regarding how to use this capability to achieve a balance of cost and value-add. Typically, companies at Level 2 have "inherited" distributed operations through mergers and acquisitions, but this was an adjunct to some other strategy and not a primary strategy in and of itself.
- True Global Product Development begins at **Level 3 – Discrete Services,** where companies deploy a relatively conservative strategy to retain control of product development projects and core activities in-house and onshore, but "farm out" various discrete support activities to offshore locations. For example, a company may retain requirements capture and core design responsibilities in high-cost regions, but shift drafting, technical publications, and even simulation and testing activities toward lower-cost offshore resources. Companies who are at Level 3 may achieve as much as 30% portability (to low cost regions) of their product development activities.
- At **Level 4 – Co-Development,** companies become more aggressive and begin to segment their overall product portfolio in order to identify select subsets that can be "carved out" and transferred with full responsibility to their offshore counterparts. Examples of Level 4 would include transferring responsibility for a complete subassembly design for a new product effort, sustaining engineering for existing products, or a specific value-engineering project aimed at improving profitability of an existing design. Most companies in high-cost regions envision getting to Level 4 over a period of time.
- A small minority of companies envision getting to the **Level 5 – Transformational Outsourcing** model as the basis for a complete

reinvention of how their company does business. In Level 5, the onshore resources capture customer requirements, and become the interface to the offshore operation, which in turn designs and perhaps even manufactures the final product. The risk of completely losing product development capabilities keeps most companies from seriously considering Level 5.

Operational Considerations

The key to implementing Global product development is to reconfigure product development activities in a global manner to optimize the alignment of value add and cost. This must be done in a considered and evolutionary fashion, however, to avoid the real risk of a damaging disruption to the output of the product development process.

The key is **balance.** Be too conservative and you risk leaving money on the table—money that could make an important difference in profitability or competitive advantage. Go too fast and you risk disrupting the process with resulting missed deliverables and product launches — a potentially catastrophic situation for the business. Go too far and you risk the loss of institutional knowledge that may compromise the company for years to come. A methodical approach, implemented in phases over a period of time, affords the necessary balance.

What to Offshore?

In order to proceed with the implementation of a Global Product Development strategy, it is necessary to analyze product development activities and segregate higher value-add activities from lower value-add activities. Separately, it is necessary to identify the degree to which various activities are indeed portable without disruption to the overall product development process. Some activities, though potentially characterized as lower value-add, might require higher degrees of institutional knowledge or physical co-location with the customer. These activities may be poor candidates for relocation.

The analytical approach to be followed when answering **"what to offshore?"** varies depending on the desired outcome as measured by the Global Product Development Maturity Model presented earlier. Companies that want to achieve a "Level 3 – Discrete Services" level of maturity will retain overall management and control for all products and projects onshore, but try to identify those supporting tasks and roles that could be relocated offshore. This outcome essentially requires that companies take an approach that could be characterized as "modular process design".

In other words, breaking their process into a series of discrete steps, all of which have defined inputs and outputs. Companies who want to proceed to a **"Level 4 – Co-Design"** level of maturity need to take a different approach. These companies will analyze their portfolio of products and identify those products or projects that can be moved offshore in their entirety. These companies are more likely to focus on "modular product design".

To help companies proceed with this segregation, various analytical models that examine each task within a typical electromechanical product development process and ranked those tasks in terms of their value-add and portability. This analysis shows how companies can achieve the 30% resource portability level at **"Level 3–Discrete Services"** of the Global Product Development Maturity Model, which is the natural and more conservative starting point for most companies who are contemplating Global Product Development. **Figure 6.2** shows the summary results from this analytical model.

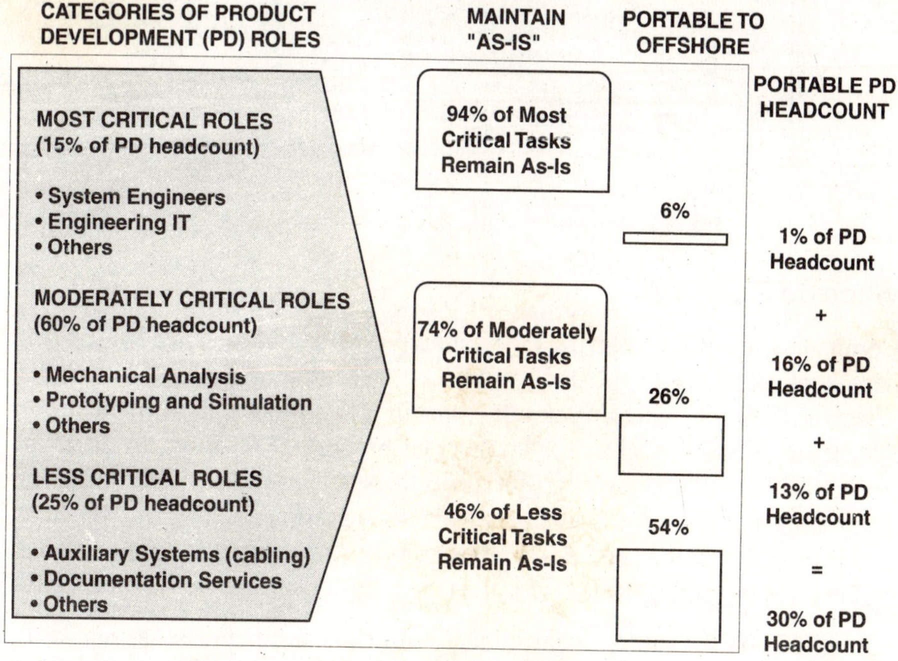

Fig. 6.2: Summary Analysis of Partability by Role

There are two other key considerations when contemplating what activities to offshore: business strategy and product lifecycle. Each business must understand what its strategy is and the required core competencies in product development that support that strategy. For example, a company that focuses on a specific type of technological innovation in its products would keep those related activities in-house. The second consideration is the lifecycle of each product or platform. In general, more product development activities related to older product lines can be off-shored versus the number of similar activities related to new products, as indicated in **Figure 6.3.** The relative value added for sustaining engineering on older products is generally less than the value of new product development associated with new, yet to be launched products. However, there are opportunities to utilize global product development strategies for new and old products to take advantage of cost and time-to-market benefits.

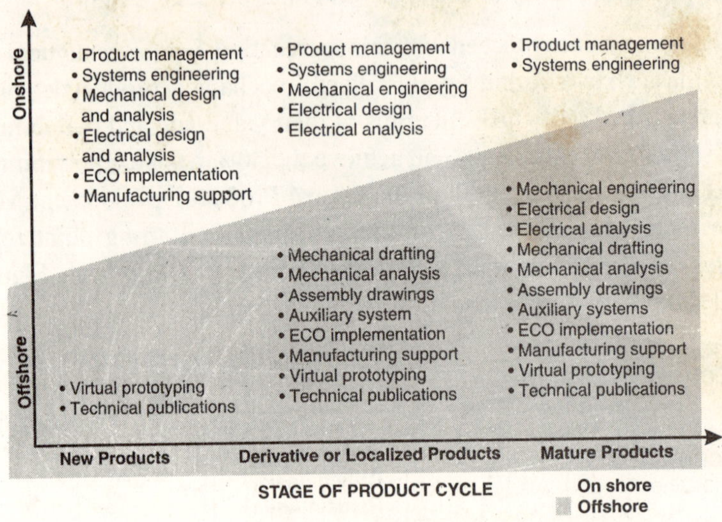

Fig. 6.3: Assessing Portability by Product Li fecycle

Where to Offshore?

Companies that have identified which activities can be relocated must next decide where to relocate those activities. There are a number of criteria that affect this decision, including cultural capabilities for product development, cost advantage, cultural respect for intellectual property, education levels of the population as well as their language capabilities, the business environment, and the existing provider base. A summary model using various ranking and weighting factors is shown in **Figure 6.4**. Different companies are likely to apply different ranking and weighting factors to reflect their particular interests and concerns.

As **Figure 6.4** shows, today, India is the prime destination—especially for English-speaking countries —for companies that want to implement Global Product Development. In addition to strong English-language skills, India enjoys a relatively strong educational system that produces more than 200,000 new engineers each year. In fact, it is these same engineering schools that supplied technical recruits who were repurposed to feed the IT boom that has transpired in India since the mid-1990's. Therefore, India has a large existing supply of engineers as well as strong annual recruitment.

There are other strong players on the global scene as well, and certain alignments are proving repeatable. It is common to see Western European countries transfer work to Eastern European and former Soviet countries due to a stronger alignment of culture and language. Similarly, Japanese companies are more likely to transfer product development activities to China and other Asian countries.

Country	Rank	Store	Product Develop-ment Capabilities	Cost	IP Security	People	Environ -ment	Provider
India	1	3.3	3	4	2	3	2	4
Czech Republic	2	3.0	3	3	3	3	3	2
China	3	2.8	3	4	1	1	1	3
Russian Federation	4	2.7	3	4	0	2	1	1
Poland	5	2.7	3	3	2	3	1	2
Hungary	6	2.7	3	2	4	3	3	1
Malaysia	7	2.5	3	3	3	2	2	1
South Korea	8	2.5	3	1	3	3	4	3
Canada	9	2.4	3	0	4	4	4	4
South Africa	10	2.1	3	1	4	3	3	3
Israel	11	2.1	3	0	4	3	4	4
Mexico	12	2.0	3	2	3	3	2	2
Brazil	13	1.7	3	1	2	2	3	3
Argentina	14	1.6	3	2	1	3	1	1
		Weig-hting	25%	40%	15%	10%	5%	5%

Legend
4 = Highly Attractive 0 = Relatively Unattractive

Fig. 6.4: Global Product Development Destinations

How to Offshore?

Once a company has decided "what" and "where" to offshore it must then make the selected engineering design work portable. This requires both process changes and technology infrastructure.

Process Change

A degree of consideration must be given to the need for realignment of product development processes to support Global Product Development. Ad hoc processes that may work fine when the team is familiar and physically co-located are easily thwarted when the team becomes separated by geographic, corporate, and cultural divides.

For companies who desire to adopt the "Level 3–Discrete Services" approach to Global Product Development, consideration must be given to instituting a formalized "modular **process**" where each main step or "module" has clear inputs, outputs, and responsibilities. By formalizing these interactions, companies gain the ability to transition certain "modules" to offshore facilities or partners, with clear expectations of how the process will work when some work is done offshore and the majority remains onshore.

Companies who elect to pursue "Level 4 – Co-Design" strategies need to give strong consideration to how to segregate major products or projects so that they may be transitioned offshore in their entirety. However, when the strategy calls for transitioning sub-components of a new product design, then additional thought must be given to "modular **product** design". Unlike modular process design that formalizes interfaces between people, modular product design is a methodology activities can proceed more independently with the assurance that the results will integrate nicely in the final product.

Required Infrastructure

It is the advancement of information technology that has made Global Product Development a practical reality. The family of CAD, CAM, CAE, PLM, and related IT technologies that companies have been deploying for internal automation purposes for the last decade now also provide the necessary enablement for Global Product Development. In order to facilitate Global Product Development, an effective IT infrastructure must enable the product development process to:

- **Get Digital:** By eliminating paper, and by moving to a pure digital product modeling approach, companies can make their intellectual property highly portable between locations and team members. It is this portability that allows a US engineer to work on a design during the day, have that same design advanced in India during the night, and then be ready for review again in the morning. The consistent use of CAD, in particular, is a prerequisite to any meaningful Global Product Development strategy, but the use of CAM, CAE, and Visualization technologies is required to realize its full potential.
- **Get Automated:** An effective information and process management environment enables companies to capture digital data content, securely control its various versions and configurations, manage concurrent changes, and automate the flow of information between members of the product development team. Like CAD, a baseline of information and process control is a critical prerequisite to avoid disabling chaos during the transition to, and ongoing operation of, Global Product Development.

- **Get Global:** The introduction of Internet-based collaboration technologies enables the establishment of "virtual team rooms" that allow dynamic sharing of digital product information across both geographic and company boundaries. When collaboration and data management solutions are integrated, companies can share enterprise information with offshore partners in a select and secure manner, enabling productivity without compromising the proprietary nature of intellectual property.

Risks and Challenges

The degree to which Global Product Development is viewed as "politically incorrect" suggests the magnitude of risks people have associated with it. The topic of off-shoring, especially white-collar jobs, has been the source of many heated debates. To protect their own economies, some local and national governments have even proposed legislation to prevent the migration of jobs to low-cost regions. When viewed at the global level, this protectionist approach is inefficient and prevents businesses from achieving optimal productivity levels.

Furthermore, protectionist legislation usually invites counter-productive retaliation in the form of trade sanctions that further limit global economic growth. Most people would agree that the free market should remain free to pursue its natural equilibrium. While governments can mandate short-term policies, pure economics manages to win out over the longer timeframe. There is a long list of potential risks and challenges associated with Global Product Development, but in aggregate they could be characterized in four primary forms that merit discussion:

- Political
- Business
- Technical
- Organizational

POLITICAL CONCERNS

Global Product Development ultimately results in the transition of innovation activities offshore. Many Western countries are sensitive about ceding economic power that is underpinned by innovation. The following are some common arguments that address this issue, and typical responses.

Brain Drain

- **Argument:** As we shift product development work to low-cost countries, we will ultimately be arming them to become skilled innovators. This will someday weaken the leadership position of the high-cost countries and put them at a disadvantage politically.

- **Reply:** In fact, just the opposite will occur. As low-cost countries strengthen their economies, their purchasing power will rise and they will demand increasingly sophisticated goods and services from high-cost countries. Furthermore, as the low-cost countries accept the rote and mundane activities of product development, they will free up more time for higher-cost engineers to work on higher-level, innovation-oriented work. If anything, the high-cost countries will become intellectually stronger—not weaker.

Job Loss

- **Argument:** Moving engineering jobs to low-cost countries will compromise the economies of the higher-cost countries. Unemployed workers do not spend money, which creates a drag on the high-cost country's economy.
- **Reply:** Same argument as above – but with the added distinction that, as low-cost country economies began to demand more goods and services from high-cost country economies, local firms would have to increase staff to meet demand. In short, on a localized basis, jobs may decline, but across the entire economy, increased demand will spur job growth in adjacent industries and activities. The off-shoring of manufacturing did not coincide with an economic crash in high-cost countries, but actually fueled growth and prosperity.

Threat to National Security

- **Argument:** Many high-cost countries are prohibited from sending defense-oriented intellectual property outside the country.
- **Reply:** This is, indeed, true. Global Product Development will not be appropriate in all circumstances. However, there are proven ways to disaggregate defense-oriented work to isolate those components of the work that can be done offshore, so, one should not necessarily assume that none of the work is applicable for Global Product Development.

BUSINESS CONCERNS

Given that economic strength plays such a strong role in world politics today, it's not surprising that there are a series of business-oriented criticisms to Global Product Development. These criticisms operate at a level below international competition and focus more on competitiveness of the individual firm. Samplings of these challenges are as follows:

Intellectual Property (IP) Theft

- **Argument:** Many low-cost nations have no formal IP laws and lack respect for intellectual property rights. For example, software piracy is rampant in many low-cost countries. For this reason, high-cost country firms are hesitant to distribute their own IP (e.g., product designs, CAD models, assembly instructions) outside of nations where they can ensure its safety.
- **Reply:** While this is certainly true, there are measures that can be taken to mitigate IP risk. These measures include a thoughtful and strategic up-front assessment of which IP to send and which to keep, as well as using information technology, organizational, and physical deterrents to control access to sensitive information, or portions thereof. Additionally, a number of low-cost countries recognize IP protection as a requirement to grow their services businesses and they are working on legislation and enforcement.

Non-Standard Processes

- **Argument:** Some companies argue that their innovation processes are not "standard" enough to be decomposed and reconfigured for Global Product Development. In other words, they never conduct product development the same way twice.
- **Reply:** While aspects of this may be true, most manufacturing companies have taken steps to control their product development processes. In fact, the Product Development and Management Association (PDMA) recently conducted a survey indicating that 72% of companies surveyed now have a formal, cross-functional product development process. In addition, for those that still do not, Global Product Development can serve as a focal point around which to pilot and then instill process discipline.

Customers will Complain

- **Argument:** Many companies in high-cost countries feel that they will be viewed as "unpatriotic" in the eyes of their customers for sending work outside of the home country, and they worry about losing business as a result.
- **Reply:** While customers might view the migration of work as unpatriotic, they will certainly not complain about lower prices or products getting to market faster. Assuming that a portion of the Global Product Development entitlement is passed back to the customer, any initial negative reactions will not be sustained. As evidence, today virtually all products have some components that are manufactured offshore, and yet, customers show widespread acceptance.

TECHNICAL CONCERNS

Technology has played a pivotal role in the rise of Global Product Development. The ability to digitize work products, the increased bandwidth available in low-cost countries, and the proliferation of networks and computers have all contributed. While technology has great power to enable new business models, because of its naturally dynamic nature, it can cause skepticism and even fear in those who are not comfortable with it. Some common objections are:

Non-Digital Product Development Process

- **Argument:** Some high-cost country companies still do not use digital technology (three-dimensional CAD, Product Lifecycle Management, etc.) to orchestrate product development. So to effectively participate in Global Product Development, they would first have to "digitize" their basic product development operations, which can create a great deal of concurrent business changes.
- **Reply:** Over the past decade, the world of product development has advanced rapidly, and those who have not adopted modern techniques and technologies are now in a small minority and already at serious risk of competitive disadvantage. Global Product Development can be seen as a focal point for driving an initiative to upgrade product development to be a fully digital, automated, and collaborative process. This investment will pay productivity dividends locally in the high-cost country, as well as contribute toward the Global Product Development initiative.

Viability of the Technology

- **Argument:** Since Global Product Development is a relatively new concept, some home country manufacturers might question the viability of the underlying technology to actually support it.
- **Reply:** Global Product Development is simply a more advanced application of the "Design Anywhere – Build Anywhere (DABA)" concept, which is a well–understood and proven practice. The same Product Lifecycle Management applications that have been enabling DABA enable Global Product Development; they are well-understood and stable.

ORGANIZATIONAL CONCERNS

Global Product Development implies a radical shift in the way that work gets accomplished – this shift occurs across many different dimensions from process, to capabilities, to organization. Many would argue that organizational issues are, perhaps, the most critical, given the importance of smooth collaboration to the success of Global Product Development.

Communication

- **Argument:** Management in high-cost countries may be wary of telling employees that Global Product Development will entail local staff reductions, for fear that morale and productivity will be compromised. Off-shoring strategies can cause difficulty with labor unions as well. These reasons alone might be enough to prevent a Global Product Development initiative from happening.
- **Reply:** Like offshore manufacturing, Global Product Development is a reality whether we like it or not. Early adopters embrace the opportunity to gain competitive advantage through better productivity. Competitors have to follow to regain competitive parity, or they risk suffering even worse consequences. Either way, management may have a tough message for some employees, but business failure can be far more drastic.

The dramatic changes in consumption and consumer patterns together with the growth of international mega brand products have put heavy pressure on industry to change its way of doing business, especially its New Product Development (NPD). Strategies such as transfer, merger, acquisition and collaboration are becoming the growing trend nowadays. The success of new products depends mostly on the new product development process and management.

Success in the worldwide marketplace demands that designers and engineers excel at product innovation, creating better products faster and more cost-effectively. This often means embracing new partnerships and collaborating with colleagues, engineers and vendors from across the globe. Designers need to create partnerships that not only infuse new ideas into product development, but also take advantage of the design capabilities and manufacturing efficiencies that make today's manufacturing environment so competitive.

They need to turn a global competitive threat into a product development advantage by leveraging design collaboration, design reuse and publishing technologies in order to design, engineer and manufacture products with greater innovation.

Globalization pressures have begun to have a major impact on the practice of product development across a wide range of industries. A new paradigm has emerged whereby companies are utilizing skilled engineering teams dispersed around the world to develop products in a collaborative manner. Best practice in product development (PD) is now rapidly migrating from local, cross-functional collaboration to a mode of global collaboration. Global product development (GPD) therefore represents a major transformation for business, and it applies to a broad range of industries.

Factors which affect the industry are related to the types of new product development, R&D organization, the R&D and marketing interface related to new product development and nature of the business. This paper discusses the role of R&D, enterprise, and the government etc. in promoting product development.

Product-development planning remains crucial to organizations' survival. Some key challenges, and hence success factors are as follows: Development Speed: 'Faster and faster' is the mantra of product development. One way to hasten development speed is through digital design, analysis, and collaboration tools to get products to market faster.

Deployment of global resources in product development and manufacturing also creates unique constraints and challenges. Managing a virtual team from across a global enterprise and a global value chain requires the right skills, infrastructure, and business processes. Real-time global communication, ensuring a win-win strategy for all participants, IP ownership/protection and product documentation are a few of these challenges.

Product development with a virtual team also requires a certain degree of formality in the management of concurrent designs by disperse engineering groups. Definition of the interfaces of subsystems and the scope of the work and deliverables from different groups must be well documented and updated frequently to reflect changes in project direction and priority.

Leveraging globalization allows companies to meet business goals of improved time-to-market and lower development costs. When we think of globalization, most of us immediately focus on the continuing move of manufacturing away from the US, Japan and Europe and into the Asia-Pacific and other low-cost manufacturing countries. But globalization is more than manufacturing. Many large companies are not only using manufacturing in the Pac-Rim but are also establishing significant facilities in these countries to capitalize on the low-cost engineering talent that is available.

They are also outsourcing design of all or parts of their products to **ODMs** (original design manufacturers). They now have a situation where the development and delivery process for a product may be spread across a number of locations around the world. Another aspect of globalization is the necessity to market a product on a global basis. Companies need to design a product globally and then sell it to a global audience.

This all adds new meaning (and words) to an old adage: "**Design Everywhere – Build Anywhere – Sell Globally.**" For a change, let's work backward through the process.

Sell Globally

When a company produces a product for sale in various regions around the world, it often has to produce different versions of the same design. Examples might include different operating voltages for a product, different electromagnetic emissions regulations or different communication protocols for a wireless device depending on location. The less efficient and most risky way to meet these goals is to: design a specific product for each region, estimate the number of units to be sold in each region, and then manufacture and stockpile the correct number of units to be sold. The risk is you can produce more than enough for one region and not enough for another, thus wasting stock and missing market opportunity respectively. Another option is to slow down manufacturing and only produce versions as needed in the marketplace; again risking maximum sales due to the time required to re-kindle a manufacturing line to high volume.

The best option is to use the method of **"variant design".** Using this method, a single design is produced that will accommodate all of the possible variations required for the different regions. The variations are dependent on the combination of component(s) mounted and independent of the bare board. The bare boards can then be manufactured in high volumes and stockpiled. (The bare board is not nearly as expensive as the components that go on it.) Then depending on the specific volumes required for each region, have manufacturing assemble the boards with the correct set of components.

Modern communication tools and the Internet have reduced the need for product development partners to be geographically close. Indeed product development is increasingly being divided between locations, with different parts getting created in multiple centers around the globe and brought back together for integration and testing.

Build Anywhere

A common practice to reduce product costs in today's global environment is to outsource manufacturing to a lower-cost manufacturing center. A company may want to line up multiple manufacturers to meet high volume and flexible demands. Taking a product from design into a successful manufacturing process requires that decisions be made during the design process to result in a smooth transition of the design into the manufacturer(s) environment (new product introduction).

First, let's look at some decisions during design that could make the difference between a successful product and one that misses revenue goals.

One of these involves choosing components early and throughout ECOs (engineering change orders) in the design process. The choice of the wrong component (even though functionally correct) could mean an increase in product cost (high reliability and an expensive part into a consumer product). Another example is a part that requires manual versus automatic assembly, again increasing the product cost. Yet another is the ability to obtain enough parts to support your production volume.

The way to prevent these situations involves two areas requiring electronic design solution capabilities. First is the ability to produce work-in-progress BOMs and communicate those to the target procurement and manufacturing organizations. These should be produced as soon as the schematic is somewhat final and before layout begins. Given the BOMs, procurement and manufacturing can identify any potential problems.

When it comes time to transfer the design into manufacturing, it can be a daunting task if the designer is required to understand all of the target manufacturer's machine specific format and process steps. The designer can use a tool that takes all of the required design data and translates it into a common format. This common data can then be accepted by the target manufacturer(s) and automatically customized to their exact needs.

Design Everywhere

As we look at the typical large enterprise today, it often has its design resources dispersed at various locations around the country or around the world. As the company strives to meet its basic business goals of getting a competitive product to market faster with lower development costs, it needs to leverage these design resources in the most efficient manner. This involves not only the electronic designers, but all of the engineering disciplines required in the design and delivery process. The key is **collaboration.** How do you create an environment where all of these disciplines can collaborate on the same design in the most efficient manner?

Collaboration Breeds Innovation

Working collaboratively on a global scale means design team members are often on the other side of the world. In order to collaborate across vast geographic distances, design teams need a common design data environment that is accessible to all partners. The ability to share design information among team members regardless of their location, function or even the type of data they generate, is imperative for product developers who need create new products.

Providing a visual representation of product designs has become increasingly important for working with partners, suppliers and vendors on a global scale.

Tools like eDrawings, which deliver complete 2D drawings and 3D models with multiple views, geometry rotation and mark-up capabilities, can deliver design information in a format that can help engineers overcome language and data barriers.

Creating design reports automatically from analysis results is another way to communicate design information in a visual fashion.

Global Intellectual Property (IP) Management

With a company's design resources spread around the world, it is important that IP (component libraries, design constraints and intent, work-in-progress design data, design reuse data, best practices work flow, etc.) be easily created, protected and accessed by designers and manufacturing. This type of infrastructure requires a significant investment by the company to build and maintain.

CHALLENGES IN GLOBAL PRICING

Pricing means to set price or prices for the markets, aim at gaining profit for the company. There are many kinds of pricing including pricing strategies, pricing objectives, pricing policies and so on.

A number of different pricing strategies are available to global marketers. An overall goal must be to contribute to company sales and profit objective worldwide. Customer-oriented strategies such as market skimming, penetration, and market holding can be used when customer perceptions, as determined by the value of equation, are used as a guide. Global pricing can also be based on other external criteria such as the escalations in costs when goods are shipped long distances across national boundaries. The issue of global pricing can also be fully integrated in the product design process, an approach widely used by Japanese companies. Pricing in global markets must be evaluated at regular intervals and adjusted if necessary. Similarly pricing objectives may vary, depending on product's life cycle stage and the country-specific competitive situation.

Any pricing system should address price floor, price ceiling and optimum prices in each of national market in which the company operates. The pricing consideration for marketing outside the home countries are the reflection of quality in price, competitiveness, the kind of pricing objective i.e. penetration, skimming holding, the type of discount, market segmentation, the pricing option in case of costs increase or decrease, logicalness of price by the host-country, and its laws and the probable dumping.

Three major objectives known in pricing are ***market skimming, price penetration and market holding.***

Market skimming pricing strategy is an attempt to reach a market segment that is willing to pay a premium price for a product. In such case the product must create high value for buyers or the knowledge of customer regarding the technology used for the product is not sufficient. This pricing strategy is often used in the introductory phase of product life cycle, when both production capacity and competition are limited by setting high price the demand is limited to early adopters who are willing and able to pay the price. The goals of this pricing are maximize revenue on limited volume to match demand and to reinforce customers' perception of high product value.

Penetration pricing uses price as a competitive weapon to gain market position. The majority of companies, located in Pacific Rim, use this type of pricing. Scale-efficient plans and low-cost labor allow these companies to attack the market. Usually a first-time exporter do not use this type of pricing because it may call for some losses for some length of time which his company can not afford it. Some innovative companies, when their product is not patentable, use this strategy to achieve market saturation before the other competitors can copy. The sale volume it expects to achieve in the markets leads to scale economies and lower costs.

The ***market holding*** strategy is frequently adopted by companies that want to maintain their share of the market. In single-country marketing, this strategy often involves reacting to price adjustments by competitors. One of the changes factors in the price in global marketing is the currency fluctuations which often trigger price adjustments. Adjusting prices to fit the competitive situation may mean lower profit margins. A strong home currency and rising costs in the home country may also force a company to shift its sourcing to in-country or third-country manufacturing or licensing agreements, rather than exporting from home country, to maintain market share. Market holding means that a company must carefully examine all its costs to ensure that it will be able to remain competitive in target markets.

Another strategy, frequently used by companies new to exporting is ***cost-plus*** to gain to hold in global marketplace. There are two cost-plus pricing methods: historical accounting cost method which defines cost as the sum of all direct and indirect manufacturing and overhead costs, and estimated future cost method which is used mostly in recent years.

Cost –plus pricing requires adding up all costs required to get the product to destination, plus shipping and ancillary charges, and a profit percentage. It is relatively easy to arrive at a quote, assuming that accounting costs are available. This approach, however, ignores demand and competitive conditions in target market. Therefore this approach is either too high or too low in the light of market and competitive conditions.

Novice exporters do not care because they react to the market opportunities rather than having proactive seeking for them. *Price escalation is the increase in a product's price* as transportation, duty, and distributor margins which are added to the factory price.

Using Sourcing as a Strategic Pricing Tools

There are several options when addressing the problem of price escalation described earlier. Domestic manufacturers may be forced to switch to lower income, lower wages countries for the sourcing of certain components or even finished goods to keep costs and prices competitive. Some people believe low wage approach a one-time advantage, and can not be substitute for ongoing creativity which causes value. Another option is to source 100 percent of a finished product offshore near the local markets. In this case the manufacturer can enter into one of the arrangements such as licensing, joint venture, or a technology transfer agreement. In this case the manufacturer has presence in the market and high costs of home land and transportation will no longer be an issue. Another option is a through audit of the distribution structure in the target market. A *rationalization* of the distribution structure can substantially reduce the total markups required to achieve distribution in international market. Rationalization may include selecting new intermediaries, assigning new responsibilities to old intermediaries, or establishing direct marketing operations.

Exporters also encounter to dumping, which is sale of an imported product at a price lower than that normally charged in a domestic market or country of origin. Many countries have their own policies against dumping but the main point is how to prove a company is dumping and the time it take to get the losses from this action.

Environmental Factors Affecting Pricing

Marketers must deal with a number of environmental factors when making pricing decisions. Currency fluctuation, inflation, government controls and subsidies, competitive behavior, and market demand are among these factors. Some of these factors work in conjunction with others; for example, inflation may be accompanied by government controls.

When *currency fluctuation* occurs, there are two options for pricing: one is to fix the price of products in country target market. In this case, any appreciation or depreciation of the value of the currency in the country of production will lead to gain or losses for the seller. The other option is to fix the price of products in home country currency. If it is done, any appreciation or depreciation of the home country currency will result in price increases or decreases for customers and no immediate consequences for the seller. In actual practice, a manufacturer and its distributor may work together to maintain Market share in international market. Either party, or both, may choose to take a lower profit percentage. In the long term contracts, both parties agree an exchange rate clause, which allows them to agree to supply and purchase at fixed prices in each company's national currency. In this case if the exchange rate fluctuate within a specified range, say plus or minus of five percent, the agreed price will not be changed, but if more than that, say plus or minus of ten percent, then new discussion or negotiation for adjusting the prices should be opened.

Inflation, or a persistent upward change in price levels, is a worldwide phenomenon. Inflation requires periodic adjustments. These adjustments are caused by rising costs that must be covered by increased selling prices. An essential requirement when pricing in an inflationary environment is the maintenance of operating profit margins.

Government control can also limit the freedom to adjust prices, and the maintenance of margins should be compromised. In a country that is undergoing severe financial difficulties and is in the midst of a financial crisis (e.g., a foreign exchange shortage caused in part runaway inflation), government officials are under pressure to take some type of action. Governmental actions in the case of hard financial problems include use of broad or selective price controls, prior cash deposit requirements for imports, customs duties for imports, value added tariffs, proliferation of rules and regulations, and subsidization. All of these controls are against exporting pricing when a company wants to export products to an importing country which is under control of the government. In fact the more control rendered by a government the more difficult to enter in that country market. In this case the availability of this market is not so suitable.

The other fact is the study of relationship between quality and price. Recent four country international study found that there is a weak relation between price and quality. The authors concluded that the lack of strong price-quality relationship appears to be an international phenomenon.

Pricing decisions are also bounded by ***competitive action***. If competitors are manufacturing or sourcing in a lower costs country, it may be necessary to cut prices to stay competitive. Consumers with limited information rely more on product style and appearance and less on technical quality as measured by testing organizations. Still some marketers believe that this relation is strong and has the major role in product value. The recent following model shows strong relationship between price and quality which offers four strategy of *economy*, when the price and quality are both low, *penetration*, when the price low yet the quality is high to get more market share or penetrate in a new market, *skimming,* when the price is high but the quality is high and the goods are not supplied by too many competitors, and *premium,* when the price and quality are both high and there is a uniqueness about the product or service.

The knowledge of customer about the technology of new product and the amount of his or her awareness can play a major role in pricing. As much as the knowledge of a customer about the product is low, the producer can use this margin to skim the market or get a better premium from this market.

Transfer Pricing

Transfer pricing refers the pricing of goods and services bought and sold by operating units or divisions of a single company. In other word, transfer pricing concerns intra corporate exchanges-transactions between buyers and sellers that have the same corporate parent. For example Toyota subsidiaries sell to, and buy from each other. This happens when the company expands and profit centers are shaped in the corporate financial picture.

There are three alternative approaches to transfer pricing: (1) cost based pricing, (2) market based transfer pricing, and (3) negotiated prices.

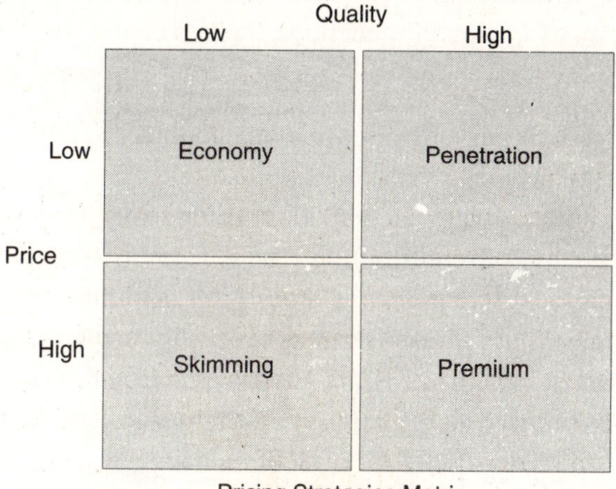

Pricing Strategies Matrix

Fig. 6.5

Some companies using ***cost- based*** approach may arrive at transfer prices that reflect variable and fixed manufacturing costs only. Alternatively, transfer prices may be based on full costs, including overhead costs from marketing, R&D, and other functional areas. The way costs are defined may have an impact on tariffs and duties sales to affiliates and subsidiaries by global companies. Cost plus pricing is also based by costs but different approach. In this approach, profit must be shown for any product or service at every stage of movement through the corporate system. It may be set at certain percentage of fixed costs such as 15 percent of cost. It is unrelated to competitive and demand conditions but many exporters use it.

Another approach to transfer pricing is ***market-based*** approach. A market-based transfer price is derived from the price required to be competitive in the international market. The volume level also plays a major role in pricing. To use market-based transfer prices to inter in a small market, third country sourcing may be required. This enables a company to establish its name or franchise in the market without committing to a major capital investment.

A third alternative is to allow the organization affiliates to negotiate transfer prices among themselves. In some instances, the final transfer price may reflect costs and market prices, but this is not a requirement. Corporate costs and profits are also affected by import duties. The higher the duty rate, the more desirable is a low transfer price. The high duty creates an increase to reduce transfer prices to minimize the customs duty.

The companies also may use three policies on worldwide pricing: ***extension ethnocentric, adaptation/poly centric*** *and* ***invention/geocentric***. The first policy indicates that the firm believes there is no need to change present product, relies on its culture preference, does not involve itself in knowing the differences of the markets and believes in their local success, that could leads to global success as well; by extension/ethnocentric, it relies on the similarities of global markets. The second policy suggests that all markets are different and we have to consider these differences and adapt our products by using product adaptation for each market.

In the **first policy**, the price of an item is the same around the world and the importer will endure freight, import charges and duties. In this policy, no information on competitive or market condition is required and the exporter does not respond to every market neither to maximize the company profits in national market nor global one. Its only advantage is to simply entering a market if it matches to their price so the exporter has no information about it.

In the **second policy** the exporter tries to match the price with any individual local market. This policy permits subsidiary or affiliate manager to establish any price they feel is most desirable in their circumstances. Yet this policy may cause product arbitrage, because of different prices in different location and enterprising business managers may use it and foster a grey market for the company's product. It may also weaken the corporate strategies of the central company because all local market managers have the freedom to set the price for their markets. Different prices for different places may have another disadvantage, because it may send a signal to the rest of the world that is contrary to company interests. A price moves anywhere in the world would instantly be known all over the world.

The **third** and the best policy to international pricing is termed invention/geocentric. Using this approach a company neither fixes a single price nor remains apart from subsidiary price decisions, but instead strikes intermediate positions. There are unique market factors, like local costs, income levels, competition, and local marketing strategies that should be recognized in arriving at pricing decisions. Local costs plus a return on invested capital and personnel fix the price floor for the long term. This approach lends itself to global competitive strategy. A global competitor will take in to account global markets and global competitors in establishing prices. Prices will support global strategy objectives rather than the objectives of maximizing performance in a single country.

Other Approaches to Pricing

There are also new approaches for pricing that has been experience in the global marketing. We will describe them below:

- **Psychological pricing** is used when the marketer wants the consumer to respond on an emotional, rather than rational basis. For example, price point perspective 99 cents not one dollar.
- **Product line pricing** can be used when where there is a range of products and pricing reflects the benefits of parts of the range.
- **Optional product pricing strategy:** Companies will attempt to increase the amount customer spend once they start to buy. Optional extras increase the overall price of the product. For example airlines will charge for optional extras such as guaranteeing a window seat.
- **Captive product pricing strategy:** Companies will charge a premium price where the consumer is captured. For example the razor price is low but its unique blades are expensive and the customer should later buy it if the razor breaks down.
- **Product bundle pricing:** Sellers combine several products in the same package. This also serves to move old stocks and CDs often sold using the bundle approach.
- **Promotional pricing** companies try to promote their sale through sale promotional, like by one get one free (BOGOF)
- **Geographical pricing** is used where there are variations in price different part of the world. For example rarity value, or where shipping costs increase price.
- **Value pricing** also is used where external factors such as recession or increased competition force companies to provide value products and services to retain sales e.g. value meals at McDonalds.

Japanese companies act different in pricing. In Japan, planned sale prices, by deducting the intended profit is considered as the target cost. In this stage the product design units, engineering and price suppliers, with the aim of developing value for the customers or rise based on the customer perception, try to close their costs to target costs so that the price of products can be reduced. After the company could reach the target costs, the production process will be started. We conclude that Japanese producers, before producing the product, consider the market price of goods and try to reach the cost feasible to sell the market. Meanwhile Japanese competitors don't care the costs of goods, before considering the acceptable costs of goods.

Particular Factors of an Export Price

The factors for developing price are *costs*, the *market and customer behavior conditions*, *competition and the company policies*. The main factor for pricing is *costs*. The price base on costs, especially when there is no information about the market and customer willingness, is a virtually easy approach and shows the fairness for value added payment of production. The costs are useful for determining the floor price of a product.

In short term, when we have extra capacity, the floor costs may be the out of pocket costs, i.e. direct costs like labor, material and transport costs. However, in the long term, the full costs must be considered for the products, but may not be considered for all products. Direct costs when using in export mean the required costs for developing income. In addition to extra capacity, direct cost pricing (margin cost pricing) for entering a market in the competitive condition or preserving a market in the competitive condition can be applied.

These reasons are: to help intermediate organizations or agents, maintaining the coworkers working together, selling a product especially out of the normal line of export and for offering a manufactured sample to a dependent or under license organization, mass customized production, in many companies, when the conditions of market are not normal, the pricing less than full costs is applied. The floor price is mostly affected by floor price. This kind of pricing is highly recommended when the company is sure that the internal market will guarantees the sale volume at least up to break even point. From that point the profit margin will be a combination of internal and global sales.

The **market condition** pricing is based on the market demand and the product attractiveness in each market. The nature of market can determine the ceiling of the price. When the demand in a market for the product is high we use higher prices for that market. Utility, or the assumed value of buyers of a product, determine the ceiling price of a product.

In demand forecasting of a market, exporter can classify the market based on the price attractiveness for customer in different price levels. Then the export manager can define a classified utilities relate to prices. The main problem of this kind of pricing is the lack of information for demand forecasting and the customer willingness particularly in developing countries. Therefore the market condition is a difficult factor for pricing.

The third and may be the most important factor of pricing is the condition of *competition.* Condition of competition helps for pricing between these two boundaries. The competitor reaction forces producer to determine new export pricing. The price of competitors affects the sale volume of exporter and the resulted decision may be less or more than price of them. When an exporter does not have enough authority for pricing a competitive market, the main problem of pricing then will be to sell the product with the assigned price or not. If the floor price of a manufacturer is less than the current price of market, the product will be produced and sold. The market condition pricing is most suitable when the new technology used for the product or service is complex or unique for that market and the knowledge of customer or market about know-how of the product is little.

Pricing can different in each market, depending on different stages of a product. When we want to enter a competitive market we may use direct costs because of the product and cherry picking character of the intermediates and possible future agents. When the product is well known and well positioned the firm may use competitive or market price suitable in that market. When the market is saturated by different competitors we may use niche pricing and stay in that market and let other competitors to leave this market or we leave the market, during the last stage of product life cycle, if we feel this market will not be profitable any more.

Developing Export Pricing Model

Kotler in pricing argument, when focuses on customer needs, classify organizations to profitable and for-profit organizations. He believes that profitable organization is the one that sell his product in the present time and tries to gain the maximum profit regarding the present situation. Meanwhile, for-profit organization focuses on long term profitability, and is presently ready, for customer satisfaction, to overlook the short term profit enabling to gain success in the market and developing fame in the customer consideration.

It seems these two different considerations in the management, is depended on the management authority and offering logical reasons. An export manager, who has enough position certainty in the future, enough delegated authority to decide and price for different market, logical and fast decision making for the price related to each market, can develop strategic prices in his plans and implement them in the long term. This manager can plot his logical reasons for penetrating, direct costs pricing etc, to board of directors and top management and gain necessary authority for pricing decisions which indeed should be delegated to him.

Another factor, which causes unwillingness for manufacturers to export their goods to foreign market, is the internal market conditions and its characteristics. Internal market favorableness or unfavorableness shows the attractiveness of the market which could be measured by factors like: internal demand situation, government industry support, future prospects of internal market, local customer support, stability of market demand and government supports and etc.

If we concern two factors of the *amount of management authority*, which is depended to delegation granted for pricing, and the *internal market conditions*, managers usually use 4 pricing strategies as follows:

Authority granted	Internal market condition: Unfavorable	Internal market condition: Favorable
High	Direct costs pricing	Global strategic pricing
Low	Floor pricing	Ceiling price based on internal price

Fig. 6.6: Model of export pricing based on amount of authority granted and internal market condition

When the authority of manager for pricing is low and internal market condition is unfavorable, manager is to set floor or finished costs prices for exporting. When the export manager authority is high and internal market condition is unfavorable, he or she may use direct costs pricing and uses the remained capacity of production. This pricing is particularly good when the company wants to enter new markets.

If the internal marketing condition is favorable and the authority of export manager is low, then the prices for export will be ceiling price based on internal prices. This kind of pricing stems from the short term profitability willingness from internal market; which has made the present top managers to be proud of it. In this approach the management uses local market values and governs the local customer's values to international prices.

Finally, if the authority of export manager is high and the internal market condition is favorable, manager take the best advantage of for-profit organization philosophy (not profitable organization) and use pricing for each market so that in future the required interests to be gained for the organization.

Top managers and owners of an organization should notice that they can cultivate a seed now and use its fruit in near future, provided to be patient enough, and plan wisely, for the potential markets to reach the profit. But this cultivation requires good farmer too, and a well marketing expert with enough experience and good strategic vision helps to make the organization takes advantage of proper strategy. So we recommend granting enough authority to such marketing manager for fast paste pricing in different markets.

INTERNATIONAL CHANNEL DISTRIBUTION AND MANAGEMENT

A distribution channel is a method of getting a product to its consumer. Distribution channels are part of a company's marketing mix. A marketing mix refers to each business' unique combination of product, price, promotion and place. Distribution affects the place or path through which consumers can buy and receive the product. A distribution channel may be an on-site store, a virtual store, a retailer, a wholesaler, an agent, a telemarketer or direct mail.

Most producers do not sell their goods directly to the final users; between them stands a set of intermediaries performing a variety of functions. These intermediaries constitute a marketing channel (also called a trade channel or distribution channel). Formally, marketing channels are sets of interdependent organizations involved in the process of making a product or service available for use or consumption. They are the set of pathways a product or service follows after production, culminating in purchase and use by the final end user.

Some intermediaries—such as wholesalers and retailers—buy, take title to, and resell the merchandise; they are called merchants. Others—brokers, manufacturers' representatives, sales agents—search for customers and may negotiate on the producer's behalf but to not take title to the goods; they are called agents. Still others—transportation companies, independent warehouses, banks, advertising agencies—assist in the distribution process but neither take title to goods nor negotiate purchases or sales; they are called facilitators.

The Importance of Channels

A marketing channel system is the particular set of marketing channels employed by a firm. Decisions about the marketing channel system are among the most critical facing management. Marketing channels also represent a substantial opportunity cost. One of the chief roles of marketing channels is to convert potential buyers into profitable orders.

In managing its intermediaries, the firm must decide how much effort to devote to push versus pull marketing. A push strategy involves the manufacturer using its sales force and trade promotion money to induce intermediaries to carry, promote, and sell the product to end users. Push strategy is appropriate where there is low brand loyalty in a category, brand choice is made in the store, the product is an impulse item, and product benefits are well understood. A pull strategy involves the manufacturer using advertising and promotion to persuade consumers to ask intermediaries for the product, thus inducting the intermediaries to order it. Pull strategy is appropriate when there is high brand loyalty and high involvement in the category, when people perceive differences between brands, and when people choose the brand before they go to the store.

Channel Development

A new firm typically starts as a local operation selling in a limited market, using existing intermediaries. The number of such intermediaries is apt to be limited: a few manufacturers' sales agents, a few wholesalers, several established retailers, a few trucking companies, and a few warehouses. Deciding on the best channels might not be a problem might be to convince the available intermediaries to handle the firm's line.

If the firm is successful, it might branch into new markets and use different channels in different markets. In smaller markets, the firm might sell directly to retailers; in larger markets, it might sell through distributors. In rural areas, it might work with general-goods merchants; in urban areas, with limited-line merchants. In one part of the country, it might grant exclusive franchises; in another, it might sell through all outlets willing to handle the merchandise. In one country it might use international sales agents; in another, it might partner with a local firm. In short, the channel system evolves in response to local opportunities and conditions.

Value Networks

A supply chain view of a firm sees markets as destination points and amounts to a linear view of the flow. The company should first think of the target market, however, and then design the supply chain backward from that point. This view has been called demand chain planning. An even broader view sees a company at the centre of a value network—a system of partnerships and alliances that a firm creates to source, augment, and deliver its offerings. A value network includes a firm's suppliers and its suppliers' suppliers, and its immediate customers and their end customers. The value network includes valued relations with others such as university researchers and government approval agencies.

Demand chain planning yields several insights. First, the company can estimate whether more money is made upstream or downstream, in case it might want to integrate backward or forward. Second, the company is more aware of disturbances anywhere in the supply chain that might cause costs, prices, or supplies to change suddenly. Third, companies can go on-line with their business partners to carry on faster and more accurate communications, transactions, and payments to reduce costs, speed up information, and increase accuracy. With the advent of the Internet, companies are forming more numerous and complex relationships with other firms.

Managing this value network has required companies to make increasing investments in information technology and software. They have invited such software firms as SAP and Oracle to design comprehensive enterprise resource planning systems to manage cash flow, manufacturing, human resources, purchasing, and other major functions within a unified framework. They hope to break up department silos and carry out core business processes more seamlessly. Marketers, for their part, have traditionally focused on the side of the value network that looks toward the customer. In the future, they will increasingly participate in and influence their companies' upstream activities and become network managers, not only product and customer managers.

Types of Channel Members

Channel activities may be carried out by the marketer or the marketer may seek specialist organizations to assist with certain functions. This section classify specialist organizations into two broad categories: resellers and specialty service firms.

Resellers

These organizations, also known within some industries as intermediaries, distributors or dealers, generally purchase or take ownership of products from the marketing company with the intention of selling to others. If a marketer utilizes multiple resellers within its distribution channel strategy the collection of resellers is termed a Reseller Network. These organizations can be classified into several sub-categories including:

- **Retailers:** Organizations that sell products directly to final consumers.
- **Wholesalers:** Organizations that purchase products from suppliers, such as manufacturers or other wholesalers, and in turn sell these to other resellers, such as retailers or other wholesalers.
- **Industrial Distributors:** Firms that work mainly in the business-to-business market selling products obtained from industrial suppliers

Specialty Service Firms

These are organizations that provide additional services to help with the exchange of products but generally do not purchase the product (i.e., do not take ownership of the product):

- **Agents and Brokers:** Organizations that mainly work to bring suppliers and buyers together in exchange for a fee.
- **Distribution Service Firms:** Offer services aiding in the movement of products such as assistance with transportation, storage, and order processing.
- **Others:** This category includes firms that provide additional services to aid in the distribution process such as insurance companies and firms offering transportation routing assistance.

CHANNEL ARRANGEMENTS

The distribution channel consists of many parties each seeking to meet their own business objectives. Clearly for the channel to work well, relationships between channel members must be strong with each member understanding and trusting others on whom they depend for product distribution to flow smoothly.

For instance, a small sporting goods retailer that purchases products from a wholesaler trusts the wholesaler to deliver required items on-time in order to meet customer demand, while the wholesaler counts on the retailer to place regular orders and to make on-time payments.

Relationships in a channel are in large part a function of the arrangement that occurs between the members. These arrangements can be divided in two main categories:

1. Independent Channel Arrangements
2. Dependent Channel Arrangement

Independent Channel Arrangements

Under this arrangement a channel member negotiates deals with others that do not result in binding relationships. In other words, a channel member is free to make whatever arrangements they feel is in their best interest. This so-called "conventional" distribution arrangement often leads to significant conflict as individual members decide what is best for them and not necessarily for the entire channel.

On the other hand, an independent channel arrangement is less restrictive than dependent arrangements and makes it easier for a channel members to move away from relationships they feel are not working to their benefit.

Dependent Channel Arrangements

Under this arrangement a channel member feels tied to one or more members of the distribution channel. Sometimes referred to as "vertical marketing systems" this approach makes it more difficult for an individual member to make changes to how products are distributed. However, the dependent approach provides much more stability and consistency since members are united in their goals. The dependent channel arrangement can be broken down into three types:

- **Corporate:** Under this arrangement a supplier operates its own distribution system in a manor that produces an integrated channel. This occurs most frequently in the retail industry where a supplier operates a chain of retail stores. Starbucks is a company that does this. They import and process coffee and then sell it under their own brand name in their own stores. It should be mentioned that Starbucks also distributes their products in other ways, such as through grocery stores and mail order. As we will see in more detail later, Starbucks is using a multi-channel structure to market their products.
- **Contractual:** Under this arrangement a legal document obligates members to agree on how a product is distributed. Often times the agreement specifically spells out which activities each member is permitted to perform or not perform. This type of arrangement can occur in several formats including:
    - **Wholesaler-sponsored:** where a wholesaler brings together and manages many independent retailers including having the retailers use the same name.
    - **Retailer-sponsored:** this format also brings together retailers but the retailers are responsible for managing the relationship.
    - **Franchised:** where a central organization controls nearly all activities of other members.
- **Administrative:** In certain channel arrangements a single member may dominate the decisions that occur within the channel. These situations occur when one channel member has achieved a significant power position. This most likely occurs if a manufacturer has significant power due to brands in strong demand by target markets (e.g., Procter & Gamble) or if a retailer has significant power due to size and market coverage (e.g., Wal-Mart). In most cases the arrangement is understood to occur and is not bound by legal or financial arrangements. (More discussion on **channel power** can be found below.)

Benefits Offered by Channel Members

When choosing a distribution strategy a marketer must determine what value a channel member adds to the firm's products. Remember, as we discussed in the Product Decisions tutorial, customers assess a product's value by looking at many factors including those that surround the product (i.e., augmented product). Several surrounding features can be directly influenced by channel members, such as customer service, delivery, and availability. Consequently, for the marketer selecting a channel partner involves a value analysis in the same way customers make purchase decisions. That is, the marketer must assess the benefits received from utilizing a channel partner versus the cost incurred for using the services. These benefits include:

- **Cost Savings in Specialization:** Members of the distribution channel are specialists in what they do and can often perform tasks better and at lower cost than companies who do not have distribution experience. Marketers attempting to handle too many aspects of distribution may end up exhausting company resources as they learn how to distribute, resulting in the company being "a jack of all trades but master of none."
- **Reduce Exchange Time:** Not only are channel members able to reduce distribution costs by being experienced at what they do, they often perform their job more rapidly resulting in faster product delivery. For instance, consider what would happen if a grocery store received direct shipment from EVERY manufacturer that sells products in the store. This delivery system would be chaotic as hundreds of trucks line up each day to make deliveries, many of which would consist of only a few boxes. On a busy day a truck may sit for hours waiting for space so they can unload their products. Instead, a better distribution scheme may have the grocery store purchasing its supplies from a grocery wholesaler that has its own warehouse for handling simultaneous shipments from a large number of suppliers. The wholesaler will distributes to the store in the quantities the store needs, on a schedule that works for the store, and often in a single truck, all of which speeds up the time it takes to get the product on the store's shelves.
- **Customers want to Conveniently Shop for Variety:** Marketers have to understand what customers want in their shopping experience. Referring back to our grocery store example, consider a world without grocery stores and instead each marketer of grocery products sells through their own stores. As it is now, shopping is time consuming, but consider what would happen if customers had to visit multiple retailers each week to satisfy their grocery needs. Hence, resellers within the channel of distribution serve two very important needs: (1) they give customers the products they want by purchasing from many suppliers (termed accumulating and assortment services), and (2) they make it convenient to purchase by making products available in single location.
- **Resellers Sell Smaller Quantities:** Not only do resellers allow customers to purchase products from a variety of suppliers, they also

allow customers to purchase in quantities that work for them. Suppliers though like to ship products they produce in large quantities since this is more cost effective than shipping smaller amounts. The ability of intermediaries to purchase large quantities but to resell them in smaller quantities (referred to as bulk breaking) not only makes these products available to those wanting smaller quantities but the reseller is able to pass along to their customers a significant portion of the cost savings gained by purchasing in large volume.

- **Create Sales:** Resellers are at the front line when it comes to creating demand for the marketer's product. In some cases resellers perform an active selling role using persuasive techniques to encourage customers to purchase a marketer's product. In other cases they encourage sales of the product through their own advertising efforts and using other promotional means such as special product displays.
- **Offer Financial Support:** Resellers often provide programs that enable customers to more easily purchase products by offering financial programs that ease payment requirements. These programs include allowing customers to: purchase on credit; purchase using a payment plan; delay the start of payments; and allowing trade-in or exchange options.
- **Provide Information:** Companies utilizing resellers for selling their products depend on distributors to provide information that can help improve the product. High-level intermediaries may offer their suppliers real-time access to sales data including information showing how products are selling by such characteristics as geographic location, type of customer, and product location (e.g., where located within a store, where found on a website). If high-level information is not available, marketers can often count on resellers to provide feedback as to how customers are responding to products. This feedback can occur either through surveys or interviews with reseller's employees or by requesting the reseller allow the marketer to survey customers.

Costs of Utilizing Channel Members

- **Loss of Revenue:** Resellers are not likely to offer services to a marketer unless they see financial gain in doing so. They obtain payment for their services as either direct payment (e.g., marketer pays for shipping costs) or, in the case of resellers, by charging their customers more than what they paid the marketer for acquiring the product (termed markup). For the latter, marketers have a good idea of what the final customer will pay for their product which means the marketer must charge less when selling the product to resellers. In these situations marketers are not reaping the full sale price by using resellers, which they may be able to do if they sold directly to the customer.

- **Loss of Communication Control:** Marketers not only give up revenue when using resellers, they may also give up control of the message being conveyed to customers. If the reseller engages in communication activities, such as personal selling in order to get customers to purchase the product, the marketer is no longer controlling what is being said about the product. This can lead to miscommunication problems with customers, especially if the reseller embellishes the benefits the product provides to the customer. While marketers can influence what is being said by training reseller's salespeople, they lack ultimate control of the message.
- **Loss of Product Importance:** Once a product is out of the marketer's hands the importance of that product is left up to channel members. If there are pressing issues in the channel, such as transportation problems, or if a competitor is using promotional incentives in an effort to push their product through resellers, the marketer's product may not get the attention the marketer feels it should receive.

MARKETING ISSUES IN CHANNELS

Product Issues

The nature of the product often dictates the distribution options available especially if the product requires special handling. For instance, companies selling delicate or fragile products, such as flowers, look for shipping arrangements that are different than those sought for companies selling extremely tough or durable products, such as steel beams.

Promotion Issues

Besides issues related to physical handling of products, distribution decisions are affected by the type of promotional activities needed to sell the product to customers. For products needing extensive salesperson-to-customer contact (e.g., automobile purchases) the distribution options are different than for products where customers typically require no sales assistance (i.e., bread purchases).

Pricing Issues

The desired price at which a marketer seeks to sell their product can impact how they choose to distribute. As previously mentioned, the inclusion of resellers in a marketer's distribution strategy may affect a product's pricing since each member of the channel seeks to make a profit for their contribution to the sale of the product. If too many channel members are involved the eventual selling price may be too high to meet sales targets in which case the marketer may explore other distribution options.

Target Market Issues

A distribution system is only effective if customers can obtain the product. Consequently, a key decision in setting up a channel arrangement is for the marketer to choose the approach that reaches customers in the most effective way possible. The most important decision with regard to reaching the target market is to determine the level of distribution coverage needed to effectively meet customer's needs.

RELATIONSHIP ISSUES IN MARKETING CHANNELS

A good distribution strategy takes into account not only marketing decisions, but also considers how relationships within the channel of distribution can impact the marketer's product. In this section we examine three such issues:

Channel Power

A channel can be made up of many parties each adding value to the product purchased by customers. However, some parties within the channel may carry greater weight than others. In marketing terms this is called channel power, which refers to the influence one party within a channel has over other channel members. When power is exerted by a channel member they are often in the position to make demands of others. For instance, they may demand better financial terms (e.g., will only buy if prices are lowered, will only sell if price is higher) or demand other members perform certain tasks (e.g., do more marketing to customers, perform more product services). Channel power can be seen in several ways:

- **Back-end or Product Power:** Occurs when a product manufacturer or service provider markets a brand that has a high level of customer demand. The marketer of the brand is often in a power position since other channel members have little choice but to carry the brand or risk losing customers.
- **Middle or Wholesale Power:** Occurs when an intermediary, such as a wholesaler, services a large number of smaller retailers with products obtained from a large number of manufacturers. In this situation the wholesaler can exert power since the small retailers are often not in the position to purchase products cost-effectively and in as much variety as what is offered by the wholesaler.

- **Front or Retailer Power:** As the name suggests, the power in this situation rests with the retailer who can command major concessions from their suppliers. This type of power is most prevalent when the retailer commands a significant percentage of sales in the market they serve and others in the channel are dependent on the sales generated by the retailer.

Channel Conflict

In an effort to increase product sales, marketers are often attracted by the notion that sales can grow if the marketer expands distribution by adding additional resellers. Such decisions must be handled carefully, however, so that existing dealers do not feel threatened by the new distributors who they may feel are encroaching on their customers and siphoning potential business. For marketers, channel strategy designed to expand product distribution may in fact do the opposite if existing members feel there is a conflict in the decisions made by the marketer. If existing members sense a conflict and feel the marketer is not sensitive to their needs they may choose to stop handling the marketer's products.

Need for Long-Term Commitments

Channel decisions have long-term consequences for marketers since efforts to establish new relationships can take an extensive period of time while ending existing relationships can prove difficult. For instance, Company A, a marketer of kitchen cabinets that wants to change distribution strategy, may decide to stop selling their product line through industrial supply companies that distribute cabinets to building contractors and instead sell through large retail home centers. If in the future Company A decides to once again enter the industrial supply market they may run into resistance since supply companies may have replaced Company A's product line with other products and, given what happened to the previous relationship, may be reluctant to deal with Company A. As another example of problems with long-term commitments, building contractors may be comfortable purchasing kitchen cabinets from industrial suppliers. If Company A decides to change their reseller network they may find it difficult to regain the building contractor customer base, who may continue to purchase from the industrial suppliers but are now purchasing products from Company A's competitors. In this case, Company A may have to give serious thought to whether breaking their long-term relationship with industrial suppliers is in the company's best interest.

Channel Evaluation

Channels of distribution may be evaluated on such primary criteria as cost of distribution, coverage of market (penetration), customer service, communication with the market, and control of distribution networks. Occasionally, such secondary factors as support of channels in the successful introduction of a new product and cooperation with the company's promotional effort also become evaluative criteria. To arrive at a distribution channel that satisfies all these criteria requires simultaneous optimization of every facet of distribution, something that is usually not operationally possible. Consequently, a piecemeal approach may be followed.

Cost of Distribution. A detailed cost analysis of distribution is the first step in evaluating various channel alternatives on a sales-cost basis. This requires classification of total distribution costs under various heads and subheads. The question of evaluation comes up only when the company has been following a particular channel strategy for a number of years. Presumably, the Channels of distribution may be evaluated on such primary criteria as cost of distribution, coverage of market (penetration), customer service, communication with the market, and control of distribution networks. Occasionally, such secondary factors as support of channels in the successful introduction of a new product and cooperation with the company's promotional effort also become evaluative criteria. To arrive at a distribution channel that satisfies all these criteria requires simultaneous optimization of every facet of distribution, something that is usually not operationally possible.

Coverage of the Market. An important aspect of predicting future sales response is the penetration that will eventually be achieved in the market. For example, in the case of a drug company, customers can be divided into three groups: (a) drugstores, (b) doctors, and (c) hospitals. One measure of the coverage of the market (or penetration of the market) is the number of customers in a group contacted or sold, divided by the total number of customers in that group. Another measure may be penetration in terms of geographical coverage of territory. But these measures are too general. Using just the ratio of customers contacted to the total number of customers does not give a proper indication of coverage because not all types of customers are equally important.

Customer Service. The level of customer service differs from customer to customer for each business. Generally speaking, the sales department, with feedback from the field force, should be able to designate the various services that the company should offer to different consumer segments. If this is not feasible, a sample survey may be planned to find out which services customers expect and which services are currently being offered by competitors. This information can be used to develop a viable service package. Then the capability and willingness of each channel alternative to provide these services may be matched to single out the most desirable channel. This can be done intuitively. A more scientific approach would be to list and assign weights to each type of service, then rate different channels according to their ability to handle these services. Cumulative scores can be used for the service ranking of channel alternatives. Conjoint measurement can be used to determine which services are most important to a particular segment of customers.

Communication and Control. **Control** may be defined as the process of taking steps to bring actual results and desired results closer together. **Communication** refers to the information flow between the company and its customers. To evaluate alternate channels on these two criteria, communication and control objectives should be defined. With reference to communication, for example, information may be desired on the activities of competitors, new products from competitors, the special promotional efforts of competitors, the attitudes of customers toward the company's and toward competitors' services, and the reasons for success of a particular product line of the company. Each channel alternative may then be evaluated in terms of its willingness, capabilities, and interest in providing the required information. In the case of wholesalers, the communication perspective may also depend on the terms of the contract. But the mere fact that they are legally bound by a contract may not motivate wholesalers to cooperate willingly. Finally, the information should be judged for accuracy, timeliness, and relevance.

Channel Modification Environmental shifts, internal or external, may require a company to modify existing channel arrangements. A shift in trade practice, for instance, may render distribution through a manufacturer's representative obsolete. Similarly, technological changes in product design may require frequent service calls on customers that wholesalers may not be able to make, thus leading the company to opt for direct distribution.

DISTRIBUTION SYSTEM

Mindful of the factors affecting distribution decisions (i.e., marketing decision issues and relationship issues), the marketer has several options to choose from when settling on a design for their distribution network. We stress the word "may" since while in theory an option would appear to be available, marketing decision factors (e.g., product, promotion, pricing, target markets) or the nature of distribution channel relationships may not permit the marketer to pursue a particular option. For example, selling through a desired retailer may not be feasible if the retailer refuses to handle a product.

For marketers the choice of distribution design comes down to the following options:

1. Direct Distribution Systems
2. Indirect Distribution Systems
3. Multi-Channel or Hybrid Distribution Systems

Direct Distribution Systems

With a direct distribution system the marketer reaches the intended final user of their product by distributing the product directly to the customer. That is, there are no other parties involved in the distribution process that take ownership of the product. The direct system can be further divided by the method of communication that takes place when a sale occurs. These methods are:

- **Direct Marketing Systems:** With this system the customer places the order either through information gained from non-personal contact with the marketer, such as by visiting the marketer's website or ordering from the marketer's catalog, or through personal communication with a customer representative who is not a salesperson, such as through toll-free telephone ordering.
- **Direct Retail Systems:** This type of system exists when a product marketer also operates their own retail outlets. As previously discussed, Starbucks would fall into this category.
- **Personal Selling Systems:** The key to this direct distribution system is that a person whose main responsibility involves creating and managing sales (e.g., salesperson) is involved in the distribution process, generally by persuading the buyer to place an order. While the order itself may not be handled by the salesperson (e.g., buyer physically places the order on-line or by phone) the salesperson plays a role in generating the sales.
- **Assisted Marketing Systems:** Under the assisted marketing system, the marketer relies on others to help communicate the marketer's products but handles distribution directly to the customer. The classic example of assisted marketing systems is e-Bay which helps bring buyers and sellers together for a fee. Other agents and brokers would also fall into this category.

Distribution Systems: Indirect

With an indirect distribution system the marketer reaches the intended final user with the help of others. These resellers generally take ownership of the product, though in some cases they may sell products on a consignment basis (i.e., only pay the supplying company if the product is sold). Under this system intermediaries may be expected to assume many responsibilities to help sell the product.

Indirect Methods Include

- **Single-Party Selling System:** Under this system the marketer engages another party who then sells and distributes directly to the final customer.

This is most likely to occur when the product is sold through large store-based retail chains or through on-line retailers, in which case it is often referred to as a trade selling system.

- **Multiple-Party Selling System:** This indirect distribution system has the product passing through two or more distributors before reaching the final customer. The most likely scenario is when a wholesaler purchases from the manufacturer and sells the product to retailers.

Distribution Systems: Multi-Channel (Hybrid)

In cases where a marketer utilizes more than one distribution design the marketer is following a multi-channel or hybrid distribution system. As we discussed, Starbucks follows this approach as their distribution design includes using a direct retail system by selling in company-owned stores, a direct marketing system by selling via direct mail, and a single-party selling system by selling through grocery stores (they also use other distribution systems).

The multi-channel approach expands distribution and allows the marketer to reach a wider market, however, as we discussed under Channel Relationships, the marketer must be careful with this approach due to the potential for channel conflict.

ESTABLISHING CHANNEL RELATIONSHIPS

Since channel members must be convinced to handle a marketer's product it makes sense to consider channel partner's needs in the same way the marketer considers the final user's needs. However, the needs of channel members are much different than those of the final customer. Resellers seek products of interest to the reseller's customers but are also concerned with many other issues such as:

- **Delivery:** Resellers want the product delivered on-time and in good condition in order to meet customer demand and avoid inventory out-of-stocks.
- **Profit Margin:** Resellers are in business to make money so a key factor in their decision to handle a product is how much money they will make on each product sold. They expect that the difference (i.e., margin) between their cost for acquiring the product from a supplier and the price they charge to sell the product to their customers will be sufficient to meet their profit objectives.
- **Other Incentives:** Besides profit margin, resellers may want other incentives to entice them especially if they are required to give extra effort selling the product. These incentives may be in the form of additional free products or even bonuses (e.g., bonus, free trips) for achieving sales goals.

- **Packaging:** Resellers want to handle products as easily as possible and want their suppliers to ship and sell products in packages that fit within their system. For example, products may need to be a certain size or design in order to fit on a store's shelf, or the shipping package must fit within the reseller's warehouse or receiving dock space. Also, many resellers are now requiring marketers to consider adding identification tags to products (e.g., RFID tags) to allow for easier inventory tracking when the product is received and also when it is sold.
- **Training:** Some products require the reseller to have strong knowledge of the product including demonstrating the product to customers. Marketers must consider offering training to resellers to insure the reseller has the knowledge to present the product accurately.
- **Promotional Help:** Resellers often seek additional help from the product supplier to promote the product to customers. Such help may come in the form of funding for advertisements, point-of-purchase product materials, or in-store demonstrations.

SUMMARY

- Globalization may be defined as "the growing economic interdependence of countries worldwide through increasing and variety of cross border transactions in goods and services and of international capital flows, and also through the more rapid and widespread diffusion of technology."
- Globalization may be considered at two levels, viz., at the macro level (i.e., globalization of the world economy) and at the micro level (i.e., globalization of the business and the firm). Globalization of the economies and globalization of business are very much interdependent.
- There are several similarities and differences between the two phases of globalization. The current phase of globalization is characterized by several new features: new markets; new technologies, new actors and new rules and norms.
- Normally, a firm passes through different stages of development before it becomes a truly global corporation. Typically, a domestic firm starts its international business by exporting. Later it may establish joint ventures or subsidiaries abroad.
- Globalization has both beneficial and harmful effects. It affects differently different countries, sectors, industries and sections of people.
- There are some essential conditions to be satisfied on the part of the domestic economy as well as the firm for successful globalization of the business. They include the following: Business freedom, required facilities, government support; resources; competitiveness and proper strategic orientation.
- India's economic integration with the rest of the world was very limited because of the restrictive economic policies followed until 1991. Indian firms

confined themselves, by and large, to the home market. Foreign investment by Indian firms was very insignificant.

- Globalization has in fact become a buzz world with Indian firms now and many are expanding their overseas business by different strategies.
- Pricing is one the marketing mix and reflects costs and competitive factors. The maximum absolute price for a product does not exist, yet for each market, the price should be fixed concerning the customer attitude. The goal of most marketing strategies is to determine a price which could be accountable for customer perception.
- Pricing strategies include increasing interests regarding the importance of the product in the market. We can use different pricing strategies, concerning the environmental factors of markets. Each company should determine competitive market, its costs for each market, the availability of them, and other environmental dimensions.
- Export managers, from their advantage point of familiarities to markets should have enough authority to determine strategic prices for each market regarding the life cycle of the product in each market an their stability and profitability for that market. Export managers should be qualified and brilliant mind knowing the corporate strategy and acting different roles in different markets.
- **Three** major objectives known in pricing are ***market skimming, price penetration and market holding.***
- The companies also may use three policies on worldwide pricing: ***extension ethnocentric, adaptation/poly centric*** *and* ***invention/geocentric***.
- Distribution channels are part of a company's marketing mix. A marketing mix refers to each business' unique combination of product, price, promotion and place.
- Decisions about the marketing channel system are among the most critical facing management. Marketing channels also represent a substantial opportunity cost. One of the chief roles of marketing channels is to convert potential buyers into profitable orders.
- Relationships in a channel are in large part a function of the arrangement that occurs between the members. These arrangements can be divided in two main categories:
  - Independent Channel Arrangements
  - Dependent Channel Arrangement
- A channel can be made up of many parties each adding value to the product purchased by customers.
- For marketers the choice of distribution design comes down to the following options:
  - Direct Distribution Systems
  - Indirect Distribution Systems
  - Multi-Channel or Hybrid Distribution Systems
- Channels of distribution may be evaluated on primary criteria such as cost of distribution, coverage of market (penetration), customer service, communication with the market, and control of distribution networks.

Chapter 7

International Strategic Planning

Strategic Planning is the process of determining an organization's basic mission and long-term objectives, and then implementing a plan of action for pursuing this mission and attaining these objectives. As companies go international, this strategic process takes on added dimensions.

The Growing Need for Strategic Planning

One of the primary reasons that MNCs such as Toyota or Citibank need strategic planning is to keep track of their increasingly diversified operations in a continuously changing international environment. This need is particularly obvious when one considers the amount of foreign direct investment (FDI) that has occurred in recent years. Recent statistics reveal that FDI has grown three times faster than trade and four times faster than world gross domestic product (GDP). These developments are resulting in a need to coordinate and integrate diverse operations with a unified and agreed on focus. There are many examples of firms that are doing just this.

One is Ford Motor, which has reentered the market in Thailand and, despite a shrinking demand for automobiles there, is beginning to build a strong sales force and to garner market share. The firm's strategic plan here is based on offering the right combination of price and financing to a carefully identified market segment. In particular, Ford is working to keep down the monthly payments so that customers can afford a new vehicle. This is the same approach that Ford used in Mexico, where the currency crisis of 1994 resulted in problems for many multinationals. However, this was not true for Ford which rolled out a carefully formulated strategy that allowed it to increase its vehicle market share in Mexico from 14 per cent in 1994 to 20 per cent three years later.

Another example of the growing need for strategic planning is provided by Bertelsmann AG, the giant German book publisher that has now entered the

Chinese market. Bertelsmann has created a giant book club that could dramatically change the way Chinese buy books. In the past two years this club has signed up over 600,000 members, opened a handful of retail stores, and sold almost 5 million volumes. Moreover, Bertelsmann is now adding 2000 new members every day, a growth rate that is easily sustainable given that approximately 180 million Chinese read books on a regular basis.

A third example of the growing need for strategic planning is provided by the German MNC Siemens. The firm used to make mobile phones but its costs were so high that it could not compete effectively. Today, thanks to its strategic plan, Siemens is back in the race. The company can now produce a phone in five minutes and the lightweight unit with long battery life sells for half that of competitive models.

Benefits of Strategic Planning

Now that the needs for strategic planning have been explored, what are some of the benefits? Many MNCs are convinced that strategic planning is critical to their success and these efforts are being conducted both at the home office and in the subsidiaries. For example, one study found that 70 per cent of the 56 U.S. MNC subsidiaries in Asia and Latin America had comprehensive 5–10 year plans.

Do these strategic planning efforts really pay off? To date, the evidence is mixed. Certainly, that the strategic plan helps an MNC to coordinate and monitor its far-flung operations must be viewed as a benefit. Similarly, that the plan helps an MNC to deal with political risk problems (see Chapter 2), competition, and currency instability cannot be downplayed.

Despite some obvious benefits, there is no definitive evidence that strategic planning in the international arena always results in higher profitability. Most studies that report favorable results were conducted at least a decade ago. Moreover, many of these findings are tempered with contingency-based recommendations. For example, one study found that when decisions were made mainly at the home office and close coordination between the subsidiary and home office was required, return on investment was negatively affected.

Another study found that *planning intensity* (the degree to which a firm carries out strategic planning) is an important variable in determining performance. Those firms with high planning intensity tended to exaggerate the emphasis, and profitability suffered. Companies that earned a high percentage of their total sales in overseas markets however did best with a high-intensity planning process and poorly with a low-intensity process. Therefore, although strategic planning usually seems to pay off, as with most other aspects of international management, the specifics of the situation will dictate the success of the process.

Approaches to Formulating and Implementing Strategy

Four common approaches to strategic planning are: (1) focusing on the economic imperative; (2) addressing the political imperative; (3) emphasizing the quality imperative; and (4) implementing an administrative coordination strategy.

Economic Imperative: MNCs that focus on the economic imperative employ a worldwide strategy based on cost leadership, differentiation and segmentation. Many of these companies typically sell products for which a large portion of value is added in the upstream activities of the industry's value chain. By the time the product is ready to be sold, much of its value has already been created through research and development, manufacturing and distribution. Some of the industries in this group include automobiles, chemicals, heavy electrical systems, motorcycles and steel.

Because the product is basically homogeneous and requires no alteration to fit the needs of the specific country, management uses a worldwide strategy that is consistent on a country-to-country basis.

Another economic imperative concept that has gained prominence in recent years is global sourcing, which is proving very useful in formulating and implementing strategy. A good example is the European PC market. Initially, this market was dominated by such well-known companies as IBM, Apple and Compaq. However, more recently, clone manufacturers have begun to gain market share. This is because the most influential reasons for buying a PC have changed. A few years ago, the main reasons were brand name, service, and support. Today, price has emerged as a major impact into the purchasing decision. Customers now are much more computer literate, and they realize that many PCs offer identical quality performance. As a result, the economic imperative dominates the strategic plans of computer manufacturers.

Political Imperative: MNCs using the political imperative approach to strategic planning are country-responsive; their approach is designed to protect local market niches. "International Management in Action: Point/Counterpoint" demonstrates this political imperative. The products sold by MNCs often have a large portion of their value added in the downstream activities of the value chain. Industries such as insurance and consumer packaged goods are examples – the success of the product or service generally depends heavily on marketing, sales and service. Typically, these industries use a country-centered or multi-domestic strategy.

Quality Imperative: This quality imperative is taking two interdependent paths: (1) a change in attitudes and a rising of expectation for service quality; and (2) the implementation of management practices that are designed to make quality improvement an ongoing process. Commonly called "total quality management", or simply TQM, the approach takes a wide number of forms, including cross-training personnel to do the jobs of all members in their work group, process re-engineering designed to help identify and eliminate redundant tasks and wasteful effort, and reward systems designed to reinforce quality performance.

TQM covers the full gamut, from strategy formulation to implementation. It briefly summarizes the following:

- Quality is operationalized by meeting or exceeding customer expectations. Customers include not only the buyer or external user of the product or service, but also the support personnel both inside and outside the organization who are associated with the goods or service.
- The quality service is formulated at the top management level and is diffused throughout the organization. From top executives to hourly employees, everyone operates under a TQM strategy of delivering quality products and/or services to internal and external customers.
- The techniques range from traditional inspection and statistical quality control to cutting-edge human resource management techniques such as self-managing teams and empowerment.

Many MNCs make quality a major part of their overall strategy, because they have learned that this is the way to increase market share and profitability. For example, while the US automakers have dramatically increased their overall quality in recent years to close the gap with Japanese auto quality, Japanese firms continue to have fewer safety recalls. Toyota and Honda continue to be ranked very high by American consumers, and Nissan's recent market performance shows that the firm is also a major competitor in this market.

Administrative Coordination: An administrative coordination approach to formulation and implementation is one in which the MNC makes strategic decisions based on the merits of the individual situation rather than using a predetermined economic or political strategy. A good example is provided by Wal-Mart, which has expanded rapidly into Latin America in recent years. While many of the ideas that worked well in the North American market served as the basis for operations in the southern hemisphere, the company soon realized that it was doing business in a market where local tasters were different and competition was strong.

Many large MNCs work to combine the economic, political, quality and administrative approaches to strategic planning. For example, IBM relies on the economic imperative when it has strong market power, the political and quality imperatives when the market requires a calculated response (European countries), and an administrative coordination strategy with rapid, flexible decision-making is needed to close the sale. Of the four, the first three approaches are much more common because of the firm's desire to coordinate its strategy both regionally and globally.

STRATEGIC PREDISPOSITIONS

In addition to the economic, political, quality and administrative approaches, most MNCs also have a strategic predisposition toward doing things in a particular way. This orientation or predisposition helps to determine the specific steps the MNC will follow. Four distinct predispositions have been identified:

- Ethnocentric
- Polycentric
- Regiocentric
- Geocentric

A company with an **ethnocentric predisposition** allows the values and interests of the parent company to guide the strategic decisions. Firms with a **polycentric predisposition** make strategic decisions tailored suite the cultures of the countries when the MNC operates. A **regiocentric predisposition** leads a firm to try to blend its own interests with those of its subsidiaries on a regional basis. A company with a **geocentric predisposition** tries to integrate a global systems approach to decision making.

If an MNC relies on one of these profiles over an extended time, the approach may become institutionalized and greatly influence strategic planning. By the same token a predisposition toward only of these profiles can provide problems for a firm if it is out of step with the economic or political environment. For example, a firm with an ethnocentric predisposition may find it difficult to implement a geocentric strategy, because it is unaccustomed to using global integration.

The Basic Steps in Formulating Strategy

The needs, benefits, approaches, and predispositions of strategic planning serve as a point of departure for the basic steps in formulating strategy. In international management, strategic planning can be broken into the following steps:

- Scanning the external environment for opportunities and threats.
- Conducting an internal resource analysis of company strengths and weaknesses.
- Formulating goals in light of the external scanning and internal analysis.

Environmental Scanning

Environmental Scanning attempts to provide management with accurate forecasts of trends that relate to external changes in geographic areas where the firm is currently doing business and/or considering setting up operations. These changes relate to the economy, competition, political stability, technology, and demographic consumer data.

Typically, the MNC will begin by conducting a forecast of macroeconomic and industry performance dealing with factors such as markets for specific products, per-capita income of the population, and availability of labor and raw materials. A second common forecast will predict likely trends in monetary exchange rates, exchange controls, balance of payments, and inflation rates. A third is the forecast of the company's potential market share in particular geographic areas as well as that of the competitors. Other considerations include political stability, government pressure, nationalism, and related areas of political risk.

These assessments are extremely important in determining the risk profile and profit potential of the region, which always is a major consideration when deciding where to set up international operations.

Internal Resource Analysis

When formulating strategy, some firms wait until they have completed their environmental scanning before conducting an internal resource analysis. Others perform these two steps simultaneously. Internal resource analysis helps the firm to evaluate its current managerial, technical, material and financial strengths and weaknesses. This assessment then is used by the MNC to determine its ability to take advantage of international market opportunities.

An internal analysis identifies the key factors for success that will dictate how well the firm is likely to do. A **key factor for success (KFS)** is a factor that is necessary for a firm to compete effectively in a market niche.

For example, a KFS for an international airline is price. An airline that discounts its prices will gain market share vis-à-vis those that do not. A second KFS for the airline is safety, and a third is quality service in terms of on-time departures and arrivals, convenient schedules, and friendly, helpful personnel.

In the automobile industry, quality of products has emerged as the number-one KFS in world markets. Japanese firms have been able to invade the US auto market successfully, because they have been able to prove that the quality of their cars is better than the average domestically built US car. Toyota and Honda have had such quality edge over the competition in recent years in the eyes of US car buyers. A second KFS is styling.

Goal Setting for Strategy Formulation

In practice, goal formulation often precedes the first two steps of environmental scanning and internal resource analysis. As used here, however, the more specific goals for the strategic plan come out of external scanning and internal analysis. Profitability and marketing goals almost always dominate the strategic plans of today's MNCs. Profitability is so important because MNCs generally need higher profitability from their overseas operation than they do from their domestic operations. The reason is quite simple: Setting up overseas operations involves greater risk and effort.

Once the strategic goals are set, the MNC wili develop specific operational goals and controls, usually through a two-way process at the subsidiary or affiliate level. Home office management will set certain parameters, and the overseas group will operate within these guidelines.

STRATEGY IMPLEMENTATION

Once formulated, the strategic plan next must be implemented. Strategy implementation provides goods and services in accord with a plan of action. Quite often, this plan will have an overall philosophy or series of guidelines that direct the process.

International management must consider three general areas in strategy implementation. First, the MNC must decide where to locate operations. Second, the MNC must carry out entry and ownership strategies. Finally, management must implement functional strategies in areas such as marketing, production and finance.

Location Considerations for Implementation

In choosing a location, today's MNC has two primary considerations: the country, and the specific locale within the chosen country. Quite often, the first choice is easier than the second, because there are many more alternatives from which to choose a specific locale.

The Country: Traditionally, MNCs have invested in highly industrialized countries and research reveals that annual investments have been increasing substantially. In 1993 over $325 billion was spent on mergers and acquisitions worldwide. By 1997 the annual total had jumped to $1.6 trillion and today it is well in excess of $2 billion. Much of this investment, especially by American MNCs, has been in Europe, Canada and Mexico.

Foreign investors are also pouring into Mexico. One reason is because it is a gateway to the American and Canadian markets. A second reason is because Mexico is a very cost effective place to manufacture goods. A third is that the declining value of the peso in the late 1990s hit many Mexican hard and left them vulnerable to mergers and acquisitions – an opportunity that was not lost on many large multinationals.

MNCs often invest in advanced industrialized countries because they offer the largest markets for goods and services. In addition, the established country or geographic locale may have legal restrictions related in imports, encouraging a local presence. Japanese firms, for example in complying with their voluntary export quotas of cars to the United States as well as responding to dissatisfaction in Washington regarding the continuing trade imbalance with the United States, have established US based assembly plants.

Still another consideration in selecting a country is restrictions on foreign investment. Traditionally, countries such as China and India have required that control of the operation be in the hands of local partners. MNCs that are reluctant to accept such conditions will not establish operations there.

Another consideration in choosing a country is the amount of government control. Traditionally, MNCs from around the world refused to do business in Eastern European countries with central planning economies. The same is true in India, although the political climate can be volatile and MNCs must carefully weigh the risks of investing here.

In addition to these considerations, MNCs will examine the specific benefits offered by host countries, including low tax rates, rent-free land and buildings, low-interest or no interest loans, subsidized energy and transportation rates and a well-developed infrastructure that provides many of the services found back home (good roads, communication systems, schools, health care, entertainment, and housing).

Local Issues: Once the MNC has decided the country in which to locate the firm must choose the specific locale. A number of factors influence this choice. Common considerations include access to market, proximity to competitors, availability of transportation and electric power, and desirability of the location for employees coming in from the outside.

Another common consideration is the nature of the workforce. MNCs prefer to locate near sources of available labor that can be readily trained to do the work. A complementary consideration that often is unspoken is the presence and strength of organized labor. Japanese firms in particular tend to avoid heavily unionized areas.

Still another consideration is the cost of doing business. Manufacturers often set up operations in rural areas, commonly called "***green field locations***", which are less expensive and do not have the problems of urban areas.

Conversely, banks often choose metropolitan areas, because they feel they must have a presence in the business district.

Some MNCs opt for locales where the cost of running a small enterprise is significantly lower than that of running a large one. In this way, they spread their risk, setting up many small locations throughout the world rather than one or two large ones. Some production firms feel that the economies of scale associated with a large-scale plant are more than offset by potential problems that can result should economic or political difficulties develop in the country.

Ownership and Entry Considerations for Implementation

There are a number of common forms of ownership in international operations. However, the most widely recognized are wholly owned subsidiaries acquired through acquisitions and alliances / mergers, joint ventures, licensing agreements, franchising and basic export and import operations. Depending on the situation, any one of these can be a very effective way to implement a MNCs strategy.

The Role of the Functional Areas in Implementation

To implement strategies, MNCs must tap the primary functional areas of marketing, production, and financc. Thc following sections examine the roles of these functions in international strategy implementation.

Marketing: The implementation of strategy from a marketing perspective must be determined on a country-by-country basis. What works from the standpoint of marketing in one locale may not necessarily succeed in another. In addition, the specific steps of a marketing approach often are dictated by the overall strategic plan, which in turn is based heavily on market analysis.

The implementation strategy of marketing strategy in the international arena is built around the well-known "four Ps" of marketing: product, price, promotion, and place. German auto firms in Japan are a good example of using marketing analysis to meet customer needs. Over the past 15 years, the Germans have spent millions of dollars to build dealer, supplier and service-support networks in Japan, in addition to adapting their cars to Japanese customers' tastes. The Japanese also provide an excellent example of how the marketing process works. In many cases, Japanese firms have followed a strategy of first building up their market share at home and driving out imported goods. Then, the firms move into newly developed countries, honing their marketing skills as they go along. Finally, the firms move into fully developed countries, ready to compete with the best available. This pattern of implementing strategy has been used in marketing autos, cameras, consumer electronics, home appliances, petrochemicals, steel, and watches.

Production: Although marketing usually dominates strategy implementation, the production function also plays a role. If a company is going to export goods to a foreign market, the production process traditionally has been handled through domestic operations. In recent years, however, MNCs have found that whether they are exporting or producing the goods locally in the host country, consideration of worldwide production is important.

If the firm operates production plants in different countries but makes no attempt to integrate its overall operations, the company is known as **multi-domestic**. A recent trend has been away from this scattered approach and toward global coordination of operations.

Finally, if the product is labor-intensive, as in the case of microcomputers, then the trend is to farm the product out to low-cost sites such as Mexico or Brazil, where the cost of labor is relatively low and the infrastructure is sufficient to support production. Sometimes, multiple sources of individual components are used; in other cases, one or two sources are sufficient. In any event, careful coordination of the production function is needed when implementing the strategy, and the result is a product that is truly global in nature.

Finance: Use of the finance function to implement strategy normally is developed at the home office and carried out by the overseas affiliate or branch. When a firm went international in the past, the overseas commonly relied on the local area for funds, but the rise of global financing has ended this practice. MNCs have learned that transferring funds from one place in the world to another, or borrowing funds in the international money markets, often is less expensive than relying on local sources. Unfortunately, there are problem in these transfers.

When dealing with the inherent risk of volatile monetary exchange rates, some MNCs have bought currency options that guarantee convertibility at a specified rate. Others have developed countertrade strategies, whereby they receive products in exchange for currency.

SUMMARY

- There is a growing need for strategic planning among MNCs. Some of the primary reasons include: foreign direct investment is increasing, planning is needed to coordinate and integrate increasingly diverse operations via an overall focus, and emerging international challenges require strategic planning.
- A strategic plan can take on an economic focus, a political focus, a quality focus, an administrative coordination focus, or some variation of the four. In addition, an MNC typically is predisposed toward an ethnocentric, polycentric, regiocentric, or geocentric orientation. Companies may use a

combination of these orientations in their strategic planning, but geocentric is the one employed most commonly by global companies.

- Strategic planning is used by more MNCs every year, although no definitive evidence proves that this process always results in higher profitability. As with other aspects of international management, the particular situation largely will dictate the success of a strategic plan.
- Strategy formulation consists of several steps. First, the MNC carries out external environmental scanning to identify opportunities and threats. Next, the firm conducts an internal resource analysis of company strengths and weaknesses. Strategic goals then are formulated in light of the results of these external and internal analyses.
- Strategy implementation is the process of providing goods and services in accord with the predetermined plan of action. This implementation typically involves such considerations as: deciding where to locate operations, carrying out an entry and ownership strategy, and using functional strategies to implement the plan. Functional strategies focus on marketing, production and finance.

Chapter 8

Country Evaluation and Selection

INTRODUCTION

Companies seldom have enough resources to take advantage of all opportunities. Committing human, technical and financial resources to one locale may mean forgoing projects in other areas. So managers must be choosy. They must know how to pick the best location for their business interests.

A company should look to those countries with economic, political, cultural, and geographic conditions that mesh with its strengths. Managers might ask, "Where can we best leverage our already developed competencies?" and "Where can we go to best sustain, improve, or extend our competencies?" A company needs to determine the order of entry into potential countries and set the allocation of resources and rate of expansion among them.

Choosing Marketing and Production Sites, and Geographic Strategy

Companies must determine where to market and where to produce. In so doing, managers will need to answer two basic questions:

"Where markets should we serve?"

"Where should we place production to serve those markets?"

The answers to these questions can be one and the same, particularly if transport costs or government regulations mean that local production is necessary for serving the chosen market. Many service industries, such as hotels, construction and retailing must locate facilities near their foreign customers, so decisions on market and production location are connected. If a company develops a product that consumers find attractive, it must still find production cost advantages so that it can price the product favorably enough to sell it.

Decisions on market and production locations may be highly interdependent for other reasons. A company many have excess production capacity already in place that will influence its ability to serve markets in different countries. Or it may find a given market very attractive but forgo sales because it unwilling to invest in needed production locations.

The process of determining an overall geographic strategy must be flexible because country conditions change. A plan must let a company both respond to new opportunities to different locations and withdraw from less profitable ones. Unfortunately, there is little agreement on a comprehensive theory or technique for choosing the best location, one that helps companies get the most out of their resources.

Nevertheless, managers can use several geographic strategies. A company may expand its international sales by marketing more of its existing product line, by adding products to its line, or by some combination of these two. Most companies begin by asking

"Where can we sell more of our products?" instead of

"What new product can we make to maximize sales in a given market?"

In this chapter we assume that for the most part, the company has pursued the first question. In essence, a company needs to decide where to operate and what portion of operations to place within each location. There are certain major steps that international business managers take in making these decisions. The following discussion examines these steps in depth.

SCAN FOR ALTERNATIVE LOCATIONS

To compare countries, managers use scanning techniques based on broad variables that indicate opportunities and risks. That way, decision makers can perform a detailed analysis of a manageable number of geographic locations. Scanning is like weeding out-it is useful in that a company might otherwise consider too few or too many possibilities.

A company can easily overlook or disregard some promising options. Some locations may be skipped rather than rejected, simply because managers either never think of them or decide to go where "everyone else has gone".

A detailed analysis of every alternative might result in maximized sales or a least-cost production location, but the cost of so many studies would erode profits. A company with 1,000 products that might locale in any of 150 countries would need 150,000 different studies. Plus, other alternatives must be considered as well, such as whether to export or to set up a foreign production unit. Companies should examine any conditions would enhance the probability of making an investment before they perform a more detailed feasibility study.

CHOOSE AND WEIGHT VARIABLES

When scanning, managers will take the **environmental climate** into consideration. The environmental climate is the external conditions in a host country that could significantly affect the success or failure of a foreign business enterprise. It can determine whether a company will make a detailed study as well as the terms under which it will initiate a project. The environmental climate reveals both opportunities and risks.

OPPORTUNITIES

Managers make investment decisions after weighing opportunities against risks. Opportunities are determined by revenues less costs. From a broad scanning perspective, there are variables that indicate the amount of revenue, cost factors, and risk that might be forthcoming from one country to another.

The factors that have the most influence on the placements of marketing and production emphasis are:

- Market size
- Ease of compatibility of operations
- Costs and resource availability
- Red tape

Some of these variables are more important for the market location decision; others are more important for the production-location decision. Some variable affect both.

Market Size: Sales potential is probably the most important variable managers use in determining where and whether to make an investment. The assumption, of course, is that sales will occur at a price above cost, so that where there are sales, there are profits.

In some cases, a company can obtain past and current sales figures on a country-to-country basis for the type of product it wants to sell. In many cases, however, such figures are unavailable, leaving managers to estimate current demand. Either way, management must make projections about what will happen to future sales. One way is to base projections on a similar or complementary product for which sales figures are available, such as Blockbuster's projections of video rental potential based on VCR data.

Ease of Compatibility of Operations: Regardless of the industry, US companies put more emphasis on Canada, the United Kingdom, and Mexico than would be indicated by those countries' economic size. Managers prefer to go where they perceive it's easier to operate. For US companies, Canada and

Mexico rank high because of geographic proximity, which makes it easier and cheaper for the companies to control their foreign subsidiaries. Moreover, since the advent of NAFTA, US companies encounter fewer border restrictions for their operations in Canada and Mexico than they do for most other locales.

After companies pare alternatives to a reasonable number, they must prepare much more detailed feasibility studies. These studies can be expensive. The more time and money companies invest in examining an alternative, the more likely they are to accept it regardless of its merits, a situation known as an ***escalation of commitment***. A feasibility study should have clear-cut decision points at which managers can cut the commitment before it escalates.

Companies also consider local availability of resources in relation to their needs. More foreign operations require local resources, a requirement that may severely restrict the feasibility of given locales. For example, the company may need to find local personnel who are knowledgeable enough about its type of technology. If local equity markets are poorly developed and local borrowing is expensive, the company locating in a different country.

Companies sometimes use a **lead-country strategy**, which is introducing a product on a test basis in a small-country market that they consider representative of a region before investing to serve larger-country markets.

Costs and Resource Availability: So far, we have discussed market-seeking operations. However, companies also go abroad to secure resources that are either unavailable or expensive in their home countries. Often, a company considers making a product or component abroad for sales where it produces or for export into other markets. It must examine the costs of labor, raw materials inputs, capital, utilities, real estate, taxes and transfer costs in relation to productivity.

Labor compensation is an important cost of manufacturing for most companies. However, capital intensity is growing in most industries, which reduces labor costs as a percentage of total costs and decreases the differences in production cost from one location to another. Labor, however, is not a homogeneous commodity. If a country's labor force lacks the specific skill levels required, a company might have to train, redesign production, or add supervision-all of which are expensive.

When companies move into emerging economies because of labor-cost differences, their advantages may be short lived because:

- Competitors follow leaders into low-wage areas.
- There is little first-in advantage for this type of production migration.
- Foreign costs rise quickly because of pressure on wage or exchange rates.

Increasingly, companies need to be near suppliers and customers in areas where the infrastructure will allow them to move supplies and finished products efficiently. Regional headquarters should reside near specialized private and public institutions such as banks, factoring firms, insurance groups, public accountants, freight forwarders, customs brokers and consular offices all of which handle international functions.

If a company is looking for a production location that will serve sales in more than one country, the ease of moving goods in and out of the country is very important. The company may compare countries in terms of their port facilities and trade liberalization agreements with other countries.

Red Tape: Companies frequently compare the degrees of red tape necessary to operate in given countries because red tape increases their operating cots. Red tape includes the difficulty of getting permission to operate, bringing in expatriate personnel, obtaining licenses to produce and sell certain goods, and satisfying government agencies on such matters as taxes, labor conditions, and environmental compliance. The degree of red tape is not directly measurable, so companies commonly rate countries subjectively on this factor.

RISKS

Should a company calculate return on investment (ROI) on the entire earnings of a foreign subsidiary or just on the earnings that can be remitted to the parent? Does it make sense for a company to accept a low return in one country if doing so will help the company's competitive position elsewhere? Is it ever rational for a company to invest in a country that has an uncertain political and economic future? These are but a few of the unresolved questions that companies must consider when making international capital-investment decisions.

Risk and Uncertainty

Companies use a variety of financial techniques to compare potential projects, including discounted cash flow, economic value added, payback period, net present value, return on sales, return on assets employed, internal rate of return, accounting rate of return and return on equity. The differences among these techniques are best explained in a finance course; however, the international implications of all of them are roughly the same.

Often, companies may reduce risk or uncertainty by insuring. However, insuring against non-convertibility of funds or expropriation is apt to be costly. In the initial process of scanning to develop a manageable number of alternatives, the company should give some weight to the elements of risk and uncertainty. At the later and more detailed stage of the feasibility study, management should determine whether the degree of risk is acceptable without incurring additional costs. If it not, management needs to calculate an ROI that includes expenditures, such as for insurance, to increase the outcome certainty of the operation.

When a company operates abroad, it usually has higher uncertainty than at home because the foreign operations are in environments with which it is less familiar. As a company gains experience in operating in a particular country or in similar countries, it improves its assessments of consumer, competitor, and government actions – thereby reducing its uncertainty.

Competitive Risk

A company's innovative advantage may be short lived. Even when it has a substantial competitive lead-time, the time may vary among markets. One strategy for exploring temporary innovative advantages is known as the **imitation lag**. To pursue this strategy, a company moves first to those countries most likely to adapt and catch up to the innovative advantage, and later to other countries.

Countries also may develop strategies to find countries in which there is least likely to be significant competition. However, companies may gain advantages in locating where competitors are. To begin with, the competitors may have performed the costly task of evaluating locations, so a follower may get a "free ride". Moreover, there are clusters of competitors in various locations. These clusters attract multiple suppliers and personnel with specialized skills. They also attract buyers who want to compare potential suppliers but don't want to travel great distances between them.

Monetary Risk

If a company's expansion occurs through direct investment abroad, exchange rates on and access to the invested capital and earnings are key considerations. The concept of liquidity preference is a common theory that helps explain companies' capital budgeting decisions in general and can be applied to their international expansion decisions.

Liquidity preference is the theory that investors usually want some of their holdings to be in highly liquid assets, on which they are willing to take a lower return. Liquidity is needed in part to make near-term payments, such as paying out dividends; in part to cover unexpected contingencies, such as stockpiling materials if a strike threatens supply; and in part to be able to shift funds to even more profitable opportunities, such as purchasing materials at a discount during a temporary price depression.

Present capital controls and recent exchange-rate stability are useful indicators of countries' monetary situation. Additionally, companies need to predict countries' likely future exchange rate deterioration and exchange controls. Some indicators of future problems are countries' negative trade balances, decreasing official reserves, high inflation, and governmental budget deficits.

Political Risk

In Chapter 2, we discussed the consequences of political risk and explained that it occurs because of changes in political leaders' opinions and policies, civil disorder, and animosity between the host and other countries – particularly with the company's home country. It may cause property takeovers, damage property, disrupt operations, and change the rules governing business. Managers use three approaches to predict political risk:

- Analyzing past patterns
- Using expert opinion
- Examining the social and economic conditions

Substantial variations in political risk frequently exist within countries' as well. Except in few countries' government takeovers of companies' have been highly selective. Similarly, unrest that leads to property damage and disruption of supplies or sales may not endanger the operations of all foreign companies. This may be because of the limited geographic focus of the unrest.

Companies may also rely on experts' opinions about a country's political situation, with the purpose of ascertaining how influential people may sway future political events affecting business.

The first step is reading statements made by political leaders both in and out of office to determine their philosophies on business in general, foreign input to business, the means of effecting economic changes, and their feelings toward given foreign countries.

The second step is for managers to visit the country and "listen". Embassy officials and foreign and local business people are useful sources of opinions about the probability and direction of change. Journalists, academicians, middle-level local governmental authorities, and labor leaders usually reveal their own attitudes, which often reflect changing political conditions that may affect the business sector.

Finally, companies may examine countries' social and economic conditions that could lead to political instability. However, there is no general consensus as to what constitutes dangerous instability or how such instability can be predicted. The lack of consensus is illustrated by the diverse reactions of companies to the same political situations.

COLLECT AND ANALYZE DATA

Companies undertake business research to reduce uncertainties in their decision process, expand or narrow the alternatives they consider, and assess the merits of their existing programs. Efforts to reduce uncertainties include attempts to answer such questions as these:

"Can qualified personnel be hired?"

"Will the economic and political climate allow for a reasonable certainty of operations?"

Alternatives may be expanded by asking,

"Where among the alternatives would operating costs be lowest?"

Evaluation and control are improved by assessing present and past performance,

"Is the distributor servicing sufficient accounts?"

"What is our market share?"

Clearly, there are numerous details that, if a company ascertains them, can be useful in its objectives.

Managers should estimate the costs of data collection and compare them with the probable payoff from the data in terms of revenue gains or cost savings.

Reasons for Inaccuracies

For the most part, incomplete or inaccurate published data result from the inability of many governments to collect the needed information. Poor countries may have such limited resources that other projects necessarily receive priority in the national budget.

Education affects the competence of governmental officials to maintain and analyze accurate records. Economic factors also hamper record retrieval and analysis, because hand calculations may be used instead of costly electronic data-processing systems. Finally cultural factors affect responses. Mistrust of how the data will be used may lead respondents to answer incorrectly, particularly if questions probe financial details.

However, not all inaccuracies are due to governmental collection and dissemination procedures. A large proportion of the studies by academicians describing international business practices are based on broad generalizations that may be drawn from too few observations, on non-representative samples, and on poorly designed questionnaires.

Comparability Problems

Countries publish census, output figures, trade statistics, and base-year calculations for different time periods. So companies need to compare country figures by extrapolating from those different periods.

There also are numerous definitional differences among countries. For example, a category as seemingly basic as "family income" may include only the nuclear family – parents and children – in some countries, but may include the extended family – the nuclear family plus grandparents, uncles and cousins – elsewhere. Similarly, some countries define literacy as some minimum level of formal schooling, others as attainment of certain specified standards, and still others as simply the ability to read and write one's name.

Another comparability problem concerns exchange rates, which must be used to convert countries' financial data to some common currency. Even if changes in exchange rates are ignored, purchasing power and living standards are difficult to compare, because costs are so affected by climate and habit. Exchange rates, even when using purchasing power purity (PPP) are a very imperfect means of comparing national data.

EXTERNAL SOURCES OF INFORMATION

Although we have indicated variables that may be useful for making locational decisions, it is impossible to include a comprehensive list of information sources. There are simply too many. The following discussion highlights the major types of information sources in terms of their completeness, reliability and cost.

Individualized Reports: Market research and business consulting companies will conduct studies for a fee in most countries. Naturally, the quality and the cost of these studies vary widely. They generally are the most costly information source because the individualized nature restricts peroration among a number of companies.

Specialized Studies: Some research organizations prepare fairly specific studies that they sell to any interested company at costs much lower than for individualized studies. These specialized studies sometimes are printed as directories of companies that operate in a given locale, perhaps with financial or other information about the companies. They also may be about business in certain locales, forms of business, or specific products.

Service Companies: Most companies that provide services to international clients – for example banks, transportation agencies, and accounting firms – publish reports. These reports usually are geared toward either the conduct of business in a given area or some specific subject of general interest, such as tax or trademark legislation. Some service firms also offer informal opinions about such things as the reputations of possible associates and the names of people to contact in a company.

Governmental Agencies: Governments and their agencies are another source of information. Different countries' statistical reports vary in subject matter, quantity and quality. When a government or governmental agency wants to stimulate foreign business activity, the amount and type of information it makes available may be substantial.

International Organizations and Agencies: Numerous organizations and agencies are supported by more than one country. These include the United Nations (UN), the World Trade Organizations (WTO), the International Monetary Fund (IMF), the Organization for Economic Cooperation and Development (OECD) and the European Union (EU). All of these organizations have large research staff that compile basic statistics as well as prepare reports and recommendations concerning common trends and problems.

Trade Associations: Trade associations connected to various product lines collect, evaluate, and disseminate a wide variety of data dealing with technical and competitive factors in their industries. Many of these data are available in the trade journals published by such associations; others may or may not be available to non-members.

The Internet: Printed publications are quickly becoming archives that are older than information one may find on the Internet. This is because Internet changes appear immediately, whereas changes for periodicals must be printed, disseminated, cataloged, and shelved before they are available. The amount of materials available on the Internet and WWW is expanding very rapidly; however, finding these materials is still somewhat haphazard because of cataloging methods.

ALLOCATING AMONG LOCATIONS

These are useful in allocating operational emphasis among countries, but there are factors companies need to consider. We shall now discuss three of these:

- Reinvestment versus harvesting
- The interdependence of locations
- Diversification versus concentration

Reinvestment Versus Harvesting

A company usually makes new foreign investments by transferring capital abroad. If the investment is successful, the company will earn money that it may remit back to headquarters or reinvest to increase the value of the investment. Over time, most of the value of company's foreign investment comes from reinvestment. If the investment is unsuccessful or if its outlook is less favorable than possible investments in other countries, the company may consider harvesting the earnings to use elsewhere or even to discontinue the investment.

Reinvestment Decisions: Companies treat decisions to replace depreciated assets or add to the existing stock of capital from retained earnings in a foreign country somewhat differently from original investment decisions. Once committed to a given locale, a company may find it doesn't have the option of moving a substantial portion of the earnings elsewhere-to do so would endanger the continued successful operation of the given foreign facility.

Another reason a company treats reinvestment decisions differently is that once it has experienced personnel within a given country, it may believe they are the best judges of what is needed for that country, so headquarters managers may delegate certain investment decisions to them.

Harvesting: Companies commonly reduce commitments in some countries because those countries have poorer performance prospects than do others, a process is known as **harvesting** or **divesting**.

Some indications suggest that companies might benefit by planning divestments better and by developing divestment specialists. Companies have tended to wait too long before divesting, trying instead expensive means of improving performance. Local managers, who fear losing their positions if the company abandons an operation, propose additional capital expenditures.

Companies may divest by selling or closing facilities. They usually prefer selling because they receive some compensation. A company that considers divesting because of a country's political or economic situation may find few potential buyers except at very low prices. In such situations, the company may try to delay divestment, hoping the situation will improve.

A company cannot always simply abandon an investment either. Governments frequently require performance contracts, such as substantial severance packages to employees that make a loss from divestment greater than the direct investment's net value.

Interdependence of Locations

The derivation of meaningful financial figures is not easy when foreign operations are concerned. Profit figures from individual operations may obscure the real impact those operations have on overall company activities. Much of the sales and purchases of foreign subsidiaries may be made from and to units of the same parent company. The prices the company charges on these transactions will affect the relative profitability of one unit compared to another. By stating a high value, a government may permit the company to repatriate a larger portion of its earnings.

Diversification Versus Concentration

The term diversification strategy is when the company moves rapidly into many foreign markets, gradually increasing its commitments within each. The company eventually will increase its involvement by taking on activities that it first contracted to other companies.

At the other extreme, with a **concentration strategy**, the company will move to only one or a few foreign countries until it develops a very strong involvement and competitive position there. There are, of course, hybrids of these two strategies; for example, moving rapidly to most markets but increasing the commitment in only a few.

Growth Rate in Each Market: When the growth rate in each market is high, a company usually should concentrate on a few markets because it will cost a great deal to expand output sufficiently in each market. Further, costs per unit are typically lower for the market shareholder. Slower growth in each market may result in the company's having enough resources to build and maintain a market share in several different countries.

Sales Stability in Each Market: A company's earnings and sales may be smoothed because of operations in various parts of the world. This smoothing results from the leads and lags in the business cycle. In addition, a company whose assets and earnings base are in a variety of countries will be less affected by occurrences within a single one; for example, a strike or expropriation will affect earnings from only a small portion of total corporate assets. Although diversification is usually of secondary importance as a motive for foreign expansion, it is nevertheless an added advantage from operating abroad.

Competitive Lead Time: The first company to enter a market often gains advantages in terms of brand recognition and because it can line up the best suppliers, distributors, and local partners. This is called **first-in advantage** and may be difficult for followers to counteract. If a company determines that it has a long lead time before competitors are likely to be able to copy or supersede its advantages, then it may be able to follow a concentration strategy and still bear competitors into other markets.

Spillover Effects: Spillover effects are situations in which the marketing program in one country results in awareness of the product in other countries. They are advantageous because additional customers may be reached with little additional cost. When marketing programs reach many countries, such as by cable television or the Internet, a diversification strategy has advantages.

Need for Product, Communication, and Distribution Adaptation: Companies may have to alter products and their marketing to sell in foreign markets, a process that, because of cost, favors a concentration strategy. The adaptation cost may limit the resources the company has for expanding in many different markets. Further, if the adaptations are unique to each country, the company cannot easily spread the costs over sales in other countries to reduce total unit costs.

Program Control Requirements: The more a company needs to control its operations in a foreign country, the more it should develop a concentration strategy. This is because the company will need to use more of its resources to maintain that control. Its need for more control could result for various reasons, including the fear that collaboration with a partner will create a competitor or the need for highly technical assistance for customers.

Extent of Constraints: If a company is constrained by the resources it needs to expand internationally compared to the resources it can muster, it will likely follow a concentration strategy.

MAKING FINAL COUNTRY SELECTIONS

So far we have examined comparative opportunities on a very broad basis. At some point, a company must perform a much more detailed analysis of specific projects and proposals in order to make allocation decisions. For new investments, companies need to make on-site visits and detailed estimates of all costs and expenses. They will need to evaluate whether they should enter the market alone or with a partner. For acquisitions, they will need to examine financial statements in detail. For expansion within countries where they are already operating, managers within those countries will most likely submit capital budget requests that include details of expected returns.

Because companies have limited resources at their disposal, it might seem that they maintain a storehouse of foreign investment proposals that they may rank by some predetermined criteria. If this were so, management could simply start allocating resources investments. Companies tend to evaluate investment proposals separately, and their decision is commonly known as a **go-no-go decision**.

Two major factors restricting companies from comparing investment opportunities are cost and time. Clearly, some companies cannot afford to conduct very many investigations simultaneously. If they are conducted simultaneously, they are apt to be in various stages of completion at a given time. The time interval between completions probably would invalidate much of the earlier results and necessitate updating, added expense and further delays. Another time-inhibiting problem is governmental regulations that require a decision within a given period. Also, other companies may impose time limits on partnership proposals.

During all of this evaluating and selecting, companies still have the pressure of satisfying stockholders and employees. Few companies can afford to let resources lie idle or be employed for a low rate of return during a waiting period. This applies not only to financial resources but also to such resources as technical competence, because the companies reduce their lead-time over competitors when they make decisions.

SUMMARY

- Because companies seldom have sufficient resources to exploit all opportunities, two major considerations facing managers are which markets to serve and where to locate the production to serve those markets.
- Scanning techniques aid managers in considering alternatives that might otherwise be overlooked. They also help limit the final detailed feasibility studies to a manageable number of those that appear most promising.
- The ranking of countries is useful for determining the order of entry into potential markets and for setting the allocation of resources and rate of expansion to different markets.
- The amount, accuracy, and timeliness of published data vary substantially among countries. Managers should be particularly aware of different definitions of terms, different collection methods, and different base years for reports, as well as misleading responses.
- Sources of published data on international business include consulting firms, governmental agencies, international agencies and organizations that serve international businesses. The cost and specificity of these publications vary widely.
- Because of the interdependence of operations in different countries, it is difficult to derive meaningful financial figures to evaluate the effects or return from operations in a single country.
- Companies normally treat reinvestment decisions separately from new investment decisions because a reinvestment may be necessarily to protect existing resources' viability and because there are people on location who can better judge the worthiness of proposals.
- Using a similar amount of internal resources, a company may choose initially to move rapidly into many foreign markets with only a small commitment in each (a diversification strategy) or to pursue a strong involvement and commitment in one or a few locations (a concentration strategy).
- The major variables a company should consider when deciding whether to diversify or concentrate are the growth rate and sales stability in each market, the expected lead time over competitors, the spillover effects, the degree of need for product and marketing adaptation in different countries, the need to maintain control of the expansion program, and the constraints the company faces.
- Companies must develop locational strategies for new investments and devise means of de-emphasizing certain areas and divesting if necessary.

Chapter 9

WTO and Trade Liberalization

INTRODUCTION

The World Trade Organization (WTO) is an international organization designed by its founders to supervise and liberalize international capital trade. The organization officially commenced on January 1, 1995 under the Marrakesh Agreement, replacing the General Agreements on Tariffs and Trade (GATT), which commenced in 1947.

The World Trade Organization deals with regulation of trade between participating countries; it provides a framework for negotiating and formalizing trade agreements, and a dispute resolution process aimed at enforcing participants' adherence to WTO agreements which are signed by representatives of member governments and ratified by their parliaments.

Most of the issues that the WTO focuses on derive from previous trade negotiations, especially from the **Uruguay Round (1986–1994).** The organization is currently endeavoring to persist with a trade negotiation called the **Doha Development Agenda (or Doha Round)**, which was launched in 2001 to enhance equitable participation of poorer countries which represent a majority of the world's population. However, the negotiation has been dogged by "disagreement between exporters of agricultural bulk commodities and countries with large numbers of subsistence farmers on the precise terms of a 'special safeguard measure' to protect farmers from surges in imports. At this time, the future of the Doha Round is uncertain.

The WTO has 153 members, representing more than 95% of total world trade and 30 observers, most seeking membership. The WTO is governed by a ministerial conference, meeting every two years; a general council, which implements the conference's policy decisions and is responsible for day-to-day administration; and a director-general, who is appointed by the ministerial conference. The WTO's headquarters is at the Centre William Rappard, Geneva, Switzerland.

HISTORY

ITO and GATT 1947

- The WTO's predecessor, the **General Agreement on Tariffs and Trade** (GATT), was established after World War II in the wake of other new multilateral institutions dedicated to international economic cooperation - notably the **Bretton Woods** institutions known as the World Bank and the International Monetary Fund.
- A comparable international institution for trade, named the International Trade Organization was successfully negotiated. The ITO was to be a United Nations specialized agency and would address not only trade barriers but other issues indirectly related to trade, including employment, investment, restrictive business practices, and commodity agreements.
- But the ITO treaty was not approved by the United States and a few other signatories and never went into effect.

GATT Rounds of Negotiations

- The GATT was the only multilateral instrument governing international trade from 1948 until the WTO was established in 1995.
- Despite attempts in the mid 1950s and 1960s to create some form of institutional mechanism for international trade, the GATT continued to operate for almost half a century as a semi-institutionalized multilateral treaty regime on a provisional basis.

From Geneva to Tokyo

- Seven rounds of negotiations occurred under the GATT. The first GATT trade rounds concentrated on further reducing tariffs.
- Kennedy Round in the mid-sixties brought about a GATT anti-dumping Agreement and a section on development.
- The Tokyo Round during the seventies was the first major attempt to tackle trade barriers that do not take the form of tariffs, and to improve the system, adopting a series of agreements on non-tariff barriers, which in some cases interpreted existing GATT rules, and in others broke entirely new ground.
- Several of these codes were amended in the Uruguay Round, and turned into multilateral commitments accepted by all WTO members.
- Only four remained pluri-lateral (those on government procurement, bovine meat, civil aircraft and dairy products), but in 1997 WTO members agreed to terminate the bovine meat and dairy agreements, leaving only two.

WTO MINISTERIAL CONFERENCES

FIRST MINISTERIAL CONFERENCE

The inaugural ministerial conference was held in Singapore in 1996. Disagreements between largely developed and developing economies emerged during this conference over four issues initiated by this conference, which led to them being collectively referred to as the **"Singapore issues".**

SECOND MINISTERIAL CONFERENCE

Was held in Geneva in Switzerland.

THIRD MINISTERIAL CONFERENCE

The third conference in Seattle, Washington ended in failure, with massive demonstrations and police and National Guard crowd control efforts drawing worldwide attention.

FOURTH MINISTERIAL CONFERENCE

Was held in Doha in Persian Gulf nation of Qatar. The **Doha Development Agenda (DDA)** was launched at the conference. The conference also approved the joining of China, which became the 143rd member to join.

FIFTH MINISTERIAL CONFERENCE

The ministerial conference was held in Cancún, Mexico, aiming at forging agreement on the Doha round. An alliance of 22 southern states, the G20 developing nations (led by India, China and Brazil), resisted demands from the North for agreements on the so-called "Singapore issues" and called for an end to agricultural subsidies within the EU and the US. The talks broke down without progress.

SIXTH MINISTERIAL CONFERENCE

The sixth WTO ministerial conference was held in Hong Kong from 13–18 December 2005. It was considered vital if the four-year-old Doha Development Agenda negotiations were to move forward sufficiently to conclude the round in 2006. In this meeting, countries agreed to phase out all their agricultural export subsidies by the end of 2013, and terminate any cotton export subsidies by the end of 2006. Further concessions to developing countries included an agreement to introduce duty free, tariff free access for goods from the Least Developed Countries, following the everything but Arms initiative of the European Union — but with up to 3% of tariff lines exempted. Other major issues were left for further negotiation to be completed by the end of 2010.

SEVENTH MINISTERIAL CONFERENCE

The WTO General Council, on 26 May 2009, agreed to hold a seventh WTO ministerial conference session in Geneva from 30 November–December 2009.

A statement by chairman Amb. Mario Matus acknowledged that the prime purpose was to remedy a breach of protocol requiring two-yearly "regular" meetings, which had lapsed with the Doha Round failure in 2005, and that the "scaled-down" meeting would not be a negotiating session, but "emphasis will be on transparency and open discussion rather than on small group processes and informal negotiating structures".

URUGUAY ROUND–EIGHT MINISTERIAL CONFERENCE

Discussed in detail later in this chapter

DOHA ROUND–NINTH MINISTERIAL CONFERENCE

Discussed in detail later in this chapter

FUNCTIONS OF WTO

The main functions of the WTO can be described in very simple terms. These are:

- To oversee implementing and administering WTO agreements;
- To provide a forum for negotiation; and
- To provide a dispute settlement mechanism.

The goals behind these functions are set out in the preamble to the Marrakech Agreement. These include:

- Raising standards of living;
- Ensuring full employment;
- Ensuring large and steadily growing real incomes and demand; and
- Expanding the production of and trade in goods and services.

These objectives are to be achieved while allowing for the optimal use of the world's resources in accordance with the objective of sustainable development, and while seeking to protect and preserve the environment. The preamble also specifically mentions the need to assist developing countries, especially the least developed countries, secure a growing share of international trade.

PRINCIPLES OF THE TRADING SYSTEM

The WTO agreements are lengthy and complex because they are legal texts covering a wide range of activities. They deal with: agriculture, textiles and clothing, banking, telecommunications, government purchases, industrial standards and product safety, food sanitation regulations, intellectual property, and much more. But a number of simple, fundamental principles run throughout all of these documents. These principles are the foundation of the multilateral trading system.

A closer look at these principles:

Trade without Discrimination

1. **Most-favored-nation (MFN): Treating other People Equally** Under the WTO agreements, countries cannot normally discriminate between their trading partners. Grant someone a special flavor (such as a lower customs duty rate for one of their products) and you have to do the same for all other WTO members.

   This principle is known as most-favored-nation (MFN) treatment. It is so important that it is the first article of the General Agreement on Tariffs and Trade (GATT), which governs trade in goods. MFN is also a priority in the General Agreement on Trade in Services (GATS) and the Agreement on Trade-Related Aspects of Intellectual Property Rights (TRIPS), although in each agreement the principle is handled slightly differently. Together, those three agreements cover all three main areas of trade handled by the WTO.

   Some exceptions are allowed. For example, countries can set up a free trade agreement that applies only to goods traded within the group—discriminating against goods from outside. Or they can give developing countries special access to their markets. Or a country can raise barriers against products that are considered to be traded unfairly from specific countries. And in services, countries are allowed, in limited circumstances, to discriminate. But the agreements only permit these exceptions under strict conditions. In general, MFN means that every time a country lowers a trade barrier or opens up a market, it has to do so for the same goods or services from all its trading partners — whether rich or poor, weak or strong.

2. **National Treatment: Treating foreigners and locals equally** imported and locally-produced goods should be treated equally —at least after the foreign goods have entered the market. The same should apply to foreign and domestic services, and to foreign and local trademarks, copyrights and patents. This principle of "national treatment" (giving others the same treatment as one's own nationals) is also found in all the three main WTO agreements (Article 3 of GATT, Article 17 of GATS and Article 3 of TRIPS), although once again the principle is handled slightly differently in each of these.

National treatment only applies once a product, service or item of intellectual property has entered the market. Therefore, charging customs duty on an import is not a violation of national treatment even if locally-produced products are not charged an equivalent tax.

Freer Trade: Gradually, through Negotiation

Lowering trade barriers is one of the most obvious means of encouraging trade. The barriers concerned include customs duties (or tariffs) and measures such as import bans or quotas that restrict quantities selectively. From time to time other issues such as red tape and exchange rate policies have also been discussed.

Since GATT's creation in 1947–48 there have been eight rounds of trade negotiations. A ninth round, under the Doha Development Agenda, is now underway. At first these focused on lowering tariffs (customs duties) on imported goods. As a result of the negotiations, by the mid-1990s industrial countries' tariff rates on industrial goods had fallen steadily to less than 4%.

But by the 1980s, the negotiations had expanded to cover non-tariff barriers on goods, and to the new areas such as services and intellectual property.

Opening markets can be beneficial, but it also requires adjustment. The WTO agreements allow countries to introduce changes gradually, through "progressive liberalization". Developing countries are usually given longer to fulfill their obligations.

Predictability: Through Binding and Transparency

Sometimes, promising not to raise a trade barrier can be as important as lowering one, because the promise gives businesses a clearer view of their future opportunities. With stability and predictability, investment is encouraged, jobs are created and consumers can fully enjoy the benefits of competition—choice and lower prices. The multilateral trading system is an attempt by governments to make the business environment stable and predictable.

The Uruguay Round Increased Bindings

Percentages of tariffs bound before and after the 1986–94 talks

	Before	After
Developed countries	78	99
Developing countries	21	73
Transition economies	73	98

(These are tariff lines, so percentages are not weighted according to trade volume or value)

In the WTO, when countries agree to open their markets for goods or services, they "bind" their commitments. For goods, these bindings amount to ceilings on customs tariff rates. Sometimes countries tax imports at rates that are lower than the bound rates. Frequently this is the case in developing countries. In developed countries the rates actually charged and the bound rates tend to be the same.

A country can change its bindings, but only after negotiating with its trading partners, which could mean compensating them for loss of trade. One of the achievements of the Uruguay Round of multilateral trade talks was to increase the amount of trade under binding commitments. In agriculture, 100% of products now have bound tariffs. The result of all this: a substantially higher degree of market security for traders and investors.

The system tries to improve predictability and stability in other ways as well. One way is to discourage the use of quotas and other measures used to set limits on quantities of imports— administering quotas can lead to more red-tape and accusations of unfair play. Another is to make countries' trade rules as clear and public ("transparent") as possible. Many WTO agreements require governments to disclose their policies and practices publicly within the country or by notifying the WTO. The regular surveillance of national trade policies through the Trade Policy Review Mechanism provides a further means of encouraging transparency both domestically and at the multilateral level.

Promoting Fair Competition

The WTO is sometimes described as a "free trade" institution, but that is not entirely accurate. The system does allow tariffs and, in limited circumstances, other forms of protection. More accurately, it is a system of rules dedicated to open, fair and undistorted competition.

The rules on non-discrimination—MFN and national treatment—are designed to secure fair conditions of trade. So too are those on dumping (exporting at below cost to gain market share) and subsidies. The issues are complex, and the rules try to establish what is fair or unfair, and how governments can respond, in particular by charging additional import duties calculated to compensate for damage caused by unfair trade.

Many of the other WTO agreements aim to support fair competition in agriculture, intellectual property, services, for example. The agreement on government procurement (a "plurilateral" agreement because it is signed by only a few WTO members) extends competition rules to purchases by thousands of government entities in many countries and so on.

Encouraging Development and Economic Reform

The WTO system contributes to development. On the other hand, developing countries need flexibility in the time they take to implement the system's agreements. And the agreements themselves inherit the earlier provisions of GATT that allow for special assistance and trade concessions for developing countries.

Over three quarters of WTO members are developing countries and countries in transition to market economies. During the seven and a half years of the Uruguay Round, over 60 of these countries implemented trade liberalization programs autonomously. At the same time, developing countries and transition economies were much more active and influential in the Uruguay Round negotiations than in any previous round, and they are even more so in the current Doha Development Agenda.

At the end of the Uruguay Round, developing countries were prepared to take on most of the obligations that are required of developed countries. But the agreements did give them transition periods to adjust to the more unfamiliar and, perhaps, difficult WTO provisions—particularly so for the poorest, "least-developed" countries. A ministerial decision adopted at the end of the round says better-off countries should accelerate implementing market access commitments on goods exported by the least-developed countries, and it seeks increased technical assistance for them. More recently, developed countries have started to allow duty-free and quota-free imports for almost all products from least-developed countries. On all of this, the WTO and its members are still going through a learning process. The current Doha Development Agenda includes developing countries' concerns about the difficulties they face in implementing the Uruguay Round agreements.

The GATT Years: From Havana to Marrakesh

The WTO's creation on 1 January 1995 marked the biggest reform of international trade since after the Second World War. It also brought to reality — in an updated form— the failed attempt in 1948 to create an International Trade Organization.

Much of the history of those 47 years was written in Geneva. But it also traces a journey that spanned the continents, from that hesitant start in 1948 in Havana (Cuba), via Annecy (France), Torquay (UK), Tokyo (Japan), Punta del Este (Uruguay), Montreal (Canada), Brussels (Belgium) and finally to Marrakesh (Morocco) in 1994. During that period, the trading system came under GATT, salvaged from the aborted attempt to create the ITO. GATT helped establish a strong and prosperous multilateral trading system that became more and more liberal through rounds of trade negotiations. But by the 1980s the system needed a thorough overhaul. This led to the Uruguay Round, and ultimately to the WTO.

GATT: 'Provisional' for Almost Half a Century

From 1948 to 1994, the General Agreement on Tariffs and Trade (GATT) provided the rules for much of world trade and presided over periods that saw some of the highest growth rates in international commerce. It seemed well-established, but throughout those 47 years, it was a provisional agreement and organization.

The original intention was to create a third institution to handle the trade side of international economic cooperation, joining the two "Bretton Woods" institutions, the World Bank and the International Monetary Fund. Over 50 countries participated in negotiations to create an International Trade Organization (ITO) as a specialized agency of the United Nations. The draft ITO Charter was ambitious. It extended beyond world trade disciplines, to include rules on employment, commodity agreements, restrictive business practices, international investment, and services. The aim was to create the ITO at a UN Conference on Trade and Employment in Havana, Cuba in 1947.

Meanwhile, 15 countries had begun talks in December 1945 to reduce and bind customs tariffs. With the Second World War only recently ended, they wanted to give an early boost to trade liberalization, and to begin to correct the legacy of protectionist measures which remained in place from the early 1930s.

This first round of negotiations resulted in a package of trade rules and 45,000 tariff concessions affecting $10 billion of trade, about one fifth of the world's total. The group had expanded to 23 by the time the deal was signed on 30 October 1947. The tariff concessions came into effect by 30 June 1948 through a "Protocol of Provisional Application". And so the new General Agreement on Tariffs and Trade was born, with 23 founding members (officially "contracting parties").

The 23 were also part of the larger group negotiating the ITO Charter. One of the provisions of GATT says that they should accept some of the trade rules of the draft. This, they believed, should be done swiftly and "provisionally" in order to protect the value of the tariff concessions they had negotiated. They spelt out how they envisaged the relationship between GATT and the ITO Charter, but they also allowed for the possibility that the ITO might not be created. They were right.

The Havana conference began on 21 November 1947, less than a month after GATT was signed. The ITO Charter was finally agreed in Havana in March 1948, but ratification in some national legislatures proved impossible.

The most serious opposition was in the US Congress, even though the US government had been one of the driving forces. In 1950, the United States government announced that it would not seek Congressional ratification of the Havana Charter, and the ITO was effectively dead. So, the GATT became the only multilateral instrument governing international trade from 1948 until the WTO was established in 1995.

For almost half a century, the GATT's basic legal principles remained much as they were in 1948. There were additions in the form of a section on development added in the 1960s and "plurilateral" agreements (i.e. with voluntary membership) in the 1970s, and efforts to reduce tariffs further continued. Much of this was achieved through a series of multilateral negotiations known as "trade rounds" — the biggest leaps forward in international trade liberalization have come through these rounds which were held under GATT's auspices.

In the early years, the GATT trade rounds concentrated on further reducing tariffs. Then, the Kennedy Round in the mid-sixties brought about a GATT Anti-Dumping Agreement and a section on development. The Tokyo Round during the seventies was the first major attempt to tackle trade barriers that do not take the form of tariffs, and to improve the system. The eighth, the Uruguay Round of 1986-94, was the last and most extensive of all. It led to the WTO and a new set of agreements.

The Tokyo Round: A First try to Reform the System

The Tokyo Round lasted from 1973 to 1979, with 102 countries participating. It continued GATT's efforts to progressively reduce tariffs. The results included an average one-third cut in customs duties in the world's nine major industrial markets, bringing the average tariff on industrial products down to 4.7%. The tariff reductions, phased in over a period of eight years, involved an element of "harmonization"—the higher the tariff, the larger the cut, proportionally.

In other issues, the Tokyo Round had mixed results. It failed to come to grips with the fundamental problems affecting farm trade and also stopped short of providing a modified agreement on "safeguards" (emergency import measures). Nevertheless, a series of agreements on non-tariff barriers did emerge from the negotiations, in some cases interpreting existing GATT rules, in others breaking entirely new ground. In most cases, only a relatively small number of (mainly industrialized) GATT members subscribed to these agreements and arrangements. Because they were not accepted by the full GATT membership, they were often informally called "codes".

They were not multilateral, but they were a beginning. Several codes were eventually amended in the Uruguay Round and turned into multilateral commitments accepted by all WTO members. Only four remained "plurilateral"

—those on government procurement, bovine meat, civil aircraft and dairy products. In 1997 WTO members agreed to terminate the bovine meat and dairy agreements, leaving only two.

Did GATT Succeed?

GATT was provisional with a limited field of action, but its success over 47 years in promoting and securing the liberalization of much of world trade is incontestable. Continual reductions in tariffs alone helped spur very high rates of world trade growth during the 1950s and 1960s — around 8% a year on average. And the momentum of trade liberalization helped ensure that trade growth consistently out-paced production growth throughout the GATT era, a measure of countries' increasing ability to trade with each other and to reap the benefits of trade. The rush of new members during the Uruguay Round demonstrated that the multilateral trading system was recognized as an anchor for development and an instrument of economic and trade reform.

But all was not well. As time passed new problems arose. The Tokyo Round in the 1970s was an attempt to tackle some of these but its achievements were limited. This was a sign of difficult times to come.

GATT's success in reducing tariffs to such a low level, combined with a series of economic recessions in the 1970s and early 1980s, drove governments to devise other forms of protection for sectors facing increased foreign competition. High rates of unemployment and constant factory closures led governments in Western Europe and North America to seek bilateral market-sharing arrangements with competitors and to embark on a subsidies race to maintain their holds on agricultural trade. Both these changes undermined GATT's credibility and effectiveness.

The problem was not just a deteriorating trade policy environment. By the early 1980s the General Agreement was clearly no longer as relevant to the realities of world trade as it had been in the 1940s. For a start, world trade had become far more complex and important than 40 years before: the globalization of the world economy was underway, trade in services—not covered by GATT rules—was of major interest to more and more countries, and international investment had expanded. The expansion of services trade was also closely tied to further increases in world merchandise trade. In other respects, GATT had been found wanting. For instance, in agriculture, loopholes in the multilateral system were heavily exploited, and efforts at liberalizing agricultural trade met with little success. In the textiles and clothing sector, an exception to GATT's normal disciplines was negotiated in the 1960s and early 1970s, leading to the Multi-fiber Arrangement. Even GATT's institutional structure and its dispute settlement system were causing concern.

These and other factors convinced GATT members that a new effort to reinforce and extend the multilateral system should be attempted. That effort resulted in the Uruguay Round, the Marrakesh Declaration, and the creation of the WTO.

GATT Trade Rounds

Year	Place/name	Subjects covered	Countries
1947	**Geneva**	Tariffs	23
1949	**Annecy**	Tariffs	13
1951	**Torquay**	Tariffs	38
1956	**Geneva**	Tariffs	26
1960–1961	Geneva **Dillon Round**	Tariffs	26
1964–1967	Geneva **Kennedy Round**	Tariffs and anti-dumping measures	62
1973–1979	Geneva **Tokyo Round**	Tariffs, non-tariff measures, "framework" agreements	102
1986–1994	Geneva **Uruguay Round**	Tariffs, non-tariff measures, rules, services, intellectual property, dispute settlement, textiles, agriculture, creation of WTO, etc	123

Trade Rounds: Progress by Package

They are often lengthy—the Uruguay Round took seven and a half years— but trade rounds can have an advantage. They offer a package approach to trade negotiations that can sometimes be more fruitful than negotiations on a single issue.

- The size of the package can mean more benefits because participants can seek and secure advantages across a wide range of issues.
- Agreement can be easier to reach, through trade-offs — somewhere in the package there should be something for everyone.

This has political as well as economic implications. A government may want to make a concession, perhaps in one sector, because of the economic benefits. But politically, it could find the concession difficult to defend. A package would contain politically and economically attractive benefits in other sectors that could be used as compensation.

So, reform in politically-sensitive sectors of world trade can be more feasible as part of a global package—a good example is the agreement to reform agricultural trade in the Uruguay Round.

- Developing countries and other less powerful participants have a greater chance of influencing the multilateral system in a trade round than in bilateral relationships with major trading nations.

But the size of a trade round can be both strength and a weakness. From time to time, the question is asked: wouldn't it be simpler to concentrate negotiations on a single sector? Recent history is inconclusive. At some stages, the Uruguay Round seemed so cumbersome that it seemed impossible that all participants could agree on every subject. Then the round did end successfully in 1993–94. This was followed by two years of failure to reach agreement in the single-sector talks on maritime transport.

Did this mean that trade rounds were the only route to success? No. In 1997, single-sector talks were concluded successfully in basic telecommunications, information technology equipment and financial services.

The debate continues. Whatever the answer, the reasons are not straightforward. Perhaps success depends on using the right type of negotiation for the particular time and context.

URUGUAY ROUND – VIII ROUND OF WTO TALKS

The Uruguay Round is the name given to the eighth round of international talks and agreements on economic issues undertaken by the General Agreement on Tariffs and Trade (GATT). The Uruguay Round was the replacement for the earlier meeting of the GATT that took place in Geneva in 1982. The original meeting took place in Punta del Este in Uruguay in September of 1986, and continued until April of 1994.

On December 15, 1993, 117 countries concluded a major agreement to reduce barriers blocking exports to world markets, to extend coverage and enhance disciplines on critical areas of trade, and to create a more fair, more comprehensive, more effective, and more enforceable set of world trade rules.

The Uruguay Round agreement is the most comprehensive trade agreement in history. The existing set of trade rules was incomplete; it was unreliable; and it was increasingly unresponsive to major concerns of US exporters.

The United States is uniquely positioned to benefit from the Uruguay Round trade agreement and the new world trade system it will create. US workers will gain from significant new employment opportunities and additional high—paying jobs associated with the increased production of goods for export. US companies will gain from significant opportunities to export more agricultural products, manufactured goods and services. U.S. consumers will gain from greater access to a wider range of lower priced, higher quality goods and services.

This Historic Agreement will

- cut foreign tariffs on manufactured products by over on-third, the largest reduction in history;
- protect the intellectual property of U.S. entrepreneurs in industries such as pharmaceuticals, entertainment, and software from piracy in world markets;
- ensure open foreign markets for U.S. exporters of services such as accounting, advertising, computer services, tourism, engineering and construction;
- greatly expand export opportunities for U.S. agricultural products by limiting the ability of foreign governments to restrict trade through tariffs, quotas, subsidies, and a variety of other domestic policies and regulations;
- ensure that developing countries follow the same trade rules as developed countries and that there will be no free riders;
- establish an effective set of rules for the prompt settlement of disputes, thus eliminating shortcomings in the current system that allowed countries to drag out the process and to block judgments they did not like; and
- create a new World Trade Organization (WTO) to implement the agreements reached.

This Agreement will not

- impair the effective enforcement of U.S. Laws;
- limit the ability of the United States to set its own environmental and health standards and to pass its own laws; or
- erode the sovereignty of the United States to pass its own laws.

How the Uruguay Round Agreement Benefits Americans

- The Uruguay Round Agreement provides a needed boost to the world economy, which is currently stalled.
- The Uruguay Round Agreement helps ensure long-term U.S. economic growth.
- The Uruguay Round Agreement benefits consumers by effectively raising incomes.

- The Uruguay Round Agreement helps to level the playing field for U.S. farmers, businesses, and workers by strengthening trade rules.
- The Uruguay Round Agreement ensures fair and prompt resolution of trade disputes.
- The Uruguay Round Agreement addresses environmental issues in international trade.
- The Uruguay Round Agreement supports transitions to democracy.

KEY AREAS URUGUAY ROUND FOCUS

Market Access

Expanding U.S. exports, jobs and growth. In an economy increasingly reliant on trade, opening up new markets is absolutely essential to creating jobs and growth.

Since World War II, international trade negotiations have lowered tariffs by about 85 per cent, resulting in unprecedented export-led economic growth and ushering in an era of prosperity among the trading nations. Before the Uruguay Round, however, significant barriers remained.

The agreement on market access for goods will:

- Eliminate tariffs in major industrial markets and significantly reduce or eliminate tariffs in many markets, in the following areas:
  - Construction equipment
  - Distilled spirits
  - Agricultural equipment
  - Beer
  - Medical equipment
  - Pharmaceuticals
  - Steel
  - Paper
  - Furniture
  - Toys
- Make deep cuts ranging from 50 to 100 per cent on important electronics items (such as semiconductors, computer parts, and semiconductor manufacturing equipment) by major U.S. trading partners;
- Harmonize tariffs of developed and major developing countries in the chemical sector at very low rates (0, 5.5 and 6.5 per cent); and,

- Cut European tariffs on goods imported from the United States by over 50 per cent.

Moreover, the Uruguay Round agreement will sharply limit the non-tariff barriers to imports—such as quotas and voluntary export restraints — that have often sprouted to replace falling tariffs.

The rules of the new World Trade Organization will help ensure that all WTO members play by the same rules. These new global trade rules will enable our companies and workers to compete on a more level playing field.

Specifically, the World Trade Organization will have more effective rules in the following areas:

- **Dispute Settlement:** A swift, sure, and effective mechanism to resolve trade disputes will ensure that the United States will have recourse to a speedy remedy when foreign countries violate international rules and raise new trade barriers.
- **Dumping:** Under the new rules, the United States retains its ability to take effective action against unfair dumping practices, while U.S. exporters are ensured fair application of anti-dumping laws by foreign countries.
- **Subsidies:** The new agreement strengthens our ability to combat unfairly subsidized foreign products that compete against non-subsidized U.S. Products.
- **Import Safeguards:** New rules will enable the United States to take temporary actions against surges in imports without having to pay compensation. At the same time, the new rules will ensure that other countries will follow the same kind of objective and transparent procedures that the United States follows.
- **Product Standards:** Stronger, more comprehensive rules will ensure that product standards are not used to keep out imports, while allowing each country to set its own standards for the protection of human life, health, and the environment. The United States will not have to change any of its health and safety standards, because they are based on objective, scientific criteria and are not used as trade barriers.

The **Uruguay Round** will more fully integrate developing countries into the world economy by:

- opening their markets to goods, services, and investment;
- committing them to following the same rules of fair, open trade as all other countries; and

- moving away from a system of obligations in which developing countries enjoy the benefits of the trading system without adhering to the rules.

IMPACT OF THE URUGUAY ROUND AGREEMENTS OF RELEVANCE TO THE AGRICULTURAL SECTOR

The Uruguay Round was a turning point in the evolution of agricultural policy. For the first time, a large majority of countries agreed a set of principles and disciplines to reduce the trade distortions caused by agricultural policies. This chapter summarizes the main accomplishments of:

- Agreement on Agriculture (AoA) and the other Uruguay Round Agreements of relevance to agriculture and food security issues includes
- Agreement on the Application of Sanitary and Phytosanitary Measures (SPS)
- Agreement on Technical Barriers to Trade (TBT)
- Agreement on Trade Related Aspects of Intellectual Property Rights (TRIPS)

AGREEMENT ON AGRICULTURE

The Agreement on Agriculture (AoA) brought national agricultural policies under multilateral rules and disciplines, with the long-term objective of establishing "a fair and market-oriented agricultural trading system through substantial progressive reductions in agricultural support and protection". The AoA includes specific binding commitments by WTO members to improve market access and to reduce production and trade-distorting domestic support and export subsidies.

A basic motivation for the AoA was the need to reduce surplus production caused by rising levels of support and protection in a number of developed countries during the 1980s and early 1990s. This was known as a period of "disarray" in global commodity markets as some of the largest agricultural exporters competed on the basis their governments' ability to subsidise production and exports while limiting access to their markets for products from lower-cost suppliers. By agreeing to cap and reduce these subsidy levels and import barriers, the developed countries hoped to bring an end to the "subsidy wars" that were draining their national budgets and driving down world commodity prices.

The vast majority of developing countries, on the other hand, entered the Uruguay Round with under-developed agricultural sectors and insufficient resources to raise productivity and output in line with their food needs and production potential. Their farmers were forced to compete with the treasuries of the world's richest countries in export markets and in their home markets.

While consumers in developing countries could be said to "benefit" from the availability of subsidised supplies, the situation was unstable and unsustainable.

Prior to implementation of the AoA most studies of the impact on world markets and trade predicted trade gains for developing country exporters and slightly higher and more stable real world commodity prices. Subsequent analyses based on actual trade developments, however, could not distinguish between the impacts of specific policy changes resulting from the AoA and other factors having an impact on trade, such as macroeconomic shocks, weather-induced supply-side variations, civil strife etc.

Policy Impact

- **Domestic Support to Agriculture**
  - **Commitments for the Reduction of Domestic Supports:** The Agreement categorized domestic support policies according to their potential to distort production and trade, and capped and reduced measures that were considered to cause distortions. These are known as the "Amber Box" policies.
  - **Reformulation of Agricultural Supports:** Many developed countries changed their agricultural policies in significant ways in anticipation of and following the implementation of the AoA. For example, the EU, the United States and Canada have all moved away—in varying degrees—from market price supports that tend to encourage excess production towards direct income payments and other measures that are less distorting, although not necessarily completely production and trade-neutral.
  - **Imbalances in Support Limits:** The upper limits agreed on domestic support were based on the actual level of "distorting" support provided by each country during the 1986–88 base period.
  - **Domestic Support** in developed countries remains high despite the disciplines agreed in the AoA.
- **Export Subsidies**
  - **Commitments on Export Subsidies:** Subsidy levels were capped and reduced both in terms of value and volume. Countries that did not subsidize exports during the base period were prohibited from doing so, except for certain exceptions agreed for developing countries.
  - **Export Subsidies** have been reduced somewhat on several products, but they remain high, particularly for meat and dairy products as well as cereals. Export subsidies not only distort

competition on global markets but also destabilize world prices. Countries tend to use subsidies more when world prices are low, thus further depressing prices, but subsidizes tend to fall when world prices are high, just at the time when importing countries might be said to "benefit" from subsidized supplies.

- **Market Access**
  - **Commitments on Tariffs:** Countries agreed to replace their non-tariff import barriers with bound tariffs and, in many cases, to reduce these tariffs.
  - **Agricultural Tariffs** *remain high and complex* despite these improvements, especially for temperate-zone products (horticulture, sugar, cereals, dairy products and meat). There is a high degree of variance in agricultural tariffs both within and between individual countries, and tariff escalation (higher tariffs on more processed products, which gives greater protection to the processing industry of the importing country) still prevails in several important product chains (e.g. coffee, cocoa, oilseeds, vegetables, fruit and nuts and hides and skins).
  - **Tariff Rate Quotas** were created to ease the process of converting non-tariff measures to tariffs. Countries that chose to use this mechanism agreed to provide market access at a low or zero tariff for a fixed quantity of product, while additional quantities could be charged a higher tariff. While tariff rate quotas have created some new trading opportunities, a number of implementation issues have arisen. As a result, only about 60-65 per cent of the potential trade under tariff rate quotas has actually occurred.
  - **Special Safeguard** (SSG) provisions were made available for countries that converted their non-tariff barriers to tariff-only regimes according to the procedure known as "tariffication". The SSG allows an importer to increase tariffs above their bound rate in response to a surge in imports or a sharp decline in import prices. Most developing countries did not use the tariffication procedure, choosing instead to follow a simpler procedure for which the SSG was not made available. Most developed countries, in contrast, used the tariffication procedure and reserved the right to use the SSG, typically for temperate zone products such as meat, cereals, fruit and vegetables, oilseeds and oil products and dairy products.
  - **Actual Protection Rates** *in agriculture are still high and market access terms have not improved much.* Recent statistics show that nominal protection rates in the OECD countries have declined

somewhat but remain high on the whole. Bound tariffs are also high in many developing countries, although their applied rates are generally lower. A number of developing countries have raised their applied tariffs in recent years — within their bound rates — in an effort to protect domestic producers from the disruptive effects of very low world market prices.

SPS and TBT Agreements

The SPS and TBT Agreements confirm the right of WTO members to apply measures necessary to protect human, animal and plant life and health. These include the setting of technical regulations and standards governing quality requirements for food, packaging, marking and labeling, and national zoo and phyto-sanitary measures to protect animal and plant life and health.

These Agreements define rules for setting national measures so that they do not unduly restrict traffic and trade. SPS measures must be based on scientific principles and not maintained without sufficient evidence. The SPS and TBT agreements encourage international harmonization through the establishment of international sanitary and phytosanitary standards by, respectively, the Codex Alimentarius, the OIE and the International Plant Protection Convention.

Major challenges faced by many countries, particularly the developing countries and countries with economies in transition, are:

- to meet the sanitary, phytosanitary and technical requirements of importing countries,
- to provide scientific justification for their own sanitary, phytosanitary and technical measures, and
- to participate in a meaningful manner in the development and adoption of international standards. The gap in the technical and financial ability of countries to meet such standards is wide.

An additional challenge is faced by these countries when new standards are introduced on risk assessment grounds that are stricter than those currently in place, as the time and resources required to ensure conformity with these standards may be considerable. On the other hand, the risk assessment paradigm applied in the SPS Agreement in particular has had the effect of eliminating out-of-date, ineffective or arbitrary standards that may have provided a false sense of security. The transition to risk-based standard setting has required major changes in legislative, regulatory and administrative practices in most countries all of which have implied significant cost.

With some exceptions, disputes under the SPS and TBT Agreements involving food and agricultural products have not involved developing countries as few of them have standards that are stricter than those established by the international standards-setting bodies and therefore have not been challenged by other WTO Members (the main exceptions have been challenges by the US, Canada and Australia against practices in the Republic of Korea over various measures).

Few developing countries (or none at all) have used the formal dispute settlement mechanism and the SPS/TBT Agreements to challenge measures applied by importing countries that are believed to be arbitrary or unjustified. On the other hand, developing countries have been active in the SPS and TBT Committees in raising issues of importance to them with the intention of resolving such issues in the informal or consultative processes of the WTO.

The SPS and TBT agreements contain promises of financial and technical assistance for the developing countries. However, translating these promises into concrete action has not yet been achieved. Finally, the level of participation of these countries, in both number and effectiveness, in international standard-setting bodies remains an issue.

INTELLECTUAL PROPERTY: PROTECTION AND ENFORCEMENT

The WTO's **Agreement on Trade-Related Aspects of Intellectual Property Rights (TRIPS)**, negotiated in the 1986-94 Uruguay Round, introduced intellectual property rules into the multilateral trading system for the first time.

Origins: into the rule-based trade system

Ideas and knowledge are an increasingly important part of trade. Most of the value of new medicines and other high technology products lies in the amount of invention, innovation, research, design and testing involved. Films, music recordings, books, computer software and on-line services are bought and sold because of the information and creativity they contain, not usually because of the plastic, metal or paper used to make them. Many products that used to be traded as low-technology goods or commodities now contain a higher proportion of invention and design in their value—for example brand named clothing or new varieties of plants.

Creators can be given the right to prevent others from using their inventions, designs or other creations—and to use that right to negotiate payment in return for others using them. These are "intellectual property rights". They take a number of forms. For example books, paintings and films come under copyright; inventions can be patented; brand names and product logos can be registered as trademarks; and so on. Governments and parliaments have given creators these rights as an incentive to produce ideas that will benefit society as a whole.

Types of Intellectual Property

The areas covered by the TRIPS Agreement

- Copyright and related rights
- Trademarks, including service marks
- Geographical indications
- Industrial designs
- Patents
- Layout-designs (topographies) of integrated circuits
- Undisclosed information, including trade secrets

The **agreement** covers five broad issues:

- how basic principles of the trading system and other international intellectual property agreements should be applied
- how to give adequate protection to intellectual property rights
- how countries should enforce those rights adequately in their own territories
- how to settle disputes on intellectual property between members of the WTO
- special transitional arrangements during the period when the new system is being introduced.

How to Protect Intellectual Property: Common Ground-rules

The second part of the TRIPS agreement looks at different kinds of intellectual property rights and how to protect them. The purpose is to ensure that adequate standards of protection exist in all member countries. Here the starting point is the obligations of the main international agreements of the World Intellectual Property Organization (WIPO) that already existed before the WTO was created:

- The Paris Convention for the Protection of Industrial Property (patents, industrial designs, etc)
- The Berne Convention for the Protection of Literary and Artistic Works (copyright).

Some areas are not covered by these conventions. In some cases, the standards of protection prescribed were thought inadequate. So the TRIPS agreement adds a significant number of new or higher standards.

COPYRIGHT

The TRIPS agreement ensures that computer programs will be protected as literary works under the Berne Convention and outlines how databases should be protected.

It also expands international copyright rules to cover rental rights. Authors of computer programs and producers of sound recordings must have the right to prohibit the commercial rental of their works to the public. A similar exclusive right applies to films where commercial rental has led to widespread copying, affecting copyright-owners' potential earnings from their films.

The agreement says performers must also have the right to prevent unauthorized recording, reproduction and broadcast of live performances (bootlegging) for no less than 50 years. Producers of sound recordings must have the right to prevent the unauthorized reproduction of recordings for a period of 50 years.

TRADEMARKS

The agreement defines what types of signs must be eligible for protection as trademarks, and what the minimum rights conferred on their owners must be. It says that service marks must be protected in the same way as trademarks used for goods. Marks that have become well-known in a particular country enjoy additional protection.

Industrial Designs

Under the TRIPS Agreement, industrial designs must be protected for at least 10 years. Owners of protected designs must be able to prevent the manufacture, sale or importation of articles bearing or embodying a design which is a copy of the protected design.

Patents

The agreement says patent protection must be available for inventions for at least 20 years. Patent protection must be available for both products and processes, in almost all fields of technology. Governments can refuse to issue a patent for an invention if its commercial exploitation is prohibited for reasons of public order or morality. They can also exclude diagnostic, therapeutic and surgical methods, plants and animals (other than microorganisms), and biological processes for the production of plants or animals (other than microbiological processes).

If a patent is issued for a production process, then the rights must extend to the product directly obtained from the process. Under certain conditions alleged infringers may be ordered by a court to prove that they have not used the patented process.

Integrated Circuits Layout Designs

The basis for protecting integrated circuit designs ("topographies") in the TRIPS agreement is the Washington Treaty on Intellectual Property in Respect of Integrated Circuits, which comes under the World Intellectual Property Organization. This was adopted in 1989 but has not yet entered into force. The TRIPS agreement adds a number of provisions: for example, protection must be available for at least 10 years.

Technology Transfer

Developing countries in particular, see technology transfer as part of the bargain in which they have agreed to protect intellectual property rights. The TRIPS Agreement includes a number of provisions on this. For example, it requires developed countries' governments to provide incentives for their companies to transfer technology to least-developed countries.

Anti-dumping Actions

If a company exports a product at a price lower than the price it normally charges on its own home market, it is said to be "dumping" the product. Is this unfair competition? Opinions differ, but many governments take action against dumping in order to defend their domestic industries. The WTO agreement does not pass judgment. Its focus is on how governments can or cannot react to dumping — it disciplines anti-dumping actions, and it is often called the "**Anti-Dumping Agreement**". (This focus only on the reaction to dumping contrasts with the approach of the Subsidies and Countervailing Measures Agreement.)

TRADE RELATED INVESTMENT MEASURES (TRIMS)

The Agreement on Trade Related Investment Measures (TRIMs) is one of Agreements covered under Annex IA to the Marrakech Agreement, signed at the end of the Uruguay Round (UR) negotiations. The Agreement addresses investment measures that are trade related and that also violate Article III (National treatment) or Article XI (general elimination of quantitative restrictions) of the General Agreement on Tariffs and Trade. An illustrative list of the measures that are violative of the provisions of the Agreement is annexed to the text of the Agreement. These pertain broadly to local content requirements, trade balancing requirements and export restrictions, attached to investment decision making.

ILLUSTRATIVE LIST OF PROHIBITED TRIMS

TRIMS that are inconsistent with the obligation of national treatment provided for in GATT 1994 include those which are mandatory or enforceable under domestic law or under administrative rulings, or compliance with which is necessary to obtain an advantage, and which require:

- The purchase or use by an enterprise of products of domestic origin or from any domestic source, whether specified in terms of particular products, in terms of volume or value of products, or in terms of a proportion of volume or value of its local production; or
- That an enterprise's purchase or use of imported products be limited to an amount related to the volume or value of local products that it exports.

TRIMS that are inconsistent with the obligation of general elimination of quantitative restrictions provided GATT 1994 include those which are mandatory or enforceable under domestic law or under administrative rulings, or compliance with which is necessary to obtain an advantage, and which restrict:

- The importation by an enterprise of products used in or related to its local production, generally or to an amount related to the volume or value of local production that it exports;
- The importation by an enterprise of products used in or related to its local production by restricting its access to foreign exchange to an amount related to the foreign exchange inflows attributable to the enterprise; or
- The exportation or sale for export by an enterprise of products, whether specified in terms of particular products, in terms of volume or value of products, or in terms of a proportion of volume or value of its local production

India's Notified TRIMs

As per the provisions of Article 5.1 of the TRIMs Agreement India had notified three trade related investment measures as inconsistent with the provisions of the Agreement:

- Local content (mixing) requirements in the production
- Local content requirement in the production
- Dividend balancing requirement in the case of investment in 22 categories consumer goods.

Such notified TRIMs were due to be eliminated by 31st December, 1999. None of these measures is in force at present. Therefore, India does not have any outstanding obligations under the TRIMs agreement as far as notified TRIMs are concerned.

Investment Policy and Competition Policy

In the course of this review, the Council for Trade in Goods shall consider whether the Agreement should be complemented with the provisions on investment policy and competition policy. The Singapore Ministerial Conference which established the two parallel Working Groups to study the relationship between Trade and Investment on the one hand and Trade and Competition Policy on the other had stipulated that future negotiations, if any, regarding multilateral disciplines in these areas will take place only after explicit consensus decision by the Members. The Working Group process is still on.

DOHA DEVELOPMENT AGENDA (DDA) – IX ROUND

The Doha Development Agenda (DDA or Doha Round) is the **ninth round** of multilateral trade negotiations to be carried out since the end of World War II. The Doha Development Round or Doha Development Agenda (DDA) is the current trade-negotiation round of the World Trade Organization (WTO) which commenced in November 2001. Its objective is to lower trade barriers around the world, which allows countries to increase trade globally. As of 2008, talks have stalled over a divide on major issues, such as agriculture, industrial tariffs and non-tariff barriers, services, and trade remedies.

The most significant differences are between developed nations led by the **European Union (EU)**, the **United States (USA)**, and Japan and the major developing countries led and represented mainly by **India, Brazil, China and South Africa.** There is also considerable contention against and between the EU and the U.S. over their maintenance of agricultural subsidies—seen to operate effectively as trade barriers.

The goal of the DDA is to reduce trade barriers in order to expand global economic growth, development, and opportunity. The main focus of the negotiations under the DDA is in the following areas: **agriculture; industrial market access; services; trade facilitation;** WTO rules (i.e., trade remedies, fish subsidies, and regional trade agreements); and development.

The agenda of the Doha Round is much broader than past global trade negotiations and is specifically targeted at addressing the needs of developing countries. The focus of negotiations has been on reforming agricultural subsidies, improving the access to global markets and ensuring that new liberalization in the global economy respects the need for sustainable economic growth in developing countries.

EU PRIORITIES FOR DOHA

The basic EU priorities in the Doha Round are as follows:

- In market access for the **industrial goods sector,** the EU wants to create significant new trade flows by cutting tariffs in both developed countries and the growing emerging economies such as China, Brazil and India. The goal is to create new trade between developed countries, but also between developing countries.
- For the **agriculture sector** the EU is committed to an agreement that reforms farm subsidy programs throughout the rich world in line with the EU's wide-ranging 2003 reform of the Common Agricultural Policy. As part of the Doha Round, the EU has offered to cut farm tariffs by 60%, reduce trade distorting farm subsidies by 80% and eliminate farm export subsidies altogether. The EU also wants to see new market access opportunities for its own processed agricultural exports.
- In market access negotiations for the **services trade,** Doha should bring considerable and real market opportunities for business as well as benefits to consumers world-wide. However, the EU does not seek general deregulation or privatization of sectors where principles of public interest are at stake, and the EU is also committed to defending the right of WTO members to promote cultural diversity.
- The EU wants the Doha Round to agree a package of development measures including: a special agreement to address trade distortions caused by subsidies to cotton farmers in developed countries; the extension of unlimited markets access to all Least Developed Countries by as many countries as possible; a new global package of 'aid for trade' assistance to help the poorest build the capacity to trade; special measures to help the poorest countries implement any Doha Agreement effectively and without long-term harm to their economies.
- The EU wants the Doha Round to agree a new set of rules to govern the **use of trade defence instruments** so that they are not abused, and a complete update of the WTO's rulebook for trade facilitation, the standard practice for customs and other border related procedures world wide – a potential source of huge savings for traders, especially in developing countries. The EU also wants to use the Doha Round to improve the protection of **geographical indications** – the special legal identity given to products like Parma Ham and Roquefort cheese that are closely linked to a particular place and tradition of production.

DOHA DEVELOPMENT AGENDA (CURRENT ISSUES)

The Doha negotiations incorporated negotiations already underway on agriculture and services. Agriculture and services were the only areas where negotiations on further trade liberalization had been mandated in the Uruguay Round WTO Agreements (see **Agreement on Agriculture:** General Issues).

The Doha Ministerial Declaration sets out the basic mandate for the negotiations. With over three quarters of WTO members identifying themselves as developing countries, the Doha Declaration gives developing country issues a high priority in the negotiations. This is reflected in the decision to refer to the negotiations as the Doha Development Agenda and by members committing themselves to addressing the interests and concerns of developing countries—especially the least developed countries (LDCs)—in the multilateral trading system. The Doha Declaration also states that "special and differential treatment for developing countries shall be an integral part of all elements of the negotiations."

The **main objectives** for agriculture found in the **Doha Declaration** are for:

- "Substantial improvements in market access; reductions of, with a view to phasing out, all forms of export subsidies; and substantial reductions in trade distorting domestic support."
- To "take note of the non-trade concerns reflected in the negotiating proposals submitted by members and confirm that non-trade concerns will be taken into account in the negotiations as provided for in the Agreement on Agriculture."
- Most countries accept that agriculture has functions other than producing food and fiber—non-trade concerns—such as food security, environmental protection, structural adjustment, rural development, poverty alleviation, and animal welfare.
- Non-trade concerns have not received much attention in the Doha negotiations, as countries have concentrated on negotiating cuts in tariffs, domestic support, and export subsidies, while providing for the special and differential needs of developing countries.

IMPORTANT EVENTS IN DDA

November 9, 2001: Doha Ministerial

WTO Members launched the Doha Round, with the goal of incorporating developing countries into the international trading system.

September 10, 2003: Cancun Ministerial

At the Cancun Ministerial, Members were unable to reach a consensus on the way forward on the main issues negotiated under the Doha Round.

July 13, 2004: Geneva Mini-Ministerial

As a result of U.S. efforts to reinvigorate the negotiations, Members reached a "Framework-Agreement," which addressed issues such as **NAMA** (Non-Agricultural Market Access) flexibilities and the elimination of agricultural export subsidies.

October 10, 2005: U.S. Proposal for Agriculture Negotiations

The United States tabled a comprehensive proposal for the agriculture negotiations to eliminate all tariffs and subsidies in a two-phase process. The proposal was contingent on others adopting these bold reforms.

December 13, 2005: Hong Kong Ministerial

At the Hong Kong Ministerial, limited progress was made. In NAMA, the Swiss formula to calculate NAMA tariff cuts was agreed to by WTO Members as the "standard formula".

July 27, 2006: Suspension of Negotiations

A July 2006 gathering of trade ministers in Geneva highlighted the wide gap that existed on fundamental questions about securing a meaningful market opening DDA outcome. Director-General Lamy recommended to the WTO General Council on July 27, 2006, that the Doha Round negotiations be suspended.

July 2006–July 2007: Resuming Negotiations

After the July 2006 suspension, the United States led the way over the following months to revive the DDA negotiations. This resulted in an informal resumption of negotiations in Geneva before the close of the year. On January 31, 2007, Director-General Lamy called for a "full resumption" of negotiations.

Agriculture and NAMA Negotiating Texts

The Chairs of the Agriculture and NAMA negotiating groups circulated initial draft texts for the "modalities" (the frameworks and formalities needed to be agreed upon in order to move the negotiations into the final phase) on July 17, 2007. Revised draft texts were issued on February 8, 2008, May 19, 2008, and July 10, 2008.

Elements of a Services Negotiating Text

The Chair of the Services negotiating group circulated an initial report on the elements required for the completion of the services negotiations on February 13, 2008. A revision was issued on May 26, 2008.

Draft Rules Negotiating Text

The Chair of the Rules negotiating group issued texts on anti-dumping, subsidies and countervailing measures, and fisheries subsidies on November 30, 2007.

July 21, 2008: Geneva Ministers Meetings

Ministers and other senior officials will meet in Geneva the week of July 21, 2008, in an effort to reach agreement that will establish modalities for Agriculture and NAMA, allowing negotiations to enter the final phase of work. Ministers will also meet in a special conference to signal future offers and set the services negotiations on a path to a strong market-opening outcome.

NON-AGRICULTURAL MARKET ACCESS (NAMA)

The Non-Agricultural Market Access (NAMA) negotiations are based on the Doha mandate of 2001 that calls for a reduction or elimination in tariff peaks, tariff escalation, high tariffs, and non-tariff barriers, particularly on goods that are of export value and therefore of interest to developing countries.

NAMA refers to all those products that are not covered by the Agreement on Agriculture or the negotiations on services. In practice, NAMA products include manufacturing products, fuels and mining products, fish and fish products, and forestry products.

The NAMA negotiations have been considered important by the WTO because NAMA products account for almost 90% of the world's merchandise exports.

HISTORY

After the Doha Declaration was adopted in 2001, negotiations on NAMA formally began in January 2002 after the creation of the **Negotiating Group on Market Access (NGMA)**. In the beginning, negotiations on non-agricultural products were to be concluded by 1 January 2005. However, this deadline was missed and the negotiations are still under way.

Pierre Louis Girard, Chairman of the NGMA, made the first proposal in 2003 before the Cancun Ministerial about the modalities regarding how to take the process forward. However, Girard's proposal faced severe opposition from the developed members, as it proposed a smaller tariff cut than the one that the developed member countries had been advocating.

However, by the time the Cancun Ministerial was held in 2003, the second text on NAMA was opposed by the developing countries for moving away from the first NAMA draft, especially by the G90 and African Caribbean and Pacific (ACP) countries.

The deadlock on NAMA negotiations was broken in July 2004, which was the first agreement amongst the countries after the collapse of Cancun. The July 2004 agreement also laid the framework for establishing future modalities.

The aim of NAMA is to reduce tariffs in these areas, particularly industry. Developing countries tend to have the highest tariffs, usually in place to protect national industries. Those arguing for reductions in these tariffs say that only free trade can lead to the creation of efficient new industries and forestry and fishing sectors. However, others argue that nearly all developed countries, and the emerging economies of Asia used tariffs to protect new industries, and that there is a case for tariff protection for infant industries that are not yet profitable. Tariffs are also an efficient and effective way of raising government revenue in the form of taxes.

MAJOR ISSUES

The key U.S. NAMA objective is to achieve an ambitious outcome that results in significant new market access through cuts in applied tariff rates in both developed and key developing country member markets.

In **2008,** WTO members focused on a number of substantive elements relating to tariff liberalization in NAMA:

- The tariff-cutting formula and specifics on the level of ambition to be achieved by developed and developing country members;
- The scope of exceptions available to developing countries applying the tariff-cutting formula;
- Flexibilities to be provided for least-developed country (LDC) members and other developing country members;
- A sectoral tariff component; and
- Work on non-tariff barriers.

Members attempted to finalize these elements at the WTO Ministerial in Geneva in July 2008. Discussions resumed in September and continued to the end of the year.

The United States supports a combination of tariff cuts achieved through applying a Swiss formula with different coefficients for developed and developing Members and sectoral tariff elimination initiatives to most effectively achieve the objectives laid out in the Doha mandate.

The United States also believes that all the elements of NAMA from the Framework in the July 2004 Package must be considered in tandem. There is an inextricable link between the formula, flexibilities, and sectoral initiatives.

Prospects for 2011

In 2011, the United States will continue to seek an ambitious NAMA outcome that will deliver new market access in key developed and developing country

Member markets, while supporting elements of flexibility for developing country Members that does not operate to undermine the overall level of ambition.

The United States remains committed to the view that true development gains can best be achieved through further real market liberalization by both developed and developing members.

Formula Tariff Cuts

In the current NAMA negotiating text, approximately 30 self-designated developing countries are expected to apply the tariff cutting Swiss formula, choosing between the three available coefficients in the Chair's text, each linked with a different level of flexibilities.

These countries include nine members of the so-called NAMA-113, which has advocated a high developing country coefficient in the formula and expanded flexibilities for developing countries, as well as the members of Middle Ground group, which has generally supported stronger market opening results and more limited exceptions to the formula.

Also among the countries expected to apply a developing country coefficient are the four Recently Acceded Members (RAMs) that are not considered small, vulnerable economies or Very Recently Acceded Members (VRAMs).

CURRENT TARIFF STRUCTURE OF NAMA

This chapter measured the initial tariff structure, bilaterally, for some countries and regions and found that the average global tariff for exports of industrial products is around 6.22%. It is noteworthy that there have been major tariff reductions on industrial products over a number of decades and this market is clearly more open than the market for agricultural products. A tariff of 4.57% is applied to Africa as against the rest of the world, which is slightly lower where African exporters are seeking developed-country markets.

Indeed, the average tariff level is around 4.23% in regard to the tariffs applied by developed countries on African exports. Europe and the United States apply lower tariffs than the average for developed countries (1.31% and 1.69% respectively). This can be explained by the various preferential facilities extended to African countries. The tariffs applied in the intra-African domain are among the highest and constitute a bottleneck to the continent's economic integration. In general terms, developing countries apply high industrial tariffs because of the need to protect their industrial sector and support the diversification of their economies.

However, even though the average tariff levels suggest that Africa enjoys privileged access to a number of markets, including developed-country markets, there are important exceptions in regard to industrial products and particularly in the labor-intensive sectors where developing-country competition is also intensifying.

Table: Initial (bilateral) average tariff structure

Exporter	Importer						
	Developed countries	Developing countries	EU25	Japan	USA	Africa	World
Developed Country	8.34%	10.50%	5.93%	4.82%	1.03%	16.62%	6.51%
Developing Country	6.19%	11.10%	3.10%	4.20%	2.92%	19.38%	5.75%
EU25	6.77%	9.26%	0.00%	4.65%	2.82%	16.46%	6.49%
Japan	5.21%	11.46%	4.82%	0.00%	2.33%	15.58%	7.12%
USA	5.66%	8.33%	4.60%	3.41%	0.00	14.63%	6.61%
Africa	4.23%	9.16%	1.31%	2.87%	1.69%	`6.86%	4.57%
World	6.36%	9.89%	3.86%	4.35%	2.62%	17.18%	6.22%

Source: MacMaps Database

The average industrial tariff for the United States is 1.69%. Despite the relatively low average, industrial tariffs applied in the United States frequently peak. In fact, the tariffs applied in textiles, processed dairy products and sugar are way above the average tariff level. Europe has slightly lower tariff levels (1.31%), which belies the fact that European tariffs in textiles and clothing are prohibitive against exports of sub-Saharan Africa. However, in regard to these products, North Africa enjoys more significant preferences than sub-Saharan African countries. Japan applies tariff levels in the range of 2.33% on industrial products. This figure appears quite low, but it should be noted that the tariffs applied on textiles and processed agricultural products are, respectively, three to six times the average.

The Sectoral Initiative: the Strategic Choice of these Sectors

Doha Round sectoral initiatives are voluntary agreements by WTO Members to significantly reduce or eliminate tariffs on specific categories of industrial goods.

Further progress was made on sectoral tariff initiative discussions in 2008.

The United States continued efforts to inform other Members of the benefits of sectoral liberalization and proposed specific flexibility options for developing country Members based on sensitivities they raised in sector-specific discussions.

The United States worked with other sponsors of sectoral initiatives to refine sectoral proposals and draft the structure of individual sectoral agreements. To date, Members have proposed fourteen sectors that are being considered for such agreements.

The sectoral tariff component of the negotiations is also being actively pursued by individual Members interested in seeing such an outcome in a particular sector, and who consider this an essential component of the NAMA negotiations to achieve commercially meaningful market access. African countries, which are not LDC's, should analyze the consequences of the sectoral initiatives on their economies.

Indeed, many sectors quoted by the NAMA Chairman (Electronics/ Electrical Equipment, Bicycles and Sporting Goods, Fish, Forest Products, Gems and Jewellery, Raw Materials) are important for African countries in terms of diversification and industrialization. Therefore, African countries could have the discretionary power to define the sectors they will choose with their development objectives. Any sectoral negotiations should not be linked to the determination of the appropriate formulae.

The consequences of possible NAMA modalities on African economies depend to a large extent on the nature of the implicit and explicit special and differential treatment. A pro-development outcome from the NAMA negotiations needs to address the following:

- Greater levels of flexibility in the final formula. An extended Swiss formula or a Swiss 'type' formula, which includes the country's tariff average, could take more into consideration the interests of developing countries in the NAMA negotiations and therefore could constitute a compromise among WTO members.
- Stronger special and differential treatment must be possible in the final modalities agreed upon. The final formula should be able to discriminate between developed and developing countries without any ambiguity.
- The negotiations should ensure the provision of policy space for developing countries to pursue industrial development and diversification of their economies.

Non-Tariff Barriers (NTBs)

Non-Tariff Barriers (NTBs) are measures other than a tariff that restricts imports, such as quotas or discriminatory regulations and remain an integral and equally important component of the NAMA negotiations.

In line with the Hong Kong Ministerial Declaration, WTO Members continued to consider how NTBs could be addressed horizontally (i.e., across all sectors), vertically (i.e., pertaining to a single sector), and through a bilateral request/offer process.

In **2008,** the United States tabled three draft proposed texts:

- on transparency in export licensing,
- on non-tariff barriers pertaining to safety and electromagnetic compatibility for electronic products, and
- on non-tariff barriers relating to technical barriers to trade for automotive products.

WTO DISPUTE SETTLEMENT

The dispute settlement mechanism, with its ability to deliver binding decisions, is one of the central elements of the Uruguay Round Agreements. The Dispute Settlement Understanding introduced a more structured dispute settlement process with more clearly defined stages than that which existed under GATT since 1947. A fundamental difference between the two is that under GATT a positive consensus was needed to adopt reports, so any one party could prevent formally adopting a decision. Under the DSU, dispute settlement reports are automatically adopted, unless consensus is to the contrary. This is known as "reverse consensus" and makes the decisions very difficult to reject. The DSU did, however, add a mechanism for appealing rulings to an Appellate Body.

A dispute is brought to the WTO when a member state believes that a fellow member is violating trade rules. This usually occurs when a company brings the violation to the attention of its government. The two parties to a dispute then follow a pre-defined set of procedures.

A dispute arises when one member country adopts a trade policy *measure* or takes some *action* that one or more fellow members considers to a breach of WTO agreements or to be a failure to live up to obligations. By joining the WTO, member countries have agreed that if they believe fellow members are in violation of trade rules, they will use the multilateral system of settling disputes instead of taking action unilaterally — this entails abiding by agreed procedures (Dispute Settlement Understanding) and respecting judgments, primarily of the **Dispute Settlement Body (DSB)**, the WTO organ responsible for adjudication of disputes.

FOUR PHASES OF WTO DISPUTE SETTLEMENT MECHANISM

- ***Consultations*:** Parties to a dispute are obliged to see if they can settle their differences. If consultations are not successful within 60 days, the complainant can ask the Dispute Settlement Body to establish a panel. The parties may also undertake good offices, conciliation, or mediation procedures.

- ***The Panel***: The three-member panel decides the case in a quasi-judicial process. Where the dispute involves a developing country, one panelist is from a developing country. The panel report, circulated to all WTO members within nine months of panel establishment, becomes the ruling of the DSB unless it is rejected by consensus or appealed.
- ***Appeals***: The possibility of appealing a panel ruling is a new feature in the DSM as compared with GATT. Either party can appeal the ruling of the panel based on points of law. Appeals are heard by three randomly selected members of the Appellate Body and may uphold, modify or reverse the legal findings and conclusions of the panel in a report issued within 60 to 90 days.
- ***Surveillance of Implementation***: The violating member is required to state its intentions on implementation within 30 days of the report being. The cases which we shall study are either not yet resolved, resolved through settlement, or resolved through the decision of the panel or appellate body. They show that the WTO encourages amicable settlement where possible, arbitrated settlement if necessary, and that the WTO can enforce its judgments. These facts are empirical support of the validity of the professionalisation thesis in practice as well as theory. All of the cases involve intellectual property law and all cases but one involve the US and the EU or an EU member state adopted by the DSB. If the party fails to implement the report within a reasonable period (usually between eight and 15 months), the two countries enter negotiations to agree on appropriate compensation. If this fails, the prevailing party may ask the DSB for permission to retaliate, by imposing, for example, trade sanctions, the level of which is subject to arbitration.

The DSM cannot force a state to change its laws, even if they are found to contravene WTO rules. States intent on keeping such laws can either negotiate compensation for the complainant (for example, increasing the access to markets in another area), or failing that, be subjected to retaliatory trade sanctions.

DURATION OF DISPUTE SETTLEMENT MECHANISM

These approximate periods for each stage of a dispute settlement procedure are target figures. The agreement is flexible. In addition, the countries can settle their dispute themselves at any stage. Totals are also approximate.

DURATION	MECHANISM
60 days	Consultations, mediation, etc
45 days	Panel set up and panelists appointed
6 months	Final panel report to parties
3 weeks	Final panel report to WTO members
60 days	Dispute Settlement Body adopts report (if no appeal)
Total = 1 year (without appeal)	
60–90 days	Appeals report
30 days	Dispute Settlement Body adopts appeals report
Total = 1 year 3 months (with appeal)	

Source: Understanding the WTO: Settling Disputes-A unique contribution

WTO dispute settlement is a government-to-government process in which the commercial interests of a country's nationals are taken up and pursued by its government.

WTO disputes begin with a 'diplomatic' process of consultation between states. If these fail to resolve a dispute, the matter may be referred by the WTO (through an organ called the Dispute Settlement Body or DSB) to a panel of independent trade experts. A panel's report may be appealed to the Appellate Body.

Settling disputes is the responsibility of the Dispute Settlement Body. The DSB has the exclusive authority to establish "panels" of experts to judge the case, and to accept or reject the panels' findings or the results of an appeal. It oversees the implementation of the rulings and recommendations, and has the power to permit retaliation when a country does not comply with a ruling.

First Stage: Before taking any other actions the countries in dispute are encouraged to settle their conflict themselves. This consultation may last a maximum of 45 days. If that process fails, they may request the mediation of the WTO director-general.

Second Stage: If consultations fail, the complaining country can ask for a panel to be appointed. The panel has to give his ruling within a period of time of 6 months. Also the appointment of the panel is to be done within a period of 45 days. The concerned country can block the creation of a panel once, but when the DSB meets for a second time, the panel formation cannot be stopped unless by consensus in the DSB.

The panel will submit a report to the Dispute Settlement Body. The reports conclusions have to be based on WTO agreements are crucial because the panel's report can only be rejected by consensus in the Dispute Settlement Body.

The panel submits a first draft report including descriptive facts to the two sides, giving those two weeks to comment. This report does not include findings and conclusions. The panel then submits an interim report, including its findings and conclusions, to the two sides, giving them one week to ask for a review. The period of review must not exceed two weeks.

During that time, the panel may hold additional meetings with the two sides. Countries concerned submit written rebuttals and present oral arguments at the panel's second meeting. Also, if necessary, the panel may appoint one or more experts to submit an advisory report.

The agreement describes in some detail how the panels are to work. The main stages are:

- **Before the First Hearing:** Each side in the dispute presents its case in writing to the panel.
- **First Hearing: the Case for the Complaining Country and Defence:** The complaining country (or countries), the responding country, and those that have announced they have an interest in the dispute, make their case at the panel's first hearing.
- **Rebuttals:** The countries involved submit written rebuttals and present oral arguments at the panel's second meeting.
- **Experts:** If one side raises scientific or other technical matters, the panel may consult experts or appoint an expert review group to prepare an advisory report.
- **First Draft:** The panel submits the descriptive (factual and argument) sections of its report to the two sides, giving them two weeks to comment. This report does not include findings and conclusions.
- **Interim Report:** The panel then submits an interim report, including its findings and conclusions, to the two sides, giving them one week to ask for a review.
- **Review:** The period of review must not exceed two weeks. During that time, the panel may hold additional meetings with the two sides.

Final Report: A final report is submitted to the two sides and three weeks later, it is circulated to all WTO members. If the panel decides that the disputed measures are contrary to WTO agreement or obligations, it recommends the necessary measures to be made to conform to WTO rules.

The report finally becomes the Dispute Settlements Body's ruling or recommendation within 60 days unless a consensus rejects it. The two sides can appeal the report.

The Report Becomes a Ruling: The report becomes the Dispute Settlement Body's ruling or recommendation within 60 days unless a consensus rejects it. Both sides can appeal the report (and in some cases both sides do).

Appeals

Either side can appeal a panel's ruling. Appeals have to be based on points of law such as legal interpretation and cannot reexamine existing evidence or examine new issues.

Each appeal is heard by three members of a permanent member Appellate Body setup by the Dispute Settlement Body and broadly representing the range of WTO membership. Members of the Appellate Body have four-year terms. The appeal can uphold modify or reverse the panel legal findings and conclusions. Normally appeals should not last more than 60 days with a maximum time table of 90 days.

CASES RAISED BEFORE DSB

The cases which we shall study are either not yet resolved, resolved through settlement, or resolved through the decision of the panel or appellate body. They show that the WTO encourages amicable settlement where possible, arbitrated settlement if necessary, and that the WTO can enforce its judgments. These facts are empirical support of the validity of the professionalization thesis in practice as well as theory. All of the cases involve intellectual property law and all cases but one involve the US and the EU or an EU member state.

The settlement procedure encourages dispute resolution through hierarchical procedures of trial and enforcement of judgment. Settlement is also encouraged by the fact that the mechanisms of enforcement are efficacious. Enforcement efficacy is guaranteed by the ultimate sanction of economic retaliation (counter-veiling duties, import restrictions and other barriers to trade). Because this mechanism turns the self interest of the state toward enforcement, the WTO and DSB are a working example of effective realist-functionalist state theory.

Pending Cases

The following cases are currently pending before the arbitration panel:

United States - Section 211 Omnibus Appropriations Act, complaint by the European Communities and its member States (WT/DS176/1).

Essentially, a US law prohibits the registration of a trademark which has fallen into disuse where the mark had been abandoned following confiscation of the trade mark owner's business assets located in Cuba.. Section 211 of the US Omnibus Appropriations Act is challenged for inconformity with TRIPS Article 2 and by reference the Paris Convention's articles 3, 4, 15-21, 41, 42 and 62. Canada, Japan and Nicaragua reserved their third-party rights.

European Communities - Enforcement of Intellectual Property Rights for Motion Pictures and Television Programs, complaint by the United States (WT/DS124/1).

Essentially this is a case asserting copyright infringement. The US alleges that Greek television stations regularly broadcast copyrighted movies and television programs without securing permission from their owners. The US argues that the Greek remedies are either unenforced or inadequate and asserts a violation of Articles 41 and 61 of the TRIPS Agreement. On 20 March 2001, the parties to the dispute notified a mutually satisfactory solution on the matter to the DSB.

The cases which have been taken up but which are not yet settled are examples of the first step in the process, seeking a hearing before the panel, and that request is made whilst negotiations occur to settle amicably. Either the case settles, or goes forward. If the case goes forward a decision is issued. Either the decision is appealed or enforced or avoided. If the decision is appealed either the decision may be changed. If however the decision is avoided a series of escalating retaliatory measures are allowed proportional to the injury resulting from breach of the treaty obligations. This is very similar to the process before any other court, and this similarity is further evidence of the validity of the professionalisation thesis.

COMPLETED CASES

The following cases have been completed, either through settlement or through binding arbitration. As such they illustrate the efficacity of the DSB. The parties preferred settling in 2 of the 3 cases studied which supports the professionalisation thesis since the efficacity of enforcement is key to the validity of that thesis. Were the enforcement mechanism ineffective, parties would be unlikely to settle. Yet in most cases parties prefer to settle, at least in this small case survey (which does however reach every case involving intellectual property with the US and the EU or an EU member state as parties).

SETTLED CASES

Sweden - Measures Affecting the Enforcement of Intellectual Property Rights, complaint by the United States **(WT/DS86/1).**

Here, in essence, the US argued that the Swedish remedy for infringement of intellectual property rights was inadequate and thus violated Articles 50, 63 and 65 of the TRIPS Agreement. The parties reached a mutally agreed upon settlement. This case is thus another example of the efficacity of the agreement in terms of encouraging settlements.

Portugal - Patent Protection under the Industrial Property Act, complaint by the United States **(WT/DS37).**

In that case the US argued that Portugese domestic law on (Portugal's Industrial Property Act) was in violations of Articles 33, 65 and 70 of TRIPS. Both parties notified a mutually agreed solution to the DSB. Again the procedures are effective as the encourage enforcable settlement of disputes.

Compensation and Retaliation

If all else fails, two more possibilities are set out in the DSU:

- If a member fails within the "reasonable period" to carry out the recommendations and rulings, it may negotiate with the complaining state for a mutually acceptable compensation.
- Compensation is not defined, but may be expected to consist of the grant of a concession by the respondent state on a product or service of interest to the complainant state.
- If no agreement on compensation is reached within twenty days of the expiry of the "reasonable period", the prevailing state may request authorization from the DSB to suspend application to the member concerned of concessions or other obligations under the covered agreements. The DSU makes clear that retaliation is not favored, and sets the criteria for retaliation.
- In contrast to prior GATT practice, authorization to suspend concessions in this context is semi-automatic, in that the DSB "shall grant the authorization within thirty days of the expiry of the reasonable period", unless it decides by consensus to reject the request.
- Any suspension or concession or other obligation is to be temporary. If the respondent state objects to the level of suspension proposed or to the consistency of the proposed suspension with the DSU principles, still another arbitration is provided for, if possible by the original panel members or by an arbitrator or arbitrators appointed by the Director-General, to be completed within sixty days from expiration of the reasonable period.

SUMMARY

- ❑ The WTO agreements are lengthy and complex because they are legal texts covering a wide range of activities. They deal with: agriculture, textiles and clothing, banking, telecommunications, government purchases, industrial standards and product safety, food sanitation regulations, intellectual property.

- Under the WTO agreements, countries cannot normally discriminate between their trading partners.
- Suppose country A is better than country B at making automobiles, and country B is better than country A at making bread. It is obvious (the academics would say "trivial") that both would benefit if A specialized in automobiles, B specialized in bread and they traded their products. That is a case of **absolute advantage**.
- Uruguay Round brought about the biggest reform of the world's trading system since GATT was created at the end of the Second World War.
- The WTO replaced GATT as an international organization, but the General Agreement still exists as the WTO's umbrella treaty for trade in goods, updated as a result of the Uruguay Round negotiations.
- Much of the Uruguay Round dealt with the first two parts: general principles and principles for specific sectors. At the same time, market access negotiations were possible for industrial goods.
- The objective of the **Agriculture Agreement** is to reform trade in the sector and to make policies more market-oriented. This would improve predictability and security for importing and exporting countries alike.
- Trade is distorted if prices are higher or lower than normal, and if quantities produced, bought, and sold are also higher or lower than normal — i.e. than the levels that would usually exist in a competitive market.
- A separate agreement on food safety and animal and plant health standards (the **Sanitary and Phyto-sanitary Measures Agreement** or **SPS**) sets out the basic rules.
- A **Textiles Monitoring Body (TMB)** supervised the agreement's implementation. It consisted of a chairman and 10 members acting in their personal capacity. It monitored actions taken under the agreement to ensure that they were consistent, and it reported to the Goods Council which reviewed the operation of the agreement before each new step of the integration process.
- The WTO's **Agreement on Trade-Related Aspects of Intellectual Property Rights (TRIPS)**, negotiated in the 1986-94 Uruguay Round, introduced intellectual property rules into the multilateral trading system for the first time.
- "**Anti-Dumping Agreement**": This focus only on the reaction to dumping contrasts with the approach of the Subsidies and Countervailing Measures Agreement.
- TRIMS Agreement addresses investment measures that are trade related and that also violate Article III (National treatment) or Article XI (general elimination of quantitative restrictions) of the General Agreement on Tariffs and Trade.
- WTO disputes begin with a 'diplomatic' process of consultation between states. If these fail to resolve a dispute, the matter may be referred by the WTO (through an organ called the Dispute Settlement Body or DSB) to a panel of independent trade experts. A panel's report may be appealed to the Appellate Body.

Chapter 10

International Control Strategies

INTRODUCTION

Control is management's planning, implementation, evaluation, and correction of performance to ensure that the organization meets its objectives. Top management's toughest challenge is to balance the company's global needs with its need to adapt to country-level differences.

Control is also needed so that individuals cannot make decisions that endanger the entire company. Several factors make control more difficult internationally than it is domestically.

1. **Distance:** In spite of the growth in e-mail and fax transmissions, many communications are still best handled by face-to-face or voice-to-voice contact. The geographic distance and cultural disparity separating countries increase the time, expense, and possibility of error in cross-national communications.
2. **Diversity:** This book has emphasized the need for an MNE to adjust to each country in which it operates. When market size, type of competition, nature of the product, labor cost, currency and a host of other factors differentiate operations among countries, the task of evaluating performance or setting standards to correct or improve business functions is extremely complicated.
3. **Uncontrollable:** Evaluating employees' and subsidiaries' performance is of little use in maintaining control unless there is some means of taking corrective action. Effective corrective action may be minimal because many foreign operations must contend with the dictates of outside stockholders in the foreign company, whose objectives may differ somewhat from those of the parent, and with government regulations over which the company has no short-term influence.
4. **Degree of Certainty:** Control implies setting goals and developing plans to meet those goals. Economic and industry data are much less

complete and accurate for some countries than for others. Further, political and economic conditions are subject to rapid change in some locales.

Although these factors make control more difficult in the international context, managers still try to ensure that foreign operations comply with overall corporate goals and philosophies. This chapter discusses five aspects of the **international control process:**

- Planning
- Organizational structure
- Location of decision making
- Control mechanisms
- Special situations

PLANNING

Planning is an essential element of managerial control. A company must adapt its resources and objectives to different and changing international markets and this takes planning.

The Planning Loop

Planning must mesh a company's objectives and capabilities with its internal and external environments. It must also involve continuing reassessment – thus the concept of a loop back to early steps in the planning process.

The first step (A) is to develop a long-range **strategic intent**, an objective that will hold the organization together over a long period while it builds global competitive viability. Although few companies start with such intent, most develop one as they progress toward significant international positions. Some, such as Honda and Canon, developed strategic intents to become major global competitors while they were still small domestic companies. The strategic intent may encompass whether and where a company wants to be a leader, such as dominating its domestic market, dominating a regional or global market, or attaining profit results without being the market leader.

The next planning step (B) is to **analyze internal resources**, along with environmental factors in the home country. These resources and factors affect and constrain each company differently and sometimes each product differently for the same company. For example, a small company inexperienced in foreign operations may lack financial and human resources, even though it may have unique product capabilities. Unlike a large counterpart, it may have to collaborate with another company, perhaps by licensing foreign production rather than owning facilities abroad.

Only by making an internal analysis (Step B) can a company set the overall rationale for its **international activities** (Step C). Managers must examine these activities in conjunction with the means of competing, such as by keeping prices low or differentiating through brand recognition.

Because each country in which the company is operating or contemplating operating is unique, managers must do a **local analysis** (Step D) before examining the **final alternatives** (Step E).

The selection among the alternatives in Step E determines the extent to which a company follows a global, transnational or multi-domestic strategy. These alternatives include:

- *Location of Value-added Functions:* The choice of where to locate each of the functions that comprise the entire value-added chain, from research to production to after-sales servicing.
- *Location of Sales Targets:* The allocation of sales among countries and the level of activity in each particularly in terms of market share.
- *Level of Involvement:* The choice of operating through wholly owned facilities, partially owned facilities, or contract arrangements and whether the choice varies among countries.
- *Marketing:* The extent to which a company uses the same brand names, advertising, and other marketing elements in different countries.
- *Competitive Moves:* The extent to which a company makes competitive moves in individual countries as part of a global competitive strategy.

Uncertainty and Planning

The more uncertainty there is, the harder it is to plan. It is generally agreed that conditions in the international sphere are more uncertain than those in the domestic sphere because international operations are complex. International managers have to monitor many subsidiaries – many with different products – in different foreign markets.

ORGANIZATIONAL STRUCTURE

International companies try to set up organizational structures (the formal patterns of their lines of communication and responsibilities) that group individuals and operational units in strategic ways. The structure depends on many factors, including:

- Degree of multi-domestic, global and transnational policies employed
- Location and type of foreign facilities
- Impact of international operations on total corporate performance.

The form, method, and location of operational units at home and abroad will affect taxes, expenses – and control. Consequently, organizational structure has an important effect on the fulfillment of corporate objectives. We shall now examine the major structures of companies' international operations.

As firms expand across abroad, they adopt a variety of organizational structures in order to meet the demands of the international business environment. Although a variety of specific MNE structures exist, five structures represent the most common forms. These will be described in their general format, though it will be obvious as we progress that it is possible to combine some of these general structures. A graphical illustration and a summary of they key strengths and weaknesses of each type of structure are provided.

Figure 10.1 shows simplified organizational structures of international businesses. Most companies basically use one of these structures. Note that no structure is without drawbacks.

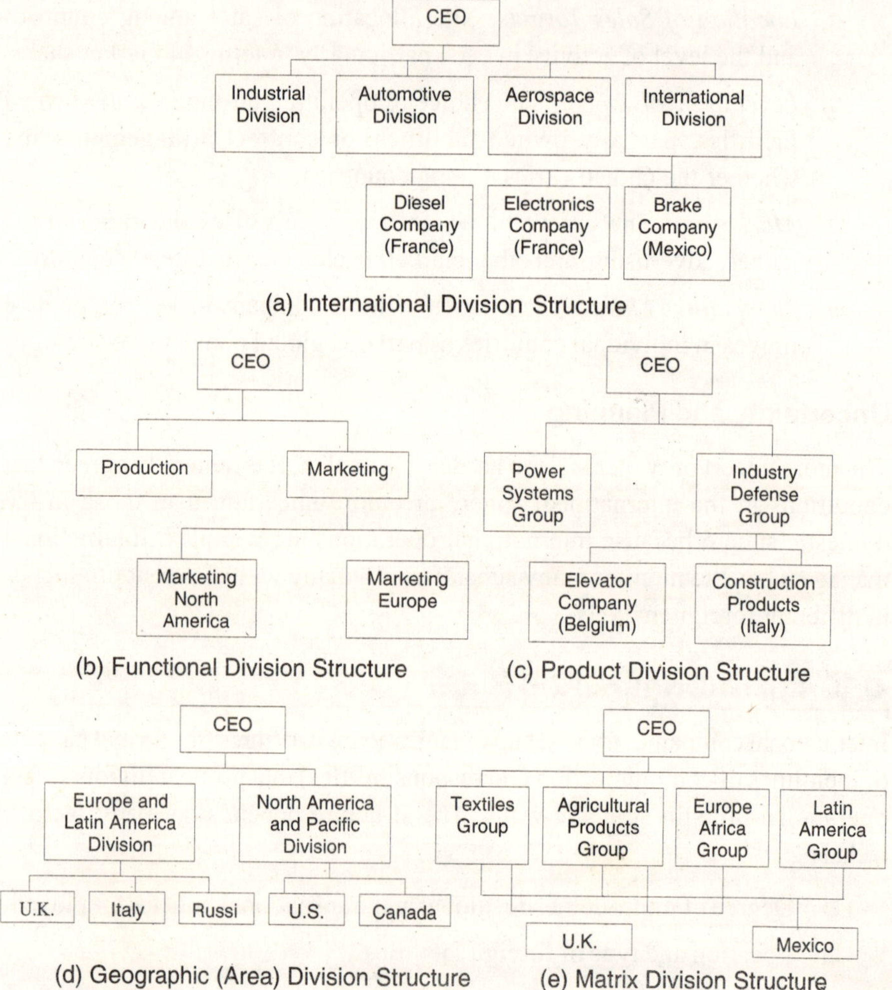

Fig. 10.1: Placement of International Activities within the Organizational Structures for International Businesses

International Division Structure: Often upon their initial entry into the international environment, firms have few products for international markets or little understanding of foreign customers and governments. Consequently, it is common for MNEs at this point to establish an international division, which is responsible for all functional activities relative to international markets. A variety of functions such as accounting, finance, marketing, and sales are generally conducted within the international division.

Figure 10.1(a) puts internationally specialized personnel together to handle such diverse matters as export documentation, foreign-exchange transactions, and relations with foreign governments. This prevents duplication of these activities in more than one place in the organization. It also creates a large enough critical mass so that personnel within the division can wield power within the organization to push for international expansion. However, an international division might have to depend on the domestic divisions for products to sell, personnel, technology and other resources.

Although this structure is not popular among European MNEs, it is popular among US MNEs. One apparent reason for this difference is that US companies depend much more on the domestic market than do European companies.

Strengths: The international division structure has a number of advantages. First, it is an efficient means of dealing with the international market when an MNE has limited experience with the international environment. The focus on international activities and issues within the division can foster a strong professional identity and career path among its members. The focus of international markets, competitors, and environments can also facilitate the development of a more focused international strategy.

Weaknesses: One of the major weaknesses is the international division's dependence upon other divisions for products and support. Because international sales of a particular product are often only a small percentage of the product's overall sales, low priority may be given to international sales. Also, other parts of the firm that supply products and services to the international division may be unwilling to make modifications that would facilitate greater international sales.

Functional Division Structure: Functional divisions, like those shown in **Figure 10.1 (b)** group personnel organizationally so that marketing people report to other marketing people, finance to other finance people and so on. Functional divisions are popular among companies with a narrow range of products, particularly if the production and marketing methods are undifferentiated among them. However, as they add new and different products this structure becomes cumbersome. This structure is most common when the technology and products that the MNE produces are similar throughout the world.

Strengths: The major advantages are that this structure reduces potential headquarters-subsidiary conflicts because operations throughout the world are integrated into their respective functional areas, and functional area executives are charged with global responsibility. This, in turn, enhances the overall international orientation of managers. The global functional structure can also facilitate centralized global coordination and control since all function heads are charged with worldwide responsibility.

Weaknesses: The weaknesses of this structure are most prevalent when the firm has a wide variety of products and these products have different environmental demands. This weakness is exacerbated when different functional areas experience different demands by geographical area. For example, if the accounting practices are similar between the US and Japan but the advertising approaches differ, this will tend to exaggerate coordination difficulties arising from different environment demands via governments, customers and so on.

Product Division Structure: Product divisions, as **Figure 10.1(c)** illustrates, are particularly popular among companies that make a variety of diverse products, especially those that have become diverse through acquisitions, such as Westinghouse. Because these divisions may have little in common, they may be highly independent of each other.

In this structure, all functional activities within each division and charges each division with worldwide responsibility. Typically, a division is formed by grouping several, related products together. As is true for the functional structure, the product division structure is well-suited for a global strategy because both the foreign and domestic operations for a given product report to the same manager, who can find synergies between the two, such as by sharing information on the successes and failures of each. Most likely, there will be duplicated functions and international activities among the product divisions.

Strengths: One of the strengths of this structure is that having common functions for all products within the division can reduce the duplication of resources. Also, for customers who tend to make purchases within a related set of products, coordination across products is easier and can facilitate customer service and satisfaction.

Weaknesses: Whereas the product focus in the global product structure can facilitate the determination of global and local elements of a product, the more diversified focus created by global divisional structure can inhibit this determination. This can increase costs by obscuring opportunities to leverage global advantages in raw materials sourcing, production, marketing or adverting.

Geographic (Area) Division Structure: Companies use geographic divisions, as in **Figure 10.1(d)**, if they have large foreign operations that are not dominated by a single country or area (including the home country). This structure is more common to European MNEs, such as Nestle, than to US MNEs, which tend to be dominated by the strong domestic market. The structure is useful when maximum economies in production can be gained on a regional rather than a global basis because of market size or the production technologies for the industry.

Strengths: One of the strengths of this structure is that it facilitates the development of an in-depth understanding of the market, customers, governments, and competitors within a given geographical area. The fact that area managers are responsible for all activities within their region also fosters a strong sense of accountability for performance, and regions are often treated as profit centers. Placing all functions under a regional umbrella also facilitates the coordination of functional activities under the region.

Weaknesses: One of the major weaknesses of this structure is that it can inhibit coordination and communication between regions. Placing all functional areas within each region can also lead to duplication of resources such as accounting, finance, human resource management and so on.

Matrix Division Structure: A global matrix structure consists of two organization structures superimposed on each other. As a consequence, there are dual reporting relationships. These two structures can be a combination of the general forms already discussed. This structure consists of product divisions intersecting with functional departments or geographical areas intersecting with global divisions. The two intersecting structures will largely be a function of what the organization sees as the two dominant aspects of its environment, such as product and functions, or product and region.

Strengths: Because of the dual intersection, global matrix structures can facilitate the flow of information throughout the organization. Before key decisions are made, the structure brings to bear the two intersecting perspectives. This tends to balance the orientation of the MNE so that no single perspective dominates.

Weaknesses: The weakness is that by bringing two perspectives together, the level of conflict is likely to rise. To the extent that effective conflict resolution mechanisms are not in place, increased levels of conflict can inhibit the organization's ability to quickly respond to changing conditions. Further, this structure means that many managers have two bosses.

LOCATION OF DECISION-MAKING

The location of decision-making may vary within the same company over time as well as by product, function, and country. In addition, actual decision-making is seldom as one-sided as it may appear. A manager who has decision-making authority may consult other managers before exercising that authority.

We usually associate centralized decision-making with a global strategy, decentralized decision-making with a global strategy, decentralized decision-making with a multi-domestic strategy, and a combination of the two with a transnational strategy. A **polycentric** attitude would cause the company to delegate decisions to foreign subsidiaries because headquarters personnel believe only people on the spot know best what to do. A **geocentric** attitude would permit more openness to capabilities either at home or abroad and be conducive to a transnational strategy.

Some conditions favor the location of decisions in one place or the other. Basically, companies should choose the location based on a combination of three trade-offs:

- Balancing pressures for global integration versus pressures for local responsiveness.
- Balancing the capabilities of headquarters versus subsidiary personnel.
- Balancing the expediency versus the quality of decisions.

CONTROL MECHANISMS

So far, we have discussed how companies group their operations for the purpose of communications and control and what companies should consider when deciding where control should be located. We shall now move to the subject of the mechanisms they can use to help ensure that control is implemented.

Corporate Culture: Every company has certain common values its employees share. These constitute its **corporate culture** and form a control mechanism that is implicit and helps enforce the company's explicit bureaucratic control mechanisms. For example, without setting explicit rules, managers may conform to company tradition in terms of how they dress, how late they work, whether they socialize with other managers, and whether they go to others in the company for advice.

MNEs have more difficulty relying on corporate culture for control because managers from different countries may have different norms and little or no exposure to the values prevalent at corporate headquarters. To try to overcome this problem, many companies encourage a worldwide corporate culture by promoting closer contact among managers from different countries. The aim is to convey a shared understanding of global goals and norms for reaching those goals, along with the transference of "best practices" from one country to another.

Using home-country nationals in subsidiaries' management or even having headquarters set the standards for local managers' selection and training may be perceived by local managers as a means of ensuring primary loyalty to the corporate culture than the subsidiary culture. Corporate culture may be effective even if the operations are only partially owned or when the parent requires long-range planning assistance from the subsidiaries.

Coordinating Methods

Because of each of type of organizational structures has advantages and disadvantages, companies in recent years have developed mechanisms to pull together some of the diverse functional, geographic (including international), and product perspectives without abandoning their existing structures. Some of these mechanisms are:

- Developing teams with members from different countries for planning to build scenarios on how the future may evolve.
- Strengthening corporate staffs (adding or creating groups of advisory personnel) so that headquarters and subsidiary managers with line responsibilities (decision-making authority) must listen to different viewpoints-whether or not they take the advice.
- Keeping international and domestic personnel in closer proximity to each other, such as by placing the international division in the same building or city as the product divisions.
- Establishing liaisons among subsidiaries within the same country so that different product groups can get combined action on a given issue.
- Developing teams from different countries to work on special projects of cross-national importance, so that they share viewpoints.
- Placing foreign personnel on the board of directors and top-level committees to bring foreign viewpoints into top-level decisions.
- Basing reward systems partially on global results so that managers are committed to global as well as local performance.

Reports

Reports are another control mechanism. Headquarters needs timely reports to allocate resources, correct plans, and reward personnel. Decisions on how to use capital, personnel and technology are almost continuous so reports must be frequent, accurate and up-to-date to assure meeting the MNE's objectives. Headquarters uses reports to evaluate the performance of subsidiary personnel so as to reward and motivate them. These personnel adhere to reports and try to perform well on what is in them so that they receive more rewards.

Written reports are more important in an international setting than in a domestic one because subsidiaries' managers have much less personal contact with managers above them. Corporate managers miss out on much of the informal communication that could tell them about the performance of the foreign operations.

Types of Reports

Most MNEs use reports for foreign operations that resemble those they use domestically. There are several reasons for this:

1. If the reports have been effective domestically, management often believes they also will be effective internationally.
2. There are economies from carrying over the same types of reports. The need to establish new types of reporting mechanisms is eliminated, and corporate management is already familiar with the system.
3. Reports with similar formats presumably allow management to better compare one operation with another.

Role of Information Systems in International Business

This discussion has centered on information headquarters management needs to evaluate the performance of subsidiaries and their management. Although this information is crucial, corporate management requires additional data to plan, take action, and share to improve performance. This might include:

- Information generated for centralized coordination, such as subsidiary cash balances and needs so that headquarters can move funds effectively.
- Information on external conditions, such as analyses of local political and economic conditions, so that headquarters can plan where to expand and constrict operations.
- Information for feedback from parents to subsidiaries, such as R&D breakthroughs, so that subsidiaries can compete more effectively.
- Information that subsidiaries can share so that they can learn from each other and be motivated to perform as well as other subsidiaries.
- Information for external reporting needs, such as to stakeholders and tax authorities.

Companies face three problems in acquiring information: the cost of information compared to its value, redundant information, and information that is irrelevant. For example, much of the information that is useful to a subsidiary, such as whom to contact to clear items at customs, is irrelevant to headquarters and should not be transmitted. To cope, companies should periodically reevaluate the information sources they use.

With expanding global telecommunications and computer links – especially the **World Wide Web and e-mail** – managers throughout the world can share information quicker and easier than ever before. On the other hand, this technology may permit more centralization, because corporate management can more easily examine the global conditions and performance. On the other hand, managers in foreign locations may become autonomous because they have more information at their disposal.

SPECIAL SITUATIONS

Acquisitions, shared ownership, and changes in strategies create control problems. We shall now discuss each of them.

Acquisitions: A policy of expansion through acquisitions can create some specific control problems. For Nestle, some of the US acquisitions resulted in overlapping geographic responsibilities and markets as well as new lines of business with which corporate management had no experience.

Another control problem is that the acquiring company's criteria for evaluating performance may be different from that of the acquired company's accustomed performance criteria. For example, US executives tend to focus more on profitability than on market potential, whereas the opposite is true in Korean companies.

Attempts to centralize certain decision-making or change operating methods may result in distrust, apprehension, and resistance to change on the part of the acquired company. These authorities may use a variety of means to ensure that decision-making remains vested within the country.

Shared Ownership

Ownership sharing limits the flexibility of corporate decision-making. Nevertheless, there are administrative mechanisms to gain control even with a minority equity interest. These mechanisms include spreading the remaining ownership among many shareholders, contract stipulations that board decisions require more than a majority, dividing equity into voting and non-voting stock, and side agreements on who will control decision-making.

A company can also maintain control over some asset the subsidiary needs, such as a patent, a brand name, or a raw material. In fact, maintaining control is a motive for having separate licensing or franchising agreements or management contracts with a foreign subsidiary.

Changes in Strategies

Most recent changes in strategies have involved movements from multi-domestic to transnational or global operations. But regardless of the type of change, there will be a need for new reporting relationships, changes in the type of information collected, and a need for new performance appraisal systems. In addition, to the practical problems of changing systems, there are human resource problems as well.

It is difficult to remove control from operations when managers are accustomed to much autonomy. These companies often have faced difficult obstacles when integrating these operations because the country managers perceive that integration brings personal and operating disadvantages. Managers who fear losses through a changed strategy continue to guard their autonomy and functional specialties and maintain existing allegiances.

Types of Subsidiaries and How they Affect Control Strategies

A company establishing a subsidiary in a foreign country can usually choose from a number of alternatives legal forms. There are too many forms to list here; however, some distinctions between them are worth mentioning so that you understand there are many considerations. In addition to differences in liability, forms vary in terms of:

- Ability of the parent to sell its ownership
- Number of stockholders required to establish the subsidiary
- Percentage of foreigners who can serve on the board of directors
- Amount of required public disclosure
- Whether equity may be acquired by non-capital contributions, such as goodwill
- Types of businesses (products) that are eligible
- Minimum capital required for establishing the subsidiary

Before making a decision on a legal operating form, an MNE, should analyze all of these differences in terms of its corporate objectives.

TYPES OF CONTROL

There are two common, complementary ways of looking at how MNEs control operations. One way is by determining whether the enterprise chooses to use internal or external control in devising its overall strategy. The other is by looking at the ways in which the organization uses direct and indirect controls.

Internal and External Control

From an internal control standpoint, an MNE will focus on the things that it does best. At the same time, of course, management wants to ensure that there is a market for the goods and services that it is offering. So the company first needs to find out what the customers want and be prepared to respond appropriately. This requires an external control focus. Normally, every MNE will give consideration to both internal and external perspectives of control. However, one is often given more attention than the other.

Cultures differ in the control approach they use. For example, among US multinationals it is common to find managers using a more internal control approach. Among Asian firms an external control approach is more typical. Table 10.1 provides some contrasts between the two.

Table 10.1: The Impact of Internal and External Oriented Cultures on the Control Process

Key Differences between	
Internal Control	**External Control**
Often dominating attitude bordering on aggressive towards the environment. Conflict and resistance means that a person has convictions. The focus is on self, function, one's own group, and one's own organization. There is discomfort when the environment seems "out of control" or changeable.	Often-flexible attitude, willing to compromise and keep the peace. Harmony, responsiveness, and sensibility are encouraged. The focus is on others such as custommers, partners, and colleagues. There is comfort with waves, shifts, and cycles, which are regarded as "natural".
Tips for Doing Business with	
Internally Controlled (for externals)	**Externally Controlled (for Internals)**
Playing "hard ball" is legitimate to test the resilience of an opponent. It is most important to "win your objective". Win some, lose some.	Softness, persistence, politeness, and long, long patience will get rewards. It is most important to maintain one's relationships with others. Win together, lose apart.

Direct Controls: Direct Control involves face-to-face or personal meetings to monitor operations. A good example is International Telephone and Telegraph (ITT), which hold monthly management meetings at its New York headquarters. The CEO of the company runs these meetings, and each ITT unit manager throughout the world submits reports.

Another common form of direct control is visits by top executives to overseas affiliates or subsidiaries. During these visits, top managers, can learn firsthand the problems and challenges facing the unit and offer assistance.

A third form is the staffing practices of MNEs. By determining who to send overseas to run the unit, the corporation can directly control how the operation will be run. The company will want the manager to make operating decisions and handle day-to-day matters, but the individual also will know which decisions should be cleared with the home office.

A fourth form is the organizational structure itself. By designing a structure that makes the unit highly responsive to home-office requests and communications, the MNE ensures that all overseas operations are run in accord with central management's desires. This structure can be established through formal reporting relationships and chain of command.

Indirect Controls: These controls use reports and other written forms of communication to control operations. One of the most common examples is the use of monthly operating reports that are sent to the home office. The home office will use these operating and financial data to evaluate how well things are going and make decisions regarding necessary changes. Three sets of financial statements usually are required from subsidiaries.

1. Statements prepared to meet the national accounting standards and procedures prescribed by law and other professional organizations in the host country.
2. Statements prepared to comply with the accounting principles and standards required by the home country.
3. Statements prepared to meet the financial consolidation requirements of the home country.

Indirect controls are particularly important in international management because of the great expense associated with direct methods. Typically, MNEs will use indirect controls to monitor performance on a monthly basis, whereas direct controls are used semiannually or annually. This dual approach often provides the company with effective control of its operations at a price that also is cost-effective.

Approaches of Control

International managers can employ many different approaches to control. These approaches typically are dictated by the MNEs philosophy of control, the economic environment in which the overseas unit is operating, and the needs and desires of the managerial personnel who staff the unit. Working within control parameters, MNEs will structure their processes so that they are as efficient and effective as possible.

Typically the tools that are used will give the unit managers the autonomy needed to adapt to changes in the market as well as to attract competent local personnel. These tools will also provide for coordination of operations with the home office, so that the overseas unit is in harmony with the MNEs strategic plan.

Some Major Differences

MNEs control operations in many different ways, and these often vary considerably from country to country. We take an example here, how do US

MNEs differ from their European counterparts? One comparative study found that a major difference is that US firms tend to rely much more heavily on reports and other performance related data. Americans make greater use of output control and Europeans rely more heavily on behavioral control. Some specific findings from this study include:

1. Control in US MNEs focuses more on the ***quantifiable***, objective aspects of a foreign subsidiary, whereas control in European MNEs tends to be used to measure more ***qualitative*** aspects.
2. Control in US MNEs requires more precise plans and budgets in generating suitable standards for comparison. Control in European MNEs requires a high level of company-wide understanding and agreement regarding what constitutes appropriate behavior and how such behavior supports the goals of both the subsidiary and the parent firm.
3. Control in US MNEs requires large central staffs and centralized information processing capability. Control in European MNEs requires a larger cadre of capable expatriate managers who are willing to spend long periods of time abroad. This control characteristic is reflected in the career approaches used in the various MNEs. Although US multinationals do not encourage lengthy stays in foreign management positions, European MNEs often regard these positions as stepping-stones to higher offices.
4. Control in European MNEs requires more decentralization of operating decision than control in US MNEs.
5. Control in European MNEs favors short vertical spans or reporting channels from the foreign subsidiary to responsible positions in the parent.

Evaluating Approaches to Control: Is one control approach any better than the other? The answer is that each seems to work best for its respective group. Some studies predict that as MNEs increase in size, however, they likely will move toward the objective orientation of the US MNEs.

Approaches to control also differ between US and Japanese firms. For example, one study surveyed the attitudes of a large sample of Japanese and US controllers and line managers. Respondents were drawn from the 500 largest industrial firms in both countries, and some of the results are presented in **Table 10.2**.

One overall finding of the research was that Japanese controllers and managers prefer less participation in the control process than their US counterparts do. In addition, the Japanese have longer-term planning horizons, view budgets as more of a communication device than a controlling tool, and prefer more slack in their budgets than the Americans. These results are extremely important in terms of adapting US approaches to Japanese owned subsidiaries.

Another thing that the researchers discovered is that sometimes performance results are not as high as they could be because of the fear of embarrassing others in the organization. For example, even though some decisions might result in higher returns on investment for the company, if these decisions put others in a bad light, they will not be made.

Table 10.2: Selection Beliefs Related to Planning and Control

	Statements of Results – Average Responses*			
	Japan		**United States**	
	Managers	**Controllers**	**Managers**	**Controllers**
To be useful in performance evaluation of managers, a budget must be revised continuously throughout the year.	3.07	3.14	2.70	2.48
It is important that budgets be very detailed.	3.38	3.31	2.93	2.97
It is appropriate to charge others activities when budgeted funds are used up.	3.01	2.91	1.96	1.52
Budgets should be developed from the bottom up rather than from the top down.	3.13	3.01	3.68	3.96
Budgets are useful for communicating the goal and planned activities of the company.	4.54	4.68	4.11	4.23
Budgets are useful in coordinating activities of various departments.	4.24	4.46	3.78	4.02
A manager who fails to attain the budgets should be replaced.	2.56	2.67	2.00	1.92
Top management should judge a manager's performance mainly on the basis of attaining budget profit.	3.25	3.38	2.27	2.07
It is important that executive compensation depend on a comparison of actual and budgeted performance.	3.18	3.18	3.55	3.56
It is important that managers who perform exceptionally well receive more money than other managers in similar positions.	3.84	3.92	4.28	4.14

Contd...

It is important for a manager to have quantitative or analytic skills as opposed to people skills.	3.12	3.15	2.04	1.96
The best way to determine the value of capital projects is through the use of quantitative analysis.	3.61	3.80	3.23	3.37
Note* The response scale was as follows: Strongly disagree 1 Disagree 2 Neutral 3 Agree 4				

Control Techniques

A number of performance measures are used for control purposes. Three of the most common types are those related to financial performance, quality performance and personnel performance.

Financial Performance

Financial performance evaluation of a foreign subsidiary or affiliate usually is based on profit and return on investment. **Profit** is the amount remaining after all expenses are deducted from total revenues. **Return on investment (ROI)** is measured through dividing profit by assets; some firms use profit divided by owners equity (return on owners' investment or ROOI) in referring to the return-on-investment performance measure.

In any case, the most important part of the ROI calculation is profits, which often can be manipulated by management. Thus, the amount of profit directly relates to how well or how poorly a unit is judged to perform. The so-called bottom-line (i.e. profit) performance of subsidiaries also can be affected by a devaluation or revaluation of local currency. For example, if a country devalues its currency, then subsidiary export sales will increase, because the price of these goods will be lower for foreign buyers, whose currencies now have greater purchasing power.

If the country revalues its currency, then export sales will decline because the price of goods for foreign buyers will rise, since their currencies now will have less purchasing power in the subsidiary's country. Likewise, a devaluation of the currency will increase the cost of imported materials and supplies for the subsidiary, and a revaluation will decrease these costs because of the relative changes in the purchasing power of local currency.

Of course, not all bottom-line financial performance is a result of manipulation or external economic conditions. Sometimes there are other forces that account for the problem.

Quality Performance

The term "quality control" (QC) has been around for a long time, and it is a major function of production and operations management. A **quality control circle** (QCC), which has been popularized by Japanese is a group of workers who meet on a regular basis to discuss ways of improving the quality of work. This approach has helped many MNEs to improve the quality of their goods and services dramatically.

Why are Japanese-made goods of higher quality than those of many other countries? The answer cannot rest solely on technology, because many MNEs have the same or superior technology or the financial ability to purchase it. There must be other causal factors.

The various reasons how Japanese firms differ from other firms. A complete analysis has been made on this regard.

- They focus on keeping the workplace clean and ensuring that all machinery and equipment was properly maintained. The Japanese firms were more careful in handling incoming parts and materials, work-in-progress, and finished products than their US counterparts. Japanese companies also employed equipment fixtures to a greater extent than US manufacturers in ensuring proper alignment of parts during final assembly.
- The Japanese minimized worker error by assigning new employees to existing work teams or pairing them with supervisors. In this way, the new workers gained important experience under the watchful eye of someone who could correct their mistakes.
- Another important difference is that the Japanese tend to build in early warning systems so that they know when something is going wrong. A good example is that incoming field data are reviewed immediately by the quality department, and problems are assigned to one of two categories: routine or emergency. Special efforts then are made to resolve the emergency problems as quickly as possible.
- Still another reason is that the Japanese work closely with their suppliers so that the latters' quality increases. In fact, research shows that among suppliers that have contracts with both American and Japanese auto plants in the US the Japanese plants get higher performance from their suppliers than do the Americans.

Personnel Performance

Besides financial techniques and the emphasis on quality, another key area of control is personnel performance evaluation. This type of evaluation can take a number of different forms, although there is a great deal of agreement from firm to firm when looking at the overall criteria that are measured. What makes these MNEs so successful? Consultants at the Hay Group made an analysis of the best global firms in a recent year and concluded that there were seven common themes that emerged.

1. Top managers at the most admired companies take their mission statements seriously and expect everyone else to do the same.
2. Success attracts the best people – and the best people sustain success.
3. The top companies know precisely what they are looking for.
4. These firms see career development as an investment, not a chore.
5. Whenever, possible these companies promote from within.
6. Performance is rewarded.
7. The firms are genuinely interested in what their employees think and they measure work satisfaction often and thoroughly.

One of the most common approaches to personnel performance evaluation is the periodic appraisal of work performance. Although the objective is similar from country to country, how performance appraisals are done differs. Other differences relate to how rewards and monitoring of personnel performance are handled. Both US and Japanese managers offered greater rewards and more freedom from close monitoring to individuals when they were associated with successful performance, no matter what the influence of the group on the performance.

An **assessment center** is an evaluation tool that is used to identify individuals with the potential to be selected or promoted to higher-level positions. A typical assessment center would involve simulation exercises such as:

- In-basket exercises that require managerial attention
- A committee exercise in which the candidates must work as a team in making decisions
- Business decisions exercises in which participants compete in the same market
- Preparation of a business plan
- A letter-writing exercise.

These forms of evaluation are beginning to gain support, because they are more comprehensive than simple checklists or the use of a test or an interview and thus better able to identify those managers who are most likely to succeed when hired or promoted.

SUMMARY

- Control of MNEs is difficult because of the geographic and cultural distances separating countries, the need to operate differently among countries, the need to operate differently among countries, the large number of uncontrollables abroad, and the high uncertainty resulting from rapid change in the international environment and problems in gathering reliable data in many places.

- Good planning should include the establishment of a long-range strategic intent, analysis of internal corporate resources, setting of international objectives, analysis of local conditions abroad, selection of alternatives and priorities, and implementation of a strategy.
- As a company expands internationally, the corporate structure must include a means by which foreign operations report. The more important the foreign operations, the higher up in the hierarchy they should report.
- Whether a company separates or integrates international operations, it usually needs to develop some control mechanism/structure to prevent costly duplication of efforts, to ensure that headquarters managers do not withhold the best resources from the international operations and to include insights from anywhere in the organization that can benefit performance.
- Even though worldwide uniformity of policies and centralization of decision-making may not be best for a particular foreign subsidiary, overall company gains may be more than enough to overcome the individual country losses. When top management prevents subsidiaries managers from doing their best job, however, there may be a negative effect on employee morale.
- Many critics in emerging economies argue that centralization of decision-making in MNEs continues emerging economies historical dependency on industrial countries. These critics are pressuring for increased decentralization of decision-making.
- Timely reports are essential for control so that corporate/headquarters management can allocate resources properly, correct plans, and evaluate and reward personnel.
- Many MNEs use international reporting systems similar to their domestic ones because home-country management is familiar with them and because uniformity makes it easier to compare different operations.
- Generally, MNEs evaluate their subsidiaries and their subsidiary managers separately. However, MNEs may use some of the same criteria, including financial and non-financial performance, for both.
- Special control problems arise for acquired operations, operations that have historical autonomy, and operations that are not wholly owned. The legal status of foreign operations may also raise control problems.
- Controlling involves evaluating results in relation to plans or objectives, then taking action to correct deviations. MNEs control their overseas operations in a number of ways. Most combined direct and indirect controls. Some prefer heavily quantifiable methods, and others opt for more qualitative approaches. Some prefer decentralized approaches; others opt for greater centralization.
- Three of the most common performance measures used to control subsidiaries are in the financial, quality and personnel areas. Financial performance typically is measured by profit and return on investment. Quality performance often is controlled through quality circles. Personnel performance typically is judged through performance evaluation techniques.

Chapter 11

International Negotiations

INTRODUCTION

Chapter 8 discussed how home and host countries evaluate MNEs. But evaluation is only part of the story. After that comes negotiation, and that's where business government relationships become difficult. Governments may refuse companies original or continued operating permission. At the same time, companies will not operate unless their terms of business are favorable. But countries and companies do come to agreements that, although not usually ideal for either party, are sufficient for an evolving relationship. The business negotiations and diplomacy between companies and governments determine the terms of international business operations. **Figure 11.1** shows the relationships.

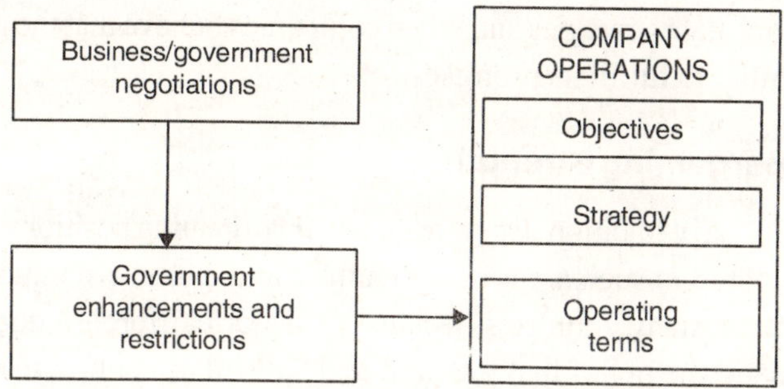

Fig. 11.1: Business–Government Negotiations in International Operations

GOVERNMENTAL VERSUS COMPANY STRENGTH IN NEGOTIATIONS

As the Saudi Aramco case illustrates, both home and host country policies greatly influence the terms under which companies operate abroad. These strengths depend on such factors as competitive changes, the resources the parties have at their disposal, validation by public opinion, and joint efforts with other parties. However, companies have different viewpoints on how much they can influence their operating terms. Governments also have different viewpoints on how much power they can exert over international companies.

Hierarchical View of Governmental Authority

Governments have regulations affecting international business. In a hierarchical view of governmental authority, companies accept regulations as "givens", in which case they comply with, circumvent, or avoid operating because of the regulations. Companies will circumvent regulations they find unacceptable through loopholes, legal or illegal. For example, a firm's ability to control a foreign subsidiary in spite of country's requirement for shared ownership might be possible if the company makes a side agreement with a local partner not to vote its shares of stock. Avoidance is simply the reverse of compliance as a company decides not to operate in a given locale because of its regulations.

Country Bargaining Strength

Generally, companies prefer to establish investments in highly developed countries because those countries offer large markets and a high degree of political stability. Countries such as the United States, Canada, and Germany are large recipients of foreign investment. Because they are such attractive countries to invest in, they make few concessions to MNEs. In all of these countries, however, regional areas via for investments by offering incentives. If incentives are used, they are most appealing when they fit closely with companies' corporate strategies and when companies believe that the government has the credibility to fulfill its promises.

Company Bargaining Strength

Some industries have traditionally enjoyed better bargaining positions than others. Foreign ownership in such areas as agriculture and extractive industries is not very welcome in many countries because of historical foreign domination of these sectors and the belief that the land and subsoil are public resources.

The bargain struck between the foreign investor and the host country also depends on the number of companies offering similar resources. Foreign investors are more likely to have a strong bargaining position in foreign operations when they have few competitors and when they control certain types of assets. These assets include:

- **Technology:** For example, governments have allowed IBM 100 per cent ownership of operations in a number of countries because of the local need for its unique technology. However, they have refused other companies the same ownership.

- **Marketing Expertise:** For example, Coca-Cola apparently has been able to gain local consumer allies who believe its differentiated products are superior.
- **Ability to Export Output from the Foreign Investment, Especially when Exports go to other Entities Controlled by the Parent Company:** These investments earn foreign exchange for the country that might otherwise not be forthcoming.
- **Product Diversity:** Governments will allow more foreign ownership when a company provides greater product diversity, probably because of variety of products can save foreign exchange through import substitution. In the past, if a company offered to invest a large amount of capital, it did not usually affect its bargaining power. At least two factors played a role here:

    1. A large investment may be examined much more closely than a small one because of the potential impact it might have on the economy. That is, the host country wants the benefits of the capital inflow but is leery of being so dependent on foreign ownership.
    2. The host-country government may be more likely to borrow funds externally to invest in large enterprises.

NEGOTIATIONS IN INTERNATIONAL BUSINESS

Negotiations are a means by which a company may initiate, carry on, or terminate operations in a foreign country. At one time, negotiations were prevalent only for direct investments. However, today they play a part in other operating arrangements, such as licensing agreements, debt repayment, and large-scale export sales.

The negotiation process often leads to multi-tired bargaining: An MNE may need to reach an agreement with a local company to purchase an interest in it, sell technology or products to it, or loan money to it. That agreement must sometimes be presented to a host-country agency that may approve, disapprove, or propose entirely new terms.

The MNE may need to negotiate with its home government to transfer technology or borrow funds. The home and host governments may negotiate loans, investment guarantees, and overall economic and political relationships.

Bargaining Process

Comprehensive bargaining among companies and governments may begin long before they agree on MNEs terms of operations. Behavioral factors in addition to economic ones affect the agreement terms. They may renegotiate these terms later.

Acceptable Zones: Before taking part in overseas negotiations, a manager probably has some experience with a domestic bargaining process similar to that in the foreign sphere. For example, collective bargaining with labor as well as agreements to acquire or merge facilities with another company usually start with an array of proposals, just like negotiations with foreign organizations. The proposals undoubtedly include provisions that one side or the other is willing either to give up entirely or to compromise on.

As in domestic negotiations, the outcome of foreign negotiations will depend partly on other recent negotiations or events, which serve as models. Finally there are zones of acceptable and non-acceptable for the proposals presented. If the acceptance zones overlap, an agreement is possible. If zones have no overlap positive negotiations are not possible.

The final agreement would depend on each party's negotiating ability and strengths and on the other concessions that each made in the process. Because each side could only speculate on how far the other was willing to go, the exact amount of ownership allowed might fall anywhere within the overlapping acceptance zones.

Range of Provisions: The major difference between domestic and foreign negotiations is a matter of degree. International negotiations may take much longer and may include provisions unheard of in the home country, such as a negotiated tax rate. Further, governments vary in their attitudes toward foreign investors, so their negotiating agendas also vary.

Most countries offer investment incentives to attract MNEs. Direct incentives that countries have offered foreign investors include tax holidays, employee training, R&D grants, accelerated depreciation, low-interest loans, loan guarantees, subsidized energy and transportation, exemption of import duties, and the construction and rail spurs and roads. Countries also provide indirect incentives, such as a trained labor force and labor laws that prevent work disruptions.

Negotiations are seldom a one-way street. Companies agree to many performance requirements aimed at helping host countries reach economic and non-economic objectives, such as a favorable balance of payments, growth, high employment, and local control over important decisions. These performance requirements include:

- Foreign-exchange deposits to cover the cost of imports and foreign-exchange payments on loans and dividends.
- Limits on payments to the parent for services it provides to its host-country subsidiary.

- Maximum prices on goods sold
- Limits on the use of expatriate personnel and on old or reconditioned equipment
- Control of prices on goods the MNE imports or exports to the host-country subsidiary
- Demands to enter into joint ventures

BEHAVIORAL CHARACTERISTICS AFFECTING NEGOTIATIONS

In international negotiations, misunderstandings are a strong possibility because of cultural differences as well as possible language differences. Further, the background and expertise of government officials may be quite distinct from those of businesspeople. Their superiors may also evaluate them on very different criteria.

Cultural Factors: Many people agree with this assessment of US performance in business negotiations abroad. But companies from other countries have problems as well. Much of the problem stems from cultural differences that lead to misunderstandings and mistrust across the conference table. Although this discussion cannot list all the possible cultural differences, the following points based on the cultural framework in Chapter 2 indicate areas of possible misunderstanding.

- Individual negotiators from some countries are more likely to have the power to make decisions than are their counterparts from some other countries in part because of differences between individualist and collectivist societies.
- Negotiators from low-context cultures want to get to the heart of the matter quickly.
- Negotiators from cultures with high trust are less prone to want to cover every possible contingency in a contract than are negotiators from cultures with low trust.

Language Factors

It may be difficult for negotiators to find words to express their exact meaning in another language, which may result in occasional pauses while translators resort to dictionaries. Negotiators find facial expressions difficult to judge because of cultural differences and the time lag caused by translation. Because English is widely understood worldwide, people with a different native language may understand quite well most of what is said in English, allowing them to cavesdrop on confidential comments and form responses while remarks are being translated into their language.

When negotiators do use interpreters, each side should have its own. Good interpreters brief their teams on cultural factors affecting the negotiation process. But even with interpreters, negotiators cannot be certain that their statements are fully understood, especially if they use slang or attempt humor that is culture specific.

Culturally Responsive Strategies

The fact that managers' counterparts in negotiations come from countries with different cultures does not necessarily mean they will behave according to their culture's norm. First, a counterpart may be an exception to the country's norm. Second a counterpart may know the other's culture and be adaptive to it. So managers should determine at the start whether they would adjust to their counterparts to adjust them, or follow some form of hybrid adjustment.

Professional Conflict

Governmental and business negotiators may start with mutual mistrust due to historic animosity or to differences in their professional status. The businesspeople may come armed with business and economic data that governmental officials don't fully understand, and the officials may counter with sovereignty considerations that are nearly incomprehensible to the businesspeople.

Negotiators may see their rewards, such as new assignments, as dependent on immediate results and perhaps not expect to be around for longer-term problems. Professional conflict has been particularly evident, as many emerging economies have attempted to sell state-owned enterprises to foreign investors. The managers within these enterprises are suspicious of MNEs, fearful of foreign domination, and worried about their jobs after privatization.

Termination of Negotiation

When one or both parties want to end serious consideration of proposals, the method of cessation can be extremely important. It may affect the negotiators positions with their superiors, who may wonder why their appointed negotiators have spent so much time and money without reaching an agreement. Also affected may be future transactions between the parties and their dealings with other organizations, both in that country and elsewhere in the world. Because termination is an admission of failure, negotiators are prone to publicly blame others to save face. Fearing adverse consequences from termination, negotiators sometimes drag out the process until a proposal eventually dies unnoticed. Although termination is stressful, when it is necessary, the parties should attempt to find means that allow each to save face and that avoid publicity.

Preparation for Negotiations

Role-playing is a valuable technique for projects requiring approval by a foreign government or agreement with a foreign company. By practicing their own roles and those of the counterpart negotiators-and by researching the country's culture and history to determine attitudes toward foreign companies – negotiators may be much better able to anticipate responses and plan their own actions.

Role-playing presupposes that the company knows who will be negotiating for the other side. Commonly, MNEs use a team approach so that people with the necessary range of functional responsibilities take part in the decision-making. It also is common to use people at different organizational levels at different points in the negotiations.

Negotiating in the "home field" gives managers an advantage because they can go home at night, eat familiar food, not have to explain travel expenses to superiors, and more easily take care of other business at the office. If managers must travel abroad for negotiators, they will likely be more alert if they arrive in time to be rested and adjust to any time changes.

MANAGING INTERNATIONAL NEGOTIATIONS

Negotiation is the process of bargaining with one or more parties to arrive at a solution that is acceptable to all. Negotiation often follows assessing political risk and can be used as an approach to conflict management. If the risk is worth it, then the MNE must negotiate with the host country to secure the best possible arrangements. The MNE and the host country will discuss the investment the MNE is prepared to make in return for certain guarantees and/or concessions.

The initial range of topics typically includes critical areas such as hiring practices, direct financial investment, taxes and ownership control. Negotiation also is used in creating joint ventures with local firms and in getting the operation off the ground. After the firm is operating, additional areas of negotiation often include expansion of facilities, use of more local managers, additional imports or exports of materials and finished goods and recapture of profits.

The Negotiation Process

There are several basic steps that can be used in managing the negotiation process. Regardless of the issues or personalities of the parties involved, this process typically begins with planning.

Planning: Planning starts with the negotiators identifying those objectives they would like to attain. Then, they explore the possible options for reaching these objectives. Research shows that the greater the number of options, the greater the chances for successful negotiations. Next, consideration is given to areas of common ground between the parties. Other areas include: (1) the setting of limits on single-point objectives, such as deciding to pay no more than $10 million for the factory and $3 million for the land; (2) dividing issues into short and long-term considerations and deciding how to handle each; and (3) determining the sequence in which to discuss the various issues.

Impersonal Relationship Building: The second phase of the negotiation process involves getting to know the people on the other side. This "feeling-out" period is characterized by the desire to identify those who are reasonable and those who are not. In contrast to negotiations in many other countries, those in the United States often given little attention to this phase; they want to get down to business immediately, which often is an ineffective approach.

Exchanging Task-Related Information: In this part of the negotiation process, each group sets forth its position on the critical issues. These positions often will change later in the negotiations. At this point, the participants are trying to find out what the other party wants to attain and what it is willing to give up.

Persuasion: This step of negotiations is considered by many to be the most important. No side wants to give away more than it has to, but each knows that without giving some concessions, it is unlikely to reach a final agreement. The success of the persuasion step often depends on: (1) how well the parties understand each other's position (2) the ability of each to identify areas of similarity and differences (3) the ability to create new options; (4) the willingness to work toward a solution that allows all parties to walk away feeling they have achieved their objectives.

Agreement: The final phase of negotiations is the granting of concessions and hammering out a final agreement. Sometimes, this phase is carried out piecemeal, and concessions and agreements are made on issues one at a time. This is the way those from the United States like to negotiate. At each issue is resolved, it is removed from the bargaining table and interest focused on the next. Asians and Russians, on the other hand, tend to negotiate a final agreement on everything, and few concessions are given until the end. Simply put, to negotiate effectively in the international arena, it is necessary to understand how cultural differences between the parties affect the process.

Negotiation Tactics

A number of specific tactics are used in international negotiation. The following discussion examines some of the most common.

Location: Where should negotiations take place? If the matter is very important, most businesses will choose a neutral site. For example, US firms negotiating with companies from the Far East will meet in Hawali, South American companies negotiating with European firms will meet halfway, in the New York City. A number of benefits derive from using a neutral site. One is that each party has limited access to its home office for receiving a great deal of negotiating information and advice and thus gaining an advantage on the other. A second is that the cost of staying at the site often is quite high, so both sides have an incentive to conclude their negotiations as quickly as possible. A third is that most negotiators do not like to return home with nothing to show for their efforts, so they are motivated to reach some type of agreement.

Time Limits: Time limits are an important negotiation tactic when one party is under a time constraint. This is particularly true when this party has agreed to meet at the home site of the other party. Time limits can be used tactically even if the negotiators meet a neutral site. For example, most Americans like to be home with their families for Thanksgiving, Christmas, and the New Year holiday. Negotiations held right before these dates put Americans at a disadvantage, because the other party knows when the Americans would like to leave.

Buyer-Seller Relations: How should buyers and sellers act? As noted earlier, Americans believe in being objective and trading favors. When the negotiations are over, Americans walk away with what they have received from the other party, and they expect the other party to do the same.

The Japanese, for example, believe that the buyers should get most of what they want. On the other hand, they also believe that the seller should be taken care of through reciprocal favors. They buyer must ensure that the seller has not been "picked clean". For example, when many Japanese firms first started doing business with large US firms, they were unaware of US negotiating tactics. As a result, the Japanese thought the Americans were taking advantage of them, whereas the Americans believed they were driving a good, hard bargain.

The Brazilians are quite different from both the Americans and Japanese. Researchers have found that Brazilians do better when they are more deceptive and self-interested and their opponents more open and honest than they are. Brazilians also tend to make fewer promises and commitments than their opponents and they are much more prone to say no. However, Brazilians are more likely to make initial concessions. Overall, Brazilians are more like Americans like Japanese in that they try to maximize their advantage, but they are unlike Americans in that they do not feel obligated to be open and forthright in their approach. Whether they are buyer or seller, they want to come out on top.

Bargaining Behaviors

Closely related to the discussion of negotiation tactics are the different types of bargaining behaviors, including both verbal and non-verbal behaviors. Verbal behaviors are an important part of the negotiating process, because they can improve the final outcome. Research shows that the profits of the negotiators increase when they make high initial offers, ask a lot of questions, and do not make many verbal commitments until the end of negotiating process. In short verbal behaviors are critical to the success of negotiations.

Use of Extreme Behaviors: Some negotiators begin by making extreme offers or requests. The Chinese and Arabs are examples. Some negotiators, however, begin with an initial position that is close to the one they are seeking. The Americans and Swedes are examples here.

Research shows that extreme positions tend to produce better results. Some of the reasons relate to the fact that an extreme bargaining position:

1. Show the other party that the bargainer will not be exploited
2. Extends the negotiation and gives the bargainer a better opportunity to gain information on the opponent
3. Allows more room for concessions
4. Modifies the opponents beliefs about the bargainer's preferences
5. Shows the opponent that the bargainer is willing to play the game according to the usual norms
6. Lets the bargainer gain more than would probably be possible if a less extreme initial position had been taken.

Promises, Threats and other Behaviors: Another approach to bargaining is the use of promises, threats, rewards, self-disclosures, and other behaviors that are designed to influence the other party. These behaviors often are greatly influenced by the culture. Graham conducted research using Japanese, US and Brazilian businesspeople and found that they employed a variety of different behaviors during a buyer-seller negotiation simulation.

The Japanese also rely heavily on recommendations and commitment. The Brazilians use a discussion of rewards, commands, and self-disclosure more than Americans and Japanese. The Brazilians also say no a great deal more and make first offers that have higher-level profits than those of the others. Americans tend to operate between these two groups, although they do make less use of commands than either of their opponents and make first offers that have lower profit levels than their opponents.

Behavior and Definition

- **Promise:** A statement in which the source indicated an intention to provide the target with a reinforcing consequence which source anticipates target will evaluate as pleasant, positive, or rewarding.
- **Threat:** Same as promise, except that the reinforcing consequences are thought to be noxious, unpleasant, or punishing.

- **Recommendation:** A statement in which the source predicts that a pleasant environmental consequence will occur to the target. Its occurrence is not under the source's control.
- **Warning:** Same as recommendation except that the consequences are thought to be unpleasant.
- **Reward:** A statement by the source that is thought to create pleasant consequences for the target.
- **Punishment:** Same as reward, except that the consequences are thought to be unpleasant.
- **Positive Normative Appeal:** A statement in which the source indicates that the target's past, present, or future behavior was or will be in conformity with social norms.
- **Negative Normative Appeal:** Same as positive normative appeal, except that the target's behavior is in violation of social norms.
- **Commitment:** A statement by the source to the effect that is future bids will not go below or above a certain level.
- **Self-disclosure:** A statement in which the source reveals information about itself.
- **Question:** A statement in which the source asks the target to reveal information about itself.
- **Command:** A statement in which the source suggests that the target perform a certain behavior.
- **First Offer:** The profit level associated with each participant's first offer.
- **Initial Concession:** The differences in profit between the first and second offer.
- **Number of No's:** Number of times the word "no" was used by bargaining per half-hour.

Non-verbal Behaviors: Non-verbal behaviors also are very common during negotiations. These behaviors refer to what people do rather than what they say. Non-verbal behaviors sometimes are called the "silent language". Typical examples include **silent periods, facial gazing, touching and conversational overlaps**.

Silent Period: The number of conversational gaps of 10 seconds or more per 30 minutes.

Facial Gazing: The number of minute's negotiators spends looking at their opponents face per randomly selected 10 – minute period.

Touching: Incidents of bargainers touching one another per half-hour (not including handshakes).

Conversational Overlaps: The number of times (per 10 minutes) that both parties to the negotiation would talk at the same time.

The Japanese tend to use silent periods much more often than either Americans or Brazilians during negotiations. In fact, in this study, the latter did not use them at all. The Brazilians did, however, make frequent use of other non-verbal behaviors. They employed facial gazing almost four times more often than the Japanese, and almost twice as often as the Americans.

In addition, although the latter two groups did not touch their opponents, the Brazilians made wide use of this non-verbal tactic. They also relied heavily on conversational overlaps, employing them more than twice as often as the Japanese and almost three times as often as Americans. Quite obviously, the Brazilians rely very heavily on non-verbal behaviors in their negotiating.

SUMMARY

- Although host countries and MNEs may hold resources that, if combined, could achieve objectives for both, conflict may cause one or both parties to withhold those resources, preventing the full functioning of international business activities.
- Both MNE managers and host-country governmental officials must respond to interest groups that may perceive different advantages or no advantage at all to the business-government relationship. Therefore, the relationship's final outcome may not be the one expected from a purely economic viewpoint.
- Negotiations are playing a more important role in determining the terms under which a company may operate in a foreign country. This negotiating process is similar to the domestic processes of company acquisition and collective bargaining. The major differences in the international sphere are the much larger number of provisions, the general lack of fixed time duration for an agreement, and cultural differences among negotiators.
- Generally, a company's best bargaining position is before it makes an investment. Once it commits resources to the foreign operation, the company may not be able to move elsewhere easily.
- Because international negotiations occur largely between parties whose cultures, educational backgrounds and expectations differ, it is difficult for these negotiators to understand each other's sentimental and present convicting arguments. Role-playing offers negotiators a means of anticipating responses and planning an approach to the actual bargaining.
- Negotiation is the process of bargaining with one or more parties to arrive at a solution that is acceptable to all. This process involves five basic steps: planning, interpersonal relationship building, exchanging task related information, persuasion and agreement. The way in which the parties are carried out often will vary because of cultural differences.
- There are a wide variety of tactics used in international negotiating. These include location, time limits, buyer-seller relations, verbal behaviors and non-verbal behaviors.

Chapter 12

Export and Import Strategy

EXPORT STRATEGY

A company's choice of entry mode to a foreign market depends on different factors such as the ownership advantages of the company, location advantages of the market, and internalization advantages of integrating transactions within the company. Ownership advantages are specific assets, international experience, and the ability to develop differentiated products. For example, Boeing capitalizes on its ownership advantage through the development of sophisticated aircraft; doing the same would be difficult for a new entrant to the market.

Location advantages of the market are a combination of market potential its size and growth potential and investment risk. Internalization advantages are the benefits of holding on to specific assets or skills within the company and integrating them into activities rather than licensing or selling them.

In general, companies that have low levels of ownership advantages either do not enter foreign markets or use low-risk entry modes such as exporting. Exporting requires a lower level of investment than other modes, such as FDI, but it also offers a lower risk-return on sales. Exporting allows significant management operational control but does not provide as much marketing control, because the exporter is farther from the final consumer and often must deal with independent distributors abroad that control many of the marketing functions.

Companies consider these questions before deciding to export.

- What does the company want to gain from exporting?
- Is exporting consistent with other company goals?
- What demands will exporting place on its key resources – management and personnel, production capacity, and financing – and how will these demands be met?

- Are the expected benefits worth the costs, or would company resources be better used for developing new domestic business?

Exporting occurs for several good reasons. Companies can export goods and services to related companies such as branches and subsidiaries, or it can export to independent customers. Sometimes companies export final goods to its related companies overseas who then sell the goods to consumers. Other times, companies export semi-finished goods that are used by its related companies in the manufacturing process.

Characteristics of Exporters

Research conducted on the characteristics of exporters has resulted in two basic conclusions:

1. The probability of being an exporter increases with company size, as defined by revenues.
2. Export intensity, the percentage of total revenues coming from exports, is not positively correlated with company size. The greater the percentage of exports to total revenues the greater the intensity.

The first conclusion is based on the idea that small companies can grow in the domestic market without having to export, but large companies must export if they are to increase sales. The exceptions are small high-tech or highly specialized companies that operate in market niches with a global demand and small companies that sell expensive capital equipment.

The largest companies such as General Electric, Boeing, and General Motors are still the biggest exporters. But small companies are expanding their export capability. A survey of 10,000 small businesses in the United States found that 36 per cent of the companies derived 15 per cent or more of revenues from sales abroad, up from 27 per cent in 1992.

Why Companies Export?

Companies export primarily to increase sales revenues. This is true for service companies as well as manufacturers. Many of the former, such as accountants, advertisers, lawyers and consultants, export their services to meet the needs of client working abroad. Grieve exported products to clients that have moved abroad. Companies that are capital and research intensive, such as biotechnology and pharmaceutical companies must export to spread their R&D expenditures over a larger sales volume.

In addition, some companies export rather than invest abroad because of the perceived high risk of operating in foreign environment. Finally, many companies export to a variety of markets as a diversification strategy. Because economic growth is not the same in every market, export diversification can allow a company to take advantage of strong growth in one market to offset weak growth in another.

Stages of Export Development

Many companies begin exporting by accident rather than by design. Consequently, they tend to encounter a number of unforeseen problems. They also may never get a chance to see how important exports can be. For these reasons, developing a good export strategy is important. As **Fig. 12.1** shows, export development has three broad phases.

These phases have little to do with company size but rather on degree of export development – both large and small companies can be at any stage. In fact, more new companies are exporting sooner in their own life cycle because there is a new generation of entrepreneurs and managers with a keen awareness of international business. In addition, the ability to generate sales on the Internet is one reason why companies are exporting faster. As a company establishes a home page, Internet surfers from all over the world can have instant access to the company's product line and even initiate sales directly.

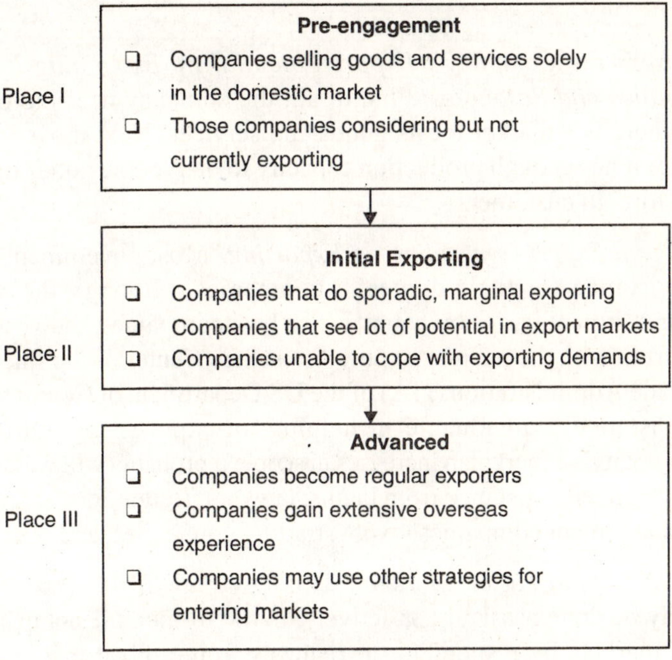

Fig. 12.1: Phases of Export Development

Potential Pitfalls of Exporting

To understand the elements in an export strategy, let's first identify the major problems that exporters often face. Aside from problems that are common to international business in general and not unique to exporting, such as language and other cultural factors, the following are mistakes companies new to exporting most frequently make.

1. Failure to obtain qualified export counseling and to develop a master international marketing plan before starting an export business.
2. Insufficient care in selecting overseas agents or distributors.
3. Insufficient commitment by top management to overcome the initial difficulties and financial requirements of exporting.
4. Neglecting export business when the domestic market booms.
5. Failure to treat international distributors on an equal basis with their domestic counterparts.
6. Unwillingness to modify products to meet other countries' regulations or cultural preferences.

Designing an Export Strategy

Designing an export strategy can help managers avoid making the costly mistakes mentioned above. To establish a successful export strategy, management must:

1. *Assess the Company's Export Potential by Examining its Opportunities and Resources:* First of all, the company needs to determine if there is a market for its goods and services. Next it needs to make sure it has enough production capacity to deliver the goods or services to foreign customers.

2. *Obtain Expert Counseling on Exporting:* Most governments provide assistance for their domestic companies, although the extent of commitment varies by country. For best companies, the best place to start is with the nearest Export Assistance Center of the International Trade Administration (ITA) of the US Department of Commerce. Such assistance is invaluable in helping an exporter get started. As a company's export plan increases in scope, it probably will want to secure specialized assistance from banks, lawyers, freight forwarders, export management companies, export trading companies, and others.

3. *Select a Market or Markets:* This key part of the export strategy may be done passively or actively. In the former, the company learns of markets by responding to requests from abroad that result from trade shows, advertisements, or articles in trade publications. A company also can determine the markets to which products like its own are currently being exported. For example, in the US setting, US Census Trade Statistics identifies the markets for different classification of exports, and the National Trade Data Bank (NTDB) provides specific industry reports for different countries. Similar forms of assistance are found in other countries.

4. *Formulate and Implement an Export Strategy:* In this step, a company considers its export objectives (immediate and long term), specific tactics it will use, a schedule of activities and deadlines to achieve its objectives, and the allocation of resources to accomplish the different activities. Then it implements the strategy by getting the goods and services to foreign consumers.

A detailed export business plan is an essential element in implementing an effective export strategy. **Table 12.1** provides a sample of such a plan. The development of the plan depends on the nature of the company. For a small or medium size company, the plan usually gets the attention of the top levels of management, as was the case with Grieve Corporation. Larger companies might establish a separate export department to deal with the export of all products. Research has shown that commitment precedes success in exporting, and the development of an export department is one indicator of commitment by top management. But whether the company is large or small, or whether the export function is centralized into an export department or diffused into different product or regional organizations, it is important to follow the steps outlined in **Table 12.1** so that an effective strategy is carried out.

Table 12.1: An Export Business Plan

1. Executive Summary ❑ Key elements of the plan ❑ Description of business and target markets ❑ Brief description of management plan ❑ Summary of financial projections	**5. Legal Decisions** ❑ Agent/Distributor agreement ❑ Patent, trademark, copyright ❑ Export/Import regulations ❑ ISO 9000 ❑ Dispute resolution
2. Business History ❑ History of company ❑ Products-services offered and their unique advantages ❑ Domestic-market experience ❑ Foreign market experience ❑ Production facilities ❑ Personnel-international experience and expertise	**6. Manufacturing and Operations** ❑ Location of production facilities ❑ Capacity of existing facilities ❑ Plans for expansion ❑ Product Modification necessary to adapt to local environment
3. Market Research ❑ Target Countries 1. Primary 2. Secondary 3. Tertiary ❑ Market Conditions 1. Existing demand 2. Competition 3. Strengths and weaknesses	**7. Personnel Strategies** ❑ Personnel needed to manage exports ❑ Experience and expertise of existing personnel ❑ Training needs of existing personnel ❑ Hiring needs in the short term and long term

4. Marketing Decisions	**8. Financial Decisions**
❑ Distribution Strategies 1. Indirect exporting 2. Direct exporting 3. Documentation 4. Direct investment 5. Strategic alliances ❑ Pricing Strategy ❑ Promotion Strategy	❑ Proforma financial statements ❑ Identification of key assumptions ❑ Current sources of funding-private and bank funding ❑ Financial needs and future sources of funding ❑ Tax consequences of export activity ❑ Potential risk and sources of protection
	9. Implementation Schedule

IMPORT STRATEGY

Importing is the bringing of goods and services into a country and results in the importer paying money to the exporter in the foreign country. Traditional goods imports are fairly easy to understand. In addition to merchandize importers, such as the Infinity XVL sedan, there are varieties of service imports. SAP software, from the German software company of the same name, is a service (even though it comes in a package, software is considered a service). Foreign banks such as Deutsche Bank that provide financial services to US customers also create service imports.

There are two basic types of imports: those that provide industrial and consumer goods and services to individuals and companies that are not related to the foreign exporter and those that provide intermediate goods and services to companies that are part of the firms global supply chain.

Why import in the first place? Companies import goods and services because they can be supplied to the domestic market at a cheaper price and better quality than competing goods manufactured in the domestic market. Specialization of production and export to markets around the world is more efficient than manufacturing every product in every market. Nike buys shoes manufactured in several Asian countries, including Korea, Taiwan, China, Thailand, Indonesia, and Vietnam because of the cheaper cost. It would be impossible to manufacture the same product in an industrial country and be able to sell it at a reasonable price because of the relatively high labor costs. Finally, companies import products that are not available in the local market. For example, North America imports bananas from tropical climates because the climate of North America is not suitable for growing bananas.

There is not as much research done on import strategies, as is the case for export strategies. However, there are three broad types of importers:

1. Those that are looking for any product around the world that they can import. They might specialize in certain types of products–such as sports

equipments or household items – but they are simply scanning the globe and looking for any product that will generate positive cash flow for them.

2. Those that are looking at foreign sourcing to get their products at the cheapest price. Soon, however, it began to branch out into decorative products for homes, so it identified manufacturers in China that could supply it with specific products for its stores.
3. Those that use foreign sourcing as part of their global supply chain. This strategy will be discussed in Chapter 13.

In fact, the export business plan in Table 12.1 could easily be adapted to an import business plan. Managers need to research potential markets, both in terms of the countries themselves and the suppliers. Then they need to determine the legal ramifications of importing the products, both in terms of the products themselves and the countries from which they come. Managers also need to deal with third party intermediates such as freight forwarders and customs agents, and they need to arrange financing for the purchase.

Importing requires a certain degree of expertise in dealing with institutions and documentation, which a company may not have. Consequently, a company may elect to work through the **import broker**. The import broker obtains various governmental permissions and other clearances before forwarding necessary paperwork to the carrier that is to deliver the goods to the importer. Import brokers in the United States are certified as such by the US Customs Service to perform the function necessary to bring products into the country.

The Role of Customs Agencies

When importing goods into any country, a company must be totally familiar with the customs operations of the importing country. In this context, "customs" are the country's import and export procedures and restrictions, not its cultural aspects. The primary duties of the US Customs Service are the assessment and collection of all duties, taxes and fees on imported merchandise, the enforcement of customs and related laws, and the administration of certain navigation laws and treaties.

A broker or other import consultant can help an importer minimize import duties by

- *Valuing Products in Such a Way that they Qualify for More Favorable Duty Treatment*: Different product categories have different duties. For example, finished goods typically have a higher duty than do parts and components.
- *Qualifying for Duty Refunds through Drawback Provisions*: Some exporters use in their manufacturing process imported parts and components on which they paid a duty. In the United States, the drawback provision allows domestic exporters to apply for a 99 per cent

refund of the duty paid on the imported goods, as long as they become part of the exporter's product.

- *Deferring Duties by using Warehouses and Foreign Trade Zones*: Companies do not have to pay duties on imports stored in bonded warehouses and foreign trade zones until the goods are removed for sale or used in a manufacturing process.
- *Limiting Liability by Properly Marking an Import's Country of Origin:* Because governments assess duties on imports based in part on the country of origin, a mistake in marking the country of origin could result in a higher import duty.

THIRD-PARTY INTERMEDIARIES

Both exporters and importers use a variety of third party intermediaries – companies that facilitate the trade of goods but that are not related to either the exporter or the importer. A company that either exports or is planning to export must decide whether its internal staff will handle certain essential activities or if it will contract other companies. Regardless, the following functions must occur:

- Stimulate sales, obtain orders, and do market research
- Make credit investigations and perform payment collection activities
- Handle foreign traffic and shipping
- Act as support for the company's overall sales, distribution, and advertising staff.

Most companies initially use external specialists and intermediary organizations to assume some or all of these functions, although a company later may develop in-house capabilities to perform them. Specialists are useful for such duties as preparing export documents, preparing customs documents in the importing country, and identifying the best means of transportation. Most companies can benefit at some time from using an intermediary organization. Some of these act as agents on behalf of the exporter, and some take title to the goods and sell them abroad.

Exporting may be either direct or indirect. Direct exports are goods and services sold to an independent party outside of the exporter's home country. Indirect exports are sold to an intermediary in the domestic market who then sells the goods in the export market. Services are more likely to be sold in a direct basis, but goods are exported both directly and indirectly.

DIRECT SELLING

Exporters undertake direct selling to give them greater control over the marketing function and do to earn higher profits. **Direct selling** is when an exporter sells through sales representatives, to distributors, to foreign retailers, or to final end users. A **sales representative** sells products in foreign markets on a commission basis, without taking title to the goods. The sales representative may have exclusive rights to sell in a particular geographic area or may have to compete with other sales representatives to have exclusive rights to a territory.

A **distributor** in a foreign country is a merchant who purchases the products from the manufacturer and sells them at a profit. Distributors usually carry a stock of inventory and service the product. They also usually deal with retails rather than end users in the market.

Companies should consider the following points about each potential foreign sales representative or distributor:

- The size and capabilities of its sales force
- Its sales record
- An analysis of its territory
- Its current product mix
- Its facilities and equipment
- Its marketing policies
- Its customer profile

Exporters can also sell directly to foreign retailers. Usually, these products are limited to consumer lines, but the growth of large retail chains around the world has facilitated the export of products to the large chains, which gives the exporter instant coverage to a wide area. Exporters can also sell directly to end-users. This can be done through catalogs or at trade shows, or the sales can be in response to foreign buyers getting a hold of company brochures or responding to advertisements in trade publications.

Direct Exporting through the Internet and Electronic Commerce

Electronic commerce is an important way for companies to export their products to end-users. It is especially important for SMEs (small and medium-size enterprises) that can't afford to establish an elaborate sales network internationally. E-commerce is easy to start, it provides faster and cheaper delivery of information, it provides quick feedback on new products, it helps to improve customer service, it is available to a global audience.

Through Internet exporting, companies can establish home pages in different languages to target different audiences. In the case of industrial products, they can install software to track hits to their home page and then send sales reps to potential customers or have local distributors contact them.

INDIRECT SELLING

In **indirect selling**, the exporter sells goods directly to or through an independent domestic intermediary in the exporter's home country that exports the products to foreign markets. The major types of indirect intermediaries are the **export management company (EMC); the export trading company (ETC);** export agents, merchants, or re-marketers; and piggyback marketers. EMCs and ETCs sometimes act as agents operating on a commission and sometimes take title to the merchandise. The larger intermediaries however, are almost always referred to as export trading companies or simply trading companies because they typically deal with both exports and imports.

Export Management Companies: An EMC usually act as the export arm of a manufacturer–although it also can deal in imports and often uses the manufacturer's own letterhead in communicating with foreign sales representatives and distributors. The EMC primarily obtains orders for its clients' products through the selection of appropriate markets, distribution channels and promotion campaigns.

EMCs operate on a contractual basis and provide exclusive representation a well-defined foreign territory. The contract specifies pricing, credit and financial policies, promotional services and basis for payment. An EMC might operate on a commission basis for sales and a retainer for other services. EMCs usually concentrate on complementary and non-competitive products so that they can present a more complete product line to a limited number of foreign importers.

Export Trading Companies: ETCs resemble EMCs and the terms are often used interchangeably. ETCs operate more on the basis of demand than of supply. ETCs are like independent distributors that match up buyers and sellers. ETCs find out what foreign customers want and they identify different domestic suppliers for the products. Rather than representing a manufacturer, an ETC looks for as many manufacturers as it can find to supply overseas customers. Because ETCs could control the foreign distribution of products and collaborate with producers of competing products, they could be open to antitrust allegations.

Piggyback Exports: Sometimes an exporter can use another exporter as an intermediary. For example, a company may agree to supply products to a foreign distributor even though it does not produce the entire range of products. Then it might look for other manufacturers to fill the gaps in the product line. In this way, the second manufacturer becomes an exporter indirectly by using the first exporter's distribution channels.

EXPORT FINANCING

From the exporters point of view, there are four major issues that relate to the financial aspects of exporting; the price of the product, the method of payment, the financing of receivables, and insurance.

Product Price: Product pricing of exports entails many of the same factors that managers consider in pricing their products for domestic markets. If the exporter bills in its own home-country currency, the importer absorbs the foreign-exchange risk and must decide whether to pass on any possible exchange-rate differences to the consumer. If the exporter bills in the currency of the importer's country, the foreign-exchange risk falls on the exporter. Another difference between domestic and export pricing is that export prices tend to escalate from transportation costs, duties, multiple wholesale channels in the importing countries, cost of insurance, and banking costs. Finally, the exporter's price may depend on dumping laws in the importing country.

Method of Payment: The flow of money across national borders is complex and requires the use of special documents. Exporters and importers must deal in foreign exchange, and the transfer of funds from one bank to another across national borders can be complicated and take time. In descending order in terms of security to the exporter, the basic methods of payment for exports are:

- Cash in advance
- Letter of credit
- Draft or bill of exchange
- Open account
- Other payment mechanisms, such as consignment sales or countertrade.

Financing Receivables: The increased distances and time of exporting can create cash flow problems for the exporter. This is especially true if the exporter extends payment through a time draft. Because exporting is risky, banks often are unwilling to provide funding for it.

Exporters can get access to funds through **factoring** and **forfeiting**. Factoring is the discounting of a foreign account receivable. Basically the factoring company is a finance provider in situations where a bank may be hesitant to lend money to the exporter. The exporter turns over its export receivables, sometimes for a small administrative fee, over to the factor. In return, the factor gives the exporter about 80 to 85 per cent of value of the receivables up front and then collects the debt itself, paying the balance to the exporter after collecting the debt.

Forfeiting is similar to factoring. A forfeiter buys from an exporter the debt due from its customer, usually in the form of a promissory note or bill of exchange. A bank in the importer's country usually guarantees these instruments. This allows the exporter to get paid immediately and does usually the exporter if it had to borrow from a bank or get credit extend a cheaper form of payments for the importer than to it.

Insurance: There are two kinds of insurance that are used most often in exports. The first kind of insurance covers the transportation of products. Damaging weather conditions, rough handling by carriers, and other hazards to cargo make insurance an important protection for exporters.

The second type of insurance covers political, commercial, and foreign-exchange risk. Some private sector insurance companies will cover these types of risks for established exporters with a proven track record, but government agencies tend to be the most important insurer for these risks.

SUMMARY

- The probability of a company's becoming an exporter increases with company site, but the extent of exporting does not directly correlate with size.
- Companies new to exporting (and also some experienced exporters) often make many mistakes. One way to avoid mistakes is to develop a comprehensive export strategy that includes an analysis of the company's resources as well as its market opportunities.
- Companies export to increase sales revenues, use excess capacity, and diversify markets.
- Importers need to be concerned with strategic issues (why import rather than buy domestically) and procedural issues (what are steps that need to be followed to get goods into the country).
- Customs agencies assess and collect duties, as well as ensure that import regulations are adhered to.
- Exporters may deal directly with agents or distributors in a foreign country or indirectly through export management companies or other types of trading companies. Internet marketing is a new form of direct exporting that is allowing many small and medium size companies to access export markets as never before.
- Trading companies can perform many of the functions for which manufacturers lack the expertise. In addition exporters can use the services of other specialists, such as freight forwarders, to facilitate exporting. These specialists can help an exporter with the complex documentation that accompanies exports.
- There are four main issues in the financial aspects of exporting – the price of the product, the method of payment, the financing or receivables, and insurance.
- Export prices are a function of domestic pricing pressures, the impact of exchange rates, and price escalation due to longer channels of distribution, tariffs, and so forth.
- In descending order in terms of security, the basic methods of payment for exports are cash in advance, letter of credit, draft, open account, and other payment mechanisms such as consignment sales or countertrade.
- A letter of credit is a financial document that obligates the importer's bank to pay the exporter.

Chapter 13

Global Manufacturing and Supply Chain Management

INTRODUCTION

Today's expansive world market offers organizations a rich environment conducive to global development. Since World War II, growth in worldwide trade has escalated greatly as independent national economies have grown more and more dependent on global trade. Additionally, foreign investment in industrialized and Third World countries has expanded. Mid-size U.S. companies are moving manufacturing operations abroad in record numbers. As transportation, communication and cost barriers decline, emphasis is shifting from distinctly national markets to global markets. Moreover, competition is flourishing as a natural byproduct of the free market system. This shift has been driven by both competition and cooperation, with one result being highly similar market segments that transcend borders.

Over the last forty years, globalization has been evolving dramatically. For example, the rise of the European community, recent perestroika in the Soviet Union and Eastern bloc, the North American Free Trade Agreement, Pacific Rim competition, and the developing of the Third World have all fueled demand for consumer and industrial goods, creating a worldwide business climate rich with opportunity. To capitalize on these opportunities, and in some cases simply to survive, companies will need to adopt a global perspective. A rich entrepreneurial global environment beckons, offering not only challenge, but also reward. As companies accept today's organizational challenges, they will expand their operations globally, integrating and refining along the way.

Expanding global operations affords an opportunity for organizations to grow and optimize. This paper describes today's rich macroeconomic climate and offers a multi-phased definition of globalization. In addition, it emphasizes the importance of worldwide operations in meeting market needs and as a competitive response to the escalating importance of quality and flexibility. Recommendations for integration and refinement of operations are also offered.

What are Global Operations?

Global operations include various levels of depth and sophistication. A basic definition includes the performance of business activities and operations that introduce and promote the flow of a company's goods and services to customers in more than one nation for a profit. To achieve this end, complementary relationships develop between firms in various nations. And, with time, education, and interaction, those relationships evolve and grow. Such relationships may take various paths, depending on the culture, values, beliefs, and behavior of the parties involved. In fact, these factors meld into the company's global strategy as it considers modes of entry into foreign markets: importing, exporting, licensing, forming joint ventures, or establishing wholly owned subsidiaries. In one form or another, each mode may identify with a key development phase. Consequently, fueled by a complex and dynamic environment, key development phases unfold. Though each phase bears distinct characteristics, phases tend to shift and overlap. Moreover, one phase often evolves into another.

In pursuing expansion of worldwide operations, choices abound as to the selection of strategies and the degree of involvement. These choices seem to manifest themselves in evolutionary development phases. For instance, the internalization of global marketing, the process by which a firm moves through successive stages, each associated with unique challenges and priorities, with moves into new stages triggered by external and internal factors.

These "triggered" stages are similar to what Staff refers to as "life cycles," whereby consumer markets change with experience and time in response to such factors as economics, the strength of particular industries, and technology. Nonetheless, each stage reflects unique emphasis, strategy, and organizational direction.

The **triggered stages** include:

- Initial
- Development and
- Advanced growth phases

Along with the accompanying profile, cultural perspective, product emphasis, market, focus, strategy, basic considerations, and likely global expansion platform associated with each phase.

Since the operations manager of today is faced with global scenarios, people and cultural skills have become more critical for success than analytical tools in a global 21st century. The main themes in production and operations management are operations strategy, productivity, and quality. These themes are manipulated to serve those involved in production and operations management including employees, customers and owners.

Experienced operations managers recognize that they accomplish their goals through people, and that the skills in dealing with people are often neglected. This operations book focuses on a new type of human-centered production management designed to broaden the operations managers' thinking in the human interactions area, and to expand problem-solving processes geographically from domestic to global.

This work should be of interest to CEOs and corporate and departmental executives who deal with operations and productions. Individuals in academic areas dealing with management, operations management, international business, and organizational behavior should also find this book of interest.

GLOBAL SPREAD OF PRODUCTION

We are moving rapidly into an age of transnational manufacturing, where things made in one country are shipped across national borders for further work, storage, sales, repair, re-manufacture, recycle, or disposal; but our laws, policies, and management practices are slow in adjusting to this reality. They are often based on inaccurate premises. This article examines these premises and suggests what they imply for management of manufacturing.

First, a common view is that manufacturing investment in the industrialized nations is declining and shifting to the developing countries. This is not true. Investment in manufacturing in both industrialized and developing nations is increasing and, in absolute value, there is a lot more investment in industrialized countries than in developing countries. **Second,** a related view argued by many is that manufacturing does not have a bright future in the rich countries.

The section discusses that manufacturers can thrive in the industrialized countries if they learn how to add more value for the end users. They must go beyond productivity improvement to producing more technologically advanced and customized products, responding faster to changing customer demands, and appending more services to their products. Doing all this is easier in the industrialized countries because the needed skills and infrastructure are more readily available there.

Third, another potentially misleading notion is related to why companies invest in manufacturing abroad. Access to low-cost production is not the main motivation in most cases; rather it is access to market. Superior global manufacturers use their foreign factories for much more: to serve their worldwide customers better, preempt competitors, work with sophisticated suppliers, collect critical marketing, technological, and competitive intelligence, and attract talented individuals into the company.

They build integrated global production networks, not collections of disjointed factories that are spread internationally. Thus their investment in manufacturing abroad is not a substitute for investment at home, it is a complement. Building and managing such integrated global factor networks is the next challenge in manufacturing.

The world is clearly entering an age of transnational manufacturing, where things made in one country are shipped across national borders for further work, packaging, assembly, storage, or sales, and products sold in a country are often shipped across national borders for repair, reuse, remanufacture, recycle, or disposal. Every indicator points to an accelerating increase in these flows.

While more products and services are produced every year, an increasing share of them cross national boundaries. Trade in manufactures (as opposed to trade in services and primary commodities) is by far the largest component of the world trade. Reduction of tariffs around the world in general and the recent economic pacts [EU (European Union), EU With EFTA (European Free Trade Agreement), ASEAN (Association of South East Asian Nations), and NAFTA (North American Free Trade Agreement)] continue to drive this trend.

Clearly the logistics of moving manufactured goods around the globe will become a greater challenge and a more critical success factor for manufacturers. This is particularly important because in a surprising number of these cross-border transfers, the same company is at both ends of the transaction, that is, transfer is intra-firm.

A more recent study of the US manufacturing multinationals shows that this intra-firm trade is rising at a striking rate: the share of the intra-firm trade of the total trade by these companies went from 37% in 1977 to 53% in 1983 to 60% in 1993 to 75% in 2003 and to 86% in 2008. (**World Investment Report 2008**) Clearly these companies are organizing or reorganizing their cross-border production activities in an efficiency-oriented, integrated fashion, capitalizing on their assets around the globe. They are locating the various parts of the value-added chain where they contribute most to the company's overall success.

Manufacturing is the single largest type of foreign direct investment in most countries. Nearly 60% of the estimated 39,000 companies around the globe that have foreign affiliates are in manufacturing. A substantial share of all foreign direct investment continues to go into the establishment, expansion or acquisition of factories. About a third of all foreign direct investment by the largest investing countries (United States, Japan, Germany, France, United Kingdom, Italy and Canada) is in manufacturing. As trade barriers fall, as transportation becomes easier, and as communication technologies improve, there are more options for location of production and new challenges for global manufacturers.

Analysis of the options in producing abroad is therefore becoming more complex, especially as one considers the number of possible arrangements for cross-border production: building a green-field site, acquiring an existing factory, forming a joint venture or an alliance, licensing production rights, or subcontracting. Adding to all this possible choices in working with foreign suppliers, distribution centers, logistic systems, and repair services shows the full complexity of cross-border manufacturing decisions. The complexity is not only for business managers but also for public policy makers, tax authorities, and financial analysis who must regulate and deal with these decisions.

Transnational Production: The Next Challenge in Manufacturing

A clear indicator of the spread of transnational manufacturing is the current controversy over what constitutes country of origin for many manufactured goods. As production spreads around the globe, the number of products that can justifiably carry the label of made in one country is decreasing.

For many products, from cars to computers, medical instruments to pharmaceuticals, telephones to refrigerators, it is already difficult to establish what the country of origin really is: where major components were made, where they were put into sub-assemblies, and where final assembly and packaging were done. Keeping track of all this is not only for academic interest; tariffs, quotas, safety regulation and a host of other factors depend on how the country of origin is determined.

For example, a recent ruling in the United States defines the country of origin for a car essentially on the basis of where it was assembled (different from the most common international practice and different from how it is done for other products in the United States itself). As one might expect, this ruling is a subject of dispute and, given all the politics involved, its resolution is not simple.

The difficulty in establishing the country of origin is the harbinger of the new issues raised by increasing transnational manufacturing. Perhaps the awkward label "Made in the World" captures what lies ahead in production more accurately than the traditional label of made in any one country. It forces a new mindset and points out the changes we need to make in public policies and management practices.

For managers of manufacturing companies, it is especially important to appreciate the potential strategic benefits and competitive threats of transnational manufacturing. When considering a factory abroad, settling for simplistic answers, limited benefits, and modest expectations would result in underutilization of the company's resources, but in the managerial debates over establishing, acquiring, expanding, shrinking, or closing foreign factories, often the most measurable and incontestable benefits and losses overwhelm other arguments. Savings in the direct costs of production, gains in foreign exchange, dazzles of financial subsidies, savings in transportation costs, and protection from trade barriers are examples of the tangible factors that can easily dominate the discussion and thinking.

The real mastery of the superior world class manufacturers is that they recognize that a factory in a foreign land can have long-term benefits also in areas beyond production. They use foreign factories to enter new markets, support their domestic factories, generate new knowledge, and bring needed skills and talented people to the company.

Rather than minimal investment, they invest for the long term and encourage development of the managerial competence to perform all that they expect at these sites. They use these factories strategically as a part of a robust global network to deal with foreign exchange and other risks, a network in which the factories reinforce each other. That is different from a company that spreads its production in a series of opportunistic moves in chase of cheap labor, tax benefits, capital subsidies, or getting inside trade barriers, and ends up with a collection of disjointed factories in different countries.

Management of an integrated global factory network is a challenge that manufacturing managers will be facing with increasing frequency. They need all the valuable lessons that they have learned about improving the operations inside individual factories and their supply chains but must also learn new ways of transferring knowledge between factories and crafting strategic charters for each factory in the network.

Leveraging the global network is a potent source of creating competitive advantage. It is not only for the big multinationals; smaller manufacturers can also do that too. Even those companies that do all their production in one country must adjust their strategies to cope with this trend. Soon, if not already, they will be competing with transnational manufacturers at their doorsteps. They can lobby for protection but that is clearly myopic; they can abandon manufacturing by outsourcing their production but that is giving up an important weapon in the competitive battle, or, as the chapter have explained earlier, move into high value-adding manufacturing. Perhaps the most effective strategy is do the same themselves. They too can spread their production into an integrated global network.

Advantages of Global Production

There are many advantages which the companies can avail by production of its products globally. Which includes cheap labor cost every country have its own preferences and the standard rate of living set he governments are different in different countries. So the companies are getting benefit of the cheap labors which is available internationally.

The second thing is cheap raw material companies prefer to put their production plants in those countries where the raw material is easily available and cheap raw material can be obtained. The other benefit the organizations can have is availability of skilled labor the companies like to move in those countries where the people are highly skilled so that they can make better and competitive products.

The global displacement of those activities are not only adopted my the big companies but there are many small companies who are striving to go to multinationals are also adopting these policies of global production to get the maximum benefit.

Some companies just put their production in those countries where natural resources like oil, gas and other minerals are easily available the advantage of this to those companies they can save the transportation cost and they can easily access the raw material to make its finished products.

Global Production Networks and Location Strategies

Global production networks can be structured into two categories; multi-domestic and globally integrated structures:

- **Multi-domestic:** Concerns operations where each market is serviced independently. Can relate to simple products that are easy to replicate but difficult to transport over long distances. Production can be integrated globally, while the marketing is multi-domestic, reflecting cultural and consumer preferences differences. The goal is therefore to better answer the needs of every market. There is also and independency in productivity, meaning that the efficiencies and productivities achieved in each market are unrelated to those taking place in other markets.
- **Globally Integrated:** System of production located in several countries and commonly involving complex products. Logistics activities are highly important as production and distribution capabilities need to be effectively reconciled. This implies an interdependency in productivity, as each component of the supply chain directly impacts the cost and the quality of the final product.

Four major **location strategies** for Global Production Networks can be identified:

- **Centralized Global Production:** The entire production occurs within only one nation (or region) and is exported thereafter on the global market. This is particularly the case for activities that are difficult to relocate, such as goods linked to the location of resources, difficult to reproduce (e.g. luxury and craft) or depending on massive economies of scale.
- **Regional Production:** Takes place within each region that manufactures a good with the size of the production system related to the size of the regional market. This system depends more on a regional accessibility than on economies of scale. It particularly applies to well known manufacturing technologies and/or to products having high distribution costs (e.g. soft drinks).
- **Regional Specialization:** This global production network involves a spatial division of the production based on the theory of comparative advantages. Each region specializes on the production of a specific good and imports from other regions what it requires.
- **Vertical Transnational Integration:** This global production network is another variant of specialization. Different stages of the production occur at locations offering the best comparative advantages. Raw materials are extracted from locations where they are the most accessible, while assembly is performed in regions having low labor costs or high levels of expertise depending on the type of product or the stage in its manufacturing.

Each production sectors has a different production network. The automotive and electronics sectors are good examples of vertical integration. For instance, the manufacture of a television generally implies stages of research and development in the United States and Japan (as well as being important markets). Several nations, such as England, South Korea and Germany provide components. The assembly takes place in low wages countries such as China, Mexico and Thailand. Labor costs are a key element of this system, but also its level of expertise.

QUALITY

Quality is defined as meeting or exceeding the expectations of the customer. More specifically, it is the conformance to specifications, value, and fitness for use, support and psychological impressions. For example, no one wants to buy computer software that has a lot of bugs. However, the need to get software to market quickly may mean getting the product to market as soon as possible and correcting errors later. In the airline industry, service is a key. Some airlines, such as Singapore Air, have developed a worldwide reputation for excellence in service.

Quality can mean zero defects, an idea perfected by Japanese manufacturers who refuse to tolerate defects of any kind. Before the strong emphasis on zero defects, US companies operated according to the premise of **acceptable quality level (AQL)**. This premise allowed an acceptable level of bad quality. It held that unacceptable products would be dealt with through repair facilities and service warranties.

Total Quality Management

The Japanese approach to quality is **total quality management (TQM)**. TQM is a process that stresses three principles: customer satisfaction, employee involvement and continuous improvements in quality. The goal of TQM is to eliminate all defects, TQM often focuses on benchmarking world-class standards, product and service design, process design and purchasing.

TQM is a process of continuous improvement at every level of the organization –from the mailroom to the boardroom. It implies that the company is doing everything it can to achieve quality at all stages of the process, from customer demands, to product design to engineering. Although benchmarking – determining the best processes used by the best companies – is an important part of TQM, using the best practices of other companies is not intended to be a goal. TQM means that a company will try to be better than the best.

The continuous improvement process is also known as kaizen, which means identifying problems and enlisting employees at all levels of the organization to help eliminate the problems. The key is to make continuous improvement a part of the daily work of every employee.

Quality Standards

There are three different levels of quality standards: a general level, an industry-specific level and company level. The first level is a general standard, such as the Deming Award, which is presented to firms demonstrating excellence in quality, and the Malcolm Baldridge National Quality Award, which is presented annually to companies that demonstrate quality strategies and achievements. However, even more important than awards is certification of quality.

Basically, under ISO 9000, companies must document how workers perform every function that affects quality and install mechanisms to ensure that they follow through on the documented routine. ISO 9000 certification entails a complex analysis of management systems and procedures, not just of quality-control standards. Rather than judging the quality of a particular product, ISO

9000 evaluates the management of the manufacturing process according to standards it has created in 20 domains, from purchasing to design to training. A company that wants to be ISO certified must fill out a report and then be certified by a team of independent auditors.

ISO 9001 is the most comprehensive and detailed standard in the series of ISO standards. It is used when the company has to assure conformance to customers for specific requirements for design, development, production, installation and servicing. ISO 9002 is directed to sites not dealing with design and after-market service and therefore is intended to assure conformance to specific requirements for production and installation.

SUPPLIER NETWORKS

Sourcing is the firm's process of having inputs (raw materials and parts) supplied to it for the production process. Global sourcing is the first step in the process of materials management; also called logistics, which includes sourcing, inventory management and transportation between suppliers, manufacturers and customers.

For example, Ford assembles cars in Hermosillo, Mexico and ships them into the United States for end-use consumers. The cars are designed by Mazda, a Japanese company, and use some Japanese parts. Ford can purchase parts manufactured in Japan and ship them to US for final assembly and sale in the US market, or it can have Japanese and US made parts shipped to Mexico for final assembly and sale in the US, some from Japan, and a small percentage from Mexico.

Sourcing in the home country enables companies to avoid numerous problems, including those connected with language differences, long distances and lengthy supply lines, exchange-rate fluctuations, wars and insurrections, strikes, politics, tariffs and complex transportation channels.

Companies pursue global sourcing strategies for a number of reasons:

1. To reduce costs–due to less expensive labor, less restrictive work rules, and lower land and facilities costs.
2. To improve quality.
3. To increase exposure to worldwide technology.
4. To improve delivery of supplies.
5. To strengthen the reliability of supply by supplementing domestic with foreign suppliers.
6. To gain access to materials available only abroad, possibly because of technical specifications or product capabilities.
7. To react to competitors' offshore sourcing practices.

Three major configuration of outsourcing have emerged:

- Vertical integration.
- Arm's length purchases from outside suppliers.
- Japanese *keiretsu* relationships with suppliers.

Vertical integration in where the company owns the entire supplier network or at least a significant part of it. It may have to purchase raw materials from outside suppliers, but the company produces the most expensive parts. Arm's length purchases is the same as outsourcing. The Japanese *keiretsu* are a group of independent companies that work together to manage the flow of goods and services along the entire value-added chain.

MAKE OR BUY DECISIONS

The make-or-buy decision is the act of making a strategic choice between producing an item internally (in-house) or buying it externally (from an outside supplier). The buy side of the decision also is referred to as outsourcing. Make-or-buy decisions usually arise when a firm that has developed a product or part—or significantly modified a product or part—is having trouble with current suppliers, or has diminishing capacity or changing demand.

Make-or-buy analysis is conducted at the strategic and operational level. Obviously, the strategic level is the more long-range of the two. Variables considered at the strategic level include analysis of the future, as well as the current environment. Issues like government regulation, competing firms, and market trends all have a strategic impact on the make-or-buy decision. Of course, firms should make items that reinforce or are in-line with their core competencies. These are areas in which the firm is strongest and which give the firm a competitive advantage.

Discussions on vertical integration - about whether products, parts, or services should be produced in-house or outsourced - can often become heated exchanges between managers holding opposing business beliefs.

- Is it a question of optimizing the cost structure, or destroying jobs?
- Of making fixed costs variable, or losing knowhow?
- Of gaining flexibility, or plunging into dependence?

Not surprisingly, **the make or buy**, debate almost invariably runs into contentious areas. Some see in it an opportunity to thrust forward into a spectacular hi-tech investment. Others see it as representing a misguided sense of loyalty to the business's in-house team. Criteria for an objective decision are neither easy to find nor easy to apply, since every case is different.

However, the good news is that make or buy considerations can be expressed in objective terms. What is not such good news is that these considerations have to go much farther and deeper than normal or convenient. To be useful, changes in a company's level of integration should make its entire value-added chain more effective - not just consist of spinning off units or adding on operations or processes in a piecemeal fashion. And when we talk of vertical integration, we include all elements of the chain, not just production.

Clearly, every company must find its own optimum level of Integration. **Vertical integration** should be used as a means to reinforce existing effectiveness in technology or operations. Thus, if a company is technologically or operationally superior to its competitors and suppliers, a high level of vertical Integration will give it a competitive advantage. If it is weaker, on the other hand, the same level of integration will be a disadvantage.

Outsourcing to compensate for operational or technological weaknesses only works if the elements that are farmed out have nothing to do with what differentiates a company in the market. Companies that outsource production simply because they are not cost-competitive must be prepared to be overtaken by more efficient competitors, or even by their suppliers entering the market in direct competition.

Component manufacturers rarely achieve strategic differentiation with a superior product concept, their strengths are more likely to lie in operational excellence, larger economies of scale, a superior process, and first-rate logistics. As a result, the best among them tend to have higher levels of integration than do the less successful.

In some cases, such as the automotive industry, optimizing vertical Integration actually means reducing it, only in this way can companies make the necessary 30 to 40 per cent cost reductions. This can raise difficult social and political concerns. But ignoring the issue could prove fatal, given the strength of international competition. Creative solutions are called for. They might Include such moves as spinning off component manufacturing facilities to create Independent companies with their own development departments as profit centers, or contracting out entire manufacturing stages to suppliers.

The increased existence of firms that utilize the concept of lean manufacturing has prompted an increase in outsourcing. Manufacturers are tending to purchase sub-assemblies rather than piece parts, and are outsourcing activities ranging from logistics to administrative services. It prescribes that a firm outsource all items that do not fit one of the following three categories:

- the item is critical to the success of the product, including customer perception of important product attributes;

- the item requires specialized design and manufacturing skills or equipment, and the number of capable and reliable suppliers is extremely limited; and
- the item fits well within the firm's core competencies, or within those the firm must develop to fulfill future plans. Items that fit under one of these three categories are considered strategic in nature and should be produced internally if at all possible.

Make-or-buy decisions also occur at the operational level. This chapter suggest these considerations that favor making a part in-house:

- Cost considerations (less expensive to make the part)
- Desire to integrate plant operations
- Productive use of excess plant capacity to help absorb fixed overhead (using existing idle capacity)
- Need to exert direct control over production and/or quality
- Better quality control
- Design secrecy is required to protect proprietary technology
- Unreliable suppliers
- No competent suppliers
- Desire to maintain a stable workforce (in periods of declining sales)
- Quantity too small to interest a supplier
- Control of lead time, transportation, and warehousing costs
- Greater assurance of continual supply
- Provision of a second source
- Political, social or environmental reasons (union pressure)
- Emotion (e.g., pride)

Factors that may influence firms to buy a part externally include:

- Lack of expertise
- Suppliers' research and specialized know-how exceeds that of the buyer
- Cost considerations (less expensive to buy the item)
- Small-volume requirements
- Limited production facilities or insufficient capacity
- Desire to maintain a multiple-source policy
- Indirect managerial control considerations
- Procurement and inventory considerations

- Brand preference
- Item not essential to the firm's strategy

The two most important factors to consider in a make-or-buy decision are cost and the availability of production capacity. Cost considerations should include all relevant costs and be long-term in nature. Obviously, the buying firm will compare production and purchase costs. This chapter provide the major elements included in this comparison. Elements of the "make" analysis include:

- Incremental inventory-carrying costs
- Direct labor costs
- Incremental factory overhead costs
- Delivered purchased material costs
- Incremental managerial costs
- Any follow-on costs stemming from quality and related problems
- Incremental purchasing costs
- Incremental capital costs

Cost considerations for the **"buy" analysis** include:

- Purchase price of the part
- Transportation costs
- Receiving and inspection costs
- Incremental purchasing costs
- Any follow-on costs related to quality or service

One will note that six of the costs to consider are incremental. By definition, incremental costs would not be incurred if the part were purchased from an outside source. If a firm does not currently have the capacity to make the part, incremental costs will include variable costs plus the full portion of fixed overhead allocable to the part's manufacture.

If the firm has excess capacity that can be used to produce the part in question, only the variable overhead caused by production of the parts are considered incremental. That is, fixed costs, under conditions of sufficient idle capacity, are not incremental and should not be considered as part of the cost to make the part.

While cost is seldom the only criterion used in a make-or-buy decision, simple break-even analysis can be an effective way to quickly surmise the cost implications within a decision. Suppose that a firm can purchase equipment for in-house use for \$250,000 and produce the needed parts for \$10 each. Alternatively, a supplier could produce and ship the part for \$15 each. Ignoring the cost of negotiating a contract with the supplier, the simple break-even point could easily be computed:

$$\$250{,}000 + \$10Q = \$15Q$$

$$\$250{,}000 = \$15Q - \$10Q$$

$$\$250{,}000 = \$5Q$$

$$50{,}000 = Q$$

Therefore, it would be more cost effective for a firm to buy the part if demand is less than 50,000 units, and make the part if demand exceeds 50,000 units. However, if the firm had enough idle capacity to produce the parts, the fixed cost of $250,000 would not be incurred (meaning it is not an incremental cost), making the prospect of making the part too cost efficient to ignore.

Firms have started to realize the importance of the make-or-buy decision to overall manufacturing strategy and the implication it can have for employment levels, asset levels, and core competencies. In response to this, some firms have adopted total cost of ownership (TCO) procedures for incorporating non-price considerations into the make-or-buy decision.

The Purchasing Function

The purchasing agent is the link between the company's outsourcing decision and its supplier relationships. Just as companies go through stages of globalization, so does the purchasing agents scope of responsibilities. Typically purchasing goes through four phases before becoming "global":

- Domestic purchasing only
- Foreign buying based on need
- Foreign buying as part of procurement strategy
- Integration of global procurement strategy

Phase 4 occurs when the company realizes the benefits from integration and coordination of purchasing on a global basis and is most applicable to the MNE as opposed to, say, the exporter. When purchasing becomes this global, MNEs often face the centralization/decentralization dilemma.

The primary benefits of decentralization include increased production facility control over purchases, better responsiveness to facility needs, and more effective use of local suppliers. The primary benefits of centralization are increased leverage with suppliers, getting better prices, eliminating administrative duplication, allowing purchasers to develop specialized knowledge in purchasing techniques, reducing the number of orders processed, and enabling purchasing to build solid supplier relationships.

Companies pursue five major sourcing strategies as they move into phases 3 and 4 in the preceding list (foreign buying as part of procurement strategy and integration of global procurement strategy):

- Assign domestic buyer(s) for international purchasing.
- Use foreign subsidiaries or business agents.
- Establish international purchasing offices.
- Assign the responsibility for global sourcing to a specific business unit or units.
- Integrate and coordinate worldwide sourcing.

INVENTORY MANAGEMENT

Whether a company decides to source parts from inside or outside the company or from domestic of foreign sources, it needs to manage the flow and storage of inventory. This is true of raw materials and parts sourced from suppliers, work in-progress and finished goods inventory inside the manufacturing plant, and finished goods stored at a distribution center.

If the company sources parts from a variety of suppliers from around the world, distance, time, and the uncertainty of the international political and economic environment can make it difficult for managers to determine correct reorder points for the manufacturing process. Rapidly changing international events can ruin a smoothly running inventory control system.

Just-in-Time Systems

JIT systems focus on reducing inefficiency and unproductive time in the production process to improve continuously the process and the quality of the product or service. The JIT system gets raw materials, parts, and components to the buyer "just in time" for use, sparing companies the cost of storing large inventories. That is why companies need to develop solid supplier relationships to ensure good quality and delivery times if JIT is to work.

JIT implies that inventories must be small, but foreign sourcing almost always requires large inventories to counteract the risk of interruption in supply. A company's inventory management strategy – especially in terms of stock sizes and whether or not JIT will be used – determines frequency of needed shipments. The less frequent the delivery, the more likely the needs to store inventory somewhere. Because JIT requires delivery just as the inventory is to be used, some concession must be made for inventory arriving from foreign suppliers.

JIT typically implies sole sourcing for specific parts in order to get the supplier to commit to the stringent delivery and quality requirements inherent in

JIT. However, if the only supplier is a foreign supplier, it would be too risky to permit just one supplier. That means cultivating multiple suppliers, at least one of which may be a foreign supplier. One strategy is that buyers may use a sole supplier for all but critical inputs. Then it is best to cultivate solid secondary suppliers.

FOREIGN TRADE ZONES

In recent years, **foreign trade zones (FTZs)** have become more popular as an intermediate step in the process between import and final use. FTZs are areas in which domestic and imported merchandize can be stored, inspected, and manufactured free from formal customs procedures until the goods leave the zones. The zones are intended to encourage companies to locate in the country by allowing them to defer duties, pay fewer duties, or avoid certain duties completely.

FTZs can be general-purpose zones or sub-zones. A general-purpose zone usually is established near a port of entry, such as shipping port, a border crossing, or an airport and usually consists of a distribution facility or an industrial park. A sub-zone usually is physically separate from a general-purpose zone but is under the same administrative structure.

FTZs are used worldwide. In Japan, they are being established for the benefit of foreign companies exporting products to that country. Japanese zones serve as warehousing and repackaging facilities at which companies can display consumer goods for demonstration to Japanese buyers.

The exports for which these FTZs are used fall into one of the following categories:

- Foreign goods transshipped through US zones to third countries.
- Foreign goods processed in US zones, then transshipped abroad.
- Foreign goods processed or assembled in US zones with some domestic materials and parts, then re-exported.
- Goods produced wholly of foreign content in US zones and then exported.
- Domestic goods moved into a US zone to achieve export status prior to their actual exportation.

TRANSPORTATION NETWORKS

For a firm, the transportation of goods in an international context is extremely complicated in terms of documentation, choice of carrier (air or ocean), and the decision on whether to establish its own transportation department or outsource to a third-party intermediary. Transportation is one of the key elements of a logistics system. The key is to link together suppliers and manufacturers and manufacturers and final consumers.

Third-party intermediaries are an important dimension to transportation networks. For example, Emery Worldwide is a division of CNF Transportation Inc., a company that specializes in transportation and logistics solutions for companies. It is a $2.5 billion integrated carrier providing global air and ocean freight transportation, logistics management, customs brokerage, and expedited services to manufacturing, industrial, and retail and government customers.

Singapore has one of the largest container ports in the world. Most goods are transported internationally by container. Goods can be loaded into containers and sent to ports by rail or truck. Then they can be sent overseas by airfreight or ocean freight. The transportation company, like Emery, can try to fill up a container just with the company's products, or it can combine the products with those of another company to share container space.

STRATEGIC ROLE OF FOREIGN FACTORIES

Many companies are not tapping the full potential of their foreign factories. They establish and manage their foreign plants to benefit only from tariff and trade concessions, cheap labor, capital subsidies and reduced logistics costs. Therefore, they assign a limited range of work, responsibilities, and resources to those factories.

But there are companies that expect much more from their foreign factories and, as a result, get much more out of them. They use them not only to gain access to the usual incentives but also to get closer to their customers and suppliers, to attract skilled and talented employees, and to create centers of expertise for the entire company. These factories perform functions beyond mere production—functions such as after-sales service and product engineering.

For example, Hewlett-Packard Company's factory in Guadalajara, Mexico, not only assembles computers but also designs computer memory boards. 3M's operations in Bangalore, India, manufacture software and write that software, as well. In Singapore, workers have designed and manufactured two popular pagers for Motorola. And Alcatel Bell's factories in Shanghai are two of the most innovative plants in its worldwide manufacturing network.

Managers do not consider manufacturing to be a source of competitive advantage, they are likely to establish foreign factories with a narrow strategic scope; they then provide those factories with limited resources. In contrast, if managers regard manufacturing as a major source of competitive advantage, they generally expect their foreign factories to be highly productive and innovative, to achieve low costs, and to provide exemplary service to customers throughout the world.

Expecting More from Foreign Factories

- It is difficult if not impossible to prove quantitatively how much any factor, let alone an attitude or approach, is responsible for a company's overall success.
- Nevertheless, after decades of studying and working with multinationals, companies that treat their foreign plants as a source of competitive advantage are rewarded in the form of higher market share and greater profits.
- Because of increasing global competition, the gap between the companies that treat their foreign plants as a source of competitive advantage and those that do not is widening.
- Indeed, managers with a limited view of what a foreign factory can or should achieve are falling out of step with three current realities of global business.

First, declining tariffs are reducing the importance of establishing foreign factories as a means of overcoming trade barriers. Tariffs have declined worldwide from an average of 40% in 1940 to 7% in 1990 to 5% in 2008. Trade pacts—GATT, the European Union, NAFTA, Mercosur, and others—are accelerating that reduction. GATT has recently propelled governments from Indonesia to Argentina to issue their first multi-year schedules for reducing tariffs.

Second, the increasing sophistication of manufacturing and product development and the growing importance of having world-class suppliers are causing more multinationals to place less emphasis on low wages when they are choosing foreign manufacturing sites. According to the latest data compiled by the United Nations Conference on Trade and Development, in 2003 ten industrialized countries—the United States, the United Kingdom, France, Germany, Spain, Canada, Australia, Holland, Belgium, and Italy—received half of the world's foreign direct investments and accounted for two-thirds of the world's accumulated stock of foreign direct investments.

The largest recipient was the United States: by 2005, foreign multinationals had more than $800 billion invested in the United States, up from $500 billion in 1994. That cumulative investment nearly equaled the total amount that multinationals had invested in the world's 175 developing countries. Britain, with $230 billion, was the second-largest recipient, followed by France and Germany.

None of these recipients offers cheap wages, materials, or capital costs. Clearly, leading manufacturers recognize that low wages, grants, and subsidies do not necessarily mean low total costs. Indeed, the low wages available in many countries, after adjusting for productivity, lose their attraction. For example, although manufacturing wages in India and the Philippines are much lower than those in the United States, their average manufacturing labor cost is higher after adjustments are made for productivity.

Types of Foreign Factories

- **Offshore Factory:** It is established for the low-cost production of specific items that are then exported either for further work or for sale. Local managers mainly follow the instructions and plans handed down to them. The factory is not responsible for innovations, developments, and engineering. Foreign factories located in Special Economic Zone in China are examples of offshore factories. They were dedicated to production of simple labor-intensive components at a low cost.
- **Source Factory:** It is also established for low-cost production, but unlike an offshore factory, it has the ability to produce a product or a part as the best factory in the company's global network. Its managers have greater authority over procurement (including the selection of suppliers), production planning, process changes, outbound logistics and production-customization and redesign decisions. By the mid-1980s HP's factory in Singapore offered low wages, low taxes and efficient production. In addition, it had its own R&D group and was actively involved in redesigning and developing products.
- **Server Factory:** It is a production site that supplies specific national or regional markets. It has relatively more autonomy than an offshore plant to make minor modifications in products and production methods to fit local conditions, but its authority and competence in this area are very limited. For example, Coca-Cola company, has many server factories around the world, each of which serves a relatively small geographic market. These plants adhere to the company standards and even minor adjustments in the formula require approval from regional or corporate headquarters.
- **Contributor Factory:** It serves a specific national or regional market, and also assumes responsibility for product customization, process improvements, product modifications or product development. Since late 1980s, Sony's Bridgend factory has shifted its role from a server to a contributor factory. It not only served the European market has also became more independent from Sony Japan. The Bridgend factory

produced most parts itself, and purchased more parts from European suppliers. The plant also worked on customizing product design and development.

- **Outpost Factory:** It is established to gain access to the knowledge or skills that the company needs. The primary role is to be close to competitors and key suppliers and to learn about technological development. All outpost factories have a secondary strategic role as a server or an offshore, making products and serving markets. For example, lots of non-US firms launch their outpost factories in Silicon valley.
- **Lead Factory:** Creates new processes, products, and technologies for the entire company. Its managers make decisions on key suppliers and also participate in joint development work with suppliers. It employees directly deal with end customers, suppliers, research laboratories and other centers of knowledge. They also initiate innovations frequently. For example HP's Singapore plant in the 90s turned into a lead factory from an offshore factory. The plant had full responsibility for a business (developing a new DeskJet printer), which included the whole spectrum of activities from the redesign, production and distribution, to the creative marketing of the product in a new market.

MANAGING GLOBAL SUPPLY CHAIN ISSUES

Supply chains are continually subjected to forces, internal and external, that are in constant states of flux. Managing a supply chain is therefore a demanding activity that requires a thorough understanding of the concepts and mechanisms that underpin the operation of the supply chain and the factors that influence its performance. In a global environment, these factors are many, often interrelated and beyond the reach of most organizations to influence or control. Knowing what these factors are and understanding how they are likely to impact on the strategic and operational decisions that must be made while managing the global supply chain is critical.

With increased globalization and offshore sourcing, global supply chain management is becoming an important issue for many businesses. Like traditional, supply chain management, the underlying factors behind the trend are reducing the costs of procurement and decreasing the risks related to purchasing activities. The big difference is that global supply chain management involves a company's worldwide interests and suppliers rather than simply a local or national orientation.

Effective global supply chain management is a key issue for many businesses. As with traditional local or national supply chain management in the past, today's increasing focus on this aspect of business operations is driven by a need to reduce the costs of procurement and minimise risks related to sourcing goods. However, because global supply chain management can involve several countries or continents, this itself can bring issues and difficulties that need to be managed.

Because global supply chain management usually involves a plethora of countries, it also usually comes with a plethora of new difficulties that need to be dealt with appropriately. One that companies need to consider is the overall costs. While local labor costs may be significantly lower, companies must also focus on the costs of space, tariffs, and other expenses related to doing business overseas. Additionally, companies need to factor in the exchange rate. Obviously, companies must do their research and give serious consideration to all of these different elements as part of their global supply management approach.

Time is another big issue that should be addressed when dealing with global supply chain management. The productivity of the overseas employees and the extended shipping times can either positively or negatively affect the company's lead time, but either way these times need to be figured into the overall procurement plan. Other factors can also come into play here as well. For example, the weather conditions on one side of the world often vary greatly from those on the other and can impact production and shipping dramatically. Also, customs clearance time and other governmental red tape can add further delays that need to be planned for and figured into the big picture.

Besides contemplating these issues, a business attempting to manage its global supply chain must also ask itself a number of other serious questions. First, the company needs to make decisions about its overall outsourcing plan. For whatever reason, businesses may desire to keep some aspects of supply chain closer to home. However, these reasons are not quite as important as other countries advance technologically. For example, some parts of India have now become centers for high-tech outsourced services which may once have been done in-house only out of necessity. Not only are provided to companies by highly qualified, overseas workers, but they are being done at a fraction of the price they could be done in the United States or any other Western country.

Another issue that must be incorporated into a global supply chain management strategy is supplier selection. Comparing vendor bids from within the company's parent-country can be difficult enough but comparing bids from an array of global suppliers can be even more complex. How to make these choices is one of the first decisions companies must make, and it should be a decision firmly based on research. Too often companies jump on the lowest price instead of taking the time to factor in all of the other elements, including those related to money and time which were discussed above. Additionally, companies must make decisions about the number of suppliers to use. Fewer supplies may be easier to manage but could also lead to potential problems if one vendor is unable to deliver as expected or if one vendor tries to leverage its supply power to obtain price concessions.

Factors Considered in Global Supply Chain

The plethora of factors that must be considered can make judging where to manufacture a product difficult. Although there are always trends as to which countries are perceived as providing the most competitive supply, the most effective sourcing location will vary greatly from company to company. In the clothing and textile industries, for example, China and India are currently popularly perceived as attractive locations due to their large pools of skilled workers and their relatively low labor costs. The most competitive place to source from, however, will vary greatly according to the market niche a company occupies, the size of their typical orders, the materials that need to be utilized and so forth. Pakistan and Bangladesh, for instance, may be cheaper than China for jeans and shirts, which are both very important markets for these countries.

When calculating the overall cost of sourcing or manufacturing overseas, it is essential to take into account the exchange rate and tariffs as well as the additional transportation costs, to which governmental taxes and charges must often be added. While labor costs may be low, these expenses could significantly decrease the profit margin to be gained through offshore supply if they are not planned for and managed appropriately. Other issues which must be factored in include extended shipping times, the customs clearance period and other governmental red tape, labor movement and possible future wage inflation, as well as, in some cases, unpredictable weather conditions which can impact production and shipping.

Naturally one of the most crucial aspects to consider in global supply chain management is supplier selection and the set-up of supplier relationships. Companies sourcing offshore must make decisions about which suppliers to use and how many companies to work with. It is important to weigh up the ease of managing fewer suppliers against the potential problems that could arise should a supplier relied upon for a large percentage of stock be unable to deliver as expected. It is also crucial for a business to consider how they will ensure effective communication with suppliers, as misinterpretations due to language and cultural differences could have a significant impact on your bottom line.

Ethical Sourcing

Socially responsible trading became a growing issue during the 1990s when companies with global supply chains - particularly those in the clothing and food industries - were coming under rising pressure form consumer groups, governments and trade unions to ensure decent working conditions for those producing their goods. Since then, numerous media campaigns, such as the recent BBC *Panorama* program, highlighting the poor working conditions in factories and farms in developing countries have encouraged consumers to purchase ethically sourced products. Moreover, corporate investment companies are increasingly screening their investments according to a range of social and environmental criteria, including an organization's efforts to secure adequate labor conditions in addressing their supply chain.

As a result, ethical sourcing is now part of the corporate responsibility agenda of most major organizations, with many implementing corporate codes of practice to ensure that the working conditions of workers producing for them meet or exceed international labor standards. What's more, ever increasing customer demand for ethically sourced items, particularly in higher income groups, means this aspect of global supply chain management is gradually descending from niche to mainstream. With a greater number of companies endeavoring to minimize the exploitation of labor resources in a supply chain, being able to track items and components back to a source has become an important aspect of global supply chain management.

Technologies Help to Manage Global Supply Chain

With today's emphasize on cutting costs and streamlining expenses, many companies are looking to improve their bottom lines with more effective supply chains. Unfortunately, many people involved with companies don't have a clear understanding of what a supply chain is or how it fits into the companies overall strategy.

Technology also plays an important role in the success of supply chain management. Even though the supply chain concept pre-dates the Internet, only through the use of web-based software and communication can it truly reach its full potential. Before the Internet, companies were limited because they were not able to receive or to send updates, feedback, or other important information in a timely fashion. Additionally, companies were limited in their ability to work with global partners because of language barriers and time differences. Using the Internet to handle most of the elements involved in supply change management, including procurement and communication, makes the exchange of data and the running of the supply chain faster.

Supply chains include a company's entire manufacturing and distribution process. They involve every step of the production from planning to manufacturing to handling defective goods. The overall goal of these chains is to keep the process running smoothly at all times and to keep all of the components (i.e. vendors, warehouses, etc.) connected. One of the biggest benefits technology has given to the supply chain concept is the ability for companies to collaborate. These collaborations are designed for the mutual benefit of all parties.

For example, a supplier of consumer goods may be linked up via the Internet to one of its distributors so that when the supply gets too low an order for more of those goods can be placed automatically. In this way, the distributor never has to worry about running out of a product and disappointing customers and the supplier doesn't have to worry about maintaining a large inventory in expectation of demand. Similar systems have also been constructed to send out multiple requests to vendors when an order is placed. Collaborating this way makes better use of existing resources and paves the way for a larger profit margin on all sides of the equation.

Businesses are increasingly turning to the latest software applications in order to control their supply chains and achieve operational excellence on a global scale. Indeed Enterprise Resource Planning **(ERP)** and Product Development Management **(PDM)** systems are often key to enabling companies to manage their global supply chain in an efficient, competitive and profitable manner.

In fact, supply chains often work best in conjunction with an **ERP** system but they are not meant to replace or to use instead of such a system because **ERP** systems involve a multitude of business activities, including customer service and production planning that are not a part of supply chains. Supply chains are generally concerned with the flow of raw materials, manufacturing, production, and distribution. However, the **ERP** system does organize a lot of the information supply chains use to run efficiently and without that system most companies run into problems effectively setting up their supply chains.

Organizations with global supply chains are realizing that complete visibility is paramount in order to obtain effective control. Using a PDM product alongside your ERP system can give you even greater control and help you select suitable suppliers from the design stage of a product.

The software can also be used to group suppliers, so for example, a company with a proactive attitude towards social responsibility can group suppliers that meet ethical and fair trade codes of practice into a preferred supplier list. The 'what if' analysis function can be used to immediately see what impact a change of supplier will have on the cost of producing an item and 'where used' reports allow a business to calculate the impact a discontinued or late supply of a material will have on production by identifying where specific fabrics or components are being utilized.

For companies that need to make more detailed order information available to their suppliers, **web-based PDM** systems can help. This type of scftware can enable suppliers to view the designs, styles and specifications they are manufacturing and even video demonstrations of the required component handling.

While the benefits of supply chain management are many, using technology to achieve those benefits does have two main drawbacks: one is resistance from vendors and the other is resistance from employees. Suppliers of goods are often hesitant to jump on-board because of the initial costs involved in setting up their own end of supply chain management system and because most vendors do not have a trusting relationship with their buyers. To overcome this obstacle, the strong relationship must be present and the seller needs to be able to see the profit potential on their end of the arrangement.

Likewise, many employees have learned to develop a hate-hate relationship with new technology. After all, it costs them their jobs and often makes them feel that their work is more tedious or more complicated. Plus, software mistakes, which are inevitable at the beginning, may cause other employees to lose faith in the system altogether. Employees need to trust the system, the company, and their ability to use the program if they are going to adopt the supply chain management software.

Landed Cost Calculation

The local functionality offered by systems designed to work on a global scale can help companies take into account additional factors, such as local tax and regulatory requirements, which affect the landed costs of items. Trade agreements can also be set up to work on a supplier level in certain ERP systems, so you can have supplier specific pricing rules.

Many fully integrated ERP systems now have direct links between demand and supply sides of the business. This means that if, for example, the demand profile for a product changes this will ripple through the system to purchase and production orders. In global supply chain management, where long distance shipping means longer lead times and smaller windows of opportunity in which to respond to market changes, this is vital. "In clothing and textile sectors, for example."

Performance Monitoring

The increased complexity of global supply networks can make it difficult to judge how particular aspects of a business are performing and where improvements need to be made. Companies with global supply chains require agile systems that deliver key business intelligence, identifying bottlenecks and monitoring aspects like lead times and supplier performance. "What's more, today's fast-paced market means such key performance indicator **(KPI)** reports must be available instantly.

Going Global

We now live in a world where more and more products are made abroad or from parts sourced across the globe. Indeed the trend to move manufacturing offshore and source goods from overseas is affecting companies in virtually all sectors, with even distinctively British brands like Burberry and HP Sauce now moving at least some aspect of production abroad. With this come the issues of more complex supply chain networks, making manufacturing offshore a potentially daunting prospect. However, more and more businesses recognize the benefits of extending their supply chain, or indeed view it as the only viable option. For theses companies, having the correct systems and infrastructure in place is crucial.

Global Crisis Economic Demands in Managing Global Supply Chains

Technology can become a critical weapon in managing inventories and uncertainty in a global supply chain during uncertain, as well as prosperous, economic conditions. Companies should augment their SCM application portfolios with tools that can help them monitor, plan and react to volatile conditions in their global supply chains.

Historically, when supply chains were more localized, enterprises had greater flexibility in responding to demand and supply volatility caused by economic conditions. If demand slowed, they could cancel orders with suppliers on short notice; if demand increased, they could place new orders with suppliers and be assured that suppliers could respond in a reasonable period of time. The reasonably short lag time in this process (days or weeks) enabled organizations to let conditions evolve a bit longer, allowing for a clearer understanding of demand before taking action. This said, however, the downstream effects of this, often referred to, as the "bullwhip effect," were still traumatic to trading partners; even so, the response time was shorter than with global supply chains. When able to cancel an order with a day's notice, businesses could wait until things got pretty bad before they had to worry. The inventory reduction programs that many companies instituted during the past decade, or strategies such as just-in-time, demand-driven or lean, were built on the premise that the end company held minimal amounts of inventory, assuming they could get what they needed quickly.

Pipeline Levels of Inventory: Although supply chain globalization principally pursued lower costs, globalization has exposed organizations to greater risk in volatile economic conditions. Demand-driven has been the SCM mantra for several years, but, paradoxically, as organizations became more global, they made becoming truly demand-driven less achievable. The ability to let current "real" demand drive inventory replenishment only works if the demand and resupply lead times are similar. However, in global supply chains, demand lead times can be measured in days, while resupply lead times can be measured in months. Consequently, by the time an organization sees a downturn in demand, it likely has too much inventory already in the pipeline.

One problematic issue for enterprises today compared with 15 or 20 years ago is that, given the prevalence of global off-shoring, cutting inventories is much more difficult. First, some of the inventories that enterprises are sitting on are the buffer stocks needed to cover the longer international lead times companies have today. Short of selling what they have, possibly at a steep discount, there's no easy solution. Long lead times, often eight weeks or longer, required for resupply are creating another dilemma, as this inventory is often owned or under contractual obligations for businesses to buy.

Timeliness of Response: The next problem impacts upstream trading partners that often take actions months in advance of their customers placing firm orders to be prepared to support future demand. For example, factories that produce intermediary goods started building products many months ago, which means that raw-material or producer-owned intermediary goods inventories will also increase if upstream businesses cancel their orders. This situation is often referred to as the bullwhip effect, where oscillating upstream demand is magnified as it ripples through the multiple echelons in the extended supply chain. In global supply chains, this ripple effect will take longer to play out than it did in the past, again because the end-to-end, resupply lead time is so long. In all likelihood, upstream suppliers will hold additional inventories that there is no longer demand for.

On the back-side of the crisis, the long lead times of global supply chains will also negatively impact turnaround times, because it will take significantly longer to get goods flowing again once things improve. In good times, the lead time from raw material to consumer can be a year or more, which suggests that, in some industries, there could be upward of a year-long lag time to turn things around once demand improves.

The long-term trend in SCM has been to push inventory risk and cost up the supply chain by making suppliers responsible for inventory costs and replenishment efforts. Suppliers were ready and willing to take this inventory risk because, as long as demand continually increased, there was no realized risk, only a theoretical risk. Few suppliers got burned in these relationships, because even if there was an order cancellation, they could, many times, sell the inventory elsewhere.

Enterprises should ask which enterprise is in the best position to manage inventory risk, because that will be the enterprise that can most efficiently hold the risk. Then, relationships should be structured so that the enterprise best positioned to hold the risk does.

Some technologies that enterprises should consider for addressing issues related to global SCM are:

- ***Long-term Forecasting:*** The long lead time, pull-based, international supply chain demands that companies get much better at forecasting in the long term. Emphasis has been on demand planning as of late, and leaders will be those organizations that do a better job responding to the longer-term forecast, say beyond three months, but more likely six to 12 months out.
- ***Strategic Sourcing Optimization:*** Purchase price has and continues to be the primary driver of global outsourcing decisions. The current crisis emphasizes the need for significantly more-robust strategic sourcing capabilities that take into account true delivered cost, as well as balancing the risks of too little or too much inventory.
- ***Global Inventory/Shipment Visibility:*** Because inventory is in transit for longer amounts of time, knowing what and how much is on the way, and where it is, is increasingly important. Today, many companies are incapable of realistically predicting exactly what their inventory positions will be even a few weeks in advance, because a large amount of inventory is not yet on their books but is in transit. Additionally, having visibility into global inventories and shipments allows companies to make decisions more rapidly as conditions change, such as diverting a shipment while en-route based on new information.
- ***Product Portfolio Analysis:*** Product proliferation makes forecasting more difficult, and can cause inventories to vacillate uncontrollably because there is significant overlap and the potential for product substitution. Weeding out under performers or places where the marginal advantage of having a product extension is overshadowed by inventory risk is beneficial.
- ***Supply Chain and Product Performance Management (PPM):*** Continuously monitoring and evaluating the condition and performance of your supply chain is always prudent, but this becomes critical in volatile economic conditions. As stated previously, too many companies are incapable of answering the question, What is my total inventory position, including in-transit stock? Even fewer companies are able to monitor supply chain conditions so they can project how things will be in days or weeks. A critical new question that enterprises must be able to answer is, What part of the supply chain is the most-efficient owner of risk at each part of the supply chain—and how much is that risk

worth? Part of the issue is that SCM information is often housed in multiple siloed applications, and there is no place where this information can be aggregated to answer fundamental questions or provide analysis of conditions across the extended supply chain.

Managing Supply Disruptions in Global Supply Chain

In the current era of global sourcing, most of the organizations have started determining strategies to handle the impact of supply disruptions. It is also well understood that the disruptions cannot be removed completely in the order fulfillment process. However, most global organizations have mitigation plans embedded in the processes, along with appropriate systems and technologies to minimize the impact of disruptions on the key metrics of the organization.

The mitigation strategies that are put in place to handle the supply chain disruptions are dependent on number of factors such as the nature of the global supply chain (Multi-echelon), product complexity, order decoupling points, logistics enablers, and compliance procedures. Additionally, organizations have separate strategies to handle disruptions in the short and long terms of the fulfillment cycle.

Disruptions in the supply chain are caused by both internal and external factors. Factors internal to the organization are as follows:

- Poor Procurement Planning
  - Procurement planning
  - Material Resource Planning (MRP) parameters planning
  - Lead time and safety stock miscalculations
- Poor Demand Planning and Forecasting
  - Mismanagement of high number of options in the BOM (Bill of Materials)
  - Improper demand conversion to material forecast
  - Lack of reviews of demand and supply such as Sales and Operations Planning (S&OP) Planning
  - Changes in customer demand within procurement lead times
- Lack of flexibility in the supply chain network planning
  - Inadequate buffer in the supply chains (to enhance operating efficiency)
  - Focus on lower transportation cost than total cost of procurement from the source to the destination.

The factors which are extraneous to the organization can also cause disruptions in the supply chain. These factors are as follows:

- Over dependency on single source for material procurement.
- Dependency on logistics service providers without tight control on their operations across the value chain.
- Synchronization or lack of it, in the IT systems managing the different components of the supply chain network.
- Outsourcing of key operations to various agencies without verifying their inter dependence and compatibility.
- Other extraneous factors such as social and political scenarios, administrative procedures, weather, terrorism and acts of God.

SUMMARY

- A company's supply chain encompasses the coordination of materials, information and funds from the initial raw material supplier to the ultimate customer.
- Suppliers can be related to or independent from the manufacture. Suppliers can be related to or independent from the manufacturer. Suppliers can be domestic or foreign.
- Logistics, or materials management, is that part of the supply chain process that plans, implements, and controls the efficient, effective flow and storage of goods, services, and related information from the point of origin to the point of consumption in order to meet customers' requirements.
- Companies can manufacture products or enter into virtual manufacturing through subcontracting to other manufacturers.
- The success of global manufacturing strategy depends on compatibility, configuration, coordination and control.
- Cost-minimization strategies and the drive for global efficiencies often force MNEs offshore to low-cost manufacturing areas, especially in Asia and Eastern Europe.
- Three broad categories of manufacturing configuration are one centralized facility, regional facilities, and multi-domestic facilities.
- Layout planning involves decisions about the physical arrangement of economic activity within a manufacturing facility.
- Quality is defined as meeting or exceeding the expectations of customers.
- Total quality management is a process that stresses customer satisfaction, employee involvement, and continuous improvements in quality.
- Quality standards can be general (ISO 9000), industry specific, and company specific.
- Global sourcing is the process of a firm having raw materials and parts supplied to it from domestic and foreign sources.

- Under the make or buy decisions, companies have to decide if they will make their own parts or buy them from an independent company.
- Just-in-time focuses on reducing inefficiency and unproductive time in the production process to improve continuously the process and quality of the product or service.
- The transportation system links together suppliers with manufacturers and manufacturers with customers.
- Global operations include the performance of business activities and operations that introduce and promote the flow of a company's goods and services to customers in more than one nation for a profit.
- Managing a supply chain is a demanding activity that requires a thorough understanding of the concepts and mechanisms that underpin the operation of the supply chain and the factors that influence its performance.
- Foreign factories establish and manage their foreign plants to benefit only from tariff and trade concessions, cheap labor, capital subsidies, and reduced logistics costs. Therefore, they assign a limited range of work, responsibilities, and resources to those factories.

Chapter 14

International Conflicts

INTRODUCTION

Whenever two or more individuals have to reach an agreement over issues such as product specifications, information credibility, vendor capabilities, multiple sourcing, contract terms, order routines, the potential over conflicts arises in International business.

The potential for conflict emanates from differences in expectations regarding suppliers, differences in evaluative criteria employed, differences in buying objectives and differences in buying objectives and differences in decision-making styles of the individuals involved.

Whether conflict is good or bad depends upon the type of conflict that emerges and how it is resolved. A conflict that supports the goals of the organizations and improves the firm's performance rather than hinders it is good.

When conflict is resolved through cooperation and the search for a mutually beneficial solution joint decision making tends to be rational. However, when conflict is resolved thorough bargaining, joint decision making tends to be based on irrational criteria.

MANAGING CONFLICT

What is Conflict?

Conflict is a natural disagreement resulting from individuals or groups that differ in attitudes, beliefs, values or needs. It can also originate from past rivalries and personality differences. Other causes of conflict include trying to negotiate before the timing is right or before needed information is available.

The Ingredients of Conflict

Needs: Needs are things that are essential to our well-being. Conflicts arise when we ignore others' needs, our own needs or the group's needs. Be careful not to confuse needs with desires (things we would like, but are not essential).

Perceptions: People interpret reality differently. They perceive differences in the severity, causes and consequences of problems. Misperceptions or differing perceptions may come from: self-perceptions, others' perceptions, differing perceptions of situations and perceptions of threat.

Power: How people define and use power is an important influence on the number and types of conflicts that occur. This also influences how conflict is managed. Conflicts can arise when people try to make others change their actions or to gain an unfair advantage.

Values: Values are beliefs or principles we consider to be very important. Serious conflicts arise when people hold incompatible values or when values are not clear. Conflicts also arise when one party refuses to accept the fact that the other party holds something as a value rather than a preference.

Feelings and Emotions: Many people let their feelings and emotions become a major influence over how they deal with conflict. Conflicts can also occur because people ignore their own or others' feelings and emotions. Other conflicts occur when feelings and emotions differ over a particular issue.

Conflict is not always negative. In fact, it can be healthy when effectively managed. Healthy conflict can lead to:

1. Growth and innovation
2. New ways of thinking
3. Additional management options.

If the conflict is understood, it can be effectively managed by reaching a consensus that meets both the individual's and society's needs. This results in mutual benefits and strengthens the relationship. The goal is for all to "win" by having at least some of their needs met.

How Public and Private Conflicts Differ?

Most of us have experience with conflict management and negotiation in private disputes (with a salesman, among family members or with your employer).

Public conflicts, like those that can occur during watershed management efforts and other environmental issues often are rooted in trying to balance environmental protection and economic growth and jobs. Keep in mind, however, that effective watershed management can result in both economic and environmental benefits. Some complicating factors include:

Distribution of Costs and Benefits. Those who benefit may not be the same as those who pay the costs.

Perceptions of Problems. People tend to blame others for causing the problem.

Speed of Clean-up or Other Actions. Some will want changes to take place more quickly than others.

STEPS FOR MANAGING CONFLICT

There are five steps to managing conflict. These steps are:

- Analyze the conflict
- Determine management strategy
- Pre-negotiation
- Negotiation
- Post-negotiation

Step 1: Analyze the Conflict.

The first step in managing conflict is to analyze the nature and type of conflict. To do this, you'll find it helpful to ask qucstions.

Answers may come from your own experience, your partners or local media coverage. You may want to actually interview some of the groups involved. Additional information regarding analyzing conflicts can be found in the guide to Information and Resources.

Step 2: Determine Management Strategy.

Once you have a general understanding of the conflict, the groups involved will need to analyze and select the most appropriate strategy. In some cases it may be necessary to have a neutral facilitator to help move the groups toward consensus.

Conflict Resolution Actions

- Collaboration
- Compromise
- Competition
- Accommodation
- Avoidance

Collaboration: This results from a high concern for your group's own interests, matched with a high concern for the interests of other partners. The outcome is "win/win". This strategy is generally used when concerns for others are important. It is also generally the best strategy when society's interest is at stake. This approach helps build commitment and reduce bad feelings. The drawbacks are that it takes time and energy. In addition, some partners may take advantage of the others' trust and openness. Generally regarded as the best approach for managing conflict, the objective of collaboration is to reach consensus.

Compromise: This strategy results from a high concern for your group's own interests along with a moderate concern for the interests of other partners. The outcome is "win some/lose some." This strategy is generally used to achieve temporary solutions, to avoid destructive power struggles or when time pressures exist. One drawback is that partners can lose sight of important values and long-term objectives. This approach can also distract the partners from the merits of an issue and create a cynical climate.

Competition: This strategy results from a high concern for your group's own interests with less concern for others. The outcome is "win/lose". This strategy includes most attempts at bargaining. It is generally used when basic rights are at stake or to set a precedent. However, it can cause the conflict to escalate and losers may try to retaliate.

Accommodation: This results from a low concern for your group's own interests combined with a high concern for the interests of other partners. The outcome is "lose/win". This strategy is generally used when the issue is more important to others than to you. It is a "goodwill gesture". It is also appropriate when you recognize that you are wrong. The drawbacks are that your own ideas and concerns don't get attention. You may also lose credibility and future influence.

Avoidance: hese results from a low concern for your group's own interests coupled with a low concern for the interests of others. The outcome is "lose/lose". This strategy is generally used when the issue is trivial or other issues are more pressing. It is also used when confrontation has a high potential for damage or more information is needed. The drawbacks are that important decisions may be made by default.

Conflict Analysis Exercise

Think of a controversial issue to analyze. On a separate sheet of paper, answer these questions.

Groups Involved

- Who are the groups involved?
- Who do they represent?
- How are they organized?
- What is their power base?
- Are the groups capable of working together?
- What are the historical relationships among the groups?

Substance

- How did the conflict arise?
- How are the main and secondary issues described?
- Can negative issues be reframed positively?
- Are the issues negotiable?
- Have positions been taken and, if so, are there common interests?
- What information is available and what other information is needed?
- What values or interests are challenged?

Possible Strategies

- Would consensus serve all interests
- Are there external constraints or other influences that must be accommodated?
- What are the past experiences (if any) of the groups working together?
- What is the timeline for a decision?
- How will the public and the media be involved and informed?
- Will an outside negotiator be needed?

Step 3: Pre-negotiation.

To set the stage for effective negotiation, the groundwork must be laid. The following should occur prior to negotiation.

Initiation: One partner raises the possibility of negotiation and begins the process. If no one is willing to approach the others to encourage them to reach an agreement, a trusted outsider could be brought in as a facilitator.

Assessment: Conditions must be right for negotiation to be successful. Key players must be identified and invited. Each side must be willing to collaborate with the others. Reasonable deadlines and sufficient resources to support the effort must exist. Spokespersons for each group must be identified and involved. Parties need to determine which issues are negotiable and which are not.

Ground Rules and Agenda: The groups must agree on ground rules for communication, negotiation and decision making. They should agree on the objectives of the negotiation process. An agenda of issues to be covered needs to be developed.

Organization: Meeting logistics must be established, including agreed upon times and places. People must be contacted and encouraged to attend. Minutes must be taken so that information can be distributed before and after meetings.

Joint Fact-Finding: The groups must agree on what information is relevant to the conflict. This should include what is known and not known about social and technical issues. Agreement is also needed on methods for generating answers to questions.

Step 4: Negotiation.

Interests: When negotiating be sure to openly discuss interests, rather than stated positions. Interests include the reasons, needs, concerns and motivations underlying positions. Satisfaction of interests should be the common goal.

Options: To resolve conflicts, concentrate on inventing options for satisfying interests. Do not judge ideas or favor any of the options suggested. Encourage creativity, not commitment.

Evaluation: Only after the partners have finished listing options, should the options be discussed. Determine together which ideas are best for satisfying various interests.

Written Agreement: Document areas of agreement and disagreement to ensure common understanding. This helps ensure that agreements can be remembered and communicated clearly.

Commitment: Every partner must be confident that the others will carry out their parts of the agreement. Discuss and agree upon methods to ensure partners understand and honor their commitments.

When evaluating options...

- Use objective criteria for ranking ideas
- Make trade-offs among different issue
- Combine different options to form acceptable agreements

Step 5: Post-negotiation.

Once negotiation is complete, the group will need to implement the decisions made. Some key steps include:

Ratification: The partners must get support for the agreement from organizations that have a role to play in the agreement. These organizations should be partners and should have been involved in the previous steps. Each organization will need to follow its own procedures to review and adopt the agreement.

Implementation" You and your partners' jobs are not done when you've reached agreement. Communication and collaboration should continue as the agreement is carried out. The partnership will need to have a plan to monitor progress, document success, resolve problems, renegotiate terms and celebrate success.

Negotiation Skills

Negotiation is an important skill for coming to an agreement when conflicts develop at home, at work and when dealing with issues like those related to watershed management. When negotiating...

Separate People from the Problem

When negotiating, remember you're dealing with people who have their own unique needs, emotions and perceptions.

Some conflicts are based on differences in thinking and perceptions. These conflicts may exist mainly in peoples' minds. It helps for each party to put themselves into the other's shoes so they can understand each other's point of view.

Identify and openly discuss differences in perceptions, being careful not to place blame. In addition, recognize an.d understand the other side's emotions as well as your own.

Interest vs. Position

People often confuse interests with positions. An interest may be reducing litter in roadside ditches. There are many possible ways of addressing this interest. One might be the position of mandatory recycling. Another position might be a deposit on bottles and cans. Still another could be organizing a clean-up day.

Focus on Interests, Not Positions

Focusing on interests, rather than positions, makes it possible to come up with better agreements. Even when people stand on opposite positions, they usually have a few shared interests.

It takes time and effort to identify interests. Groups may not even be clear about their own interests. It helps to write down each group's interests as they are discovered. It helps to ask why others take the positions or make the decisions they do. Partners will have multiple interests. Interests involving important human needs (such as security, economic well-being, a sense of belonging, recognition and control over one's life) are difficult to negotiate.

Develop Optional Solutions

When developing optional solutions that meet the interests of all sides, try to meet as many of each side's interests as possible. Start by inviting all sides to brainstorm ideas (before reaching a decision).

Some obstacles to developing innovative options are:

- Judging and rejecting prematurely
- Searching for a single best answer
- Putting limits on scope or vision
- Considering only your own interests

To overcome these obstacles, view the situation through the eyes of different partners. Focus on shared interests to make the process smoother for all involved. Look for meaningful opportunities, not simple solutions.

Developing Objective Criteria

When developing criteria for selecting or combining possible alternatives, revisit the conflicting interests. These can't be ignored or "wished" away. Instead discuss them as you begin developing criteria for judging alternatives. Also keep in mind principles such as fairness, efficiency and scientific merit.

Strive for criteria that are legitimate, practical and unbiased. You may also find it helps to explore the criteria used in making past decisions and discuss criteria with your partners or outside experts

DEALING WITH CONFLICT

Conflict occurs when individuals or groups are not obtaining what they need or want and are seeking their own self-interest. Sometimes the individual is not aware of the need and unconsciously starts to act out. Other times, the individual is very aware of what he or she wants and actively works at achieving the goal.

About Conflict:

- Conflict is inevitable;
- Conflict develops because we are dealing with people's lives, jobs, children, pride, self-concept, ego and sense of mission or purpose;
- Early indicators of conflict can be recognized;
- There are strategies for resolution that are available and DO work;
- Although inevitable, conflict can be minimized, diverted and/or resolved.

Beginnings of Conflict:

- Poor communication
- Seeking power
- Dissatisfaction with management style
- Weak leadership
- Lack of openness
- Change in leadership.

Conflict Indicators:

- Body language
- Disagreements, regardless of issue
- Withholding bad news

- Surprises
- Strong public statements
- Airing disagreements through media
- Conflicts in value system
- Desire for power
- Increasing lack of respect
- Open disagreement
- Lack of candor on budget problems or other sensitive issues
- Lack of clear goals
- No discussion of progress, failure relative to goals, failure to evaluate the superintendent fairly, thoroughly or at all.

Conflict is Destructive when it:

- Takes attention away from other important activities
- Undermines morale or self-concept
- Polarizes people and groups, reducing cooperation
- Increases or sharpens difference
- Leads to irresponsible and harmful behavior, such as fighting, name-calling.

Conflict is Constructive when it:

- Results in clarification of important problems and issues
- Results in solutions to problems
- Involves people in resolving issues important to them
- Causes authentic communication
- Helps release emotion, anxiety and stress
- Builds cooperation among people through learning more about each other;
- Joining in resolving the conflict
- Helps individuals develop understanding and skills.

Techniques for Avoiding and/or Resolving (Board-Superintendent) Conflict:

- Meet conflict head on
- Set goals
- Plan for and communicate frequently
- Be honest about concerns
- Agree to disagree - understand healthy disagreement would build better decisions

- Get individual ego out of management style
- Let your team create - people will support what they help create
- Discuss differences in values openly
- Continually stress the importance of following policy
- Communicate honestly - avoid playing "gotcha" type games
- Provide more data and information than is needed
- Develop a sound management system.

Causes of Board-Superintendent Conflict:

How does a school board cause conflict with a superintendent?

- Trying to be administrators; overstepping authority
- Making promises as board members individually
- Involving themselves in labor relations or budgetary minutia
- Not doing their "homework" and failing to prepare for meetings
- Not following procedures for handling complaints
- Not keeping executive session information confidential
- Failing to act on sensitive issues
- Failing to be open and honest with the superintendent
- Making decisions based on preconceived notions
- Not supporting the superintendent - lack of loyalty
- Springing surprises at meetings
- Having hidden agendas.

How does a superintendent cause conflict with a school board?

- Not treating board members alike
- Not informing the board members of public concerns
- Not providing adequate financial data or adequate information
- Using poor public management practices
- Making public statements before informing the board
- Failing to be open and honest with the board
- Not providing alternatives in an objective manner
- Not adjusting to the new reality of an involved board
- Not support the board - lack of loyalty
- Springing surprises at meetings
- Having hidden agendas.

Elements of Strong Board-Superintendent Partnerships:

- Full disclosure
- Frequent two-way communication
- Careful planning
- Informal interaction
- Periodic evaluation
- Mutual support.

Courageous Decision Controversies:

The controversies usually involve:

- Changes in the way "we've always done things"
- Notions of fundamental values
- Determined, articulate advocates for every side
- Inability to compromise
- Rampant rumors
- Threats of retaliation at the polls at the next bond, levy or school
- Board election.

Resolving Conflict

Searching for the causes of conflict is essential to be successful in resolving the conflict. Nine possible causes of conflict include:

- Conflict with self
- Needs or wants are not being met
- Values are being tested
- Perceptions are being questioned
- Assumptions are being made
- Knowledge is minimal
- Expectations are too high/too low
- Personality, race, or gender differences are present

Reaching Consensus through Collaboration

Groups often collaborate closely in order to reach consensus or agreement. The ability to use collaboration requires the recognition of and respect for everyone's ideas, opinions, and suggestions. Consensus requires that each participant must agree on the point being discussed before it becomes a part of the decision. Not every point will meet with everyone's complete approval. Unanimity is not the goal. The goal is to have individuals accept a point of view based on logic. When individuals can understand and accept the logic of a differing point of view, you must assume you have reached consensus.

Follow these guidelines for reaching consensus:

- Avoid arguing over individual ranking or position. Present a position as logically as possible.
- Avoid "win-lose" statements. Discard the notion that someone must win.
- Avoid changing of minds only in order to avoid conflict and to achieve harmony.
- Avoid majority voting, averaging, bargaining, or coin flipping. These do not lead to consensus. Treat differences of opinion as indicative of incomplete sharing of relevant information, keep asking questions.

  Keep the attitude that holding different views is both natural and healthy to a group.
- View initial agreement as suspect. Explore the reasons underlying apparent agreement and make sure that members have willingly agreed.

International Agencies to Resolve Conflicts:

1. The Inter-American Commercial Arbitration Commission
2. The Canadian-American Commercial Arbitration Commission for Disputes between Canadian and US businesses
3. The London Court of Arbitration
4. The American Arbitration Association
5. The International Chamber of Commerce
6. The Commercial Dispute Resolution Centre.

SUMMARY

- Conflict is a natural disagreement resulting from individuals or groups that differ in attitudes, beliefs, values or needs. It can also originate from past rivalries and personality differences.
- The various steps to analyze the conflict are: (1) Analyze the conflict (2) Determine management strategy (3) Pre-negotiation (4) Negotiation (5) Post-negotiation.
- The various conflict resolution strategies are: (1) Collaboration (2) Compromise (3) Competition (4) Accommodation (5) Avoidance.
- The conflict indicators which we know between the two parties are: (1) Body Language (2) Disagreements regardless of issue (3) Surprises (4) Strong public statements (5) Conflicts in value system (6) Increasing lack of respect.
- Consensus requires that each participant must agree on the point being discussed before it becomes a part of the decision. Not every point will meet with everyone's complete approval. Unanimity is not the goal.
- When individuals can understand and accept the logic of a differing point of view, you must assume you have reached consensus.

Chapter 15

Human Resource Development Across Cultures

TRAINING IN INTERNATIONAL MANAGEMENT

Training is the process of altering employee behavior and attitudes in a way that increases the probability of goal attainment. This training process is particularly important in preparing employees for overseas assignments because it helps ensure that their full potential will be tapped. One of the things that training can do is to help expat managers, better understand the customs, cultures, and work habits of the local people and thus avoid blunders.

The simplest training, in terms of preparation time, is to place a cultural integrator in each foreign operation. This individual is responsible for ensuring that the operation's business systems are in accord with those of the local culture. The integrator advises, guides and recommends actions needed to ensure this synchronization.

Unfortunately, although using an integrator can help, it is seldom sufficient. Recent experience clearly reveals that in creating an effective global team, the MNE must assemble individuals who collectively understand the local language, have grown up in diverse cultures or neighborhoods, have open, flexible minds, and who will be able to deal with high degrees of stress.

MNEs need a well-designed training program that is administered before the individuals leave for their overseas assignment and then evaluated later to determine its overall effectiveness. Some of these findings included the following:

- Of organizations with cultural programs, 58 per cent offer training only to some expatriates, while 42 per cent offer it to all of them.
- Ninety-one per cent offer cultural orientation programs to spouses, and 75 per cent offer them to dependent children.
- The average duration of the cultural training programs is 3 days.

- Cultural training is continued after arrival in the assignment location 32 per cent of time.
- Thirty per cent offer formal cultural training programs.
- Of those without formal cultural programs, 37 per cent plan to add such training.

The most common topics covered in cultural training include:

1. Social etiquette
2. Customs
3. Economics
4. History
5. Politics
6. Business etiquette

This is because countries tend to have distinctive human resource management (HRM) practices that differentiate them from other countries. For examples, the HRM practices that are prevalent in the United States are quite different from those in France and Argentina. This has been clearly illustrated by Sparrow and Budhwar, who compared data from 13 different countries on the basis of HRM factors. Five of these factors included the following:

- Structural empowerment that is characterized by flat organization designs, wide spans of control, the use of flexible cross-functional teams, and the rewarding of individuals for productivity gains.
- Accelerated resource development that is characterized by the early identification of high potential employees, the establishment of both multiple and parallel career paths, the rewarding of personnel for enhancing their skills and knowledge and the offering of continuous training and development education.
- Employee welfare emphasis that is characterized by firms offering personal family assistance, encouraging and rewarding external volunteer activities and promoting cultures that emphasize equality in the workplace.
- An efficiency emphasis in which employees are encouraged to monitor their own work and to continually improve their performance.

The Impact of Overall Management Philosophy on Training

The type of training that is required of expatriates is influenced by the firm's overall philosophy of international management. Briefly, four basic philosophic positions of multinational environment (MNEs) can influence the training program:

1. An **ethnocentric MNE** puts home-office people in charge of key international management positions. The MNE headquarters group and the affiliated world company managers all have the same basic experiences, attitudes, and beliefs about how to manage operations. Many Japanese firms follow this practice.
2. A **polycentric MNE** places local nationals in key positions and allows these managers to appoint and develop their own people. MNE headquarters gives the subsidiary managers authority to manage their operations just as long as these operations are sufficiently profitable. Some MNEs use this approach in East Asia, Australia, and other markets that are deemed too expensive to staff with expatriates.
3. A **regiocentric MNE** relies on local managers from a particular geographic region to handle operations in and around that area. For example, production facilities in France would be used to produce goods for all EU countries. Similarly, advertising managers from subsidiaries in Italy, Germany, France and Spain would come together and formulate a "European" advertising campaign for the company's products.
4. A **geocentric MNE** seeks to integrate diverse regions of the world through a global approach to decision making. Assignments are made based on qualifications and all subsidiary managers throughout the structure are regarded as equal to those at headquarters.

The Impact of Different Learning Styles on Training and Development

Another important area of consideration for development is learning styles. **Learning** is the acquisition of skills, knowledge, and abilities that results in a relatively permanent change in behavior. Over the last decade a growing number of multinationals have tried to become a "learning organizations" which is typified by a continual focus on activities such as training and development.

Of course, the way in which training takes place can be extremely important. A great deal of research has been conducted on the various types and theories of learning. However, the application of these ideas in an international context often can be quite challenging because cultural differences can affect the learning and teaching.

One study investigated learning styles by giving a learning style questionnaire to British Middle managers, Indian mid-career managers, and East African mid-career managers. Two dimensions of learning styles were measured: **analysis and action.**

The analysis dimension measures the extent to which the learner adopts a theory building and test approach as opposed to using an intuitive approach.

The action dimension measures the extent to which the learner uses a trial-and-error approach as opposed to employing a contemplative or reflective approach. The researchers found important differences in learning style between the three cultures. Indian managers were much higher on analysis than the other two groups. British managers were much higher on action. East African managers were the lowest on both analysis and action scores.

In addition to these conclusions, those responsible for training programs must remember that even if learning does occur, the new behaviors will not be used if they are not reinforced. For example, if the head of a foreign subsidiary is highly ethnocentric and believes that things should be done the way they are in the home country, new managers with intercultural training likely will find little reward or reinforcement for using their ideas.

Reasons for Training

Training programs are useful in preparing people for overseas assignments for many reasons. These reasons can be put into two general categories: organizational and personal.

Organizational Reasons: Organizational reasons for training relate the enterprise at large and its efforts to manage overseas operations more effectively. One primary reason is to help **ethnocentrism**, the belief that one's way of doing things is superior to that of others. Ethnocentrism is common in many large MNEs where managers believe that the home office's approach to doing business can be exported intact to all other countries, because this approach is superior to anything at the local level. Training can help home-office managers to understand the values and customs of other countries so that when they are transferred overseas, they have a better understanding of how to interact with local personnel.

Another organizational reason for training is to improve the flow of communication between the home office and the international subsidiaries and branches. Quite often, overseas managers find that they are not adequately informed regarding what is expected of them while the home office place close controls on their operating authority. This is particularly true when the overseas manager is from the host country. Effective communication can help to minimize these problems.

Finally, another organizational reason for training is to increase overall efficiency and profitability. Research shows organizations that closely tie their training and human resource management strategy to their business strategy tend to outperform those that do not. One of the ways in which almost all of these organizations did this was by giving their managers global assignments that not only filled technical and managerial needs but also provided developmental experiences for the personnel – and this assignment strategy included managers from every geographic region where the firms were doing business.

Personal Reasons: Although there is overall organizational justification, the primary reason for training overseas managers is to improve their ability to interact effectively with local people in general and their personnel in particular. One early study that surveyed 75 countries in England, Holland, Belgium, and Germany found that some of the biggest complaints about managers by their personnel revolved around personal shortcomings in areas such as politeness, punctuality, tactfulness, orderliness, sensitivity, reliability, tolerance and empathy. As a result, an increasing number of training programs now address social topics such as how to take a client to dinner, effectively apologize to a customer, appropriately address one's overseas colleagues, communicate formally and politely with others, and learn how to help others "save face".

A particularly big personal problem that managers have in an overseas assignment is arrogance. This is the so-called Ugly American problem the US expatriates have been known to have. Many expatriate managers find that their power and prestige are much greater than they were in their job in the home country. This often results in improper behavior, especially among managers at the upper and lower positions of overseas subsidiaries. This arrogance takes a number of different forms, including rudeness to personnel and inaccessibility to clients.

Another common problem is expatriate managers overruling of decisions, often seen at lower levels of the hierarchy. When a decision is made by a superior who is from the host country and the expatriate does not agree with it, the expatriate may appeal to higher authority in the subsidiary. Host-country managers obviously resent this behavior, because it implies that they are incompetent and can be second-guessed by expatriate subordinates.

In addition to helping deal with these types of personal problems, training can be useful in improving overall management style. Research shows that many host-country nationals would like to see changes in some of the styles of expatriate managers, including their leadership, decision-making, communication and group work.

Types of Training Programs

There are many different types of multinational management training programs. Some last only a few hours; others last for months. Some are fairly superficial; others are extensive in coverage. There are certain key considerations that influence development of these programs. Training programs consists of nine phases to follow:

1. In the first phase the overall objective of the program to increase the effectiveness of expats and/or repatriated executives is emphasized.
2. The second phase focuses on recognition of the problems that must be dealt with in order to reach the overall objectives.
3. The third phase is the identification of the developmental objectives.
4. The fourth phase consists of determining the amount of development that will be needed regarding each of these objectives.
5. The fifth phase entails choosing the specific methods to be used in the development process from types or pre-departure training to language instruction to re-entry training.
6. The sixth phase is an intermediate evaluation of how well things are going and the institution of any needed mid-stream corrections.
7. The seventh phase is an evaluation of how well the expat managers are doing, thus providing evaluation feedback of the developmental process.
8. The eighth phase is of the effectiveness of the executives after they have returned.
9. The ninth, and final, phase is an evaluation type of planning model.

By carefully laying out this type of planning model, MNEs ensure that their development training programs are both realistic and productive. In this process they often rely on both standardized and tailor-made training and development approaches.

Standardized vs. Tailor-made

Some management training is standard or generic. For example, participants often are taught how to use specific decision-making tools, such as quantitative analysis, and regardless of where the managers are sent in the world, the application is the same. These tools do not have to be culturally specific. Research also shows that small firms usually rely on standard training programs. Larger MNEs, on the other hand, tend to design their own. Some of the larger MNEs are increasingly turning to specially designed video and power point programs for their training and development needs.

Tailor-made training programs are created for the specific needs of the participants. Inputs for these offerings usually is obtained from managers who currently are working in the country to which the participants will be sent as well as from local managers and personnel who are citizens of that country. These programs often are designed to provide a new set of skills for a new culture. For example, MNEs are now learning that is managing in China, there is a need to provide directive leadership training because many local managers rely heavily on rules, procedures, and orders from their superiors to guide their behaviors. So training programs must explain how to effectively use this approach.

One of the most common types of training in both standard and tailor-made packages is that of self-evaluation. Participants in such training are provided personal insights about their behaviors. For example, managers will be given tests to determine if their managerial style is basically factual, intuitive, analytical or normative.

A **factual manager** looks at the available information and makes decision based on the data. An **intuitive manager** is imaginative, innovative, and can jump from one idea to another. A **normative manager** is idealistic and concerned with how things should be done. An **analytical manager** is systematic, logical, and carefully weighs alternatives to problems. Every manager will be some combination of all four types, but by learning their individual preferences, participants gain insights into their own approach to dealing with people.

Table 15.1: Cultural Characteristics of Managerial Styles and Activities

Activity	Factual Style	Intuitive Style	Analytical Style	Normative Style
Planning	Focus on the present, on the here-and-now. The manager clarifies the existing situ-ation, what is	Focus on the future. The manager sets up objectives	Relate past, present, and future. The manager works on strategies and tactics.	Focus on the past. The manager reviews and assesses what has been done to direct new action.
Performance Appraisal	Deal with skills. (Register the facts)	Concentrate on potential. (Look for possibilities)	Assess performance according to several factors.	Insist on the performance appraisal process, the relationship, the sharing of perceptions.
Decision-making	Decision are based on facts and on thorough investigations; they are always well documented	Decision are related to hunches, imagination, guesses	Decisions are the result of a systematic options, alternatives	Decisions are closely linked to the value systems, which exist in the team, organization.
Coaching	Each individual has to find his or her own way. The manager can only facilitate the process by clarifying the facts.	The manager motivates the employee in describing a "could be" situation appealing to him or her.	Coaching is systematically organized, in a kind of step-by-step approach.	The basic assumption that underlines the evaluative approach toward coaching is that weaknesses and strengths should be fairly evaluated and taken care of.

Table 15.1 shows how these managerial styles will influence the way that an individual plans, appraises performance, makes decisions, and coaches. For example, a factual manager will focus on how things are done here-and-now, while an intuitive manager will focus more on the future. Similarly, an analytical manager will integrate consideration of the past, present, and future into his or her planning activities, while a normative manager will focus heavily on reviewing what has happened in the past and use this to determine new directions. Simply put, different managers use different styles in doing their jobs.

Table 15.2 illustrates this in more depth showing how each of the management styles will differ based on the cultural background of the trainees. A close look at the table, for example, shows that a factual management style applied in European cultures would need to emphasize theoretical as opposed to factual information, while in North America a much more pragmatic approach would be required if the training were to be effective.

Similarly, when using an intuitive management style, North American trainees to look for ideas which can be applied, while in African cultures perceptions are often given much greater importance than basic facts, and in South American cultures the intuitive style often results in a great deal of excitement and emotion regarding how the information can be used – in sharp contrast to the more subdued approach used by North Americans. Additionally, when an analytical style is used in European cultures, the focus is often on getting things done through a hierarchical, bureaucratic design, while North Americans tend to process analytical information in terms of how it can be used in a decentralized, empowered structure.

Table 15.2: Management Styles Applied to Three Cultures

Management Style	European Cultures	North American Cultures	Asian Cultures
Factual	Meanings are in individuals Theoretic as opposed to practical Inconsistent	Individuals rely on the spoken words Professional experience are perceived as important	Meanings are everywhere; in people, things. No clear-cut separation between the internal and external worlds
Intuitive	Like to play with ideas Creative and imaginative	Look for ideas which can be used Enjoy learning	Highly spiritual A good sense of unity is shared by many people
Analytical	Deductive Rigid organizational structures	Inductive Flexible organizational structure	Accept ambiguity Open to many options
Normative	Overcritical Quality of life is highly valued	Getting the job done is the priority	Simplicity and humility are highly valued.

Finally, a normative approach will also have to be modified to meet the needs of the participant's culture. Europeans place a great deal of attention on quality of work life and are often on getting things done and achieving self-esteem for their professional accomplishments.

A close evaluation of the material in **Table 15.2** shows that the training approaches that are successful in one geographic region of the world may need to be heavily modified if they are to be as effective elsewhere. This finding has been echoed by Sergeant and Frenkel who recently conducted interviews with expatriate managers with extensive experience in China.

In the final analysis, the specific training program to be used will depend on the needs of the individual. Tung, after surveying managers in Europe, Japan and United States, has found that there are six major types of cross-cultural training programs:

- Environmental briefings used to provide information about things such as geography, climate, housing and schools.
- Cultural orientation designed to familiarize the individual with cultural institutions and value systems of the host country.
- Cultural assimilators using programmed learning approaches designed to provide the participants with intercultural encounters.
- Language training.
- Sensitivity training designed to develop attitudinal flexibility.
- Field experience, which sends the participant to the country of assignment to undergo some of the emotional stress of living and working with people from a different culture.

In addition to training expats and their families, effective MNEs also are developing carefully crafted programs for training personnel from other cultures who are coming into their culture. These programs, among other things, have materials that are specially designed for the target audience. Some of the specific steps that well-designed cultural training programs follow include:

1. Local instructors and a translate, typically someone who is bicultural, observe the pilot training program and/or examine written training materials.
2. The educational designer then debriefs the observation with the translator, curriculum writer, and local instructors.
3. Together, the group examines the structure and sequence, icebreaker, and other materials that will be used in the training.
4. The group then collectively identifies stories, metaphors, experiences, and examples in the culture that will fit into the new training program.
5. The educational designer and curriculum writer make the necessary changes in the training materials.

6. The local instructor is trained to use the newly developed materials.
7. After the designer, translator, and native-language trainers are satisfied the materials are printed.

Cultural Assimilators

The cultural assimilator has become one of the most effective approaches to cross-cultural training. A **cultural assimilator** is a programmed learning technique that is designed to expose members of one culture to some of the basic concepts, attitudes, role perceptions, customs and values of another. These assimilators are developed for each pair of cultures, customs and values of another.

In most cases, these assimilators require the trainee to read a short episode of a cultural encounter and choose an interpretation of what has happened and why. If the trainee's choice is correct, he or she goes on to the next episode. If the response is incorrect, the trainee is asked to re-read the episode and choose another response.

Choice of Content of the Assimilators: One of the major problems in constructing an effective cultural assimilator is deciding what is important enough to include. Some assimilators use critical incidents that are identified as being important. To be classified as a critical incident, a situation must meet at least one of the following conditions:

1. An expatriate and a host national interact in the situation.
2. The situation is puzzling or likely to be misinterpreted by the expatriate.
3. The situation can be interpreted accurately if sufficient knowledge about the culture is available.
4. The situation is relevant to the expatriate's task or mission requirements.

Validation of the Assimilator: The term validity refers to the quality of being effective, of producing the desired results. It means that an instrument – in this case, the cultural assimilator – measures what it is intended to measure. After the cultural assimilator critical incidents are constructed and the alternative responses are written, the process is validated. Making sure that the assimilator is valid is the crux of its effectiveness.

A second validation step is to ask the sample group to rate how important each episode is. This helps to identify those incidents that should be included and those that are of only marginal value and can be omitted.

After the final incidents are chosen, they are sequenced in the assimilator booklet and today can be put on-line to be taken electronically. Similar cultural concepts are placed together are presented, beginning with simple situations and progressing to more complex ones.

The Cost-Benefit Analysis of Assimilators: The assimilar approach to training can be quite expensive. A typical 75–100-incident program often requires approximately 800 hours to develop. Assuming that a training specialist is costing the company $50 an hour including benefits, the cost is around $40,000 per assimilator. This cost can be spread over many trainees, however, and the program may not need to be changed every year. An MNE that sends 40 people a year to a foreign country for which an assimilator has been constructed is paying only $200 per person for this programmed training. In the long run, the costs often are more than justified. In addition, the concept can be applied to virtually all cultures. Many different assimilators have been constructed.

SUMMARY

- Training is the process of altering employee behavior and attitudes to increase the probability of goal attainment. Many expatriates need training before their overseas stay. A number of factors will influence a company's approach to training. One is the basic type of MNE: ethnocentric, polycentric, regiocentric, or geocentric. Another factor is the learning style of the trainees.
- There are two primary reasons for training: organizational and personal. Organizational reasons include overcoming ethnocentrism, improving communication, and validating the effectiveness of training programs.
- Personal reasons include improving the ability of expatriates to interact locally and increasing the effectiveness of leadership styles. There are to types of training programs: standard and tailor-made. Research shows that small firms usually rely on standard programs and larger MNEs tailor their training. The six major types of training include environmental briefings, cultural orientation, cultural assimilators, language training, sensitivity training and field experience.
- A cultural assimilator is a programmed learning approach that is designed to expose members of one culture to some of the basic concepts, attitudes, role perceptions, customs and values of another. Assimilators have been developed for many different cultures. Their validity has resulted in the improved effectiveness and satisfaction of those being trained as compared with other training methods.

Chapter 16

Multinational Finance Function

INTRODUCTION

Why do you need to understand capital markets, cash management and financial risk? Having a good product idea is not sufficient for success. MNEs need to get access to capital markets in different in order to finance expansion. Indeed, finance is integral to firms' international strategies. The small company involved only tangentially in international business may be concerned primarily about the foreign exchange function of its commercial bank and not global capital market. It may use the bank to buy and sell foreign exchange and hedge foreign-exchange risk, but it probably doesn't think about borrowing money or issuing stock on foreign capital markets.

This chapter examines external sources of funds available to companies operating abroad and internal sources of funds that arise from inter-company links. It also examines global cash management, risk-management strategies, and international dimensions of the capital investment decision.

THE FINANCE AND TREASURY FUNCTIONS IN THE INTERNATIONALIZATION PROCESS

One of the most important people on the management team, crucial to a company's success, is the vice-president of finance, also known as the chief financial officer (CFO). The functions of the CFO are often divided into the controllership and treasury functions. This chapter focuses on the CFO's most important global treasury responsibilities. The Vice-President of finance, also known as the Chief Financial Officer (CFO), reports directly to the President and Chief Operating Officer of the company, who reports to the Chairman and Chief Executive Officer, who reports to the Board of Directors.

The Finance function in the firm focuses on cash flows. The management activities related to the cash flows can be divided into four major areas:

- Capital Structure: determining the proper mix of debt and equity.
- Capital Budgeting: analyzing investment opportunities.
- Long-term Financing: selection, issuance, and management of long-term debt and equity capital, including location (in the company's home country or elsewhere) and currency (the company's home currency or a foreign currency).
- Working Capital Management: proper management of the company's currency assets and liabilities (cash, receivables, marketable securities, inventory, trade receivables, short-term bank debt).

The CFO's job is more complex in a global environment than in the domestic setting because of forces such as foreign-exchange risk, currency flows and restrictions, different tax rates and laws pertaining to the determination of taxable income, and regulations on access to capital in different markets.

GLOBAL DEBT MARKETS

The CFO must determine the degree to which a firm funds the growth of the business by debt, which is known as leverage. The degree to which companies use leverage instead of equity capital – known as stocks or shares – varies from country to country. Country-specific factors are a more important determinant of a company's capital structure than is any other factor because companies tend to follow the financing trends in their own country and their particular industry within their country. Leveraging is often perceived as the most cost-effective route to capitalization, because the interest companies pay on debt is a tax-deductible expense, while the dividends paid to investors are not.

However, leveraging may not be the best approach in all countries for two major reasons. First, excessive reliance on long-term debt increases financial risk and so requires a higher return for investors. Second, foreign subsidiaries of an MNE may have limited access to local capital markets, making it difficult for the MNE to rely on debt to fund asset acquisition.

In addition, different tax rates, dividend remission policies, and exchange controls may cause a company to rely more on debt in some situations and more on equity in others. It is important to understand that the different debt and equity markets discussed in this chapter have different levels of importance for companies worldwide.

An MNE that needs to raise capital through debt markets has a number of options. The local domestic debt market is the first source that a company will tap. This means Japan for Japanese companies, but it could also mean Japan for the Japanese subsidiary of a US company. Toyota lists several types of long-term debt in its annual report. It issued 200 Yen billion (about $1.6 billion) bonds maturing at two different times, but it also issued US dollar bonds as well. So, companies can tap international banks for local currency borrowings or Eurodollar borrowings, as well as the longer-term bond markets.

Sometimes, the subsidiaries of foreign companies can obtain credit easier than local companies can because of their access to hard currency. They can enter into **back-to-back loans** during periods when interest rates are high or credit is frozen. A back-to-back loan is one made between a company in country A with a subsidiary in country B and a bank in country B with a branch in country A.

EUROCURRENCIES

The Eurocurrency market is an important source of debt financing for the MNEs to compliment what they can find in their domestic market. A **Eurocurrency** is any currency that is banked outside of its country of origin. Currencies banked inside of their country of origin are also known as onshore, and currencies banked outside of the country of origin are also known as offshore.

The Eurocurrency market started with the deposit of US dollars in London banks, and it was called the Eurodollar market. As other currencies entered the offshore market, the broader *eurocurrency* name is used for the market. Given the introduction of the euro as the new currency in Europe, the term Eurocurrency is confusing, but the Eurocurrency market predates in euro, and the confusion will probably not go away. Eurocurrencies could be dollars or yen in London, euro in the Bahamas, or British pounds in New York.

The major sources of Eurocurrencies are:

- Foreign governments or individuals who want to hold dollars outside of the United States.
- Multinational corporations that have cash in excess of current needs.
- European banks with foreign currency in excess of current needs.
- Countries such as Germany, Japan, and Taiwan that have large balance-of-trade surpluses held as reserves.

The Eurocurrency market is both short and medium-term. Short-term borrowing has maturities of less than one year. Anything over one year is considered as **Eurocredit**, which may be loan, line of credit, or other form of medium and long-term credit, including **syndication**, in which several bank pool resources to extend credit to a borrower.

Eurocurrency deposits tend to yield more than domestic deposits do, and loans tend to be cheaper than they are in domestic markets. Traditionally, loans are made at a certain percentage above the **London Inter-Bank Offered Rate (LIBOR),** which is the deposit rate that applies to inter-bank loans within London.

INTERNATIONAL BONDS: FOREIGN, EURO AND GLOBAL

Many countries have active bond markets available to domestic and foreign investors. Japan is one such country. The earlier long-term debt example of Toyota involves bonds issued in Japan. One bond issue for 50 Yen billion matures (must be paid back) in 2018 at an interest rate of 3 per cent, and another bond issue for 150 Yen billion matures in 2008 at an interest rate of 2 per cent. Even though the domestic bond market dominates total bond issues, with the US market offering the best opportunities, the international bond market still fills an important niche in financing.

The international bond market can be divided into foreign bonds, Eurobonds and global bonds. **Foreign bonds** are sold outside of the borrower's country but are denominated in the currency and country of issue. For example, a French company floating a bond issue in Swiss francs in Switzerland would be selling a foreign bond. Foreign bonds typically make up about 18 per cent of the international bond market.

A **Eurobond** is usually underwritten by a syndicate of banks from different countries and sold in countries other than the one in whose currency the bond is denominated. A bond issue floated by a US company in dollars in London, Luxembourg, and Switzerland is a Eurobond. Eurobonds make up approximately 75 per cent of the international bond market.

The **global bond**, introduced by the World Bank in 1989, is a combination of a domestic bond and a Eurobond in that it must be registered in each national market according to that market's registration requirements. It also is issued simultaneously in several markets, usually those in Asia, Europe and North America. Global bonds are a small but growing segment of the international bond market.

EQUITY SECURITIES AND THE EUROEQUITY MARKET

Another source of financing is equity securities, where an investor takes an ownership position in return for shares of stock in the company and the promises of capital gains – an appreciation in the value of the stock – and may be dividends. One way a company can get access to capital is through a private placement with a venture capitalist. In this case, a wealthy venture capitalist will invest money in a new venture in exchange for stock.

In addition, to private placements, companies can access the equity capital market, more commonly known as the stock market. Companies can raise new capital by listing their stocks on a stock exchange, and they can list on their home country exchange or on a foreign exchange. The growth in globalization has forced companies to look at equity markets as an alternative to debt markets and banks as a source of funds.

Another significant event in the past decade is the creation of the **Euroequity market**, the market for shares sold outside the boundaries of the issuing company's home country. Prior to 1980, few companies thought of offering stock outside the national boundaries of their headquarters country. Since then, hundreds of companies worldwide have issued stock simultaneously in two or more countries in order to attract more capital from a wider variety of shareholders.

In some cases, companies list on only one foreign exchange. It is expensive to list on foreign exchanges and so companies often list on one big one, such as the New York Stock Exchange or the London Stock Exchange. However, some companies list on different exchanges, especially if they have foreign investments in several countries and are trying to raise capital in those countries.

The New York Stock Exchange identifies four major reasons why a foreign company should list on the NYSE (and these reasons could apply to US companies trying to determine the benefits of listing on a foreign exchange):

- NYSE provides opportunities to develop a broad shareholder constituency in the United States through exposure to the widest possible range of individual and institutional investors.
- NYSE facilitates US mergers and acquisitions through the use of an NYSE listed security as acquisition currency.
- NYSE increases the visibility of a company, its products and services, and the trading of its shares in the United States.
- NYSE supports a company's incentive program for its US employees by providing a liquid market in the United States for its shares.

The most popular way for a Euroequity to get a listing in the US is to issue an **American Depository Receipt (ADR)**. ADRs are traded like share of stock with each one representing some number of shares of the underlying stock. The US is not the only market for Euroequities. There are also Global Depositary Receipts and European Depository Receipts, but the US market dominates the DR market. However, a much larger percentage of the total shares traded on the London Stock Exchange belong to foreign companies than is true for the NYSE, even though the total trading volume in the United States is quite large.

OFFSHORE FINANCIAL CENTERS

Offshore financial centers are cities or countries that engage in a variety of financial transactions and that provide significant tax advantages to companies and individuals who do business there. Usually, the financial transactions are conducted in currencies other than the currency of the country and are thus the centers for the Eurocurrency market. Generally, the markets in these centers are regulated differently, and usually more flexibly, than domestic markets. Offshore financial centers have one or more of the following characteristics.

- Large foreign-currency (Eurocurrency) market for deposits and loans (that in London, for example).
- Market that is a large net supplier of funds to the world financial markets (that in Switzerland, for example).
- Market that is an intermediary or pass-through for international loan funds (those in the Bahamas and the Cayman Islands, for example).
- Economic and political stability.
- Efficient and experienced financial services.
- Official regulatory climate favorable to the financial industry, in the sense that it protects investors without unduly restricting financial institutions.

These centers are either operational centers, with extensive banking activities involving short-term financial transactions, or booking centers, where little actual banking activity take pace but where transactions are recorded to take advantage or secrecy and low tax rates.

Offshore financial centers are good locations for establishing finance subsidiaries that can raise capital for the parent company or its other subsidiaries. They allow the finance subsidiaries to take advantage of lower borrowing costs and tax rates.

INTERNAL SOURCES OF FUNDS

Although the term funds usually means "cash", it is used in a much broader sense in business and generally refers to working capital; that is, the difference between current assets and current liabilities. A company that wants to expand operations or needs additional capital can look not only to the debt and equity markets but also to sources within itself. For an MNE, the complexity of internal sources is magnified because of the number of its subsidiaries and the diverse environments in which they operate.

Funds also can go from subsidiary to parent. The subsidiary could declare a dividend to the parent as a return on capital or could loan cash directly to the parent. If the subsidiary declared a dividend to the parent, the parent could lend the funds back to the subsidiary. The dividend would not be tax deductible to the subsidiary, but it would be included as income to the parent, and the parent would have pay tax on the dividend. If the subsidiary loaned money to the parent, the interest paid by the parent would be tax deductible to the parent and would be taxable income to the subsidiary.

Inter-company financial links become extremely important as MNEs increase in size and complexity. Goods as well as loans can travel between subsidiaries, giving rise to receivables and payables. Companies can move money between and among related entities by paying quickly (leading payments) or can accumulate funds by deferring payment (lagging payments). They also can adjust the size of the payment by arbitrarily raising or lowering the price of inter-company transactions in comparison with the market price, a transfer pricing strategy.

Multilateral Netting

An important cash-management strategy is netting cash flows internationally. Netting means a company establishes one center to handle all internal cash, and financial transactions. For example, an MNE with operations in four European countries could have several different inter-company cash transfers resulting from loans, the sale of goods, licensing agreements and the like.

Table 16.1: Net Positions of Subsidiaries in Four Countries

Subsidiary	Total Receivables	Total Payables	Net Position
French	250,000	350,000	(100,000)
German	250,000	100,000	150,000
Italian	150,000	300,000	(150,000)
UK	300,000	200,000	100,000

Table 16.1 identifies the total receivables, payables and net position for each subsidiary. Rather than have each subsidiary settle its accounts independently with subsidiaries in other countries, many MNEs are establishing cash-management centers in one city to coordinate cash flows among subsidiaries from several countries.

Figure 16.1 illustrates that can subsidiary in a net payable position (where its payments out exceed its receivables in) transfers funds to the central clearing account. The clearing account's manager then transfers funds to the accounts of the net receiver subsidiaries. In this example only four transfers funds to the accounts of the net receiver subsidiaries. The clearing account manager receives transactions information and computes the net position of each subsidiary at least monthly. Then the manager orchestrates the settlement process. The transfers take place in the payer's currency and the foreign-exchange conversion takes place centrally.

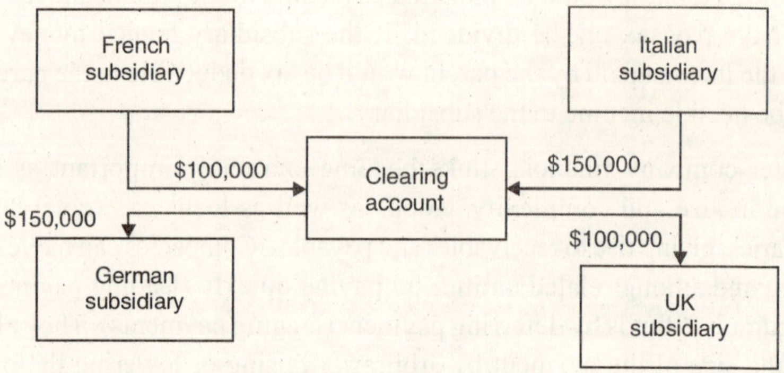

Fig. 16.1: Multilateral Netting

The advantages of establishing their clearing accounts and mechanisms for transferring funds across national boundaries include:

- Optimizing the use of excess cash.
- Reducing interest expenses and maximizing interest yields.
- Reducing costly foreign exchange, swap transactions, and inter-company transfers.
- Minimizing administrative paperwork.
- Centralizing and speeding information for tighter control and improved decision making.

The multilateral netting process has several advantages over having each foreign operation of an MNE handle payments independently:

1. Savings in foreign-exchange conversion costs, because the central manager can affect large exchanges.
2. Savings of transfer charges and commissions, again due to the large size and smaller number of transactions.
3. Quicker access to the funds.

Even though there are significant benefits to netting activities, not every MNE uses netting techniques. One reason is that for netting to work, companies need to establish custom software that not only does the netting at a central location where the MNE nets cash flows but also allows subsidiaries to link to the netting center to upload receivables and payables data automatically. Netting also becomes more economically feasible the more subsidiaries and currencies involved.

Exposure Management Strategy

To protect assets adequately against risks from translation, transaction, and economic exposure of exchange-rate fluctuations, management must:

- Define and measure exposure.
- Organize and implement a reporting system that monitors exposure and exchange rate movements.
- Adopt a policy assigning responsibility for minimizing – or hedging – exposure.
- Formulate strategies for hedging exposure.

Defining and Measuring Exposure: Most MNEs will see all three types of exposure: translation, transaction and economic. To develop a viable hedging strategy, an MNE must forecast the degree of exposure differ, the actual exposure in each major currency in which it operates. Because the types differ, the actual exposure by currency must be kept track of separately.

A key aspect of measuring exposure is forecasting exchange rates. Estimating exchange rates is similar to fortune telling: Approaches range from gut feelings to sophisticated economic models, each having varying degrees of success. Some companies develop in-house capabilities to monitor exchange rate, using economists who also try to obtain a consensus of exchange-rate movements from the banks with whom they deal. Their concern is to forecast the direction, magnitude, and timing of an exchange-rate change. Other companies contract out this work.

A Reporting System: Once the company has decided how to define and measure exposure and estimate future exchange rates, it must create a reporting system that will assist in protecting it against risk. To achieve this, substantial participation from foreign operations must be combined with effective central control. Central control of exposure protects resources more efficiently than letting each subsidiary and branch manage its own exposure. Each organizational unit may be able to define its own exposure, but the company also has an overall exposure.

Management of an MNE should devise a uniform reporting system for all of its subsidiaries. The report should identify the exposed accounts the company wants to monitor, the amount of exposure by currency of each account, and the different time periods under consideration. The time periods on the report depend on the company. Companies can identify their exposure position for different periods into the future, such as thirty, sixty and ninety days; six, nine, and twelve months; or two, three and four years. The reason for the longer time frame is that operating commitments, such as plant construction and production runs, are fairly long-term.

A Centralized Policy: It is important for management to decide at what level hedging strategies will be determined and implemented. Several hedging strategies will be discussed in the next section. To achieve maximum effectiveness in hedging, top management should determine hedging policy. However, the company may have to decentralize some exposure management decisions so it can react quickly to a more rapidly changing international monetary environment. However, such decentralization should stay within a well-defined policy established at the corporate level. Some companies run their hedging operations more as profit centers and nurture in-house trading desks.

Formulating Hedging Strategies: Once a company has identified its level of exposure and determined which exposure is critical, it can hedge its position by adopting numerous strategies, each with cost-benefit implication as well as operational implications. The safest position is a balanced position in which exposed assets equal exposed liabilities.

Operational strategies involve adjusting the flow of money and resources in normal operations in order to reduce foreign-exchange risk. First, management must determine the working capital needs of a subsidiary. Then it needs to adjust the flow of receivables, payables and inventory. Although it may be wise to collect receivables as fast as possible in a country in which the local currency is expected to depreciate, the company must consider the competitive implications of doing so.

Another operational strategy leads and lags, protects cash flows among related entities, such as a parent and subsidiaries. A **lead strategy** means collecting foreign currency receivables before they are due when the foreign currency is expected to weaken or paying foreign-currency payables before they are due when the foreign currency is expected to strengthen. With a **lag strategy**, a company delays collection of foreign-currency receivables if that currency is expected to strengthen or delays payables when the currency is expected to weaken. In other words, a company usually leads into and lags out of a hard currency and leads out of and lags into a weak currency.

THE CAPITAL BUDGETING DECISION IN AN INTERNATIONAL CONTEXT

The last international dimension of the treasury function that we will discuss in the chapter is the capital budgeting decision whereby the MNE needs to determine which projects and countries will receive its capital investment funds. The parent company must compare the net present value or internal rate of return of a potential foreign project with that of its other projects and that of others available in the host country to determine the best place to invest its resources. The technique used to compare different projects is capital budgeting. Several aspects of capital budgeting are unique to foreign project assessment.

1. Parent cash flows must be distinguished from project cash flows. Parent cash flows refer to cash flows from the project back to the parent in the parent's currency.
2. Remittance of funds to the parent, such as dividends, interest on loans, and payment of intra-company receivables and payables, is affected by differing tax systems, legal and political constraints on the movement of funds, local business norms, and differences in how financial markets and institutions function.
3. The parent must consider the possibility of unanticipated exchange-rate changes because of their direct effects on the value of cash flows, as well as their indirect effects on the foreign subsidiary's competitive position.

SUMMARY

- The corporate finance function deals with the acquisition of financial resources and their allocation among the company's present and potential activities and projects.
- CFOs need to be concerned with the international dimensions of the company's capital structure, capital budgeting decision, long-term financing, and working capital management.
- Two major sources of funds external to the MNEs normal operations are debt markets and equity markets.
- A Eurocurrency is any currency banked outside of its country of origin, but primarily dollars banked outside the United States.
- The major sources of internal funds for an MNE are dividends, royalties, management fees, loans from parent to subsidiaries and *vice versa*, purchases and sales of inventory, and equity flows from parent to subsidiaries.
- Companies can enter into operational or financial strategies for hedging exposures. Operational strategies include balancing exposed assets, with exposed liabilities, using leads and lags in cash flows, and balancing revenues in one currency with expenses in the same currency. Financial strategies involve using forward contracts, options, or other financial instruments to hedge an exposed position.

Chapter 17

Multinational Corporations

THE CONCEPT

Multinational corporations are business entities that operate in more than one country. The typical multinational corporation or MNC normally functions with a headquarters that is based in one country, while other facilities are based in locations in other countries. In some circles, a multinational corporation is referred to as a multinational enterprise (MBE) or a transnational corporation (TNC).

Multinational corporation (or **transnational corporation**) (MNC/TNC) is a corporation or enterprise that manages production establishments or delivers services in at least two countries. Very large multinationals have budgets that exceed those of many countries. Multinational corporations can have a powerful influence in international relations and local economies. Multinational corporations play an important role in globalization; some argue that a new form of MNC is evolving in response to globalization: the 'globally integrated enterprise'.

A multinational corporation (MNC) is a business organization which has its headquarters in one country but has operations in a range of different countries. There are numerous examples of such organizations, car manufacturers like Ford, Toyota, Honda and Volkswagen, oil companies like Shell, BP and Exxon Mobil, technology companies like Dell, Microsoft, Hewlett Packard and Canon and food and drink companies such as Coca Cola, Inter-brew and McDonalds.

These firms, by their very nature, are large organizations. Their size means they often have considerable power and influence and as a result have come in for some criticism of their actions. One of the most famous of such cases was the problem faced by Nestlé in marketing its baby milk in Africa. Critics pointed out that Nestlé was pushing the product on people when it was likely to cause harm to babies.

Multinational companies usually provide a broader base of markets in which to sell their goods/services. This makes them somewhat more resilient in national depressions. However, it is also far more challenging to understand different cultures and their buying patterns without substantial market research. Likewise, many countries tend to be at least somewhat protectionist about their domestic companies and try to give them slight advantages via subsidies or tariffs. This means it is often risky and expensive to break into foreign markets. There are far more answers, but these are a few of the major ones.

A multinational corporation (MNC) is a corporation or enterprise that manages production establishments or delivers services in at least two countries. Very large multinationals have budgets that exceed those of many countries. Multinational corporations have powerful influence in international relations and local economies. Multinational corporations plays an important role in globalisation leading to the evolution of "globally integrated enterprise" overcoming the barriers raised by state control or regulation.

Why the Drive to MNCs?

For many companies, the following might be some or all of the reasons to expand into different countries:

- Reduce transport and distribution costs.
- Avoid trade barriers.
- Meet different rules and regulations (avoid non-tariff barriers).
- Secure supplies of raw materials or markets.
- Cost advantages—for example low labor costs.

ROLE OF MULTINATIONAL CORPORATIONS

Multinational corporations stand at the heart of the debate over the merits of global economic integration. Their critics portray them as bullies, using their heft to exploit workers and natural resources with no regard for the economic well being of a country or community. Their advocate see multinationals as triumph for global capitalism, bringing advanced technology to poorer countries and low cost products to the wealthier ones.

Both of these stereotypes have some truth to them. But it would be wrong to portray the multinational corporation as either good or evil. Companies become multinational in many different ways and for many different reasons. Their impact on the global economy is far from simple to determine.

There is no doubting that multinationals matter. They are one of the main conducts through which globalization takes place. In 1995, the last year for which the United Nations has figures, multinationals cranked out some $7 trillion in sales through their foreign affiliates an amount greater than the world's total export. In addition, the UN's 1997 world investment report estimates that 70% of all international royalties on technology involve payments between parent firm and their foreign affiliates, showing that multinationals play a key role in disseminating technology around the globe. There is no denying the fact that multinationals are the main force behind world-wide flows of capital, goods and services.

MULTINATIONAL CORPORATE STRUCTURE

Multinational corporations can be divided into three broad groups according to the configuration of their production facilities:

- **Horizontally integrated multinational corporations** manage production establishments located in different countries to produce the same or similar products. (example: McDonalds)
- **Vertically integrated multinational corporations** manage production establishment in certain country/countries to produce products that serve as input to its production establishments in other country/countries. (example: Adidas)
- **Diversified multinational corporations** manage production establishments located in different countries that are neither horizontally or vertically integrated. (example: Microsoft)

CLASSIFICATION OF MULTINATIONAL CORPORATIONS DEPENDING ON ORIGIN

- **Ethnocentric Approach:** In ethnocentric approach, the home country practice prevails. The head office from the home country makes major key decisions. Also employees from the home country hold important positions, and the subsidiaries have to follow the home country practice.
- **Poly-centric Approach:** In the poly-centric approach, each of the subsidiaries manages on the local basis. Also local employees will head the subsidiaries because the assumption is that the head office employees are not considered to have adequate local knowledge. In this case, local subsidiaries mainly develop their own human resource management practices locally.
- **Geo-centric or Global:** In this approach, the organization that applies the global integrated business strategy, basically manages and staffs the organization on a global basis. It recruits and develops a group of global managers from diverse countries, who then, will be able to manage

business at any place. Such global employees are used in a variety of facilities as the need arises. A geocentric or global approach develops practices for worldwide use.

MODELS OF MULTINATIONAL CORPORATIONS

The exact model for an MNC may vary slightly. One common model is for the multinational corporation is the positioning of the executive headquarters in one nation, while production facilities are located in one or more other countries. This model often allows the company to take advantage of benefits of incorporating in a given locality, while also being able to produce goods and services in areas where the cost of production is lower.

Another structural model for a multinational organization or MNO is to base the parent company in one nation and operate subsidiaries in other countries around the world. With this model, just about all the functions of the parent are based in the country of origin. The subsidiaries more or less function independently, outside of a few basic ties to the parent.

A third approach to the setup of an MNC involves the establishment of a headquarters in one country that oversees a diverse conglomeration that stretches to many different countries and industries. With this model, the MNC includes affiliates, subsidiaries and possibly even some facilities that report directly to the headquarters.

REASONS AND GROWTH OF MULTINATIONAL CORPORATIONS

In the public mind, globalization and Multinational Corporation are closely related. Several reasons have been cited for the prominence of MNC's at the end of the 20th century.

- The most common explanation for multinational growth is economies of scale. In certain industries, the argument goes firms can become more efficient by becoming bigger and producing more. What better way to accomplish this than by serving a global market?
- Another explanation for the growth of multinationals is vertical integration. In some industries, the interdependence of suppliers and uses of a particular resource makes it difficult for such firms to operate at arms length, since there is always the risk that one will try to undermine the other. This is the reason many firms integrate vertically, buying up their suppliers or their customers. Sometimes those suppliers or customers will be abroad, turning the acquiring firms into a multinational.
- A third reason for the spread of multinationals is that they tend to be successful. In many businesses, inefficient firms will eventually fold,

giving way to those that can earn higher profits. As the world economy becomes more integrated, it is to be expected that the companies most adept at crossing borders are those that prosper. It should come as no surprise that firms from richer countries do this best. As a rule, they have been exposed to more competition in their home markets and are therefore well equipped for international competitive battles.

- There is yet one other reason for firms to operate as multinationals: because everyone else is doing it. Many companies exist to serve other companies, rather than household consumers. If multinational car manufacturer wants to use the same headlights in cars assembled in different countries, then head light manufacturers must become multinational, too. This is why consulting firms and accountabilities have been falling over one another to build seamless global networks.

CRITICISMS OF MULTINATIONAL CORPORATION

For one thing, multinationals size and scale can make it possible for them to exert power in an exploitative way. A Company whose facilities are located in a single country has no alternative but to comply with that country's laws and social norms, unless it wishes to import products made by others rather than making them itself. A multinational however can move production: if India's worker safety law or trade unions are too restrictive, the company can move its factory to Sri Lanka. It can also lower its tax bill by using internal pricing to shift profits from high tax countries to low tax ones.

This flexibility may make it harder for governments to raise revenue, protect the environment and promote the worker safety. Critics fear an undesirable "**race to the bottom**", with governments reducing desirable social protections to attract investments by multinationals.

Others point out that the race can be healthy in so far as it forces government to be careful before imposing costly regulations and taxes. Certainly, many developing countries are eager to be "exploited" by as many multinationals as possible.

Another important criticism is that multinationals are exporting jobs to low wage countries. This may be true in some industries, such as textiles and electronics. But in most cases it is exaggerated. Labour costs now make up only 5–10% of production costs in OECD countries.

Although the social impacts are often misstated, some multinational expansions are indeed unequivocally bad, with no offsetting benefits. Whenever they get an opportunity they tend to expand through a merger or a direct foray into a new market. In some cases they represent a wasteful use of shareholder's capital.

ADVANTAGES OF MNC

- Multinational companies are able to sell far more than other type of company.
- Multinational companies can avoid transport costs.
- Multinationals can take advantage of different wage levels in different countries (as in some countries only women and children work, so they wages can be low).
- Multinationals can achieve great economies of scale.
- Multinationals have less chance of going bankrupt than small companies.
- Multinationals can carry out a lot of research and development.

Economic Growth and Employment

The essence of a MNC is that they bring inward investment to countries that are not their home base. If they choose to expand by building production facilities they will be bringing in inward investment into the country. This investment is likely to provide a boost, not only to the local economy but also the national economy.

It can also be expected that the additional income will find its way through the local economy. If additional people are hired, they will receive an income which they spend. For existing workers, increased orders might equate to job security and they too might feel more confident in spending on new items—furniture, house extension, new white goods, holidays and so on. Inward investment therefore can act as a trigger to generating wealth in the local economy. If a MNC is attracted to an area then this might also lead to other smaller firms in the supply chain deciding to locate in those areas. Other firms providing services to these firms are then attracted to the area and so on.

For less developed countries, inward investment can again act as a catalyst for other forms of investment. The effects of the investment might be less dramatic but nevertheless, it can be something that is seen as essential for helping a country escape from poverty.

Skills, Production Techniques and Improvements in the Quality of Human Capital

It can be argued that MNCs bring with them new ideas and new techniques that can help to improve the quality of production and help boost the quality of human capital in the host country. Many will not only look to employ local labour but also provide them with training and new skills to help them improve productivity and efficiency.

In Sunderland, one of Europe's most productive car manufacturing plants, the workers have had to get used to different ways of working and different expectations than many might have been used to if working for other British firms. In some cases this can prove a challenge but in others it can lead to improvements in motivation and productivity. The skills that workers build up can then be passed on to other workers and this improves the supply of skilled labour in the area. This makes the area even more attractive to new industry as it helps to reduce the costs of training and skilling of workers.

Availability of Quality Goods and Services in the Host Country

In some cases, production in a host country may be primarily aimed at the export market. However, in other cases, the inward investment might have been made to gain access to the host country market to circumvent trade barriers. In the case of many Japanese car manufacturers the investment made into UK production has enabled them to get a foothold in the EU and to avoid tariff barriers. The UK has had access to high quality vehicles at cheaper prices and the competition this has created has also led to improvements in working practices, prices and quality in other related industries.

Tax Revenues

For the host country, there is a likelihood that the MNC will have to be subject to the tax regime in that country. As a result, many MNCs pay large sums in taxes to the host government. In less developed countries the problem might be that there is a large amount of corruption and bad governance and as a result MNCs might not contribute the tax revenue they could and even if they do it might not find its way through to the government itself.

Improvements in Infrastructure

In addition to the investment in a country in production or distribution facilities, a company might also invest in additional infrastructure facilities like road, rail, port and communications facilities. This can provide benefits for the whole country.

The Costs of Multinationals

The costs can be summarized in the points below-for the most part, the costs are closely linked to the benefits but it will depend on the extent of the benefits that might arise as a result of the activity of the MNC.

- Employment might not be as extensive as hoped - many jobs might go to skilled workers from other countries rather than to domestic workers.
- There might be a limit in the effect on the local economy - it will depend on how big the investment into the local economy actually is.

- Some MNCs may be 'footloose'; this means that they might locate in a country to gain the tax or grant advantages but then move away when these run out. As a result there might not be a long-term benefit to the country.
- How many new jobs are created depends on the type of investment. Investment into capital intensive production facilities might not bring as many jobs to an area as hoped.
- The size and power of multinationals can be used, it is argued, to exploit weak or corrupt governments to get better deals for the MNC. Mittal, for example, a major steel producer, negotiated a $900 million deal to secure rights to mine iron ore in Liberia. The government that negotiated the deal was not elected. When a new, elected government came to power, they re-negotiated the deal and took the investment to well over $1 billion.
- Pollution and environmental damage. Some countries may have less rigorous regulatory authorities that monitor the environmental impact of MNC activities. This can cause long-term problems. In India, Coca-Cola has been accused of using up water supplies in its bottling plant in Kerala in Southern India and also of dumping waste products onto land and claiming it was useful as fertilizer when it appeared to have no such beneficial properties.
- De-merit goods. Some companies might be producing goods that are not beneficial. Examples might include tobacco products and baby milk - mentioned earlier.
- Repatriation of profits. Profits might go back to the headquarters of the MNC rather than staying in the host country - the benefits, therefore, might not be as great.

DISADVANTAGES OF MNC

- Firstly, multinational companies can severely impact the local industries because it increases the competition in the economy.
- Secondly, multinational companies can negatively impact the culture of the economy.
- Thirdly, because of the trade restrictions the multinational companies can face various problems.
- The availability of resources are limited in an economy and when multinational companies are opened then resources can get scarce.
- Moreover, though a company can grow because of investments brought by multinational companies but still the economies can grow more if the local investors make these investments.

On the Home Country

- Loss of jobs.
- Loss of tax revenue.
- Flexibility of operation is reduced in a foreign political system and thus causes instability.
- Competitive advantage of multinationals over domestic firms.

On the Host Country

- Remittance of dividends and profits that can result in a net outflow of capital.
- MNCs engage in anti-competitive activities such as formation of cartels and dumping.
- MNCs offer higher wages to its employees in the host countries,which is much more than any other domestic firm.
- Obsolete technology may be used in the host country.

INDIA'S CONTRIBUTION TO MULTINATIONAL CORPORATIONS

- In recent years, India have become two of the most important markets in terms of sales, low-cost manufacturing and R&D operations. The future progress will increase the competitive advantage for both countries and attract MNC's from all over the world to invest.
- Nevertheless, success is not guaranteed, even with the large business opportunities that India provide. A MNC has to be aware of various challenges that both countries pose, such as government interventions, underdeveloped infrastructures or copyright violations.
- MNC's need efficient strategies in order to compete and improve their position in these markets. Particularly the implementation of an efficient innovation and knowledge strategy has become a crucial aspect.
- Effectiveness in local product adjustments, globalizing R&D, tailoring talent management, mastering the complexity of global value chains, and managing risks are success factors that have to be considered.
- Multiple failures of MNC's in India demonstrate that it is important to adapt a company's strategy to the local customer needs and to obtain a competitive advantage in the field of innovation.
- In the last 10 to 20 years the term emerging market has become very important in the international business context because India grew heavily and created new, enormous market segments. Companies from all over the world are seeking to do business in economically developing countries because of their great potential.

- Gross domestic product (GDP) per capita figures exceeding 10 per cent a year, a business environment of over five billion people (approximately 80 per cent of the global population), a growing domestic customer group of wealthy people, excellently educated workers and opportunities for low-cost production are changing emerging markets as South Korea, Mexico or India on a daily basis.
- Global companies like Coca-Cola, IKEA, Microsoft or Procter & Gamble have already realized the enormous potential and have expanded their business greatly into these markets.
- For example, HP benefited from the target segment in the Indian computer industry that nearly doubled each year since 1996 (from a market value of $3.34 billion in 1996 to over $35 billion in 2006).
- Already today, the 10 largest emerging markets have a GDP of more than $14 trillion (which is as big as the economy of the United States) and cannot be ignored by multinational corporations (MNC's) due to their huge business opportunities.
- Third-quarter earnings releases by UK telecom giant Vodafone Group and by Switzerland-based Holcim, the world's second-largest cement maker, reflected growing contributions from India's increasingly assertive domestic market on the earnings statements of global corporations.
- India have the highest residential figures which account for approximately 37 per cent of the world's population. In both countries roughly 700 million people will be living in the mid-income segment by 2010, which is more than the population of the United States (US), Europe and Japan combined.
- In fact, this segment is growing everyday. This means that a large number of people to sell new products/services to is emerging.
- India will become an increasingly important strategic choice for MNC's.
- However, especially an efficient innovation strategy is essential for MNC's because domestic customers are more demanding and enterprises need to adapt their products towards the local needs to gain regional market share.
- An increasing number of global companies are already highly successful by shifting their competences to India.
- Emerging market leaders like Unilever or Colgate-Palmolive already earn 5 per cent to 15 per cent of their global revenues from India, mainly because they successfully implemented an efficient strategy focusing on innovation.

ROLE OF INFORMATION TECHNOLOGY IN INTERNATIONAL BUSINESS

Computerization has changed the way business is conducted the world over. No aspect of business has remained untouched by the information technology (IT) revolution. This is especially true of international business where people located in different parts of the world conduct transactions with each other. The activities of international business include manufacturing, in-land transportation, customs and excise matters, port operation, shipping, clearing and forwarding, etc.

During the course of these transactions, a large number of documents are created and exchanged, many of these documents or the information contained therein is repeated, while creating and mailing these documents before the advent of IT, hundreds of man-hours would be lost in repetitive operation, innovations in IT have revolutionized international business; the use of technology in managing and processing information. Especially in large organizations helps save time, bring down costs, and reduce manpower, manual data input and transfer has now become not only obsolete, but also irrational.

Information technology has made a tremendous development in respect of our approach at a mass level. It opens the door of several avenues as well as has brought in several threats, which should be analyzed carefully. Due to development in technology, the information can be transferred from one place to another in very short span of time, earlier which required lot of time.

Transfer of large information and storing capacity for a long period also has some draw backs, inherent in the process itself. For example manipulation of message is very easy and it requires small level of technical literacy. It is also observed that master in a subject may not be many times able to express his views effectively as compared to a person having less knowledge of subject but more computer literacy, who can make better presentations. Here the knowledge part of the core subject has been compromised with proficiency with technology.

In international business today, IT finds maximum utility in the following areas:

- Electronic procurement
- Electronic marketing
- Electronic logistics.

A modern competitive enterprise seeks to hold an edge over the market. IT helps provide this competitive advantage through its various applications tools. By adapting these tools in various areas of business, the organization can gain many advantages in terms of accessibility to a customer or supplier in any part of the world, speed of operations, reduction in man power, etc. due to the reach of the Internet it is possible to conduct buying and selling transactions irrespective of geographical location.

Internet banking helps in the speedy execution of payments and settlement of accounts. A website can be a virtual showroom, where products can be displayed, demonstrated, and sold. Such a website can also provide various after sales service tips and suggestions, launch discussions forums, ask for customer feedback, and educate the customer. IT application such as electronic data interchange (EDI) has also enabled logistics operations to be paperless.

ROLE OF EXPATRIATES IN GLOBAL ENVIRONMENT

As organizations become globalize, there is an increasing challenge to use expatriates on international assignments to complete strategically critical tasks. Multinational Enterprises (MNEs) use expatriates, not only for corporate control and expertise reasons in vital global markets, but also to facilitate entry into new markets or to develop international management competencies.

While it is recognized that Human Resource Management (HRM) problems are more complex in the international environment, there is also increased evidence to suggest that the management of international human resources is increasingly being acknowledged as a major determinant of success or failure in international business. For renowned and established MNEs, failure to be able to communicate and coordinate their activities in international business has the potential to plunge them into a crisis. The crises confronting MNEs include failed assignments due to premature return of expatriates and the loss of their returned expatriates due to poor repatriation.

Hence, to avoid a crisis in expatriate management is threefold. The first challenge for international human resource is planning effectively for the selection of expatriates for overseas assignments. The second, return of expatriates has to be attended and the subsequent job assignment for returned expatriate in their home country is a priority for managerial attention. Essentially, the primary crisis management roles of international human resource (IHR) professionals are those of record custodian, crisis management team member, communicator, and contributing writer to the emergency plan (Williamson 1991). This multifaceted role of IHR includes providing professional counseling to help employees and their families to deal with the psychological problems associated with a hostage or an evacuation situation, to concentrate on the well-being of their workforce, but they also addressed compensation and benefits issues, reassignment issues, legal issues, health, safety and security issues.

Many organizations now find it essential to operate on a global level to maintain a competitive advantage. About 80 per cent of mid-size and large companies have employees working abroad, and 45 per cent anticipate increasing their expatriate workforce in the future. Roughly 10 to 20 per cent of people sent on expatriate assignments return early, and about a third of those who remain do not perform up to their supervisor's expectations while in these assignments, both of which are extremely costly for the organization.

It has been proposed that one reason for the high rate of expatriate failure is utilization of poor selection methods. Despite concerns about the use of poor selection methods for expatriate assignments, no thorough assessment of actual practices and decision-making of HR professionals for selecting expatriates has been undertaken.

The intent of this chapter was to fill this gap by determining how expatriates' characteristics, including gender, domestic performance/technical competence, extra-version, stress tolerance, and international experience, are incorporated in selection decisions.

Managing Expatriate Crises

International crises experienced by MNCs include premature return of their expatriates due to failed assignments and poor retention of their returned expatriates due to failed repatriation. Researchers have analyzed the causes of failure in overseas assignments and have introduced Human Resource (HR) practices that would help organizations to select, develop, and retain competent expatriates. Consequently, multinational corporations are striving to improve their capability in managing human resources internationally.

Important Features of these Initiatives Include

- The nature and length of the planning for the selection and training of expatriates for overseas assignments,
- The return of expatriate, and
- The subsequent assigned work for these repatriates in the home country.

EXPATRIATE SUCCESS

Prior to developing valid and effective selection methods, expatriate success must be clearly defined. Expatriate success has at least three aspects: **adjustment, performance and turnover.**

- Many researchers try to predict adjustment of the expatriate to the new culture, to new work responsibilities, or to interacting with people from the host country.
- Other researchers attempt to predict turnover or turnover intentions, because if expatriates leave their assignment early it is expensive for employers.

- Still others use ratings of expatriate job performance as a criterion of expatriate success.

Each of these criteria is likely to be of importance to the overall success of the expatriate and suggests the inherent relationship among the three elements of expatriate success. If employees are unable to adjust to their new surroundings, they may be unable to perform their job activities proficiently, or they might terminate the assignment early.

For example, an expatriate who does not adjust to interacting with host nationals may not be able to obtain the information needed to perform effectively or to adjust to daily liie in the new culture. As another example, an expatriate who fails to adjust to living and working in the new culture is more likely to perform ineffectively, experience stress or negative emotions, and desire an early return to the home country.

USE OF LOCALS (VS) EXPATRIATES

It becomes quite clear that (in light of cost-cutting strategies) the managers of today's internationalized companies are increasing their efforts to find new ways of minimizing the costs of their global expansions by questioning the costs of their expatriates in terms of adjustments of expatriate compensation packages and increased use of younger and more globalized employees.

Managers should determine the advantages of both types of employees (expatriates or locals) with regard to the general strategic goals, costs and productivity of their companies. Different strategic objectives of a company will typical dictate when to send expatriates and when to localize the business, so it is therefore crucial to determine whether expatriates can meet these objectives most effectively or whether local nationals can accomplish them as well.

If the manager looks at the value of each of the above four reasons for sending someone from the home office, then the business case should become more clear because of the fact that if the assignment fits into all of these four common reasons, then the price of an expatriate might be worth paying. We recognize, however, that even if the above reasons speak for expatriation, there surely are abundant difficulties as well, when choosing to expatriate. From the expense of moving an individual or family overseas to dual-career concerns to the down-time that it takes for expatriates to adjust to culture and life abroad, expatriates can be "high maintenance" and present a raft of complications in administration.

On the other hand, if a company already has a strong global mindset, it will most likely be able to find talent anywhere around the world and assign them based on expertise - and not on geography - and then the company should consider using local talents as soon as possible, as local staff brings its own set of benefits:

- Understanding the local business environment and how to transact business most effectively;
- Knowing the local culture and the nuances that are important in that country;
- Grasping the marketplace from an insider's perspective and being more in-tune with the quickly changing market;
- Providing insight into local marketing, sales and product development. However, using local staff also has its challenges - from availability of talent to training so they understand the corporate culture of the home office.

Though, choosing locals are not without costs as practical evidence shows that when managers discuss staffing overseas, they often see local employees as cheaper, as they do not actually stop to consider the real costs of bringing a local on-board (as these costs can be considerably higher than the cost of a expatriate employee because of a wide range of regulations regarding overtime, mandatory time off, and severance benefits).

Further, some local laws (i.e. Germany) require a thirteenth month pay, and there can be enormous issues surrounding retirement and social security, so a company's labor costs can therefore skyrocket depending upon the location that the company chooses.

EXPATRIATE SELECTION

- Traditionally, most selection of expatriates appears to be done solely on the basis of successful records of job performance in the home country.
- Although technical and managerial competence, as reflected in domestic performance records, are important to the success of expatriates, arguably, the cross-cultural aspects of the environment require other competencies for success.
- Further, because most employees considered for international assignments are already a rather homogeneous group in terms of professional competence, other characteristics are likely to play a role in predicting success.

Certain selection characteristics or traits have been identified as predictors of expatriate success. These include technical ability, managerial skills, cultural empathy, adaptability, diplomacy, language ability, positive attitude, emotional stability, maturity and adaptability of family.

One of the earliest reports was provided by Tung (1987), who examined expatriate selection practices across 80 U.S. MNEs, and subsequently, identified four general categories which may contribute to expatriate success. These are broadly described as:

- Technical competence on the job,
- Personality traits or relational abilities,
- Environmental variables, and
- Family situation.

This is further supported by Ronen's (1989) model that incorporates the dimensions of expatriate success identified by Tung (1981). Ronen (1989), describes five categories of attributes of success:

- Job factors,
- Relational dimensions,
- Motivational state,
- Family situation, and
- Language skills.

The five categories and their specific aspects are outlined in **Table 17.1**.

Table 17.1: Categories of Attributes of Expatriate Success

Job Factors	Relational Dimensions	Motivational State	Family Situation	Language Skills
Technical skills	Tolerance for ambiguity	Belief in the mission	Willingness of spouse to live abroad	Host country language
Familiarity with host country and HQ operations	Behavioral flexibility	Congruence with career path	Adaptive and supportive spouse	Non-verbal communi-cation
Managerial skills	Non-judgementalism	Interest in overseas experience	Stable marriage	
Administrative competance	Cultural empathy and low ethnocentrism	Interest in specific host country culture		
	Interpersonal skills	Willingness to acquire new patterns of behavior and attitudes		

Ronen (1989) identified these five selection attributes (Table 17.1) as contributing to greater expatriate success in international assignments as compared to the customary selection of expatriates based solely on technical abilities.

EXPATRIATE TRAINING AND DEVELOPMENT

Once an employee has been selected, pre-departure training becomes the next critical step in attempting to ensure the expatriates effectiveness and success abroad. Career counselling for the spouse is becoming necessary because the dual career dilemma is becoming more important, especially with the increase of women in the workforce. Part of this training is cultural awareness, a well designed cultural training program can be extremely helpful as it seeks to foster an appreciation of the host countries culture so the expatriates behave accordingly.

Examples include:

- Peter Dowling goes on to cite an example of the Middle East, in this region emphasis is placed on personal relationships, trust and respect; couple this with an emphasis on religion that permeates every aspect of life.
- Another example of a Middle Eastern cultural difference, it is considered impolite in the Middle East to show the bottom of your shoe or foot therefore, crossing ones legs in the Middle East is impolite as your host or guest would see the bottom of your shoe or foot.
- We have all heard of the "ugly American," who when told a price in local currency has responded by asking "how much is that in real money". Needless to say, the local currency IS real money.
- Another example is, the French have a beautiful language and would prefer to use their national language particularly in France.

If an expatriate is assigned to France, French language lessons would probably make him or her more successful. These language lessons should also be provided to the expatriates family, at no cost to the expatriate.

Another useful tool in expatriate pre-departure training is a preliminary visit to the assigned country. These visits often allow the expatriate and his family to become familiar with the environment in which they will be living. The preliminary visit should be sufficiently long so that people may assess the suitability of the environment.

Given the difficulties of re-entry, expatriates and their families need help to readjust back into their home country. The two most important issues are:

- career planning and
- 'reverse culture shock'.

To assist the expatriate and family to re-adapt to work and life in general and to help overcome reverse culture shock, re-entry training such as counseling workshops and career development consultations prove useful in the adjustment process.

Cross-cultural adjustment has been defined as "the degree of psychological comfort with various aspects of a host country". For expatriates unfamiliar with the customs, cultures and work habits of the local people, pre-departure training may be critical to their effectiveness and success in their overseas assignments. It is also important to include the family in these training programs. Extensive studies indicate that training is beneficial in reducing expatriates' perceived need to adjust.

Mendenhall et al. (1987) distinguish between three types of training, namely:

- Information giving approaches, which have a relatively low level of rigour;
- Affective approaches which address people's feelings as well as 'facts'; and
- Immersion approaches which are in-depth methods covering a broad range of topics and methods. These training programs are designed to improve relational skills which are crucial to effective performance in expatriate job assignments.

Training is described as the process of altering employee behavior and attitudes to increase the probability of goal attainment. The provision of a more comprehensive (high rigour) cross culture training will increase the social support that the expatriate and family need (i.e., in country support). This intensive training can provide the encouragement and motivation to seek the social network and activities that will make the new stressors more bearable. For the expatriate, training can reduce many of the uncertainties associated with the new role.

THE RETURN OF EXPATRIATES

One of the hidden costs linked with expatriation is the inability to retain the expatriate upon return to the home country. The preparedness phase of crisis management has relevance for better preparing expatriates for homecoming. Repatriation programs that assist in the development of organizational policy and job definition for repatriates combined with financial and career counseling and family orientation are initiatives that can be implemented as part of the overall process of career development and international human resource management.

Failure to address repatriation problems may lead to disillusionment and high turnover. Therefore, the challenge for organizations is to view repatriation as reverse expatriation, posing many of the same problems and warranting many of the same solutions.

Repatriation Agreement

Successful assignments begin with repatriation planning at the time of expatriation. At the onset of an overseas assignment a repatriation agreement should be determined between the employee and the employer in order to develop a repatriation process to help manage the employee's goals and expectations. The elements of a repatriation agreement are very likely to include provision of a specified period of the assignment and a return incentive payment.

On return, the expatriate should have an assurance of a job that is mutually acceptable (i.e., one equal to or better than the one held before leaving), and a provision of re-entry training combined with a repatriation program to support the repatriate and help the family readjust back into their home country.

Relocation benefits such as arranging pre-repatriation home country 'house hunting', school registration and the shipment of personal goods, would further reduce the problems associated with a return home.

Repatriation Programs

The effectiveness of a repatriation program rests on its ability to address the following questions: "Will I get a good job when I return? Will my career be enhanced and will my newly acquired skills and perspective be valued and well utilized in the home organization?"

Repatriation programs which are likely to be based on knowledge acquired from the responsiveness phase of an organizational crisis, consist of activities that provide a comparable position or a promotion from the job held before repatriation and assistance for the employee and family in assimilating back into their home culture, these programs are crucial in demonstrating supportiveness to the returnees.

These repatriation strategies are likely to improve repatriation success rates by emphasizing the commitment of the organization to its expatriate staff and may encourage expatriates to feel that their best interests were a priority, leading to enhanced expatriate commitment to the parent firm. In addition, it helps to develop commitment to the new local work unit, thereby facilitating the retention of these strategic human resources.

The repatriation process is the most overlooked in the whole of the expatriation assignment. Often a company has not prepared well and in advance for the eventual return of their employees. While it may seem a trivial matter to some, there are many issues for the returning employee and his family. A well thought out plan for repatriation should be at least as well thought out as the departure plan for the expatriate. There should be a physical relocation plan, a transition plan for the employee and an allowance for readjustment. Just as their may have been culture shock in the transition to the expatriate assignment there may likely exist reverse cultural shock on the repatriate and his family. This reverse culture shock should not be dismissed as unimportant.

There are also job related factors that concern the repatriated employee. One of these is a clear signal from upper management that career advancement is contingent on successful completion of a foreign assignment. This should be honored upon the employee's return. Another concern by returning employees is the perceived lack of a suitable position for the returning employee. This can create quite a lot of anxiety for returning employees. It should not be left until the last minute. Ericsson had a policy of explaining the repatriation process and assignment midway through the expatriate assignment.

EXPATRIATE COMPENSATION

Very few people want extended work abroad just for the experience. However, more global companies than ever now expect their talent pool to have international experience as a prerequisite for promotions into the highest levels of the company. Because companies recognize the reticence of employees to go abroad for "possible future consideration", they usually offer some form of financial incentive to those willing to consider relocation for periods of 2–3 years.

Developing international compensation policies requires that it be consistent with overall corporate strategy, structure of a global corporation. The policy must be competitive and take into account incentives for Foreign Service, tax equalization and reimbursement of expenses. Other factors that determine whether or not the compensation package will be acceptable to the potential expatriate are social security, health and medical benefits, and cost of living factors in the foreign location.

Expatriate assignments can challenge both the employee and his/her family. Companies recognize this challenge and compensate their expatriates. Expectations for the expatriate incentive package run very high. Individuals may know of other expatriates (who bought a large house or a nice cottage upon their return from a foreign assignment).

The main **components** of an international compensation plan are **base salary, Foreign Service inducement, allowances and benefits**. The base salary in domestic terms is the cash compensation, bonus and benefits are in addition to this amount. For an expatriate the base salary is a primary component of the compensation package, of which Foreign Service inducement, cost of living allowance and other costs may be a percentage of this amount. Foreign Service inducement can vary from country to country.

Managing employee expectations is the responsibility of Human Resources professionals. Their responsibility is to balance the genuine need for good salary and benefits for individuals, with the financial needs of the corporations. Their responsibility to the individual and the company means designing expatriate assignments to be win-win situations for the company and the individual, both short-term and long-term. Here are some things to expect from expatriate packages.

Direct Compensation

Salary increases should take into consideration two factors at the same time — changes in the cost of living and increases due to changes in experience and/or responsibilities-and equitable compensation plans take both aspects into consideration. In the case of expatriate assignments, both changes can be drastic:

- Foreign assignments often include a significant increase in responsibility. For example, managing a plant of outside the home country is a significantly greater responsibility than managing one in the home country, because of the more restricted access to corporate support and of the cultural challenges.
- Living in or near any large South American city is likely to be much more expensive than in a smaller or outlying city.

Insightful Human Resources professionals plan to give expatriates two separate figures, one for the change in cost of living and one for the change in responsibilities. This simplifies expatriate package negotiations in several respects:

- It improves consistency when a corporation sends people to different countries with widely different costs of living and helps prevent comments like: "Maria went to Buenos Aires two years ago and her salary was doubled. Why is mine increasing only by 20%?"
- It also helps prepare expatriates for their return to the home country. Companies find it easier to remove the adjustment made for the change in cost of living if it is explicitly separated from the salary than if it is part of one's salary. This helps prevent expatriates from feeling demoted upon their return to the home country because their salary was decreased significantly.

Note that cost of living adjustments should be based on the expatriate life style rather than the life style of locals. For example, expatriates living in some developing countries find that food and lodging is relatively inexpensive, while international telephone charges are very high. Given the amount of money that most expatriates spend on telephone, this may make the new place less affordable after all.

U.S. Department of State has published hardship post differential guidelines to determine level of payment. While the hardship guidelines may dictate a high differential cost the Cost of Living Allowance (COLA) may tend to pull this figure down. It is difficult to determine the actual cost of living in a particular country. One method to determine cost of living is according to Philippe Lasserre, Purchasing Power Parity (PPP) which is for example, a cup of coffee that cost $5.00 in New York City may cost €6.00 in France due to spot exchange rates these would be identical in cost however, the housing in Paris may be more than in New York City.

To determination this can be quite extensive, housing costs must be considered, as must the cost of entertainment and food. Another cost that should be considered is education costs for children. The spouse may also decide to attend school at the foreign location to fill in any gap in the employment record she may be encountering due to her husbands foreign posting. Care should be exercised in the selection of schools both for the children and the spouse as the accreditation of the foreign school may not be acceptable in the home country. Most international schools in Europe have an acceptable accreditation in the United States. At the university level the "American University," in London has a Untied States accreditation, please see their web site listed in the bibliography for more information.

Benefits

Because of their very different situations and needs, the benefits offered to expatriates generally go beyond the benefits offered to other employees. Many companies offer benefits in the areas of taxation, moving, accommodations, visa, immigration, and language training.

Other benefits that are less commonly offered can significantly ease expatriate package negotiations:

- **Cross-cultural Training** helps manage expatriates' expectations. By learning more about their future lives, they can understand better what will be important to them in their assigned destination. They can also calibrate their expectations versus the experience of other expatriates in that destination. For example, some expatriates are asking to live in very large houses in cities where such accommodations simply do not exist. On the professional side, they may expect to achieve objectives that may be essentially unrealistic in their new context; in this case, they may expect rewards that may never come.

- **Family Benefits:** It is critical to keep in mind the fact that the whole family is affected, and particularly the spouse. Family adjustment and lifestyle issues are the leading causes of early return [1]. Support and financial help in finding adequate schooling for the expatriate's children is often a prerequisite for the family to accept the assignment. In the case of dual-career families, recognition for the spouse's efforts can come in several forms:
    - Helping the spouse obtain a work visa and a job.
    - Helping him/her find suitable unpaid activities (studies, volunteer work in non-profit associations, or hobbies) when local immigration laws preventing him/her from receiving a salary. This can be done through dedicated career counseling.
    - Compensating the spouse for his/her loss of income.
- **Career Counseling:** Providing career coaching/mentoring to them throughout their assignment, and particularly during the first and last six months of their assignment, and after they return to the home office helps them ensure that both they and the organization reap the benefits of their newly-acquired experience. It also helps manage their expectations for their subsequent assignments - some expatriates come back to their home country hoping that they will hold far more senior positions than they should realistically hope for.
- **Repatriation Training:** Expatriate families and employees benefit from repatriation training to help readjust to living in the home country and returning to the original work environment. Length of the training often depends on the length of the assignment and the ages of the children.
- **Reassignment:** If the leading motivator of the expatriate is the long-term career aspect, the company needs to provide a challenging assignment upon return to the home office or shortly thereafter. If this is not feasible, communication about future plans for such an assignment and the timing needs to come from a mentor or senior manager or the company risks losing its entire investment to turnover of returning expatriates.

One size does not fit all expatriate packages. A young, single engineer who is going to work on an oil extraction platform in Indonesia has very different expectations and needs compared with a senior, married-with-teenage-children manager who is going to start and lead a plant in Spain. A significant degree of flexibility should be provided to both to be able to design packages that suit their own needs within a given budget - just like flexible health benefit plans.

Seeking External Advice

In many cases, neither the expatriate nor the HR manager has gone through an expatriate assignment. As a result, their understanding of what the expatriate and his/her family will need in the assigned destination may be significantly off. Seeking informal advice from other expatriates or obtaining formal advice from consulting firms specialized in setting up expatriate packages may help ensure that the most important needs of prospective expatriates are addressed.

Types of Expatriate Compensation Packages

When designing a compensation package, companies usually choose among the following six approaches:

- **Negotiation:** When firms first start sending expatriates abroad (and while they still have only few expatriates), the common approach to determine compensation and benefits for those expatriates is to negotiate a separate compensation package for each individual expatriate. This approach is build up around each expatriate, and because of the inexperience of the company of sending expatriates, it can be a difficult task to find the right balance of compensation. In such cases, the expatriates are often overcompensated, and it can lead to inconsistencies between many expatriates and the firm.
- **Localization:** It is a relatively new approach used to address problems of high cost and perceived inequality among staff in foreign subsidiaries. The expatriates are paid comparably to local nationals, which can make it relatively simple to administer. However, since expatriates come from different standards of living than they experience in the foreign country, special supplements may still have to be negotiated.
- **Lump Sum:** To avoid intrusion into expatriates life-styled decisions, the lump sum approach can be used. Here the firm determines a total salary for the expatriate, and then lets the expatriate determine how to spend it.
- **Cafeteria:** This approach is increasingly used by highly salaried expatriate executives to provide a set of choices of benefits. This enables the expatriate to gain benefits such as a company car, insurance, company-provided housing, and the like that do not increase the expatriates income for tax purposes.
- **Regional systems:** For expatriates who make commitment to job assignments within a particular region of the world, some firms are developing a regional compensation and benefits systems to maintain equity within that region.

- **Balance Sheet:** As this approach is followed by most companies when their international business expands to the point where the firm has a larger number of expatriates, we have chosen to dwell on this approach for a moment. The balance sheet approach is primarily used when the MNEs are sending expatriates from the parent firm to its foreign subsidiaries. It is particularly used for experienced senior and mid-level expatriates and keeps them whole compared to their home country peers while encouraging and facilitating their movement abroad and return home at the end of their assignment. In essence, the balance sheet approach involves an effort by the multinational to ensure that its expatriates are "made whole" (that is at a minimum the expatriates should be no worse off for accepting an overseas assignment).

Ideally, the compensation package should also provide incentive to take the foreign assignment, to remove any worry about compensation issues while on that assignment, and to ensure that the individual and his or her family feel good about having been on the assignment. The balance sheet approach of an expatriates compensation begins with the employee's existing parent-company compensation in form of salary, benefits etc. To this is added two more components: A series of incentives to accept and enjoy the foreign posting and a series of equalization components that ensure the expatriate does not suffer from foreign-country differences in salary or benefits. These components should cover the foreign compensation the expatriates are to receive.

A fair compensation package should therefore consist of two components:

- Financial (extrinsic) and
- Non-financial (intrinsic) compensation.

Financial Extrinsic Compensation Approach

One of the key complications in the balance sheet approach is the determination of the base upon which to add incentives and adjustments. A number of possibilities exist, including: Parent-country salaries; International standards; Regional standards; and Host country salaries. The choice of which base to use should be related to the nature of the company as well as the kind of expatriation the company is using. For example, if the company is using long international assignments, and the assignees often go from one foreign-country assignment to another, then an international standard is probably most appropriate. To date most companies compensate their expatriates based on either a home or a host country philosophy.

Once the base salary has been determined, the firm must then decide which incentives that are necessary in order to convince its employees that it will be to the employees' financial advantage to take the assignment abroad. Additional incentives usually include housing allowances, either to ensure the expatriate lives as well as his ore her foreign peers or to make the expatriates housing comparable to what he or she had "back home". In addition to the many incentives that firms have offered to their expatriates, MNE's have also traditionally provided a number of equalization adjustments, like compensation for any fluctuation in exchange rates between the expatriates parent-country currency and that of the foreign assignments.

Intrinsic Compensation Approach

"Intrinsic compensation" to describe the incentives that companies use to motivate their expatriates - that is incentives, where the expatriates do not directly get "money in the pocket" compensation but more in terms of benefits, instead. Intrinsic compensation includes scope for development, career movement, and personal development. An interesting job could compensate for a comparably low pay or long transportation hour or even move abroad. One example could be to give fast track managers experience in running a larger organization without close oversight from headquarters.

SUMMARY

There has also been a trend lately to devalue the foreign assignment. People often take foreign assignments to accelerate their careers, if upon return the message that was given by upper management prior to the assignment has not been taken into account; the returning employee may be placed in a lateral or lower position. This will not be perceived well by the returning employee. There may also be a loss of pay or status.

It would be in the best interests of both the company and the employee to enter into this process contractually. The contract can mean the difference between a successful assignment which helps both parties, and a failure which does not help either party. The returning employee could also benefit in that he could be guaranteed a position upon return or a salary guarantee for a specified period, which would tend to reduce anxiety.

With point of departure in the general compensation literature, we conclude that the financial (extrinsic) and the non-financial (intrinsic) factors are crucial components for clarifying the issue of why and how companies compensate their expatriates. However, since the costs of using expatriates are estimated as three to five times as much as a comparable domestic employee, we have in this chapter focused upon some of the different ways companies can keep such costs down.

Especially younger people and shorter assignments are suggested as means to achieve lower costs, as younger people in today's world seem to consider expatriation as a combination of personal and a professional development, whereby such employees agree to make some extrinsic and intrinsic sacrifices when going abroad.

Review Questions

1. What do we understand by "Cultural Industries"?

It is generally agreed that this term applies to those industries that combine the creation, production and commercialization of contents, which are intangible and cultural in nature. These contents are typically protected by copyright and they can take the form of goods or services.

Depending on the context, cultural industries may also be referred to as "creative industries", sunrise or "future oriented industries" in the economic jargon, or content industries in the technological jargon. The notion of cultural industries generally includes printing, publishing and multimedia, audio-visual, phonographic and cinematographic productions, as well as crafts and design. For some countries, this concept also embraces architecture, visual and performing arts, sports, manufacturing of musical instruments, advertising and cultural tourism.

Cultural industries add value to contents and generate values for individuals and societies. They are knowledge and labor-intensive, create employment and wealth, nurture creativity—the "raw material" they are made from—and foster innovation in production and commercialization processes. At the same time, cultural industries are central in promoting and maintaining cultural diversity and in ensuring democratic access to culture. This twofold nature—both cultural and economic—builds up a distinctive profile for cultural industries. During the 90s they grew exponentially, both in terms of employment creation and contribution to GNP. Today, globalization offers new challenges and opportunities for their development.

2. What do we understand by cultural goods and services?

The concepts of "cultural goods" and "cultural services", which appear clearly distinct, are sometimes difficult to dissociate. In fact, their respective definitions and meanings are one of the key issues currently being discussed at the international level. The combination of both terms is commonly referred to as "cultural products", and could be tentatively defined as follows:

Cultural goods generally refer to those consumer goods convey ideas, symbols and ways of life. They inform or entertain, contribute to build collective identity and influence cultural practices. The result of individual or collective creativity - thus copyright-based-cultural goods are reproduced and boosted by industrial processes and worldwide distribution. Books, magazines, multimedia products, software, records, films, videos, audio-visual programs, crafts and fashion design constitute plural and diversified cultural offerings for citizens at large.

It is traditionally understood that cultural services are those activities aimed at satisfying cultural interests or needs. Such activities do not represent material goods in themselves: they typically consist of the overall set of measures and supporting facilities for cultural practices that government, private and semi-public institutions or companies make available to the community. Examples of such services include the promotion of performances and cultural events as well as cultural information and preservation (libraries, documentation centers and museums). Cultural services may be offered for free or on a commercial basis.

While international trade in goods is relatively simple to grasp (a product is sent from one country to another and will, eventually, incur a tariff as it crosses the border), the idea of trade in services is more diverse and harder to figure out. Telephone companies, publishing houses or news agencies all provide services in quite different ways. That makes it complex to describe the nature of the services, or to establish common rules to govern their exchange.

3. What is the growth rate of the international trade of culture goods and services?

Trade in cultural goods has grown exponentially over the last two decades. Between 1980 and 1998, annual world trade of printed matter, literature, music, visual arts, cinema, photography, radio, television, games and sporting goods surged from US$ 95.340 to 387.927 millions (*Study on International Flows of Cultural Goods*, 1980–98, Paris, UNESCO, 2000). Yet most of that trade was between a relatively small numbers of countries. In 1990, Japan, USA, Germany and UK were the biggest exporters, with 55.4% of total exports. Imports were also highly concentrated with the United States of America, Germany, United Kingdom and France accounting for 47% of total imports. The high concentration of exports and imports of cultural goods among a few countries diminished, but not substantially changed in the 90s. There are, however, new players in the scenario: by 1998, China was the third most important exporter, and the new "big five" were the source of 53% of cultural exports and 57% of imports.

Although we lack precise statistics of global cultural trade, overall trade volumes of cultural products have increased dramatically since 1991. Indeed, the above figures of cultural flows do not fully reflect the 1990s boom of multimedia, audiovisual, software and other copyright based industries. The $38,671 million global retail sales of recorded music (LPs, MCs and CDs) in 1998 compared with the $27,000 million in 1990 (Figures cover sales in over seventy countries surveyed on an annual basis by the International Federation of the Phonographic Industry), reflects the growth of content-based industries and the size and magnitude of the global cultural trade today. In 1996, cultural products (films, music, television programs, books, journals and computer software) became the largest US export, surpassing, for the first time, all other traditional industries, including automobiles, agriculture, or aerospace and defense. According to a 1998 report by the International Intellectual Property Alliance, between 1977–1996, core copyright industries in the USA grew three times as fast as the annual rate of the economy, achieving in 1996 foreign sales and exports of $60,180 million. The UK has followed a similar trend, where creative industries exports reached one year later $12,500 million.

World imports of cultural goods (in millions of dollars), 1980–1998

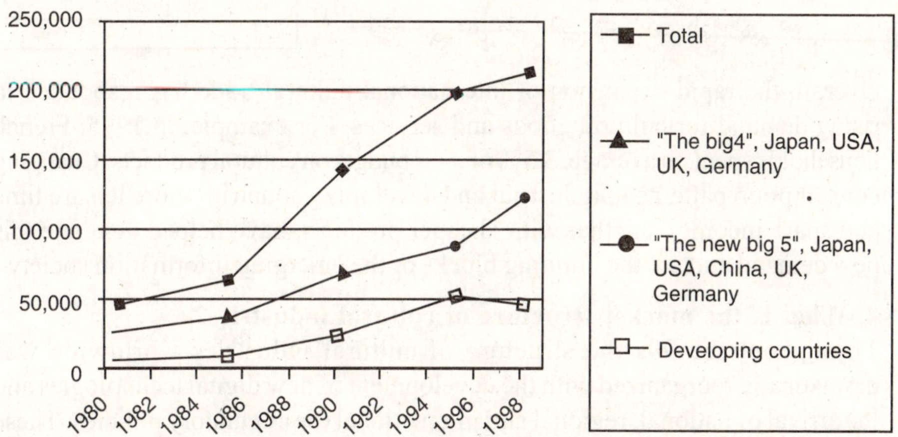

Source: "Study on International Flows of Cultural Goods between 1980–1998", UNESCO, 2000

Despite the vast problems of statistical reliability, comparability and standardization of classifications, data suggests global trade in cultural services is growing very fast, just as other commercial services are growing faster than traditional exports of merchandise goods (Definitions vary widely, even at the OECD level. In the "films and television" category of the OECD publication Services Statistics on International Transactions 1970–1994, for example, data for Japan are defined as "film rentals", for Germany as "films and television", for France as "audiovisual programs", for Canada as "films and broadcasting" and for Austria as "culture and entertainment". In addition, cross-border trade figures alone (for which data are extremely limited) may be deceptive as this trade, and activities relating to it, is often very substantial.). Available figures for the USA point in that direction: in 1994, cross-border exports including affiliated trade of audiovisual services, were about $16,120 million, while imports only $136 million. It is important to note that the biggest difficulty in consolidating and interpreting trade figures for cultural services is the fact that much intra-firm trade is not registered, whether it is between overseas affiliates or foreign owned affiliates.

World imports of cultural goods (in millions of dollars), 1980–1998

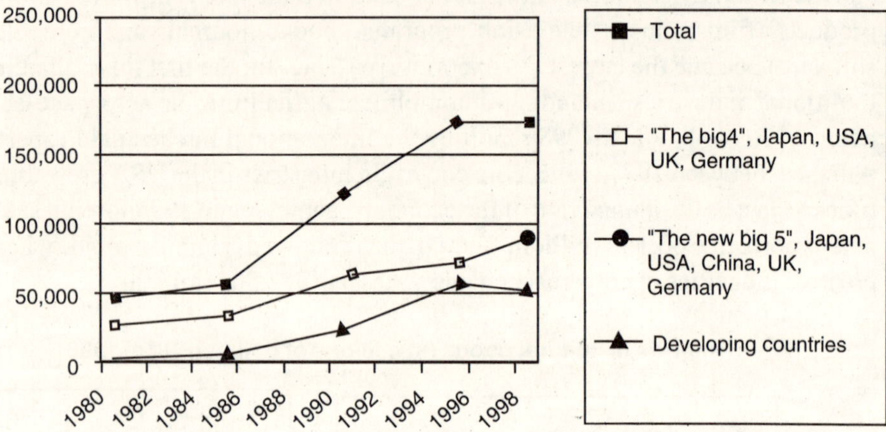

Overall, the rapid expansion of international cultural trade has responded to rising demand for cultural goods and services. For example, in 1995, French households spent on average, 3.5% of their budget on cultural products. Changing consumption patterns in industrial and developing countries more leisure time and spare income, together with cheaper products, have helped generate this new demand and are the building blocks of the emerging information society.

4. What is the market structure of cultural industries?

Throughout the 90s the structure of cultural industries worldwide was dramatically reorganized with the development of new digital technologies and the arrival of national, regional and international (de)regulatory policies. These factors have radically altered the context in which cultural goods, services and investments flow between countries today. Cultural industries have undergone a process of internationalization, realignment and progressive concentration, resulting in the formation of a few big conglomerates. This has raised concern about the creation of a new global oligopoly, which some analysts compare to the automotive business at the beginning of the century.

5. What do we mean by free trade?

In very simple terms, free trade can be defined as the absence of tariffs and import quotas on goods. This definition is based on the notion that the market is the best device to ensure consumers can access good products at the best price, and increase global wealth. The final goal of eliminating tariff barriers and national protection mechanisms is to allow the market to operate with no constraints. However, this approach to free trade takes no account of the fact that not all-trading partners are equal, and neither all products and services.

Therefore, in an integrated global economy the conventional definition of free trade will no longer do, as trade in services is surging dramatically and new barriers are replacing conventional barriers such as tariff and import quotas.

There are three categories of obstacles to international trade:

- Tariff barriers (e.g., fiscal measures such as the imposition of custom duties).
- Non-tariff measures (e.g., legal and practice barriers such as screen quotas).
- Investment barriers (e.g., restriction or limitation of foreign capital or equity participation, control of the nationality of company directors, or restriction on the repatriation of capital).

6. What is copyright and why is copyright important for cultural industries?

Copyright protection grants authors the exclusive right to freely exploit their work on a commercial/non-commercial basis by enjoying moral rights according to law. Copyright legislation is complemented by the so-called neighboring rights, which protect performers (e.g., actors, singers, and musicians) phonogram producers (e.g., sound recordings) and broadcasting organizations.

The author's rights over their literary and artistic works (e.g. books and other written works, musical compositions, paintings, sculptures, software and cinematographic works) are protected under copyright for a minimum period of 50 years after their death.

Under neighboring rights, performers have the exclusive right to authorize reproduction and public communication of their performances. Phonogram producers enjoy the exclusive right to authorize reproduction, distribution and public communication of their phonograms, and broadcasting organizations are granted the exclusive right to authorize broadcast, satellite retransmission, recording and public communication of their own broadcasts.

The main purpose of copyright and neighboring rights protection is to encourage and reward creative work, ensuring that creators are remunerated for the product of their work—a key ingredient for the successful development of cultural industries. The popularization of reproduction equipment and, more recently, the advent of digital technology has largely contributed to increasing piracy (non-authorized reproduction of protected works) damaging cultural industries' sales. Piracy is equally detrimental to authors, whose royalties on sales are diminished accordingly. The publishing industry and phonogram, audiovisual and software producers are the sectors most severely harmed by piracy.

Collecting societies are organizations created by authors and other copyright and neighboring right-holders, specifically mandated to authorize on their behalf the economic exploitation of their works. Collecting societies are responsible for collecting and distributing benefits obtained from the commercial exploitation (reproduction and public communication) of protected works, whenever the rights cannot reasonably be exercised by the right-holder, due to their complexity. Collecting societies were originally created in the area of music and theatre but nowadays operate in fields such as cinema, audiovisual, reprography, multimedia and, more recently, digital copying and electronic transmission. Collective administration of rights is crucial for copyright enforcement and constitutes a useful tool too for users, by simplifying rights clearance.

7. What is the GATT?

After the Second World War, several institutions intended to co-ordinate and regulate international economic co-operation were formed. They are referred to as the Bretton Woods institutions, known today as the World Bank and the International Monetary Fund. The original intention was to create a third institution to handle international economic co-operation: the International Trade Organization (ITO). This body was never created, but during the preparatory process, several countries started negotiations on customs tariff reduction and binding. This package of trade rules and tariff concessions accepted provisionally became known as the 1947 General Agreement on Tariffs and Trade (GATT) and entered into force in January 1948.

From 1948 to 1994, in the absence of any other regulating multilateral body, the GATT provided rules for much of world trade. Until the World Trade Organization (WTO) replaced it in 1994, the GATT was a provisional agreement and organization. During this period the GATT's basic legal text remained much as it was in 1947, through there were additions in the form of "multilateral" agreements as well as "plurilateral" ones (i.e. voluntary membership concerning only a certain number of contracting parties) and efforts to reduce custom duties and other barriers to trade continued. Much of this was achieved through a series of eight multilateral negotiations known as "trade rounds", the most recent being the Uruguay Round. While the GATT no longer exists as an ad hoc organization, the GATT Agreement lives on. The old text is now called GATT 1947; the updated version incorporated into the new WTO agreements is called GATT 1994.

8. What is the World Trade Organization?

The WTO (World Trade Organization) is a permanent intergovernmental body that deals with the global rules of trade between nations through multilateral agreements. The 1986–94 Uruguay Round of world trade talks led to the creation of the WTO and its replacement of the GATT. It was decided that the new organization would deal not only with trade in goods, as the old GATT used to, but also with trade in services and intellectual property. The main functions of the WTO are to oversee the implementation of the trade agreements adopted by member states, serve as a forum for trade negotiations, handle trade disputes, monitor and review national trade policies.

Signed in April 1994, the Marrakech Declaration endorsed the results of the Uruguay Round and the establishment of the new trade organization. The WTO was officially created on 1 January 1995. Today it has 135 member states, accounting for over 90% of world trade and over 30 others are negotiating membership.

9. What are the differences between the GATT and the WTO?

There are, at least, five main differences:

- The GATT was a set of rules for conducting international trade with no solid institutional basis (only an ad-hoc provisional secretariat). The WTO is an intergovernmental organization, and has its own secretariat.
- Although it was in place for over forty years, the GATT was a provisional agreement from a legal point of view. The WTO and its agreements are mandatory and permanent.
- The GATT dealt only with trade in goods. The WTO covers trade in services (under the General Agreement on Trade of Services, GATS), trade related aspects of intellectual property (under the TRIPS) and continues dealing with trade in goods through the so called "GATT 1994" which is an updated version of the old text "GATT 1947".
- A large number of agreements adopted under the GATT were "plurilateral", and therefore selective agreements. But WTO agreements are multilateral and all member states are concerned.
- Another major difference is the dispute settlement system, which is faster and more automatic than in the old GATT system. Its rulings cannot be blocked.

10. What are the common goals of WTO/GATT system?

The system's overriding purpose is to help trade flow as freely as possible—so long as there are no undesirable side effects. That partly means removing obstacles, ensuring that individuals, companies and governments know what the trade rules are around the world, and providing them with legal assurance regarding their international commercial transactions.

According to the GATT/WTO philosophy, the international trading system is based on five principles or main orientations, which run throughout all agreements.

- **Trade without discrimination** between trading partners (Most Favored Nation Treatment), or between national and foreign goods, services or nationals (Nation Treatment).
- **Freer trade**, with barriers progressively coming down through negotiation.
- **Predictable** policies ensured by increasing binding act that Member States have taken commitments.

- Promotion of **open and fair competition** by discouraging "unfair" practices such as exports subsidies and dumping products at below cost to gain market share.
- **Special provisions for developing countries**, giving them more time to adjust, greater flexibility, and special privileges.

11. What does "Most Favored Nation" mean?

"Most favored nation" (MFN) means that every time a member state improves the benefits that it gives to one trading partner, it has to give the same "best" treatment to all other WTO members, so that they remain equal. Countries are to grant equal treatment – not more favorable or discriminatory – to goods and services from all WTO members. This principle is found in the first article of the GATT. It is also a priority in the General Agreement on Trade in Services (GATS) and in the Agreement on Trade-Related Aspects of Intellectual Property Rights (TRIPS), although in each agreement the principle is handled slightly differently.

Some exceptions are allowed. For example, countries within a region can set up a free trade agreement that does not apply to goods from outside the group. Alternatively, a country can raise barriers against products from specific countries that are considered to be traded unfairly. And in services, countries are allowed, in limited circumstances, to discriminate. But the agreements only permit these exceptions under strict conditions.

12. What is the "National Treatment" principle?

The National Treatment principle means that imported and locally produced goods should be treated equally. The same should apply to foreign and domestic services, as well as to foreign and local trademarks, copyrights and patents. This principle of giving others the same treatment as one's own nationals is also found in all the three main WTO agreements (Article III of GATT, Article 17 of the GATS and Article III of the TRIPS), although once again it is handled slightly differently in each of these. National treatment only applies once a product, service or item of intellectual property has entered the market.

13. What is the GATS?

The GATS was adopted by the Uruguay Round and covers all internationally traded services. It is also the first multilateral agreement to provide legally enforceable rights to trade in all services including cultural ones.

The agreement defines four ways of providing an international service:

Services supplied from one country to another (e.g., banking or architectural services provided through telecommunications or regular mail), known as "*cross-border supply*". Consumers or firms using a service in another country (e.g., tourism or aircraft or ship maintenance work), known as "consumption abroad".

A foreign company setting up subsidiaries or branches to provide services in another country (e.g., Insurance companies or hotel chains) officially known as "*commercial presence*".

Individuals traveling from their own country to supply services in another (e.g., auditors, physicians, teachers, etc.), known as "*presence of natural persons*". Both national treatment and MFN principles apply to trade of all services except those provided in the exercise of governmental authority.

Governments can choose the services in which they make market access and national treatment commitments and they can limit the degree of market access and national treatment they offer. In short, every country has the right to choose the sectors in which it wishes to make an offer of liberalization, and can also establish a list of *specific commitments* it wishes to make to provide foreigners access to its' services market. Furthermore, a country does not have to apply national treatment in sectors where it has made no commitments. Even where commitments have been contracted the GATS does allow some limits on national treatment.

On the other hand, the Most Favored Nation clause and the principle of transparency are general obligations under the GATS, so they will apply even if the country has made no specific commitment to provide foreign companies access to its market. "Members shall accord immediately and unconditionally to services and service suppliers of any other Member treatment no less favorable than that it accords to like services and service suppliers of any other country" (GATS, Article II). However, special temporary exemptions to this MFN obligation have been allowed alongside the commitments, and will normally last no more than 10 years. These temporary withdrawals of MNF commitments are an integral part of the agreement. They benefit, in particular, countries within the same region that have set up special trade zones such as *custom unions* (members apply a common external tariff and eliminate tariffs between them) or free *trade areas* (trade within the group is duty free but members set their own tariffs on imports from non-members). However, they have to be sufficiently economically integrated, like the European Union and unlike the Council of Europe.

Finally there are special provisions to allow developing countries to progressively adapt and implement the commitments.

In English, GATS (General Agreement on Trade in Services); in French, AGCS (Accord Général sur le Commerce des Services).

14. What is the TRIPS?

The TRIPS is an instrument adopted by the Uruguay Round to bring intellectual property rights (copyrights, trademarks, patents, etc.) under common international GATT/WTO rules. This is an increasingly important part of trade.

The agreement requires WTO member countries to adhere to minimum standards for protection of intellectual property rights – essentially, the standards laid out in the main conventions of the WIPO, the Paris Convention for the Protection of Industrial Property and the Bern Convention for the Protection of Literary and Artistic Works. The agreement applies national and MFN treatment to intellectual property rights and sets up provisions on how best to protect them through provisions to enforce those rights and to repress counterfeiting and piracy. Finally, it makes disputes between WTO members concerning the respect of the TRIPS obligations subject to the WTO's dispute settlement procedures.

The TRIPS confirms that computer programs will be protected as literary works under the copyright regime and not under that of trademarks and patents. It grants authors of computer programs and producers of sound recordings (phonograms) the right to authorize or prohibit the commercial rental of their works to the public.

The TRIPS contains provisions related to industrial property as well, including the protection of trademarks, service marks, geographical indications, industrial designs and patents, integrated circuits layout designs, undisclosed information and trade secrets.

To provide sufficient time for Member States to introduce the system and adapt their laws and practices to conform to the agreement, the TRIPS set up special transitional periods. The deadlines for compliance are: 1 January 1995 for developed countries, 1 January 2000 for developing countries and (under certain conditions) transition economies and 1 January 2006 for least developed countries.

In English, TRIPS (Agreement on Trade-Related Aspects of Intellectual Property Rights); in French, ADPIC (Aspects des Droits de Propriété Intellectuelle qui touchent au Commerce).

15. What is the TRIMS?

The Agreement on Trade Related Investment Measures (TRIMS) applies to any measure that discriminates against foreigners or foreign products. Like the GATT, it applies only to measures that affect trade in goods. It recognizes that certain measures can restrict and distort trade, and states that no member shall apply any measure that discriminates against foreigners or foreign products (i.e. violates National Treatment). It also outlaws investment measures that lead to restrictions in quantities (violating another principle in the GATT).

An illustrative list of trade-related investment measures, agreed to be inconsistent with these GATT articles, is appended to the TRIMS. The list includes measures that require particular levels of local procurement by an enterprise ("local content requirements"). It also discourages measures that limit a company's imports or set targets for the company to export ("trade-balancing requirements"). Under the agreement, countries must inform the WTO and fellow-members of all investment measures that do not conform to the agreement. Developed countries had to eliminate these by the end of 1996; developing countries had until the end of 1999; and least developed countries were given until 1 January 2002. In addition, WTO members were to consider by 1 January 2000 whether there should also be provisions on investment policy and competition policy.

In English, TRIMS (Agreement on Trade-Related Investment Measures); in French, MIC (Accord sur les Measures concernant les Investissements et liées au Commerce).

16. What was the draft Multilateral Agreement on Investments (MAI)?

Foreign investments are increasingly an important area for international trade in general and for trade of cultural goods and services in particular. By the end of 1996, the total stock of foreign direct investment owned by companies outside their home countries was over $3 trillion and OECD members were the source of 85% of all foreign direct investment. During the Uruguay Round there was strong interest in starting new negotiations of a freestanding, enforceable multilateral investment agreement, but countries' positions on the issue were very different.

The lowest common denominator negotiators could reach was the Agreement on Trade-Related Investment Measures (TRIMS), which only deals with investments related to trade in goods and does not cover many of the areas that were discussed in the Uruguay Round negotiations, such as export performance or technology transfer requirements. The WTO continued to pursue negotiations to eliminate barriers against foreign investors, but no consensus was reached to proceed. In 1995, the OCDE started to negotiate a new Multilateral Agreement on Investments (MAI). Its main objective was to apply the WTO deregulatory agenda to investments by creating a set of global rules to replace a patchwork of 1,600 or bilateral investment treaties (BITS). The MAI was to be open to all OECD Members and to accession by non-OECD Member countries.

The MAI proposed applying the MFN principle of non-discrimination and national treatment to investment rules and foreign investors. In other words, foreign investors were to be treated as domestic investors, and all foreign investors were also to be treated equally, regardless of their country of origin. The proposal also included a ban on "Performance Requirements", so governments would not be able to impose performance measures on investors. It also proposed to protect the liberalization of investment regimes with an effective dispute settlement procedure. Like other treaties, it allowed for the application of reservations and exemptions.

However, mounting tension between negotiating parties and fierce opposition to the MAI project by global public opinion (demonstrators organized a massive protest against the agreement) led negotiators in April 1998 to decide on a six-month delay, to ostensibly give countries time to seek domestic support and carry out national consultations. After the moratorium, France announced it was withdrawing from the negotiations. Too many issues were being questioned: the impact the MAI would have on the environment, on labor rights, and particularly on the ability of governments to apply policies for the development and promotion of strategic sectors such as cultural industries. To a certain extent, the failure of the MAI has opened a new phase for multilateral negotiations. It has made evident that while there are many points of conflict and disagreement, cultural issues are particularly sensitive and controversial.

In the absence of a MAI agreement, the only multilateral rules directly or indirectly governing investments continue to be those laid down in three separate Uruguay Round agreements: the GATS, the TRIPS and the Trade Related Investment Measures (TRIMS).

- GATS recognizes commercial presence (opening shops) as a form of trade in services, though it does not oblige WTO members to open all their services industries to foreign partners.
- TRIPS obliges WTO members to grant minimum periods of protection for copyrighted works, patents and trademarks and to fight unauthorized reproduction and public communication of foreign works. Countries are also expected to prevent unauthorized use of inventions and trademarks owned by foreign investors.
- TRIMS deal with investments in manufacturing.

17. What is pending in the WTO agenda?

There are two main components of WTO's work in the coming years:

- The first is the work program included in the Uruguay Round Agreements, which established schedules for concessions and commitments and for negotiations on different areas - new or old. This is normally referred to as the "built-in" agenda, which in principle foresees from 1 January 2000 onwards, trade talks on services and agriculture.
- The second component touches upon a large number of trade related issues that remain open to negotiation, some new, some already dealt with by the GATT-WTO system, including investments, environment, subsidies, competition policies, and intellectual property, etc.
- The WTO ministerial conference in Seattle (EEUU), held in December 1999, was convened to decide on the content and schedule for the next round of negotiations, known as the Millennium Round. But after intense discussions, talks between the delegations of the 135 member states broke up, as their views were impossible to reconcile. As a backdrop to the meeting, a heterogeneous global movement of opinion used new and old media (i.e. Internet) to reject changes in the status quo.
- Since the suspension of talks on the future trade negotiating agenda during the Seattle Ministerial, the WTO General Council has decided to postpone decisions advancing further on new issues, while continuing with the built-in agenda of the Uruguay Round Agreements. Discussions

are also being held on how to reform the WTO and its functioning mechanisms, to facilitate greater consultation with specialized organizations and NGOs, and improve WTO decision-making so developing country members can participate more fully, in a more transparent system. Finally, proposals to extend transition periods for developing countries to implement various provisions of WTO agreements (e.g. TRIPS and TRIMS) and other implementation issues are being considered.

18. What co-operation strategies should be adopted at the international level?

The development and promotion of cultural industries nowadays requires a parallel effort at supranational level. This is particularly so in the case of small or non-producing countries. The international nature of cultural production and distribution makes evident that national measures on support of cultural industries, although necessary for their development, are not sufficient for their consolidation. It is essential to find competitive ways of production, new audiences and, most crucially, to ensure the ability to distribute. This can only be accomplished through a mix of national, sub-regional and regional strategies to reach a global orientation (in terms of economies of scale and efficient distribution channels) that facilitate expansion beyond the borders of national markets.

It is therefore necessary to define policies that encourage, promote and regulate the production and commercialization of cultural-industry products beyond national markets. Whether they are sub-regional, regional or transatlantic. Such common policies may target:

- Establishing or implementing specific agreements concerning customs taxes, intellectual property, foreign investment and multinationals. This can particularly benefit developing countries, since current multilateral treaties allow them to create special trade areas.
- Like in the national context, it is necessary to consider the specific needs of each sector and utilize the strengths not only of the public sector, but also of the private sector, including big corporations, small and medium size companies, and non-profit organizations. Policies should be based on the principle of negotiation and participation of all stakeholders.
- Co-ordinating investments based on specific sector research and strategic analysis of opportunities and needs in each area.
- Creating mixed funding schemes through funds contributed by member states and dedicated to supporting common projects.
- Defining common mechanisms to support and encourage export activities and developing new markets (by establishing permanent representative offices in preferential markets, mixed fund support agencies, common

facilities for film and television program dubbing and subtitling, promotional campaigns, etc.).

- Developing common policies, strategies and incentives for co-production and co-distribution projects.
- Identifying and supporting the creation of alternative distribution channels (innovative strategies to enter saturated markets).

Several key factors can be identified that enhance success of such supranational policies and strategies, including structural similarities in the markets and the target audiences, language and cultural closeness, and a pre-established tradition of cultural flows amongst participating countries. Yet, the most important prerequisite is probably political willingness and support. Such a flexible approach can potentially provide a dynamic context with variable dimensions of supranational alliances based not only on political and cultural interests but also on market ones.

International organizations also have an essential role in balancing global asymmetries. They should help build a transparent system of global trade that offers opportunities for all players, particularly developing and less developed countries. International organizations should also facilitate access to worldwide markets and respect the needs of all citizens and cultures.

19. What are the NAFTA rules of origin?

Each NAFTA country retains its external tariffs vis-à-vis non-members' goods and levies a lower tariff on the goods "originating" from the other NAFTA members. Rules of origin provide the basis for customs officials to make determinations about which goods are entitled preferential tariff treatment under the NAFTA. Negotiators of the agreement sought to make the NAFTA's rules of origin very clear so as to provide certainty and predictability to producers, exporters and importers. They also sought to ensure that the NAFTA's benefits are not extended to goods exported from non-NAFTA countries which have undergone only minimal processing in North America.

20. How does the NAFTA affect the tariff rates between Canada and the U.S.?

The NAFTA did not affect the phase-out of tariffs which had been agreed upon under the Canada-U.S. Free Trade Agreement (FTA). The phase-out of FTA tariffs was completed on January 1, 1998. As of that date, virtually all tariffs on Canada-U.S. trade in originating goods were eliminated. Some tariffs remain in place for certain products in Canada's supply-managed sectors (e.g. eggs, dairy and poultry products). In the U.S., tariffs remain in place for certain products such as sugar, dairy, peanut and cotton.

21. What is globalization?

I prefer to use the term integration, because it is more precise than globalization. Economic integration occurs when countries lower barriers such as import tariffs and open themselves up to investment and trade with the rest of the world.

22. Why were many developing countries encouraged by international institutions such as the World Bank to open themselves to international trade?

In the early 1980s, most developing countries had high barriers against imports. Many countries in Sub-Saharan Africa, for example, had small economies with high import barriers. So they were trying to develop a full range of industries in economies that did not offer sufficient scale to be efficient. It is fair to say that, as of the early 1980s, the results in terms of growth and poverty reduction were not impressive. People in Africa were struggling for new models because they felt that the old model had failed. Even very large countries such as China and India did not get good results from inward-focused development models. In India the poverty rate barely changed between independence in 1949 and 1978. China reacted to its poor economic results with it program of Gai Ge Kai Fang: "change the system, open the door." In that environment the World Bank certainly did encourage trade liberalization and in many cases gave good practical advice about gradual liberalization of import tariffs.

23. What were the results of opening up to the international economy?

In many cases the results have been good. China, India, and Vietnam have benefited dramatically and poverty rates have fallen. In Vietnam, the government conducted a household survey at the beginning of reform and went back six years later to the same households and found impressive reductions in poverty. People had more food to eat, and children were attending secondary school. Trade liberalization was one factor among many that contributed to Vietnam's success. China's reform led to the largest poverty reduction in history. India has cut its poverty rate in half in the past two decades. Uganda is an example of success in Africa.

24. But was the success shared in all cases where countries opened their economies to international trade?

In several African countries, it is hard to find encouraging progress. But the argument that liberalization has delivered bad results is not really supported by the evidence either. Many of these economies were not doing well for a variety of reasons before trade liberalization. Looking back, there was probably too much optimism that trade reform alone was going to stimulate the development of manufacturing in Africa.

25. Has the process of integrating into the international economy brought disruption to developing countries?

Globalization certainly forces a lot of adjustment. So I view this as a choice that developing countries are making. Countries have to make their own decisions and at the moment integration is popular in developing countries because they are seeing a lot of tangible benefits from it. But integration is also going to force certain types of adjustments. It's inevitable that some factories are going to go out of business, some people are going to be thrown out of work.

26. How dramatic can this process of adjustment be in a developing country?

Integration will produce adjustment costs. It will cause disruptions. So when we say that in many cases the overall income distribution measures do not change in the typical country that opens up its economy that could be the net effect of lots of change. But often the winners include a lot of poor people and, in many cases, some of the losers are relatively powerful, wealthy people.

27. Anti-globalization protests emerged again recently at Cancun. What is your view on their criticism that the World Trade Organization is dominated by rich countries and is not protecting the interests of developing countries?

What's interesting is that there is a certain inconsistency in some of the arguments coming from the anti-globalization movement. On the one hand it seems that some members of the anti-globalization movement have picked up the argument made by the World Bank to the effect that there are a lot of distortions of trade in rich countries and it would help if the rich countries would reduce agricultural subsidies or open up their markets in garments and textiles. But some of the anti-globalization elements are saying that this process of integration isn't helpful to poor countries. So if trade is not important for poor countries, then it is inconsistent to turn around and say the United States should reduce cotton subsidies. If it is true that trade is not important for poor countries, then who cares what the US is doing with agricultural subsidies?

I think that trade is important for poor countries and that it's important for the United States to reduce its cotton subsidies, for Europe to reduce its agricultural subsidies, Japan its protection of rice. One of the most powerful things that rich countries can do is create better access for developing countries to their markets. But that only makes sense as a political position if you think analytically that this process of integration has created a lot of opportunities in the developing world, and that easier access to integration will create more opportunities.

28. Is the current World Trade Organization framework beneficial to small countries or would they be better off just doing direct deals with individual rich countries?

Size matters in the global economy. At some level, trade negotiation between a country like the United States and, say, Bangladesh is inherently unfair. Whatever the international regime is, the way you settle a trade dispute is by penalizing each other. If the United States says Bangladesh can't have access to the US market that is a big problem for Bangladesh. If Bangladesh says the US can't have access to the Bangladeshi market, which is rather irrelevant to the US. So there is an inherent imbalance.

Multiple Choice Questions

Use the figure to the left, which represents the domestic market for good Z, to answer questions 1-3. (Note: P_w indicates world price of Z; P_d and Q_d indicate domestic price and quantity of Z.)

1. Assume that initially there is no trading of Z. In this case, the net gain in the domestic market from production and consumption of Z is the area:

(a) P_dAB (b) P_dEB
(c) AEB (d) $0EBQ_d$

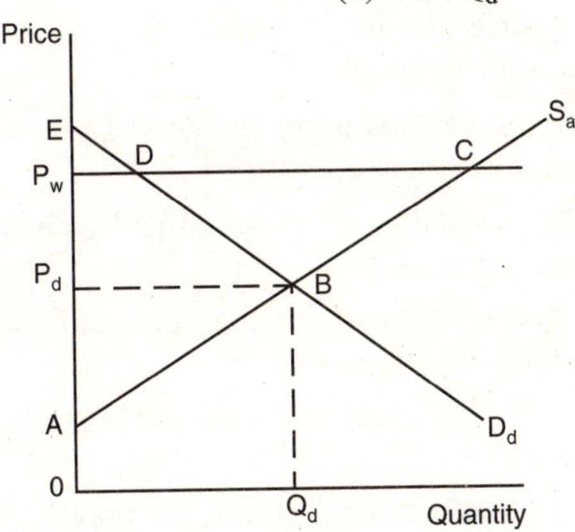

Ans. (c) Without trade, the equilibrium price is P_d and the quantity is Q_d. In this case the net gain is the sum of producers' surplus, represented by the area AP_dB, and consumers' surplus, represented by the area P_dEB. These areas add up to AEB.

2. Now assume there is world trade in Z. As a result, producer surplus will increase by the area __________, and society's net gain will increase by the area __________.

(a) AP_wC; AEB (b) P_dP_wDB; P_dEB
(c) DCB; DCB (d) P_dP_wCB; DCB

Ans. (d) Producers' surplus is the area bounded by the price line, the supply curve, and the vertical axis, in this case, AP_wC. Producers' surplus has increased by the difference between the new producer surplus and the old producers' surplus. This difference is area P_dP_wCB. Part of the new producers' surplus–P_dP_wDB–was formerly consumers' surplus. Hence, the net gain to the nation as a whole is DCB.

3. As a result of the introduction of world trade, consumer surplus has:
   (a) Increased by the area DCB.
   (b) Increased by the area P_dP_wCB
   (c) Decreased by the area P_wED.
   (d) Decreased by the area P_dP_wDB.

   Ans. (d) Prior to international trade in good Z, consumers' surplus was P_dEB. With trade in Z, consumers' surplus decreases to area P_wED. The difference is P_dP_wDB. See the answer to the previous question.

4. A "tariff" can best be described as:
   (a) a tax imposed on an imported good
   (b) a tax imposed on an exported good
   (c) a law which limits the quantity of a good that can be imported
   (d) a government payment to producers of an exportable good

   Ans. (a) This is the definition of a tariff.

5. When the world price of a good is lower than the domestic price of the same good, free trade results in:
   (a) greater domestic production of the good and less production of the good in other countries
   (b) less domestic production of the good and greater production of the good in other countries
   (c) greater domestic production of the good and greater production of the good in other countries
   (d) less domestic production of the good and less production of the good in other countries

   Ans. (b) Since the world price is lower, the good will be imported into the domestic economy and sales will be taken away from domestic producers who will respond by cutting back on production. Foreign producers will increase production to accommodate sales in the domestic economy.

6. Assume, *ceteris paribus*, that the U.S. government decides to eliminate an existing tariff on French wines. In the U.S. market for wine this will cause:
   (a) an increase in price, decrease in the quantity exchanged, and increase in the sales of domestic producers

(b) an increase price, quantity exchanged, and sales of domestic producers

(c) a decrease in price, increase in the quantity exchanged, and decrease in the sales of domestic producers

(d) a decrease in price, quantity exchanged, and sales of domestic producers

Ans. (c) This is equivalent to starting at the "price with tariff" and then moving to the "price without tariff". As such, we move down the domestic demand and supply curves. Price falls, total domestic consumption rises to Qd1, and domestic production falls to Qs1.

7. Which of the following statements is correct?

(a) Free trade does little to encourage domestic competition

(b) Free trade enables the world economy to achieve a more efficient allocation of scarce resources

(c) Free trade benefits countries only if they possess an absolute advantage in the production of the goods traded

(d) Free trade is of no benefit to underdeveloped countries

Ans. (b) The conclusions of the analysis of comparative advantage show that (b) is the only correct answer. Trade is a win-win situation for all economies, even though there may be costs borne by individuals.

8. Tariffs have the effect of:

(a) increasing the potential benefits of specialization and trade

(b) decreasing the well being of consumers

(c) decreasing the sales of domestic producers

(d) reducing the tax revenues of the government

Ans. (b) As the analysis in Figure 9-6 in the text shows, consumers are made worse off as a result of tariffs. Price is higher and quantity purchased is lower overall. However, domestic producers are better-off since their sales increase relative to what they would be with free trade. Government benefits since a tariff is a tax which results in increased revenues to the government.

9. Assume that the domestic price of good X is $10 per unit, while the world price of X is $12 per unit. Assuming there are no trade restrictions:

(a) X will be imported to the domestic market, and the domestic price will rise to some average of the current domestic and world prices

(b) X will be imported to the domestic market, and the domestic price will fall below $10 per unit

(c) X will be exported to the world market, and the domestic price will rise to the world price

(d) X will be exported to the world market, and the domestic price will rise above $12 per unit

Ans. (c) Since the world price is higher, domestic producers can realize additional profits by selling at higher prices in foreign markets. As they move up their supply curves, price increases. However, the rise in price is bounded by the existing world price of $12.

10. A "quota" can best be described as:

(a) a law which limits the quantity of a good that can be imported

(b) a government payment to producers of an exportable good

(c) a tax imposed on an imported good

(d) a tax imposed on an exported good

Ans. (a) This is the definition of a quota.

11. Which of the following arguments for trade protection is frequently cited by developing countries?

(a) The military-self-sufficiency argument

(b) The infant-industry argument

(c) The cheap-foreign-labor argument

(d) The deadweight-loss argument

Ans. (b) It is argued that firms in new industries must be protected until they are able to compete effectively on the world market with older, more experienced firms. See the discussion in the text.

12. All of the following are considered to be functions of money *except*:

(a) Store of value (b) Standard of value

(c) Medium of exchange (d) Measure of power

Ans. (d) (a), (b) and (c) are the three generally agreed upon functions of money in an economic sense.

13. Fiat currency:

(a) is a form of commodity money

(b) is rarely used in developed economies

(c) has no intrinsic value

(d) is included in M1, but not in M2

Ans. (c) This is the definition of fiat currency. Most paper currency used in developed economies today is fiat currency issued by central banks–Federal Reserve Notes are an example of this.

14. Which of the following assets is considered to be *least* liquid?

(a) Demand deposits

(b) Small denomination time deposits

(c) Money market deposit accounts

(d) Treasury bills

Ans. (d)

15. Money that is made of something of value, such as gold or silver, is referred to as:

(a) fiat money (b) bank money

(c) commodity money (d) paper money

Ans. (c) This is the definition of commodity money.

16. Which of the following functions does money serve when it used to measure the prices of different goods and services?

(a) Store of value (b) Standard of value

(c) Medium of exchange (d) Measure of power

Ans. (b) This is the definition of the standard of value.

17. Assume that a bank has $80,000 in demand deposits, total reserves of $60,000, and a reserve requirement ratio of 0.20 (20%). This bank can safely lend:

(a) $16,000 (b) $44,000

(c) $60,000 (d) $80,000

Ans. (b) The bank's required reserves are .2($80,000) = $16,000. The difference between total reserves and required reserves, $60,000 – $16,000 = $44,000, is its excess reserves, which is thc total amount the bank can lend.

18. The primary policy tools used by the Fed include the:

(a) reserve requirement ratio, moral suasion and the discount rate

(b) reserve requirement ratio, the discount rate and the prime rate

(c) federal funds ratio, the prime rate and the discount rate

(d) reserve requirement ratio, the discount rate and open market operations

Ans. (d) These are the three primary policy tools discussed in the chapter, and constitute the primary methods used by the Fed to control the money supply.

19. Which of the following statements is correct?

(a) Open market operations are the least often used monetary policy tool

(b) Changes in the reserve requirement ratio affect a bank's required reserves but not the money supply

(c) Monetary policy influences the money supply primarily by altering the amount of excess reserves held by banks

(d) Monetary policy affects the money supply, but not interest rates

Ans. (c) By altering the amount of excess reserves held by banks, the Fed influences the ability of the banking system to increase the money supply through the process of loans and deposit expansion. The other three statements are all incorrect.

20. Which of the following is considered the *most important* function of the Federal Reserve System?
   (a) Supervising member banks
   (b) Supplying the economy with paper currency
   (c) Controlling the money supply through monetary policy
   (d) Providing for the collection of checks

   Ans. (c) As our analysis of the macro-economy is beginning to make clear, changes in the money supply have significant effects on the level of real GDP and the price level.

21. If the economy is stuck in a recession, an appropriate policy for the Federal Reserve might be to:
   (a) increase the reserve requirement ratio
   (b) reduce the amount of currency in circulation
   (c) reduce excess reserve
   (d) buy bonds

   Ans. (d) By buying bonds the Fed increases banks' excess reserves, which in turn lead to an increase in the money supply and consequently lower interest rates. This has an expansionary effect on the level of aggregate demand and therefore real GDP.

22. The amount of reserves that a commercial bank is required to maintain is equal to:
   (a) the amount of its demand deposits
   (b) the sum of its demand deposits and savings deposits
   (c) its demand deposits multiplied by the reserve requirement ratio
   (d) its reserves multiplied by the reserve requirement ratio

   Ans. (c) This is the definition of required reserves.

23. If the Federal Reserve wants to decrease the money supply, it will
   (a) sell bonds
   (b) print less money
   (c) decrease the reserve requirement ratio
   (d) increase the reserves of the commercial banks

   Ans. (a) Decreasing the reserve requirement ratio or increasing the amount of excess reserves would result in an increase in the money supply. Printing money, in and of itself, has no effect on the money supply. However, selling bonds would decrease the money supply.

24. When the Fed pursues open market operations that consist of buying bonds, this has the effect of:
   (a) increasing the supply of loanable funds, increasing interest rates, and reducing the level of aggregate spending in the economy

(b) increasing the supply of loanable funds, decreasing interest rates, and reducing the level of aggregate spending in the economy

(c) decreasing the supply of loanable funds, increasing interest rates, and increasing the level of aggregate spending in the economy

(d) increasing the supply of loanable funds, decreasing interest rates, and increasing the level of aggregate spending in the economy

Ans. (d) When the Fed buys bonds this increases banks' excess reserves, which in turn leads to an increase in the money supply. The increase in the money supply leads to an increase in the supply of loanable funds. His cause's interest rates to fall and investment spending and consumption spending to increase, implying an increase in aggregate demand.

25. Assuming that banks are currently holding excess reserves, the money supply might not expand by the maximum amount possible because:

(a) banks may be unwilling to lend out all of their excess reserves

(b) people may not be willing to borrow all of the loanable funds that are available

(c) some loans may take the form of cash rather than new demand deposits

(d) all of the above

Ans. (d) As discussed in the text, (a), (b) and (c) are all factors that limit the expansion of the money supply.

26. When the Fed engages in Open Market Operations (OMOs) that involve the *selling* of government bonds, this has the effect of:

(a) reducing the money supply

(b) increasing the supply of loanable funds

(c) decreasing the interest rate

(d) increasing the demand for loanable funds

Ans. (a) When the Fed sells bonds, this reduces the amount of bank reserves and currency in circulation. Currency in circulation is a component of the money supply; therefore, the money supply is reduced.

27. Assume that a bank has demand deposits of $300,000, total reserves of $75,000 and a reserve requirement ratio (rr) of .15 (15%). This bank can safely lend:

(a) $30,000 (b) $45,000

(c) $55,000 (d) $200,000

Ans. (a) See question 17.

28. If the Federal Reserve wants to increase the money supply, which of the following is considered to be the *most likely* approach?

(a) Buy bonds

(b) Lower the discount rate

(c) Increase the reserve requirement ratio

(d) Use moral suasion

Ans. (a) Buying bonds is an example of open market operations, which are the Fed's most important and frequently-used policy tool. Buying bonds increases banks' reserves and therefore the money supply through the process of loans and deposit expansion.

29. The reserve requirement ratio enables the Federal Reserve to:

(a) alter the amount of revenue it collects from member banks

(b) prevent commercial banks from earning excess profits

(c) influence the lending ability of commercial banks

(d) prevent banks from hoarding too much vault cash

Ans. (c) By altering the reserve requirement ratio, the Fed can alter the amount of excess reserves in the banking system and consequently its lending potential.

30. Which of the following statements about the Putin re-election WSJ article is **false**?

(a) Putin is violating the "freedom of the press" building block of democracy.

(b) Most people believe that Putin's economic liberalization policies are compatible with "managed democracy".

(c) Russia's political system under Putin has been labeled "soft-authoritarianism".

(d) Putin's economic policies will be focused on opening the economy to market forces.

Ans. (a)

31. Which of the following statements about he WSJ articles is **true**?

(a) Kodak is asking the W.T.O. to stop Sony, a Japanese firm, from violating its digital imaging intellectual property rights.

(b) The disagreement between the E.U., and the U.S. over global accounting rules centers around how to account for before tax profit.

(c) Both Thailand and South Korea are attempting to adopt "transparency" as one of the building blocks of democracy.

(d) Toyota's ads for a Prado land Cruiser focused on patriotism not brand loyalty.

Ans. (c)

32. Which of the following is an attribute that distinguishes the high-need achiever?
   (a) Wanting supervisors to be responsible for finding solutions to problems.
   (b) Wanting concrete feedback on performance.
   (c) Wanting to maintain an amiable and continuing relationship with other people.
   (d) Setting moderate goals for taking calculated risks.

   Ans. (b)

33. The risks associated with doing business in a country are typically lower when countries:
   (a) are politically stable developing nations with mixed economies
   (b) are economically advanced and politically stable democratic nations
   (c) are underdeveloped, politically unstable democratic nations
   (d) have a high capacity for growth

   Ans. (b)

34. Economies of scale arise when:
   (a) average fixed costs are falling
   (b) fixed costs are large relative to variable costs
   (c) when workers are able to specialize in a particular tasks
   (d) an economy is self-sufficient in production

   Ans. (c)

35. Which of the following statements about Canada and free trade is **false**?
   (a) The most important reason for Canada to seek a free trade agreement with the U.S. was to harmonize its environmental laws with the U.S.
   (b) Canada chose not to open its cultural industries to free trade agreements
   (c) Canada felt strong competitive pressure coming from Asian firms so sought a free trade agreement with the U.S.
   (d) Canada chose a free trade pact with the U.S. since the U.S. was more willing to protect its domestic firms from foreign competition

   Ans. (a)

36. Which of the following is NOT an objective of the Single European Act?
   (a) Removal of border controls   (b) Increase competition
   (c) Create a single currency
   (d) Increase competition in the financial services industry

   Ans. (c)

37. The main redistribution effect of a tariff is the transfer of income from:

(a) domestic producers to domestic buyers
(b) domestic buyers to domestic producers'
(c) domestic producers to domestic government
(d) domestic government to domestic consumers

Ans. (b)

38. A limitation of the Porter diamond is that:

(a) companies have fewer opportunities to import factors from abroad than they did historically.
(b) it assumes companies will seek global market niches rather than responding to domestic needs.
(c) it assumes there will be little response by competitors.
(d) it emphasizes domestic conditions even though economics are becoming more open.

Ans. (d)

39. When a Swiss MNE purchases an Austrian company, it is recorded as a:

(a) credit on the Swiss current account
(b) debit on the Swiss capital account
(c) debt on the Swiss current account
(d) credit on the Austrian current account

Ans. (b)

40. What effect will variations among countries in factor proportions have on the overall volume of FDI?

(a) FDI will be stimulated due to pressures for the more abundant factors to move to countries with greater scarcity of those factors
(b) FDI will be stimulated through regional economic agreements
(c) FDI will be inhibited because of the high cost of transporting factors of production among countries
(d) FDI will be inhibited due to high unemployment rates in LDCs

Ans. (a)

41. Which of the following statements is about the euro is **false.**

(a) The euro will cause a decrease in industry mergers
(b) Price transparency will increase with the euro
(c) Euro countries will lose the ability to devalue their currencies between 1999–2001
(d) The euro will decrease currency risk and conversion costs.
(e) All of the above are false

Ans. (a)

42. With respect to the movement of labor between countries, labor in the host country:

(a) benefits as labor migrate from their country

(b) is harmed as labor migrates from their country

(c) benefits as labor migrates into their country

(d) is harmed as labor migrates into their country

Ans. (d)

43. Which of the following statements is **true**?

(a) A fixed exchange rate automatically cushions the economy's output and employment by allowing an immediate change in the relative price of domestic and foreign goods

(b) A flexible exchange rate does not automatically cushion the economy's output and employment by allowing an immediate change in the relative price of domestic and foreign goods

(c) A flexible exchange rate automatically cushions the economy's output and employment by allowing an immediate change in the relative price of domestic and foreign goods

(d) A flexible exchange rate automatically cushions the economy's output and employment by allowing an immediate change in the absolute price of domestic and foreign goods

Ans. (c)

44. Under the gold standard:

(a) exchange rates did not change for long periods of time.

(b) businesses could trade and invest with little fear of exchange rates changes

(c) the price of each currency in terms of gold was fixed

(d) inflation was a serious economic problem

Ans. (d)

45. If someone believes that the US dollar is overvalued relative to the Mexican peso, they:

(a) should buy dollars and sell pesos in advance

(b) are expecting the peso to depreciate relative to the dollar

(c) may have found that the money supply is growing faster in Mexico than the US

(d) are expecting the peso to appreciate relative to the dollar

Ans. (d)

46. The risk of exchange rate fluctuations:

(a) negates the reduction in systematic risk implied by holding an internationally diverse portfolio

(b) contributes to the low correlation between stock prices movements in different countries

(c) can only drive down the higher returns that might be available abroad for investors

(d) has essentially been eliminated as a factor when considering pan-European investments

Ans. (b)

47. Which of the following statements is **true** about the global capital markets?

(a) An increased use of the global capital market leads to a higher cost of capital

(b) Eurobonds are dominated in the currency of the country where the bonds are sold

(c) Ceilings placed on interest rates under Regulation Q fueled the growth of the Eurocurrency markets

(d) Global capital markets are more highly regulated than domestic capital markets

Ans. (c)

48. Which of the following statements is **true** about the aftermath of the Asian financial crisis?

(a) The large savings accumulated in the SE Asian nations was invested in projects with potentially high returns

(b) The banking industry in SE Asia was over-regulated

(c) Pegging Asian currency to the dollar increased its vulnerability to attacks

(d) The IMF's role helped to reduce moral hazard in the financial sector

(e) All of the above are true

Ans. (c)

49. Backlashers who are against free trade and globalization generally argue that globalization:

(a) helps spread the best of each country's culture, so as too uplift global cultural standards

(b) improves the environment by correcting for distortions caused by import competing policies

(c) causes degradation in the world's environment

(d) helps each country safeguard the best of its own culture

Ans. (c)

50. Which of the following are examples of foreign direct investment?

(a) Japanese purchase of U.S. treasury bills.

(b) An Australian purchase of bonds issued by Nippon Steel.

(c) A Japanese company's production plant in the U.S. state of Tennessee.

(d) The acquisition of a U.S. movie studio by Japan's Sony Corporation.

(e) AT&T purchasing a 3% share of the equity of Telefonos de Mexico.

(f) A McDonald's franchise in Russia owned by a Russian businessman.

Ans. (c) and (d)

51. Suppose wages in Thailand are 750 baht per worker and they are 1000 won per worker on Korea. The exchange rate is 1.4 baht per won and output per worker is as listed below:

	Televisions	Cell Phones
Thailand	150	100
Korea	200	200

Which of the following are true?

(a) Thailand has a comparative advantage in televisions

(b) Thailand has an absolute advantage in televisions

(c) Unit labor costs (ULCs) for televisions are lowest in Korea

(d) If the exchange rate were 1.6 baht per won then ULCs in Korea would be lowest for both goods

(e) If the exchange rate were 1.6 baht per won then ULCs in Thailand would be lowest for both goods

Ans. (a) and (e)

52. Consider two kingdoms (Gondor and Rohan) that trade with each other. Assume there are no other (civilized) countries in the world and labor is the only input. Productivities per hour in the three goods are shown in the first three data columns and wages per hour are in the last column. Trade costs are about 1% of the value of the goods.

	Bridles	Horseshoes	Saddles	Wages (gold pieces)
Rohan	5	15	20	6
Gonder	10	20	30	9

Which situations below are consistent with each country's competitive advantages?

(a) Gondor and Rohan can both gain from trading with each other

(b) Gondor will export bridles to Rohan and import horseshoes

(c) Gondor will export bridles and horseshoes and import saddles from Rohan

(d) Gondor will export saddles and import horseshoes and bridles from

(e) Rohan will import all three goods because it has comparatively lower productivity

(f) There are no gains from trade in saddles

Ans. (a), (b) and (f)

53. According to empirical research on international and inter-provincial trade flows based on the gravity equation:

(a) the volume of trade between neighbouring British Columbia and Washington State should be about the same as between neighbouring Ontario and Michigan

(b) a 10% increase in the distance between countries decreases trade by about 10%

(c) trade flows are proportional to the economic size of the importing country, but not the exporting country

(d) there remains a significant border effect after adjusting for distance and size of the economies involved

(e) the direction of trade can be predicted well, but not its volume

(f) distance effects on trade in goods were important before the 1990s but have since been eliminated by the "communication revolution" (fax, internet, teleconferencing).

Ans. (b) and (d)

54. Which of the following is true of WTO dispute resolution cases?

(a) The WTO ruled that Canada's tax on split-run magazines violated WTO rules

(b) Japan was applying a different tax rate on foreign whisky than Japanese whisky

(c) The WTO recognized the use of the "precautionary principle" by the EU to justify the ban on hormone treated beef

(d) Venezuela accused the U.S. of improperly levying a CVD on its gasoline

(e) The WTO ruled that the 55-day quarantine period on imported apples violated WTO rules

(f) The WTO recently ruled that Canada's voluntary restraint agreement on softwood lumber exports to the United States violates WTO rules.

Ans. (a)

Say: True/False/Uncertain

55. One need only compare Mexican wages with U.S. wages in manufacturing to see why free trade between Mexico and the U.S. will cause permanent job loss in the U.S.

Ans. False. First of all you would need to know relative productivity to compute relative unit labor costs. Second, high unit labor costs are only a problem for goods with high labor intensity. Third, you would analyze the direct and indirect trade costs associated with producing in Mexico. For goods that need to be customized and quickly delivered to consumers, it is important to produce near to consumers in the large market (U.S.). For rapidly changing industries, it might be important to locate near to headquarters and component suppliers.

56. The fact that televisions were originally produced in the U.S. and Japan and now production has moved to low-wage nations proves that the theory of comparative advantage (based on factor abundance) cannot predict the location of production.

Ans. False. The movement of production can be explained by comparative advantage if there were: (1) changes in relative abundance over time (wages may have been low in Japan when televisions were produced there) or (2) changes in factor intensity of television production (TV's evolved from a skilled-labor intensive good to an unskilled-labor intensive good).

57. Atlantis is a nation with a currency called the agar. Its nominal exchange rate is 5 agars per U.S. dollar. The price of a basket of goods in Atlantis is 800 agars and the cost of the same basket in the U.S. is $200. Based on this information, the agar in overvalued and we should expect it to quickly depreciate to a level of 4 dollars per agar.

Ans. False. The PPP exchange rate is 4 agars per dollar: $200*e = 800 agars where e = agars/dollar e = 4. Since the nominal exchange rate is 5 agars per dollar, the agar is undervalued relative to PPP. We might expect it to depreciate over a long time period towards the PPP rate of 4 agars per dollar, but experience shows currencies can be different that their the PPP levels over prolonged periods.

58. A Canadian company, CanCo, is facing anti-dumping duties on its export of widgets from Canada to the United States. The U.S. Department of Commerce has issued a preliminary finding that CanCo is selling widgets below normal value. The best strategy for CanCo is to exit the U.S. market.

Ans. Exiting is one of four strategies. The other three options are (1) concede/settle by raising the price; (2) fight (in trade "courts") the preliminary ruling through a NAFTA or WTO panel and/or fight to show that dumped imports were not a cause of injury to the U.S. widget industry; (3) circumvent by investing in the U.S. and producing there. Given the preeminence of the U.S. market, it is likely to be large enough that CanCo would not to simply exit. Conceding might be a good idea if CanCo is happy with higher prices. However, if it needs to charge low prices in the U.S. market for some reason, it may make sense to contest the ruling. Circumvention by FDI is also possible but whether it is desirable depends on many other considerations besides the ADD.

59. In France, a person drinks coffee imported from Brazil, works at a computer made in Japan, and uses gasoline from Saudi Arabia in a German automobile. This situation illustrates the concept of

(a) Empathy
(b) Scarcity
(c) Interdependence
(d) World citizenship

Ans. (c)

Explanation: Interdependence refers to the idea that nations of the world are mutually dependent on each other for the goods that they produce. A nation's goods are exported all over the world, and different items are imported from other nations.

60. Japan sells cars to the United States, the United States exports high technology to Saudi Arabia, and Saudi Arabia exports oil to Japan. Which is a valid conclusion that can be drawn from this statement?

(a) Saudi Arabia controls most of the world's natural resources
(b) The United States is the world's leading exporter
(c) Most nations of the world specialize in one export
(d) The nations of the world are economically interdependent

Ans. (d)

Explanation: Interdependence refers to the idea that nations of the world are mutually dependent on each other for the goods that they produce. A nation's goods are exported all over the world, and different items are imported from other nations.

61. Global problems of uneven economic development, environmental pollution, and hunger reflect the need for:

(a) a return to policies of economic nationalism
(b) increased military spending by all nations
(c) a reduction in foreign aid provided by industrialized nations
(d) increased international cooperation

Ans. (d)

Explanation: Interdependence refers to the idea that nations of the world are mutually dependent on each other for economic development, and are mutually responsible for the problems of environmental pollution and world hunger. The nations of the world must work cooperatively to solve these problems.

62. The Middle East is a global importance today because it:

(a) has become a model of economic and political equality

(b) allows major European powers to retain their spheres of influence

(c) provides much of the petroleum used by industrial nations

(d) remains a primary source of uranium

Ans. (c)

Explanation: Much of the industrialized world is dependent on the oil producing nations in the Middle East. This fact makes the political stability of this region of worldwide importance.

63. A major purpose of the Organization of African Unity (OAU), the Organization of American States (OAS), and the European Union (EU) is to:

(a) encourage political and economic cooperation between member nations

(b) end colonialism in member nations

(c) control overpopulation in member nations

(d) provide military assistance to member nations

Ans. (a)

Explanation: The OAU, OAS and EU were set up to encourage political and economic cooperation between member states.

64. In the past decade, Japanese automobile manufacturers have sought to improve Japanese-American trade relations by:

(a) drastically lowering the price of Japanese automobiles for American consumers

(b) allowing an unlimited number of American automobiles to be sold in Japan

(c) importing most spare parts from Mexico

(d) building an increasing number of Japanese automobiles in the United States

Ans. (d)

Explanation: The United States has a trade deficit with Japan. To offset this imbalance, Japan has agreed to create American jobs by manufacturing some of their automobiles in the United States.

65. In recent years, a major success of the European Union (EU) has been the

(a) creation of a single military force (b) rejection of national sovereignty

(c) adoption of a single language (d) elimination of trade barriers

Ans. (d)

Explanation: The European Union has recently eliminated tariffs between all member nations. This stimulates trade in a free market environment.

66. The major reason the Mexican Government strongly supported the North American Free Trade Agreement (NAFTA) was that this agreement would

(a) raise tariffs on United States products entering Mexico

(b) reduce Mexico's economic dependence on Europe

(c) promote investment and economic growth in Mexico

(d) stimulate trade between Asia and Latin America

Ans. (c)

Explanation: NAFTA eliminated tariffs between the United States, Mexico, and Canada. This has led to increased interest in investing in Mexican business and industry.

67. Within the past decade, the decision of the United States Government to grant China "most favored nation" status was important to China because this decision

(a) allowed China to join the Southeast Treaty Organization (SEATO)

(b) increased China's ability to trade with the United States

(c) helped protect China from a possible Japanese invasion

(d) eliminated Russian influence in East Asia

Ans. (b)

Explanation: Most Favored Nation status would allow China more access to markets in the United States. The intended results would be a strengthening of China's economy.

68. Modern Japan must trade to maintain its industry and living standard because Japan has

(a) a limited amount of investment capital

(b) little access to the sea

(c) a lack of communication systems

(d) few mineral resources

Ans. (d)

Explanation: Japan lacks many natural resources needed to maintain its industry and living standard. Therefore, they must develop extensive trade with other nations to offset this deficiency.

69. Peacekeeping missions are operating in more than a dozen of the world's many trouble spots. The authority to intervene and use force, if necessary, is found in several articles in the Charter. Which organization is referred to in these statements?

(a) United Nations

(b) Organization of American States (OAS)

(c) European Union (European Community)

(d) World Court

Ans. (a)

Explanation: One of the many roles of the United Nations is peacekeeping around the world.

70. Since the creation of the Organization of Petroleum Exporting Countries (OPEC), member nations have joined together to

(a) determine the supply of oil on the world market

(b) establish a policy of independence in trade

(c) maintain a low price of oil per barrel

(d) isolate themselves from the rest of the world

Ans. (a)

Explanation: Together, the nations of OPEC control a vast amount of the world's oil supply. Because of this, OPEC is able to set market price for oil around the world.

71. A main goal of the European Union (European Economic Community) in the 1990's has been to strengthen European

(a) isolationism (b) socialism

(c) interdependence (d) colonization

Ans. (c)

Explanation: The European Union has sought to bring its member nations closer together economically by issuing a standard currency and eliminating trade barriers.

72. In recent years, companies from industrialized nations have been building production facilities in Latin American nations. This economic change is mostly due to the region's

(a) favorable climate (b) supply of inexpensive labor

(c) capital resources (d) communist governments

Ans. (b)

Explanation: High population and low industrial development has given Latin America an abundant supply of cheap labor. This attracts companies from the industrialized world that wish to cut cost in manufacturing.

73. Since the end of World War II, the nations of Western Europe have improved their economic position by

(a) increasing communication and cooperation in the region

(b) colonizing African and Asian nations

(c) isolating themselves from the rest of the world

(d) rejecting membership in the United Nations

Ans. (a)

Explanation: The nations of Western Europe have increased their communication and cooperation through the creation of a series of economic communities. The current community is called the European Union, which also includes nations from Eastern Europe since the collapse of communism.

74. The principal aim of the North American Free Trade Agreement (NAFTA) and the European Union is to

(a) keep communism out of the Western Hemisphere

(b) reduce environmental pollution

(c) increase economic cooperation between the member nations

(d) eliminate global terrorism

Ans. (c)

Explanation: NAFTA and the European Union were set up to encourage economic cooperation between member states through free trade.

Annexures: Case Studies

CASE STUDY: SPAIN

Spain, which covers 195,000 square miles, is located on the Iberian Peninsula at the southwest corner of Europe, its southernmost tip is directly across from Morocco. The country has a population of approximately 46 million and gross domestic product of about $660 billion ($16,500 per capita). Until the mid 1990s, Spain, known for its sunny climate, colorful bullfights, and storybook castles, was one of the most underdeveloped countries in Western Europe. Now, it is an industrialized country whose economy relies heavily on trade, manufacturing, and agriculture. Many of the old Spanish customs, such as taking a siesta (nap or rest) after lunch, are less common. The democratic government uses a constitutional monarchy, which was adopted in 1978, in which the kind is head of state and commander-in-chief of the armed forces, but the legislative power rests in a bicameral parliament consisting of a Congress of Deputies and a Senate.

Investors Limited, a partnership based in Hong Kong and headed by Stanley Wong, owns 17 medium and large hotels throughout Asia and a total of 9 others throughout the United Kingdom, France and Germany. The group now plans of buying a large hotel in Madrid. This hotel was built at the turn of the century but was completely refurbished in 1990 at a cost of $20 million. The current owners have since decided that the return on investment, which has been averaging 5.2 per cent annually, is too small to justify continuing the operation. They have offered the hotel to the Wong group for $60 million. One-half is payable immediately, and the rest will be paid in equal annual installments over five years.

Stanley Wong believes that this is a good investment and has suggested to his partners they accept the offer. "Europe is going to boom during the new millennium," he told them, "and Spain is going to be an excellent investment. This hotel is one of the finest in Madrid, and we are going to more than triple our investment by the end of the decade".

In the past, the partnership has handled all hotel investments in the same way. A handful of company appointed managers are sent into oversee general operations and monitor financial performance, and all other matters continue to be handled by those personnel who have been with the hotel before acquisition. The investment group intends to handle the Madrid operation in the same way. "The most important thing." Stanley noted recently, "is that we keep control of key areas of performance such as costs and return on investment. If we do that and continue to offer the best possible service, we will come our just fine".

QUESTIONS

1. What are some current issues facing Spain? What is the climate for doing business in Spain today?
2. Do you think the Wong group, in running the hotel, should use centralized or decentralized decision-making?
3. What types of direct controls might the Wong group use? What types of indirect control might be employed?
4. What are some likely differences between the control measures that the Wong group would use and those that typically are used in countries such as Spain?

CASE STUDY: EXPANSION PLANS

Krandon & Associates is a very successful porcelain-manufacturing firm based in San Diego. The company has six world-renowned artists who design fine-crafted porcelain statues and plates that are widely regarded as collectibles. Every year the company offers a limited edition of new statues and plates. Last year, the company made 30 new offerings. On average, 2,500 of each line are produced, and they usually are sold within six months. The company does not produce more than this number to avoid reducing the value of the line to collectors; however, the firm does believe that additional statues and plates could be sold in some areas of the world without affecting the price in North America. In particular, the firm is thinking about setting up production facilities in Rio de Janeiro, Brazil, and Paris, France.

The production process requires skilled personnel, but there are people in both Rio de Janeiro and Paris who can do this work. The basic methods can be taught to these people by trainers from the US plant, because the production process will be identified.

The company intends to send three managers to each of its overseas units to handle setup operation and get the production process off the ground. This should take 12 to 18 months. Once this is done, one person will be left in charge, and the other two will return home.

The company believes that it will be able to sell just as much of the product line in Europe as it does in the United States. The South American market is estimated to be one-half that of the United States. Over the last five years, Kranden has had a return on investment of 55 per cent. The company charges premium prices for its porcelain but still has strong demand for its products because of the high regard collectors and investors have for the Kranden line. The quality of its statues and plates is highly regarded, and the firm has won three national and two international awards for creativity and quality in design and production over the past 18 months. Over the last 10 years, the firm has won 17 such awards.

QUESTIONS

1. In managing its international operations, should the firm use centralized or decentralized decision making?
2. Would direct or indirect controls be preferable in managing these operations?
3. What kinds of performance measures should the company use in controlling these international operations?

CASE STUDY: PERU

Peru is located in the west coast of South America. It is the third-largest nation on the continent (only Brazil and Argentina have more area), and it covers almost 500,000 square miles (about 14 per cent of the size of the United States). The land has enormous contrasts, with a desert (drier than the Sahara), the towering snow capped Andes Mountains, sparkling gross-covered plateaus, and thick rain forests. Peru has approximately 27 million people of which about 20 per cent live in Lima, the capital. More Indians (one half of the population) live in Peru than any other country in the Western Hemisphere. The ancestors of Peru's Indian are the famous Incas, who built a great empire. The rest of the population is mixed, and a small per centage is white. The economy depends heavily on agriculture, fishing, mining and services. GDP is approximately $115 billion and per-capita income in recent years has been around $4,300. In recent years the economy has gained some relative strength and multinationals are now beginning to again consider investing in the country.

One of these potential investors is a large New York bank that is considering a $25 million loan to the owner of a Peruvian fishing fleet. The owner wants to refurbish the fleet and add one more ship.

During the 1970s, the Peruvian government nationalized a number of industries and factories and began running them for the profit of the state. In most cases, these state-run ventures became disasters. In the late 1970s, the fishing fleet owner was given back his ships and allowed to operate his business as before. Since then, he has managed to remain profitable, but the biggest problem is that his ships are getting old and he needs and influx of capital to make repairs and add new technology. As he explained it to the New York banker: "Fishing is no longer just an art. There is a great deal of technology involved. And to keep costs low and be competitors on the world market, you have to have the latest component for both locating as well as catching and then loading and unloading the fish.

Having reviewed the fleet owner's operation, the large multinational bank believes that the loan is justified. The financial institution is concerned, however, that the Peruvian government might step in during the next couple of years and again take over the business. If this were to happen, it might take an additional decade for the loan to be repaid. If the government were to allow the fleet owner to operate the fleet the way he has over the last decade, the loan could be repaid within 7 years.

Right now, the bank is deciding the specific terms of the agreement. Once these have been worked out, either a loan officer will fly down to Lima and close the deal or the owner will be asked to come to New York for the signing. Whichever approach is used, the bank realizes that final agreements in the agreement will have to be made on the spot. Therefore, if the bank sends a representative to Lima, the individual will have to have the authority to commit the bank to specific terms. These final matters should be worked out within the next 10 days.

QUESTIONS

1. What are the some current issues facing Peru? What is the climate for doing business in Peru today?
2. What type of political risk does this fishing company need to evaluate? Identify and describe them.
3. What types of integrating and protective and defensive techniques can the bank use?
4. Would the bank be better off negotiating the loan in New York or in Lima? Why?

CASE STUDY: FRANCE

The French Republic is situated in Western Europe. It is bounded on the north by the English Channel: to the east by Belgium, Luxembourg, Germany, Switzerland and Italy; to the south by the Mediterranean Sea and Spain, and to the west by the Atlantic Ocean. The island of Corsica is a part of metropolitan France, white four overseas departments, two overseas collectivites territoriales and four overseas territories who form an integral part of the Republic. The principal language is French, which has numerous regional dialects; small minorities speak Breton and Basque. There are approximately 60 million residents in France.

France is one of the most economically powerful countries in Europe, and it is one of the G-7 nations. According to United Nations estimates, the country currently has a GDP of over $1.2 trillion and a per-capita GDP of about $20,000. During recent years, the GDP has continued to grow at an annual rate of 3.0 to 3.5 per cent.

Mining, manufacturing, construction and power provide around 30 per cent of French GDP, and industrial production continues go grow. Manufacturing in particular accounts for a sizable portion of economic activity, and the country is a net exporter. In 1999, France had a trade surplus of over $11 billion, and the national typically has a favorable balance of trade with the United States. Its major trading partner is Germany, however, which buys 18 per cent of all France's exports and accounts for about 19 per cent of French imports. Most of the rest of the country's import and export activity occurs between other EU nations.

Because of France's recent steady economic growth, the country has been the target of much MNE activity. The purchasing power of an average French family is far higher than that in many other EU nations, including Spain, Portugal, Greece and Finland. Additionally, MNEs from around the world doing business in Germany have found that the French economy is so interrelated that France becomes a second market. France also is a target for new expansion, as in the case of the big German auto firm DaimlerChrysler, which has recently built a new factory in France because of its faith in the workers' productivity and work ethic. On the negative side, the near future may see difficult economic times for the country. In particular the unemployment rate in France is higher than that in other economic powers, and in 2000 it stood at around 2.5 million. Additionally, the country has been running deficits in recent years.

To get the French economy moving, President Jacques Chirac promised to give tax breaks, speed up privatization and institute pension reform. Recently there have been demonstrations against these reforms and many French businesspeople still complain that the government has too much control and prevents them from making needed changes to ensure and prevents them from making needed changes to ensure the efficiency of their operations. For example, when Perrier, the world-famous French bottling MNE, wanted to cut 600 jobs to boost efficiency, the government turned down its request. When Michelin, the tire maker, tried to increase productivity by running its plants 24 hours a day, the government delayed a long time before giving the MNE permission to run one of its five plants continuously. The other four must still close on weekends, conforming to the current rules requiring French businesses to operate only five days a week. These bureaucratic rules have a negative effect on productivity and could weaken France's competitive position in the world economy.

QUESTIONS

1. Why would MNEs be interested in doing business in France?
2. How would French customers be likely to measure quality in products such as cars? Computers? Televisions? What would be looking for?
3. Why would MNEs need to have a total quality commitment if they hoped to succeed in the French market?
4. Would successful MNEs in France need to be learning organizations? Why or why not?
5. If a WCO were successful in France, might it also be well throughout the EU? Why or why not?

CASE STUDY: POLAND

Poland is the sixth largest country in Europe. It is bordered by Germany, the Czech Republic, and Slovakia in the west and south and by the former Soviet Union republics of the Ukraine in the south. Belarus in the east, and Lithuania in the northeast. The northwest section of the country is located on the Baltic Sea. Named after the Polane, a Slavic tribe that lived more than a thousand years ago, Poland has beautiful countryside and rapidly growing cities. Rolling hills and rugged mountains rise in southern Poland. There are approximately 40 million Poles, and GNP is around $270 billion. The country still is highly agricultural, and up to one-third of the population engages in farm work. The people have a rich heritage (at one point, the Poles ruled on empire that stretched across most of central Europe), have many folk traditions (which the former communist government discouraged), and strong loyalty to the Roman Catholic Church. The government is now dominated by former communists (socialists), and Lech Walesa, the democratic hero, was defeated in the 1995 presidential election by Aleksander Kwasniewski who was reelected in 2000. Today the government is still working to establish a free-market system. Predictions are that the coming years will remain very difficult as Poland continues to try to undo some of the major problems from the past.

The Poles, despite continuing problems, indeed have made some progress in establishing a viable economy. To take advantage of this economic situation, a medium-sized Canadian manufacturing firm has begun thinking about renovating a plant near Warsaw and building small power tools for the expanding Central and Eastern European market. The company's logic is fairly straightforward. There appears to be no competition in this niche, because there has been little demand for power tools in this area. As the post-communist countries continue to struggle in their transition to a market economy, they will have to increase their productivity if they hope to compete with Western European nations. Small power tools are one of the products they will need to accomplish this goal.

A second reason for the Canadian firm's interest in setting up operations in Poland is that the price of labor is still relatively low. Other nearby countries have lower wage rates, but Warsaw the company's specific choice, has a cadre of well-trained factory workers that could be recruited to this renovated factory. Product quality in the production of these tools is critical to success, so for this Canadian firm, Poland seems an ideal location.

In addition, Poland likely well continues receiving economic and moral support from Western Europe as well as Canada and United States. Exporting from Poland to Western Europe or the United States therefore should be easier than from more developed countries. Moreover, the manufacturing firm is convinced that its proximity to Russia will open up that market as well. Transportation costs to Russia will be low vis-à-vis competitors, and the Russians currently are looking for ways to increase their own worker productivity.

Finally, there likely will be little competition for the next couple of years, because small power tools do not carry a very large markup and no other manufacturer is attempting to tap what the Canadian firm views as "an emerging market for the twenty-first century". However, a final decision on this matter is going to have to wait until the company had made through evaluations of the market and the competitive nature of the industry.

QUESTIONS

1. What are some current issues facing Poland? What is the climate for doing business in Poland today?
2. Is the Canadian manufacturing firm using an economic, political or quality imperative approach to strategy?
3. How should the firm carry out the environmental scanning process? Would the process be of any practical value?
4. What are two key factors for success that will be important if this project is to succeed?

CASE STUDY: GO EAST, YOUNG PEOPLE, GO EAST

Amanda Brendhart, Jose Gutierrez, and Rhoda Schreiber founded and are partners in a small electronics firm. Electronic Visions, that has developed and patented some state-of-the-art computer components. Visions have had moderate success selling these components to large US based computer manufacturers.

The biggest problem is that in recent months, the computer market has begun to turn soft, and many of the manufacturers are offering substantial discounts to generate sales. Therefore, although Visions has found an increasing demand for its products, it now is growing less money than it was several months ago.

To increase both sales and profit, the partners have decided to expand into Asia. Although this region is known for its low-cost computer production, the group believes that countries such as China, Malaysia and Thailand soon will become more lucrative markets, because the US government will make these countries open their doors to imports more fully. If trade barriers are removed, the partners are convinced that they can export the goods at very competitive prices. In addition, the partners intend to find a partner in each market so that they have someone to help with the marketing and financing of the product. Of course, if the components can be produced more cheaply with local labor, the partnership is willing to forgo exporting and have everything produced locally.

At present, the group is trying to answer three questions. First what is the best entry strategy to use in reaching the Asian market? Second what type of marketing strategy will be most effective? Third, if production must be coordinated between the United States and the overseas country what is the best way to handle this? The partners believe that over the next 2 months, they will have a very good idea of what is going to happen regarding the opening of Asian markets. In the interim, they intend to work up a preliminary strategic plan that they can use to guide them.

QUESTIONS

1. What type of entry and ownership approach would you recommend? Defend your choice.
2. How could the partners use the four Ps of marketing to help implement strategy?
3. If production must be globally coordinated, will visions have a major problem? Why or why not?

CASE STUDY: GOING TO GDANSK

When Poland made the necessary reforms to move toward a market economy, Andrzej Jaworski from Chicago, Illinois, began thinking this might be an excellent place to set up an overseas operation. Andrzej and his two brothers own a firm that produces specialized computer chips. The company has a series of patents that provide legal protection and allow it to dominate a small but growing segment of the computer market. Their sales estimates reached $147 million within 3 years, but they believe that this could rise to $200 million if they were to expand internationally. They have thought about setting up a plant in Belgium so that they could take advantage of the European market growth. They would prefer

Poland, however, because their parents grew up there before leaving for the United States in 1948, "We feel that we know the Poles because we have grown up in a Polish household here in the Midwest." Andrzej explained to his banker. "We would like to see if the government would allow us to set up a small plant in Gdansk", train the necessary workers, and then export our product into the European Union."

One of the primary reasons that Andrzej believes that the Polish government would be agreeable to the plan is that not only in Poland moving to a market economy, but the country is still struggling with foreign debt, inflation and outmoded technology. A state-of-the-art plant could help to reduce unemployment and provide an inflow of needed capital. However, the banker is concerned that because of the political risks and uncertainty in Central Europe in general and Poland in particular, the company may either lose its investment through government expropriation or find itself unable to get profits out of the country. Given that the company will have to invest approximately $20 million, the venture could seriously endanger the company's financial status.

Andrzej understands these risks but believes that with the help of an international management consultant, he can identify and minimize the problems. "I'm determined to push ahead," he told the banker, "and if there is a good chance of making this project a success, I'm going to Gdansk,"

QUESTIONS

1. What are some of the political risks that Andrzej's firm will face if he decides to go ahead with this venture? Identify and describe two or three.
2. What strategy would you recommend that the firm use? Why?
3. In his negotiations with the Polish government, what suggestions or guidelines would you offer to Andrzej? Identify and describe two or three.

CASE STUDY: SAUDI ARABIA

Saudi Arabia is a large Middle Eastern country covering 865,000 square miles. Part of its east coast tests on the Persian Gulf, and much of the west coast rests along the Red Sea. One of the countries on its borders is Iraq. After Iraq's military takeover of Kuwait in August 1990, Iraq next threatened to invade Saudi Arabia. This, of course, did not happen, but only time will tell what will happen next in this explosive part of the world.

There are approximately 22 million people in Saudi Arabia, and the per-capita income is around $10,000. This apparent prosperity is misleading, because most Saudis are poor farmers and herders who tend their camels, goats and sheep. In recent years, however, more and more have moved to the cities and have jobs connected to the oil industry. Nearly all are Arab Muslims. The country has the two holiest cities of Islam; Mecca and Medina. The country depends almost exclusively on the sale of oil (it is the largest exporter of oil in the world) and has no public debt. The government is a monarchy, and the king makes all important decisions but is advised by ministers and other government officials. Royal and ministerial decrees account for most of the promulgated legislation. There are no political parties.

Earliest this week, Robert Auger, the executive vice president of Skyblue, a commercial aircraft manufacturing firm based in Kansas City, had a visit with a Saudi minister. The Saudi official explained in Auger that the government planned to purchase 10 aircraft over the next 2 years. A number of competitive firms were bidding for the job. The minister went on to explain that despite the competitiveness of the situation, several members of the royal family were impressed with Auger's company. The firm's reputation for high-quality performance aircraft and state-of-the-art technology gave in the inside track. A number of people are involved in the decision, however, and in the minister's words, "anything can happen when a committee decision is being made."

The Saudi official went on to explain that some people who would be involved in the decision had recently suffered large losses in some stock market speculations on the London Stock Exchange. "One relative of the King, who will be a key person in the decision regarding the purchase of the aircraft, I have heard, lost over $200,000 last week alone. Some of the competitive firms have decided to put them have given me $100,000 each. If you were to do the same, I know that it would put you a par with them, and I believe it would be in your best interests when the decision is made." Auger was stunned by the suggestion and told the minister that he would check with his people and get back with the minister as soon as possible.

As soon as he got back to his temporary office, Auger sent a coded message to headquarters asking management what he should do. He expects to have an answer within the next 48 hours. In the interim, he has had a call from the minister's office, but Auger's secretary told the caller that Auger had been called away from the office and would not be returning for at least 2 days. The individual said he would place the call again at the beginning of this coming week. In the interim, Auger has talked to a Saudi friend whom he had known back in the US who was currently an insider in the Saudi government. Over dinner, Auger hinted at what he had been told by the minister. The friend seemed somewhat puzzled about what Auger was saying and indicated that he had heard nothing about any stock market losses by the royal family or pool of money being put together for certain members of the decision making committee. He asked Auger, "Are you sure you got the story straight, or as you Americans say, is someone pulling your leg?"

QUESTIONS

1. What are some current issues facing Saudi Arabia? What is the climate for doing business in Saudi Arabia today?
2. Is it legal for Auger's firm to make a payment of $100,000 to help ensure this contract?
3. Do you think other firms are making these payments, or in Auger's firm being singled out? What conclusion can you draw from your answer?
4. What would you recommend that Skyblue do?

CASE STUDY: VIETNAM

Located in Southeast Asia, the Socialist Republic of Vietnam is bordered to the north by the People's Republic of China, to the west by Laos and Cambodia, and to the east and south by the South China Sea. The country is a mere 127,000 square miles but has a population of almost 80 million. The language is Vietnamese and the principal religion Buddhism, although there are a number of small minorities, including Confucian, Christian (mainly Catholic), Caodist, Daoist, and Hoa Hao. In recent years, the country's economy has been up and down, but average per-capita income still is in the hundreds of dollars as the peasants still remain very poor.

One of the reasons that Vietnam has lagged behind its fast-developing neighbors in Southeast Asia, such as Thailand and Malaysia, is its isolation from the industrial west, and the United States in particular, because of the Vietnam war. From the mid-1970s, the country had close relations with the U.S.S.R., but the collapse of communism there forced the still-communist Vietnamese government to work on establishing stronger economic ties with other countries. The nation recently has worked out many of its problems with China, and today, the Chinese have become a useful economically. Vietnam would most like to establish a vigorous trade relationship with the United States, however. Efforts toward this end began over a decade ago, but because of lack of information concerning the many U.S. soldiers still unaccounted for after the war, it was not until 1993 that the United States permitted U.S. companies to take part in ventures in Vietnam that were financed by international aid agencies. Then, in 1994, the U.S. trade embargo was lifted, and a growing number of American firms began doing business in Vietnam.

Caterpillar began supplying equipment for a $2 billion highway project. Mobil teamed with three Japanese partners to begin drilling offshore. Exxon, Amoco, Conoco, Unocal, and Arco negotiated production-sharing contracts with Petro Vietnam. General Electric opened a trade office and developed plans to use electric products throughout the country. AT&T began working to provide long-distance service both in and out of the country. Coca-Cola began bottling operations. Within the first 12 months, 70 U.S. companies obtained licenses to do business in Vietnam. Besides the U.S., the largest investors have been Singapore, Taiwan, Japan, South Korea and Hong Kong which collectively have put over $22 billion into the country.

In July 2000 the U.S. and Vietnam signed a bilateral trade agreement which opens up trade and foreign investment in Vietnam and gives Vietnamese exporters access to the U.S. market. The agreement is also likely to increase U.S. investment in the country over the next decade. Similar to China, many U.S. firms find doing business in Vietnam frustrating because of the numerous and changing bureaucratic roles imposed by the communist government officials, but if relations between the two countries continue on their present course, more and more opportunities should open up for American multinationals.

QUESTIONS

1. In what way does the political environment in Vietnam pose both an opportunity and a threat for American MNCs. seeking to do business there?
2. Why are U.S. multinationals so interested in going into Vietnam? How much potential does the country offer? Conversely, how much benefit can Vietnam derive from a business relationship with U.S. MNCs?
3. Would there be any opportunities in Vietnam for high-tech American firms? Why or why not?

CASE STUDY: A CHINESE VENTURE

The Durby Company is a medium-size communication technology company headquartered on the west coast of the United States. Among other things, Durby holds a patent on a mobile telephone that can operate effectively within a 5-mile radius. The phone does not contain state-of-the-art technology, but it can be produced extremely cheaply. As a result, the Chinese government has expressed interest in manufacturing and selling this phone throughout their country.

Preliminary discussions with the Chinese government reveal that some major terms of the agreement that it would like to include: (1) Durby will enter into a joint venture with a local Chinese firm to manufacture the phones to Durby's specifications (2) these phones would be sold throughout China at a 100 per cent markup, and Durby will receive 10 per cent of the profits; (3) Durby will invest $35 million in building the manufacturing facility, and these costs will be recovered over a 5 year period; and (4) the government in Beijing will guarantee that at least 100,000 phones are sold every year, or it will purchase the difference.

The Durby management is not sure whether this is a good deal. In particular, Durby executives have heard all sorts of horror stories regarding agreements that the Chinese government has made and then broken. The company also is concerned that once its technology is understood, the Chinese will work away from the agreement and start making these phones on their own. Because the technology is not state-of-the-art, the real benefits are in the low production costs, and the technological knowledge is more difficult to protect.

For its part, the Chinese government has promised to sign a written contract with Durby, and it has agreed that any disputes regarding enforcement of the contract can be brought by either side, to the World Court at the Hague for resolution. Should this course of action be taken, each side would be responsible for its own legal fees, but the Chinese have promised to accept the decision of the court as binding.

Durby has 30 days to decide whether to sign the contract with the Chinese. After this time, the Chinese intend to pursue negotiations with a large telecommunications firm in Europe and try cutting a deal with them. Durby is more attractive to the Chinese, however, because of the low cost of producing its telephone. In any event, the Chinese are determined to begin mass producing cellular phones in their country. "Our future is tied to high-tech communication," the Chinese Minister of Finance recently told Durby's President. "That is why we are so anxious to do business with your company; you have quality phones at low cost," Durby management is flattered by these kind words but still not sure if this is the type of business deal in which it wants to get involved.

QUESTIONS

1. How important is the political environment in China for the Durby Company? Explain.
2. If a disagreement arises between the two joint-venture partners and the government of China reneges on its promises, how well protected is Durby's position? Explain.
3. Are the economic and technological environments in China favorable for Durby? Why or why not?

CASE STUDY: AUSTRALIA

Australia is the smallest continent but the sixth-largest country in the world. It lies between the Indian the Pacific Oceans in the southern hemisphere and has a land mass of almost 3 million square miles (around 85 per cent the size of the United States). Referred to as being "down under" because it lies entirely within the southern hemisphere, it is a dry, thinly populated land. The outback is famous for its bright sunshine, enormous numbers of sheep and cattle, and unusual wildlife, such as kangaroos, koalas, platypuses and wombats. Australia operates under a democratic form of government somewhat similar to that of Great Britain. Gross domestic product is over $400 billion, with the largest economic sectors being services, trade and manufacturing.

A large financial-service MNE in the United States has been examining the demographic and economic data of Australia. This MNE has concluded that there will be increased demand for financial services in Australia during the next few years. As a result, the company is setting up an operation in the capital, Canberra, which is slightly inland from the two largest cities of Sydney and Melbourne.

This financial-service firm began in Chicago and now has offices in seven countries. Many of these foreign operations are closely controlled by the Chicago office. The overseas personnel are charged with carefully following instruction from headquarters and implementing centralized decisions. However, the Australian operation will be run differently. Because the country is so large and the population spread along the coast and to Perth in the west, and because of the "free spirit" cultural values of the Aussies, the home office feels compelled to give the manager of Australian operations full control over decision making. This manager will have a small number of senior level managers brought from the United States, but the rest of the personnel will be hired locally. The office will be given scales and profit goals, but specific implementation of strategy will be left to the manager and his or her key subordinates on site.

The home office believes that in addition to providing direct banking and credit card services, the Australian operation should seek to gain a strong foothold in insurance and investment services. As the country continues to grow economically, this sector of the industry should increase relatively fast. Moreover, few multinational firms are trying to tap this market in Australia, and those that are doing so are from British Commonwealth countries. The CEO believes that the experience of the people being sent to Australia will be particularly helpful in developing this market. He recently noted, "We know that the needs of the Australian market are not as sophisticated or complex as those in the United States, but we also know that they are moving in the same direction as we are. So we intend to tap our experience and knowledge and use it to garner a commanding share of this expanding market."

QUESTIONS

1. What are the some current issues facing Australia? What is the climate for doing business in Australia today?
2. What type of organizational structure arrangement is the MNE going to use in setting up its Australian operation?
3. Can this MNE benefit from any of the new organizational arrangements, such as a joint venture the Japanese concept of keiretsu, or electronic networks?
4. Will this operation be basically centralized or decentralized?

Index

Q

R

S

T